DELIBERATIVE POLICY ANALYSIS

What kind of policy analysis is required now that governments increasingly encounter the limits of governing? Exploring the new contexts of politics and policymaking, this book presents an original analysis of the relationship between state and society, and new possibilities for collective learning and conflict resolution. The key insight of the book is that democratic governance calls for a new, deliberatively oriented, policy analysis. Traditionally policy analysis has been state centred, based on the assumption that central government is self-evidently the locus of governing. Drawing on detailed empirical examples, the book examines the influence of developments such as increasing ethnic and cultural diversity, the complexity of socio-technical systems and the impact of transnational arrangements on national policymaking. This contextual approach indicates the need to rethink the relationship between social theory, policy analysis and politics. *Deliberative Policy Analysis* is essential reading for all those involved in the study of public policy.

MAARTEN A. HAJER is Professor of Public Policy and Political Science in the Department of Political Science of the University of Amsterdam. His previous publications include *The Politics of Environmental Discourse: Ecological Modernization and the Policy Process* (1995), *Living with Nature: Environmental Politics as Cultural Discourse* (edited with Frank Fischer, 1999), and *In Search of a New Public Domain* (with Arnold Reijndorp, 2001).

HENDRIK WAGENAAR is Associate Professor of Public Policy at Leiden University and Senior Researcher at the Netherlands Institute for the Study of Crime and Law Enforcement. His previous publications include *Worlds of the Mentally Ill: How Deinstitutionalization Works in the City* (with Dan Lewis and others, 1991) and *Government Institutions: Effects, Changes, and Normative Foundations* (edited, 2000).

CW00953868

THEORIES OF INSTITUTIONAL DESIGN

Series Editor
Robert E. Goodin
Research School of Social Sciences
Australian National University

Advisory Editors
Brian Barry, Russell Hardin, Carole Pateman, Barry Weingast,
Stephen Elkin, Claus Offe, Susan Rose-Ackerman

Social scientists have rediscovered institutions. They have been increasingly concerned with the myriad ways in which social and political institutions shape the patterns of individual interactions which produce social phenomena. They are equally concerned with the ways in which those institutions emerge from such interactions.

This series is devoted to the exploration of the more normative aspects of these issues. What makes one set of institutions better than another? How, if at all, might we move from the less desirable set of institutions to a more desirable set? Alongside the questions of what institutions we would design, if we were designing them afresh, are pragmatic questions of how we can best get from here to there: from our present institutions to new revitalized ones.

Theories of Institutional Design is insistently multidisciplinary and interdisciplinary, both in the institutions on which it focuses, and in the methodologies used to study them. There are interesting sociological questions to be asked about legal institutions, interesting legal questions to be asked about economic institutions, and interesting social, economic and legal questions to be asked about political institutions. By juxtaposing these approaches in print, this series aims to enrich normative discourse surrounding important issues of designing and redesigning, shaping and reshaping the social, political and economic institutions of contemporary society.

Other books in this series

Robert E. Goodin (editor), *The Theory of Institutional Design*
Brent Fisse and John Braithwaite, *Corporations, Crime, and Accountability*
Itai Sened, *The Political Institution of Private Property*
Bo Rothstein, *Just Institutions Matter*
Jon Elster, Claus Offe, and Ulrich Preuss, *Institutional Design in Post-Communist Societies: Rebuilding the Ship at Sea*
Mark Bovens, *The Quest for Responsibility*
Geoffrey Brennan and Alan Hamlin, *Democratic Devices and Desires*
Adrienne Héritier, *Policy-Making and Diversity in Europe: Escape from Deadlock*
Eric Patashnik, *Putting Trust in the US Budget: Federal Trust Funds and the Politics of Commitment*
Benjamin Reilly, *Democracy in Divided Societies: Electoral Engineering for Conflict Management*
John S. Dryzek and Leslie Holmes, *Post-Communist Democratization: Political Discourses across Thirteen Countries*

DELIBERATIVE POLICY ANALYSIS

Understanding Governance in the Network Society

Edited by

MAARTEN HAJER

University of Amsterdam

and

HENDRIK WAGENAAR

Leiden University

CAMBRIDGE
UNIVERSITY PRESS

PUBLISHED BY THE PRESS SYNDICATE OF THE UNIVERSITY OF CAMBRIDGE
The Pitt Building, Trumpington Street, Cambridge, United Kingdom

CAMBRIDGE UNIVERSITY PRESS
The Edinburgh Building, Cambridge CB2 2RU, UK
40 West 20th Street, New York, NY 10011-4211, USA
477 Williamstown Road, Port Melbourne, VIC 3207, Australia
Ruiz de Alarcón 13, 28014 Madrid, Spain
Dock House, The Waterfront, Cape Town 8001, South Africa

http://www.cambridge.org

First published 2003
Reprinted 2004

Printed in the United Kingdom at the University Press, Cambridge

Typeface Times 10/12 pt   *System* LATEX 2_ε [TB]

A catalogue record for this book is available from the British Library

ISBN 0 521 82366 8 hardback
ISBN 0 521 53070 9 paperback

Contents

Contributors

David E. Booher is a Senior Policy Adviser at the Center for Collaborative Policy of California State University, Sacramento.

Scott Noam Cook is Professor of Philosophy at San Jose State University.

Frank Fischer is Professor of Political Science at Rutgers University, New Jersey.

Herbert Gottweis is Professor of Political Science at the University of Vienna.

Patsy Healey is Professor of Urban and Regional Planning at the University of Newcastle.

Judith E. Innes is Professor of City and Regional Planning at the University of California Berkeley.

David Laws is a researcher at the Department of Urban Studies and Planning, Massachusetts Institute of Technology.

Ali Madanipour is senior lecturer at the Centre for Research in European Urban Environments, University of Newcastle.

Claudio de Magalhaes, is a researcher at the Centre for Research in European Urban Environments, University of Newcastle.

John Pendlebury is a lecturer at the Centre for Research in European Urban Environments, University of Newcastle.

Martin Rein is Professor of Urban Studies at the Department of Urban Studies and Planning, Massachusetts Institute of Technology.

Douglas Torgerson is Professor of Political Science at the University of Peterborough, Canada.

Dvora Yanow is Professor of Public Administration at the University of California at Santa Cruz.

Figures

Tables

Preface

In the early 1980s critical policy analysts began to aim their arrows at one of the key claims of positivist, technocratic policy science: its alleged neutral stance towards the politically charged issues that were the subject of its investigations and analyses. In fact, from its onset as an institutionalized discipline, the strict separation of knowledge and politics has been the *raison d'être* of traditional policy analysis. Through the application of neutral, scientific methods policy analysts would be able to generate objective knowledge that suggested optimal solutions to a broad range of social and economic problems. By systematically collecting and analysing the 'facts of the matter', traditional policy analysis claimed to be the voice of rationality, even the final cognitive arbiter, in a contested political world.

A number of critical scholars, such as Douglas Torgerson, Frank Fischer and Douglas Amy argued convincingly that this foundationalist self-image of positivist policy analysis was profoundly misguided. The neutral methods of scientific policy analysis itself presupposed strong assumptions about the constitution of society. These scholars asserted that the methodology and epistemology of positivist policy analysis tacitly assumed – and required – a certain hierarchical societal ordering. A 'scientistic', quantitative policy analysis was itself part of a particular institutional order in which political and economic elites, effectively insulated from the citizens' voice, sought to design economically efficient and technologically efficacious solutions to what they perceived as society's problems. By revealing the political bias in traditional policy analysis, these scholars turned the commonly understood relation between analysis and politics on its head. It is not so much the case, they argued, that analysis informs policy, but conversely, that a particular form of thin, representative democracy, in which, as deLeon puts it, the better informed few prescribe for the less-informed many, requires and sustains positivist policy analysis. Methodology, inevitably, entails a political stance.

Since those early days, critical policy analysis has taken off. Particularly with the publication in 1993 of Frank Fischer and John Forester's *The Argumentative Turn in Policy Analysis and Planning*, studies using methods such as interpretative analysis, the analysis of policy discourse and narratives, the socio-linguistic analysis of practitioners' stories, or the careful description and interpretation of the democratic qualities of policy deliberation, had sprung up everywhere in policy and planning. Yet, despite the range and quality of these post-positivist studies of public policy, they were almost always relegated to the periphery of the discipline. As the work was dispersed over a broad range of not always easily accessible journals and collections of papers, it hardly added up to a systematic approach, a coherent, viable alternative to traditional, scientistic policy analysis that offered prospects for further institutionalization in academic curricula, departmental hiring practices and grant policies. One reason for the relative lack of institutionalization of post-positivist policy analysis, we feel, is that during the rapid methodological development of the critical policy field, we have somehow taken our eye off the central importance of those early insights about the symbiosis between methodology and political organization. If a positivist methodology and a hierarchically ordered, Madisonian form of democracy presume and sustain each other, what kind of democratic organization then fits the interpretative, linguistically oriented methods of critical post-positivist analysis? Without a convincing answer to this question, it is not immediately obvious to the outside world what is the practical significance of post-positivist policy analysis for today's world, let alone its added value over traditional analysis.

The argument put forward in this book is that a close practical and conceptual connection exists between a post-positivist policy analysis and today's decentred world of governance. A critical policy analysis, with its assumptions about the inherently contextual nature of knowledge, seems more consistent with the contemporary situation in developed democracies of dispersed power, diminishing trust, ambiguous institutions, powerful transnational influences and increasing reflexivity. In the introductory chapter we assert that a policy analysis that is interpretative, pragmatic, and deliberative is both practically and philosophically attuned to the continuous give and take in networks of actors that, as a result of the changing political topography, have sprung up around concrete social and political issues. We have called such an approach 'Deliberative Policy Analysis'. The nine contributions to this book by major scholars in planning theory and policy analysis all elucidate the general argument of the editors' Introduction. In three sections of three chapters each, the contributors explore the possibilities of collaborative dialogue and democratic deliberation in situations of deep-seated conflict; the contribution of the analysis of discourse and practices to understanding various concrete policy controversies;

and, finally, the epistemological and philosophical foundations of the critical, non-traditional methods and concepts used in this book. We are confident that this collection of papers demonstrates that deliberative policy analysis adds up, to paraphrase Hilary Putnam's characterization of Dewey's philosophy, to a practical and epistemological justification of more direct, participatory forms of democracy.

Many people have contributed to the publication of this book. First we would like to thank the anonymous reviewers who not only saw the intellectual potential of that first loosely organized draft, but also took great pains to articulate it, and to push us and the other contributors hard to actually realize a coherent book. Bob Goodin, who edits the Institutional Design series in which this book appears, has been supportive of our project from its very inception. We are grateful for that. We are appreciative of the students in our seminar on Interpretative Policy Analysis for their critical comments on earlier versions of the manuscript. We also want to thank Teun Oosterbaan for his work in preparing the manuscript, and Chantal Laurent, who has been invaluable for the meticulous way she compiled the list of references and the index. Finally we are grateful to our copy-editor, Trevor Horwood, for his indefatigable patience in rooting out textual oddities and incomplete references.

URLs

The publisher has used its best endeavours to ensure that the URLs for external websites referred to in this book are correct and active at the time of going to press. However, the publisher has no responsibility for the websites and can make no guarantee that a site will remain live or that the content is or will remain appropriate.

Introduction

Maarten Hajer and Hendrik Wagenaar

Governance or the rise of a new vocabulary

One of the most striking developments in the analysis of politics and policy-making is the shift in vocabulary that has occurred over the last ten years. Terms such as 'governance', 'institutional capacity', 'networks', 'complexity', 'trust', 'deliberation' and 'interdependence' dominate the debate, while terms such as 'the state', 'government', 'power' and 'authority', 'loyalty', 'sovereignty', 'participation' and 'interest groups' have lost their grip on the analytical imagination. The new vocabulary prevails in spheres ranging from international relations (Finkelstein 1995; Rosenau 1995; World Bank 1997) to policy analysis and public administration (Rhodes 1996; 2000), from comparative politics to urban planning (Forester 1999; Healey 1997; Innes and Booher 1999b), from European studies (Marks et al. 1996) to political theory (Dryzek 2000; March and Olsen 1995). The shift from 'government' to 'governance' is widely proclaimed and endorsed in the political-science and policy-science communities (for an analytical overview, see especially Pierre 2000). Social science is no less immune to fads than popular culture. New concepts often have a remarkably short shelf-life. New vocabularies may signify no more than a change of rhetoric. In this case, such an explanation is too simple. The new vocabulary seems to capture changes in both the nature and topography of politics. A new range of political practices has emerged between institutional layers of the state and between state institutions and societal organizations. The new language is rooted in an appreciation of the importance of these new political practices. Authors as varied as James Rosenau, Judith Innes and John Dryzek have pointed out that it is these often transient and informal arrangements that produce solutions; not conventions among states, directives, or authoritative decisions.

Examples offer themselves readily. In California 'collaborative dialogues' have produced workable solutions to persistent problems in water management, a sensitive issue that state institutions have long sought to regulate (Innes and Booher, this volume). The importance of informal policy networks in the European Union is increasingly appreciated. Specialists have characterized the EU as 'an experiment in finding alternative forms for developing public policy' (Wallace and Young 1997: 16). The success of these networks of public administrators, scientists, experts and NGOs in resisting the pressure to become part of the formal policymaking structures and the contribution of non-governmental actors to reducing the much-discussed 'implementation deficit' are now acknowledged, even if reluctantly (Jordan 1999; Knill and Lenschaw 2000). In international politics the Arctic Council brings together eight national governments to discuss common environmental problems. Representatives from 'First Nations' (Inuit, other Native American and Sami communities), scientific experts and policy advisors from international organizations play prominent roles in the discourse (Tennberg 1998; Young and Osherenko 1993). CITES arrangements on the protection of wild animals rely heavily on the work of non-state actors.

The emerging vocabulary of governance speaks to a widely acknowledged change in the nature of politics and policymaking. The prominence of the new vocabulary also illustrates a widespread dissatisfaction with the limited reach of 'set solutions' to thorny political issues imposed through top-down government intervention. One of the virtues of the vocabulary of 'governance' is the way it opens up the cognitive commitments implicit in the thinking about governing and political decision-making. The language of 'governance' seems to help practitioners and theorists alike to unlearn embedded intellectual reflexes and break out of tacit patterns of thinking. This stimulates them to rethink governing, politics and administration against the backdrop of these changing societal processes. Thinking about institutional design nowadays requires sociological input.

Many pressing problems no longer comport with the established systems of politics, administration and society. Practical needs drive the development of co-operative efforts among new constellations of actors. Organizations themselves have become aware of how much more fluid their boundaries are. The demands of business highlight interdependencies and relationships among tasks and prompt the development of inter-organizational networks. Governments also see the tie between interaction, cooperation and results. The consequences of these new inter-organizational activities do not stop with how politics is conducted. They reshape what politics and policymaking are about. We live in an age of 'constitutional politics' (Ackerman 1992) in which constitutive rules are increasingly the object of politics. Collaborative dialogues in California, the role of the variety of committees in the European Union and of the Artic Council all suggest that politics is not 'simply' concerned with outcomes (Ackerman's 'normal' politics); we quarrel about the rules of the game themselves.

The rise of a vocabulary of governance indicates a shift away from well-established notions of politics and brings in new sites, new actors and new themes. There is a move from the familiar topography of formal political institutions to the edges of organizational activity, negotiations between sovereign bodies, and inter-organizational networks that challenge the established distinction between public and private. The disparate actors who populate these networks find nascent points of solidarity in the joint realization that they need one another to craft effective political agreements. Their efforts to find solutions acceptable to all who are involved (and to expand the circle of involvement) nibble and gnaw on the constitutional system of territorially based representative democracy. Notions of politics itself change as new themes occupy centre stage. It is probably no coincidence that these practices are more developed in 'new' spheres of politics such as the environment and the 'life politics' of food and technology.

We witness the creation of a secondary reality of political practice, in the terminology of Mark Warren of 'expansive democracy' (Warren 1992), juxtaposed with standard liberal democracy. Expansive democracy is characterized by increased participation, either by means of small-scale direct democracy or through strong linkages between citizens and broad-scale institutions, by pushing democracy beyond traditional political spheres, and by relating decision-making to the persons who are affected. Democracy has intrinsic value for those who engage in deliberative processes, value that is tied to an immanent potential for transformation and the development of capacities for citizenship that enable individuals and groups to respond directly and effectively to uncertainty and social conflict (Warren 1992: 9). This does not imply that 'classical-modernist' institutions, characterized and maintained by codified, well-established patterns of behaviour, simply fade away. Clearly, much of the business of governing is still effected by the traditional hierarchical institutions of government. However, they must now increasingly compete with open-ended, often unusual, ad hoc arrangements that demonstrate remarkable problem-solving capacity and open up opportunities for learning and change in exactly those circumstances where classical-modernist institutions have failed to deliver.

These trends shift the debate about democracy from the normative to the empirical. This does not absolve analysts from confronting the standard objections to direct democracy levelled by adherents of representative, Madisonian forms of democratic government (deLeon 1997; Warren 1992), but at least these objections can now be addressed on *empirical* grounds. What these developments show is that expansive democracy has moved from an alluring ideal to a budding reality in many regions, countries and policy domains. The new vocabulary of governance rides the back of new political strategies of cooperation that play out at the margins of traditional classical-modernist political institutions. The conceptual rhythm of these efforts pares political reality in new metres and themes.

The need for an interpretative account of governance

Many analysts and commentators seem to suggest that the new vocabulary is the logical answer to a changing world. 'Governance' and 'network management' emerge as responses to the new reality of the 'network society' in which we live. The conceptual shift is legitimized as a necessary adjustment, and a habitual quick reference to Castells (Castells 1996) is mostly seen as sufficient indication of what sort of processes of social change we should have in mind when rethinking politics and policymaking.

Involvement tends to induce myopia, but it is probably safe to say that we are going through a phase of radical social change. At the same time there is something profoundly disturbing about the change of vocabulary and the rush into a restyling of the practices of government that accompany the new vocabulary. First, the new commitments to governance are often not based on a rigorous analysis of what exactly is 'new' about our reality. There is a widespread tendency among analysts to describe the changing reality in terms of key macro-sociological processes. Technological developments (information technologies in particular), globalization, individualization and emancipation are called upon to explain the erosion of the power of the state and politics in general. Yet it might also be seen as an academically legitimated 'mantra' emphasizing various centrifugal tendencies in society without really showing the mechanisms at work. The relationship between macro-sociological change and the crisis of government is often more asserted than argued. To be sure, we would agree that the themes discussed under the headings of the 'network society', the 'risk society', or 'reflexive modernization' have grave repercussions for the character of governance, yet the field is remarkably short on empirical investigations which draw on that literature to see new manifestations of governance in the 'network society' (Beck 1999). It remains unclear how the changes and transformations that are summarized by the term 'network society' exactly challenge the activity and effectiveness of policymaking and politics. How are technological developments related to the introduction of new practices of governing, for instance? Which development causes what? What can we expect from a 'subpolitics' 'outside and beyond' the representative institutions of politics? What is the effect of the widespread usage of managerial language and practices in the new systems of governance, and how does this relate to the processes of macro-sociological change?

Concluding the first volume of his inquiries into the information age, Manuel Castells states: 'Networks constitute the new social morphology of our societies, and the diffusion of network logic substantially modifies the operation and outcomes in processes of production, experience, power and culture' (Castells 1996: 468). In a certain sense this is of course a truism as *any* social formation can be conceived of as a network. The more profound idea is, however, that we can discern *shifts in networks*: new networks eroding the power of previously powerful ones. Moreover, there is the *instability* of networks; the awareness that society experiences a 'new modernity' (Beck) in which established institutions might prove less stable and solid than we assumed and are less well positioned to keep risks at bay. Society should be conceived of as made up of *open or unstable structures* that expand, readjust, shift and evaporate; that create new chances but new risks too, of practices that mobilize on some problems, leaving others aside.

In this context the abstract language of Castells makes sense. What the rise of the vocabulary of governance makes clear is that we experience a shift in language from institutions to networks. Whereas the institutional language implies stability, networks imply fluidity. What comes out in Castells' work is that presence or absence in particular networks, combined with the inherent dynamics of each of these networks, now becomes a critical source of power (1996: 468). However, even this can be seen as a rather superficial statement. We need to know much more about the *character* of this dynamics. As R. A. W. Rhodes argued, the emergence of networks is not the end of state authority per se but the redefinition of it, characterized by a much more open mind allowing for much more diversity and experimentation (Rhodes 2000: 55; cf. also Héritier 1993; Kickert, Klijn and Koppenjan 1997). Likewise, in this context issues of power and interest are not simply rendered meaningless but are redefined and relocated. Hence to take networks and governance seriously by no means implies endorsing a quasi-Thatcherite 'rolling back of the state'. Rather what we want to do is analyse the tensions and conflicts generated by the impact of the newer 'networked' forms of policymaking and political mobilization, and also examine the potential of these new practices to search for more democratic governance. After all, as Torgerson (this volume) points out, there is hardly a reason to idealize classical bureaucracies in this regard. Endorsing this view, our task is to trace telling experiments with governance and to conceptualize the new settings in which politics and policymaking take place as well as the way in which this changes the character of the political game.

We aim to readjust this relationship between social theory and the inquiries into policymaking and politics. Rather than suggesting that these should be about the *impact* of the network society on policymaking and politics, our suggestion would be that we should focus on concrete *manifestations* of policymaking and politics in the era of the network society. In the former tradition we would try to explain various occurrences in politics drawing on macrosociological insights. However, if we focus, empirically, on the manifestations of policymaking and politics in the network society, we would analyse such issues as the way in which different actors nowadays conceive of politics, which actors participate, what they see as effective political action, how actors frame conflict, and to what extent the classical-modernist institutions indeed hamper finding effective solutions to problems people want to see resolved. The idea here clearly is not simply to 'promote' governance as an alternative approach. Likewise, the search is not for the general laws, or the 'essence' of governing in the network society. Right now we aim to focus on the variety of ways in which governing occurs. We thus try to grasp analytically what this means for our understanding of politics and policymaking, of the relationship between state and society, of our possibilities of collective learning and conflict resolution, and of the nature and role of policy analysis in all this.

This book is an attempt to do just that. We draw on the tradition of interpretative analysis of policymaking and politics, a tradition which, we think, has a much wider relevance for understanding contemporary politics than is often appreciated (for an overview, see Gibbons 1987; Rabinow and Sullivan 1979). Rooted in the tradition of the American pragmatism of John Dewey and reinforced by the work of Harold Lasswell (Lasswell 1951, 1971) and many others, the interpretative approach to public policy has already contributed to a more subtle understanding of policymaking and politics.

Over the last twenty-five years interpretative policy analysis has primarily been engaged in a methodological and foundational debate with its positivist counterpart. This has resulted in a strong body of work, in which the biases and limitations of mainstream policy analysis were systematically spelled out (Tribe 1972; Hawkesworth 1988; Dryzek 1989; Yanow 1996; Stone 1997). In this context the label 'post-positivist' policy analysis was of course useful and appropriate. However, it also may have led some to regard interpretative analysis as merely a 'counter-narrative' to the dominant narrative of mainstream, institutionalized policy analysis. It has also led some to proclaim that the postpositivists were engaged in a futile fight with a positivist straw man of their own making, as, clearly, positivism is an antiquated ideal, and no self-respecting policy analyst actually follows the positivist precepts in everyday working routines. In this book we hope to correct that picture. First, positivism is not just a set of methodological principles but, as the philosopher Leszek Kolakowski observed, above all an attitude towards knowledge (Kolakowski 1968), with deeply intertwined ramifications that range from a barely articulated ontological understanding of reality, via methodological principles of how to collect data in a proper way, to a rhetoric of accepted ways of talking about knowledge and policy. In practice this means that positivism does not restrict itself to the conduct of the social sciences, but also, and more importantly, includes normative beliefs and habits of governance and policymaking. Far from being a straw man, positivism is above all a practice of policymaking that is deeply rooted in the institutions of modern government (see also Fischer, this volume). Second, the interpretative approach has solid philosophical underpinnings that precede the policy analytic debate of the last two decades, as Gottweis and Yanow show in this book. In addition, as Fischer (this volume) argues, post-positivist policy analysis displays much greater sociological validity than mainstream analysis. Careful ethnographic observation of scientific work in research labs has shown the extent to which application of scientific methods to concrete problems involves all sorts of improvised, on-the-spot practical judgments that do not conform to the official, objective logic of science (Latour 1987; Lynch 1985).

Third, and most important, the last decade saw an attempt within post-positivist policy analysis to gauge the relationship, both normative and empirical, between policy analysis and the democratic environment in which it functions. Heeding Lasswell's call for a 'policy science of democracy', analysts such as John Dryzek and Peter deLeon have explicitly attempted to assess the place of policy analysis in contemporary representative democracy, and, given the widespread discontent with 'politics' in many western countries, explored the alternatives that might be available (Dryzek 1989). These developments within policy science merge with other developments that point towards the importance of problem formulation and practical judgment in understanding policy problems and finding policy solutions. For example, the analysis of stubborn or 'intractable' policy controversies (Schön and Rein 1994) illuminated that problem solving required a much better understanding of how various parties framed the situation, thus arguing – at least by implication – in favour of a more direct involvement of societal parties in policymaking processes. *The Argumentative Turn in Policy Analysis and Planning*, edited by Frank Fischer and John Forester (1993), and subsequent studies, established once and for all the importance of attending to the discursive dimension of public policy and politics (Fischer 1993; Hajer 1995; Yanow 1996). And solid work in planning theory demonstrated how planners in concrete situations of conflict relied on interactive and deliberative processes of discovering ends, recognizing other parties, marshalling evidence and giving reasons, exploring the implications of various value positions, and developing joint responsibility in concrete situations. Such deliberative approaches to public policy emphasize collective, pragmatic, participatory, local problem solving in recognition that many problems are simply too complicated, too contested and too unstable to allow for schematic, centralized regulation (Forester 1999; Fung 2001; Healey et al., this volume; Innes and Booher, this volume; King and Stivers 1998; Sabel, Fung and Karkkainen 1999).

This book is thus an attempt to build upon these foundations. *Deliberative Policy Analysis* explores ways in which interpretative and deliberative methods of policy analysis help us to come to grips with the political phenomena of our time. It is also an account of the intellectual development of this scholarship after seminal books such as the aforementioned *Argumentative Turn in Policy Analysis and Planning*, *Frame Reflection* or *The Deliberative Practitioner*

(Fischer and Forester 1993; Schön and Rein 1994; Forester 1999, respectively). Yet it is also a book showing that some of the themes that long dominated the critical interpretative agenda – such as the commitment to 'participation' – are in need of a critical reexamination (Innes and Booher, this volume, Torgerson, this volume, Wagenaar and Cook, this volume). In the remainder of this introduction we will spell out the focus of the book in more detail.

Policymaking and politics in the network society: five challenges for analysis

This book explores the changing manifestations of policymaking and politics. It shows new themes for analysis inspired by the macro-sociological work on the network society, the new modernity, or reflexive modernization (Beck 1999; Beck, Giddens and Lash 1994; Castells 1997, 1998; Giddens 1991, 1992; Lash and Szerszinski 1996). The essays combine this macro-sociological orientation with a strong commitment to concrete empirical work. Instead of paraphrasing the work of these sociologists, we distinguish five concrete challenges to policymaking and politics in the era of the network society. Each of them has repercussions for the analysis of policymaking and politics. Together they set the frame for the book.

The new spaces of politics

In the classical-modernist conception political institutions complied with an implicit conceptual '*matrouchka*' system. Like Russian dolls, governments were conceived to fit into one another (local fits into regional, fits into national, fits into international containers) and the political space was related to this system. This model loses its heuristic power: politics and policymaking often happen in configurations that do not conform to the old formats (Dryzek 1999; Eriksen and Fossum 2000; Held 1995). Politics in the network society is characterized by a search for 'multi-level governance', 'regimes', or 'transnational policy discourses' (Hajer 2000b). This reconstitution of political action can be observed at all levels of governing: in the domain of international politics, within the borders of the nation-state, regionally and even locally. Politics and policymaking are reinvented. Traditional top-down bureaucratic structures make way for civil servants, citizens and private sector actors who act as 'entrepreneurs' or 'problem solvers' in policy networks of their own making (Kickert, Klijn and Koppenjan 1997; Sabel, Fung and Karkkainen 1999). Party politics, once the domain of the big debates on the big decisions, finds its central role challenged. In some cases the media create political issues, in other cases it is political action from civil society that speaks to the heart of the people much more effectively than the leader-dependent, party-political practices (Manin 1997). Moreover, there is also a very concrete challenge to the practices of policymaking and politics coming from below. The emergence of 'life politics' (Giddens 1991) implies a new style of political involvement in which people combine lifestyle choices with very focused and discontinuous political activity. Bang and Sörensen captured this in the phenomenon of the 'everyday maker': a type of political activity at grassroots level that resists conceptualization in the familiar terms of participation, social movement or interest group (Bang and Sörensen 1999).

In all cases we see how the topography of politics changes as politics and policymaking is made in new spaces. Characteristically, these new spaces of politics initially exist in an *institutional void*: there are no pre-given rules that determine who is responsible, who has authority over whom, what sort of accountability is to be expected. Yet as politics takes place between organizations, all people bring their own institutional expectations and routines with them. And, as different participants follow their own 'logic of appropriateness' (March and Olsen 1995), politics in new political spaces is never only about content, but inevitably also about the rules of the game and a dynamics of credibility.

To be able to make sense of this sort of complicated communication the scholarship on the politics of symbols and meaning comes in handy. For a long time interpretative social science has focused on symbolic politics and has shown how symbols are not to be mistaken for cute epiphenomena of politics but constitute a key dimension of power and influence in an era of constitutional politics (cf. Edelman 1964). In the instability of a network society this dimension of power and influence deserves our careful attention.

Politics and policymaking under the condition of radical uncertainty

Writing on the impossibility of absolute judgments, Milan Kundera once observed that man is like somebody walking in the mist (Kundera 1992). Yet whenever he looks back to judge the behaviour of people in the past – Mayakovsky, Gottfried Benn, Heidegger – he sees no mist but only clarity. Kundera wondered who are more blind, those who do not see the mist of uncertainty that always surrounds people or those that made the decisions that we – helped by the clarity of hindsight – later see as problematic. It is a useful reminder now that we so often find the suggestion that the challenge for the analysis of policymaking and politics can be captured in terms of the enhanced complexity of society (cf., e.g., Roe 1994). Although it is tempting, it is not unproblematic to suggest that the present is more complex and unpredictable than before. So if we say that some of the most pressing problems of today require us to make 'hard' decisions with only 'soft' evidence (Ravetz and Funtowicz 1993) we should probably add that this is not particularly new.

However, in another sense the network society does indeed add something that constitutes a particular form of complexity for politics and policymaking.

The failures of classical-modernist government have created a widespread *awareness* of the ubiquity of the unintended, perverse consequences of large-scale rationalized planning and the limits to centralized, hierarchical regulation as the dominant mode of collective problem solving (Scott 1998). In its wake it has created a deep unease among citizens about the possibilities of effective and responsible state power. This new social awareness now constitutes a pool of uncertainty surrounding major projects. It is essentially a democratization of knowledge that has created *the social explosiveness* of many contemporary practices (Beck 1992). Networks are not only often 'tightly coupled' and therefore vulnerable systems (Perrow 1999), policymakers are now also forced to rethink the way in which uncertainties are dealt with *socially*. The sudden politicization of food in Europe over the twin crises of BSE and foot-and-mouth disease strongly speaks to this. Whereas within the old regulatory regime the idea prevailed that one could still employ the 'knowledge for policy' practice ('first get the facts right'), the new political reality is one in which this is no longer a credible policymaking strategy. Ulrich Beck has nicely put this condition into words, arguing that we now have an increased 'awareness of our unawareness' (1999: 123). There is a widespread appreciation that governments cannot legitimately keep up the idea that decisions can only be made once the appropriate knowledge is available. Quite the contrary, the new condition is one in which politics has to be made under conditions of 'radical uncertainty' while social protest cannot be controlled with a traditional politics of expertise (Fischer 1993).

This political-sociological shift implies the demise of the myth of absolute knowledge in the public domain. This backfires on the longstanding commitment of policy analysis to deliver knowledge for policy. Under conditions of radical uncertainty policymakers must be made aware of the limits of the (quickly) knowable. Concrete problem solving, joint responsibility, continuous performance-based and collective learning become potential building stones of a viable alternative strategy. In more practical terms, the appreciation of these limits calls for the introduction of concepts such as the 'precautionary principle', according to which we institutionally aim to *avoid* risks knowing that science might, ultimately, show the inconceivable (such as the role of previously unknown 'prions' in the BSE case) to be true. Although this awareness that the condition of radical uncertainty challenges the practices of politics and policymaking is now widespread, institutions are often slow in responding.

The increased importance of 'difference' for our understanding of politics

Modern societies have become culturally more complex. Solving public problems now almost inevitably requires us to deal with an array of groups that do not necessarily share the same language. This might often be true in the literal sense, as with the increase in the number of people who have Spanish as a first language in the USA, or with the linguistic complexity of policymaking in the European Union. Yet it is of course even more widespread if we interpret languages as general systems of signification. Various groups of people conceive of the world in different terms. Here the variety in the concepts and categories that people employ to make sense of the world complicates mutual understanding. Of course, this phenomenon of cultural difference as such is not new, and there is indeed a scholarship that has been addressing such issues in policy analysis (Yanow 1996, 2000b), yet the increased importance of difference magnifies the problem of translation: between languages, between discourses, and ultimately between people (cf. Yanow, this volume; also Torgerson, this volume). The principal meaning of difference is well understood (Benhabib 1996b) but still calls for much more empirical input in terms of its implications for the ways in which policymaking and politics are to be conducted.

Acting upon an awareness of interdependence

The fourth feature of policymaking and politics in the network society is the increased awareness of interdependence. If the condition of difference radically alters the nature of policymaking processes by posing the problem of translation, interdependence brings up the need to overcome these very real discursive barriers. If groups recognize that they are interdependent – whether this is because they share the same physical space or face the same social or environmental problems – they will recognize that they cannot solve key problems without collaboration. If the traditional forms of government are unable to deliver – either because of a lack of legitimacy or simply because there is a mismatch between the scope of the problem and the existing territorial jurisdictions – then networks of actors must create the capacity to interact and communicate. This awareness seems to facilitate a new creativity in thinking about *new modes of conflict resolution* that suggest the essence of dealing with policy conflicts might be a more substantial process of deliberation, shared problem solving and developing regimes of joint responsibility than merely interest-based bargaining. Policymaking becomes an activity of creating what Hannah Arendt once called 'communities of action', able to arrive at shared problem definitions and to agree on common paths of problem resolution.

Policymaking and the dynamics of trust and identity

Following from the above is the issue of the dynamics of trust in contemporary politics. With hindsight we see how the 'normal politics' of the postwar era could mostly rely on the trust and confidence that people collectively stored in or derived from constitutionally embedded institutions. Of course, trust was never simply there. There was an array of rituals and myths that helped sustain trust in government, from the quasi-political role of royalty in some European countries to the widespread reinforcement of governmental action in the relatively uncomplicated media landscape. Now that the magic of these practices is no longer self-evident, we can also see how they always fulfilled a key role as rituals that formed the ideological and emotive cement of national political systems.

It follows that in the 'new politics', in which, typically, actors have to collaborate by transgressing institutional boundaries, *trust cannot be assumed*. Politics and policymaking thus is not simply about finding *solutions* for pressing problems, it is as much about *finding formats that generate trust* among mutually interdependent actors. The concept of network society helps us to understand why it is that we have become interested in themes like 'trust', 'interdependence' and 'institutional capacity'. If problems cannot be solved within the preconceived scales of government, and we still feel the need to address them, we will have to invent new political practices. Here trust suddenly pops up as a key variable that we have taken for granted for a long time (Warren 1999).

The significance of this new understanding of political process as potential generator of trust sheds new light on the range of 'interactive', 'consensus-building' and 'round table' practices that have emerged in the context of the network society. After all, the new interactive policymaking practices are often *the first instance* where people who share a particular space (whether this is a region or a neighbourhood) actually meet. Policymaking thus gets a new meaning as a constitutive force in creating trust among interdependent people. As Forester and others have rightly observed, trust is made by active participation in collective action and problem solving (Forester 1999; Lave and Wenger 1991; Sabel, Fung and Karkkainen 1999). Moreover, it can be shown that the discussions within these policymaking practices generate much more than straightforward debates on solutions for shared problems. Interactive policymaking now is a practice within which people generate new identities. Understanding this dynamic of identities not only proves of great value for generating instrumental solutions for policy problems, it also turns the relationship of politics and policy on its head. Whereas previously policies were the outcome of political battles among political parties, we nowadays see how citizens themselves get worked up about various policy initiatives (or the lack thereof) and become politically active for the very first time. The mediations via political parties, with their meanings and manifestos, make way for an erratic but no less political struggle in the context of specific policy domains.

If the established institutional routines of party politics and neo-corporatist bargaining lose their heuristic value as channels of interest representation, if citizens no longer feel able to identify fully with particular leaders of parties or unions, then policymaking de facto gets a new status. One of the points shown in this volume is that present-day 'policymaking' has become much more important as a stage for politics than before. Whereas in the past we used to think of policymaking as the consequence of political will formation ('We should rebuild the inner cities!'), it now is often policymaking process that leads to political will formation (Hajer, this volume).

Towards a deliberative policy analysis

So, given this changing social and political landscape, the question we address in this book is: *what kind of policy analysis might be relevant to understanding governance in the emerging network society?* As will be obvious, we claim that an interpretative, deliberative approach to policy analysis is relevant here. This implies that a new interpretative policy analysis finds its warrant not so much by being epistemologically or methodologically different from the mainstream approach, but first of all by demonstrating its analytic fertility and practical usefulness in the context of the changes described in the preceding section.

Key to our interpretative approach is the insight that a certain conception of the way scientific method should proceed, and its grounding in beliefs about epistemology, almost inevitably lead to a certain conception of society; an understanding of how society should be organized and managed. Over the last decades the critique of positivist policy analysis has shown that epistemological beliefs, wittingly or unwittingly, have normative consequences for one's political preferences. What counts as justified belief and valid knowledge sets limits to the kind of questions and information that are acceptable in the political debate. And what has standing in societal discourse determines not only who is allowed into the halls of decision-making and who is kept out, it also designates what is considered a legitimate political argument in political discourse and what not, which rules of interpersonal political conduct are preferred over others, and, ultimately, what kind of society we envision ourselves living in. These issues gain a new relevance in a network society marked by a greater variety of value preferences, unclear rules of the game and great challenges in terms of shaping society.

Interpretative policy analysis, as both Fischer and Yanow argue in this volume, differs markedly from its positivist counterpart. Positivist epistemology is an attempt to erect a firewall between scientific procedure and political organization. Instead we suggest in this book that the way to think about this relation is in terms of *fit*: a fit between a conception of science and knowledge on the one hand and the nature of political organization on the other. The link between the two is the way that a particular conception of epistemology, and in its wake, a conception of the purpose and methods of the policy sciences, simultaneously enables and limits opportunities for collective inquiry and for knowledge thus acquired to contribute to the solution of social problems and the development of political identity.

What, then, does a policy analysis that fits the currently emerging network society look like? Given the intellectual impact of *The Argumentative Turn* on the policy field, it seems no more than fair that we take this book as our point of reference. Interestingly, only half of the 'message' of that book seems to have been taken up in the literature. Fischer and Forester sought to make the policy analysis community aware of the consequences of the role of language in policymaking. As will be remembered, they argued that language doesn't just mirror reality; it actively shapes the way we perceive and understand it. Yet this immediately brought up issues of value, distortion and outside influence on the work of the analyst. As Fischer and Forester (1993: 1) put it:

> The controversy of relevance to policy analysis and planning here involves central questions of truth and power. If analysts' ways of representing reality are necessarily selective, they seem as necessarily bound up with relations of power, agenda setting, inclusion and exclusion, selective attention, and neglect. If analysts' ways of representing policy and planning issues must make assumptions about causality and responsibility, about legitimacy and authority, and about interest, needs, values, preferences, and obligations, then the language of policy and planning analyses not only depicts but also constructs the issues at hand.

This part of their argument was enthusiastically – with hindsight perhaps somewhat too enthusiastically – embraced in the policy literature since then and resulted in reams and reams of interpretative and narrative policy analysis of dubious validity. If there was no objective reality, and if the insights of the analyst were ever so many constructions, it seemed that questions of precision, validity and generalizability were no longer important. Intrinsically, so it seemed, policy analysis represented a point of view, so why not declare this up front and side with whatever group the analyst chose to represent?

Yet in the second, and much less widely recognized, part of their argument, Fischer and Forester explicitly countervail this relativism. Here they situate policy argument in the context of *practice*. Worldviews are not made out of whole cloth, but are shaped, incrementally and painfully, in the struggle of everyday people with concrete, ambiguous, tenacious, practical problems and questions. Their deep understanding of, and respect for, the day-to-day work of planners and policymakers shapes the editors' understanding of the new face of policy analysis. People in such situations tell stories and formulate arguments to get a handle on this world of complexity and uncertainty, but stories and arguments are social commodities, not abstract armchair constructs designed by analysts far removed from the concrete policy scene. Their validity and feasibility are assessed in communities of people who are knowledgeable about the problem at hand, and who are all too conscious of the political, financial and practical constraints that define the situation for which they bear responsibility. These are people who realize that stories and arguments are always provisional, never the last word on the situation. They hold up until the situation changes, constraints are tightened or relaxed and/or a better story is told. Action, thus, structures and disciplines understanding. In this sense designing good policy arguments is itself a practice. To quote Fischer and Forester once more:

> To see policy analysis as argumentative practices is to attend closely to the day-to-day work analysts do as they construct accounts of problems and possibilities. Pecognizing these accounts as constrained, organizational accomplishments in the face of little time and poor data, we can evaluate the analysts' arguments not only for their truth or falsity but also for their partiality, their selective framing of the issues at hand, their elegance or crudeness of presentation, their political timeliness, their symbolic significance, and more. Policy and planning arguments are practical productions. (1993: 2–3)

In this book we will pick up on this view of policy analysis that Fischer and Forester outlined almost ten years ago. However, we will not just draw out and elaborate upon some of their insights that were more or less implicit in their original statement. In particular we will bring into our analytic orbit the societal context in which a new interpretative policy analysis has to play a role.

Similar to Fischer and Forester our understanding of policy analysis is geared towards the concrete, everyday activities of citizens, politicians and administrators. Thus, when there is talk of 'democracy', what we have in mind is not some abstract philosophical idea of democracy, but the concrete organization of collective social and political life 'as we know it'. Whatever we have to say about the nature and foundation of the policy sciences, its litmus test will be that it must 'work' for the everyday reality of modern democracy. Yet we also believe that the practical applicability of the policy sciences has been hampered in the past by erroneous beliefs about the nature of the social sciences, their relation to political practice and their respective philosophical foundations (cf. also Fischer, this volume). Paraphrasing a famous dictum, we believe that 'nothing is as practicable as a well-understood epistemology'. The underlying theme here is an issue that has all too often remained implicit in mainstream policy analysis: what kind of knowledge is politically relevant to society? And, to apply this to the network society: what counts as good evidence in this society of flux? How should we conceive of the relation between analysis and democracy in that context? So, wherever necessary, we will indicate the philosophical justification of what we believe policy science should look like. Although our focus is practical, on policy analysis in concrete everyday situations, our analysis of inquiry and practice takes epistemology into account.

Policy analysis for the network society

How then should we conceive of a policy science that fits the contemporary network society; a policy science that is up to the five challenges outlined in an earlier section? We will argue that a policy science whose epistemological features correspond to the nature of modern democracy rests on three pillars: interpretation, practice and deliberation. In the remainder of this introduction we will discuss in more detail these three pillars and how they relate to distinct features of the network society.

Policy analysis is interpretative

Mainstream policy analysis rests on philosophical realism. It assumes that the data and observations that form the input of its analytic techniques are non-problematical, or, as Kolakowski puts it, that 'there is no real difference between "essence" and "phenomenon" ' (1968: 3). This assumption about the way policy analysts hooks onto the external world is central to the promise of rational policy analysis to deliver objective, certain knowledge to their political taskmasters. Its scientific authority as a final arbiter of politically charged questions is intimately connected to the philosophical assumption of realism. Yet, it is precisely this assumption that has been the focus of intense criticism in post-war analytic philosophy.

In its unadulterated, naive form philosophical realism rests on the twin assumptions (a) that a world exists that is independent of our knowledge or consciousness of it, and (b) that we have access to that world in a pure form, independent of the techniques to perceive or apprehend that external world (Bailey 2000). Our images of the world are imprints on a passive mind; the workings of the mind kick in only after the imprints, the brute sense data, have been registered. Words, in this view, are nothing more than labels for stable objects in the external world (hence, the apt depiction of naive realism as the 'museum view of reference'). It is this understanding of the relation between mind and world that has been the focus of attack in post-war analytic philosophy, particularly in a number of famous articles by Quine (Quine 1961, 1969). Quine's position is that the relation between words and objects is intrinsically undetermined. That is, the semantic meaning of a word is not so much a fixed relation between a particular mental image and an object out there in the world, but arises out of our understanding of other people's behavioural dispositions towards the object in question. As Quine puts it:

> Seen according to the museum myth, the words and sentences of a language have their determinate meanings. To discover the meaning of the native's words we may have to observe his behavior, but still the meaning of the words are supposed to be determined in the native's mind. His mental museum, even in cases where behavioral criteria are powerless to discover them for us. When on the other hand we recognize with Dewey that 'meaning . . . is primarily a property of behavior', we recognize that there are no meanings, nor likenesses nor distinctions of meaning, beyond what are implicit in people's dispositions to overt behavior.   (1969: 29)

The implications of this behavioural conception of meaning and reference for the way we struggle with the meaning of words are momentous. To mention just a few: meaning is the product, not of individual mental processes, but of human communities. Behavioural disposition is a synonym for the habits and conventions of collective human practices. Second, if we leave the museum view of meaning behind, it is no longer useful to think of meaning in terms of single words. For example, the meaning of the word 'fish' is dependent on a cloud of associated meanings (and their behavioural dispositions) such as 'mammal', 'bird', 'water', etc. The argument applies *a fortiori* to the words of social reality such as 'labour' or 'natural environment', which can be understood only through a deep appreciation of the complex cultural dispositions and habits in which such terms are embedded. Third, and perhaps most important to our argument, exactly how you construct meanings out of a cluster of behavioural dispositions is undecided by the behavioural dispositions themselves. Differently put, the behavioural dispositions surrounding the term 'labour' or 'natural environment' do not themselves contain any decision rules that decide in advance how to derive in a necessary or undisputed way the 'pure' meaning of the term 'labour' or 'natural environment'. The manner in which we slice the nebula of surrounding meanings has to come from outside those meanings, for example from a particular background theory or grand narrative that serves as frame of reference, or a set of behavioural dispositions that is anchored in a particular way of life or a particular way of doing things.

What we are on to here is the ontological correlate to *The Argumentative Turn*. In concrete everyday situations people create meaning out of their behavioural dispositions, or, in the vocabulary of Fischer and Forester, by participating in practices. Like theirs, Quine's argument prevents extreme relativism in the determination of semantic meaning. Most people will have a sufficient working knowledge of terms such as 'labour' to enable them to participate in a general discussion or write a letter to the editor about, for example, the desirability or foolishness of active labour-market policies. How we interpret social reality, either as a lay person or a policy analyst, is to a large extent guided by the social rules that constitute social practices; rules we have internalized in long processes of habituation and socialization (Fay 1975: 75). Yet, the exact semantic meaning of what actors argue is not out there, visible for all, in the words and phrases that make up a discussion or letter to the editor, nor in some after-the-fact conclusion that this or that action must have been guided by such and such a social rule. Rather it is composed of the total of the underlying narratives and behavioural dispositions that make up that particular individual's life world.

The upshot of this argument is that meaning and context are only loosely coupled. Understanding of what an actor wants to convey therefore has something of the Münchhausen effect. How actors slice their context to construct semantic meaning can be understood only by reconstructing, on line, during their interactions with others, what it is that the actors want to convey. Actors and their audiences thereby rely on what they have in common; on the lifestyle and cultural content they share. Wagenaar and Hartendorp's analysis of the story of a welfare administrator (Wagenaar and Hartendorp 2000) is an example of how construction of meaning functions in the everyday world of public administration. It shows a practice of meaning-making that, although ambiguous and open-ended, is remarkably well adapted to the inconsistencies and contradictions that are characteristic of the everyday world of administrators in a fragmented bureaucratic environment characterized by power differentials and lack of coordination, and, by extension, characteristic of the world of policymakers and citizens in general.

Policy analysis is practice-oriented

The obligation to act upon the situation at hand is the decisive characteristic of the work of policymakers and public administrators. At the same time we believe that the action orientation of political and administrative work has been consistently overlooked in the policy sciences. Here we seem to struggle with the legacy of the father of positivism, Auguste Comte. Of all his beliefs and assumptions, the primacy of thought over action in the analysis of concerted social action is perhaps the most inveterate, to the point that it has become an unnoticed intellectual habit among both admirers and detractors of positivism. In all of his writings Comte proved himself to be highly suspicious of practitioners. Social reform could not be 'confided to merely practical men', and the 'spiritual' (read intellectual) and 'temporal' (read practical) power should be kept separated at all costs (Comte, in Lenzer 1975: xl). In fact, Comte saw social reform as an essentially theoretical endeavour. The design of the new social scheme, the 'ensemble', according to Comte, was a purely theoretical project, based upon the general social laws that were the fruit of the '*science social*'. The implementation of this scheme was considered an afterthought by Comte; as merely a matter of 'details' that followed seamlessly from the theoretical scheme, and that belonged to the realm of practical man. 'The *labor* of social reorganization', according to Comte, 'is in essence theoretical' (Comte in Lenzer 1975: xl, emphasis added).

All this would be mere historical curiosity if echoes of this position did not resonate through the policy sciences to this very day. In fact, the policy sciences in their modern-day institutional form are themselves based on a deep-seated suspicion of 'politics'. The promise of traditional, rational policy analysis is precisely to sanitize political decision-making from irrational politics. Moreover, the relation between analysis and implementation, as presented, for example, in a classic of policy analysis by Stokey and Zeckhauser, has the same automatic, even tautological, quality as with Comte. If the analytic techniques are applied well, then the 'one best decision' follows automatically (Stokey and Zeckhauser 1978). From the rational perspective, the analysis of social problems is at heart a cerebral, armchair activity (Allison and Zelikow 1999).

We believe that one of the main reasons for the often observed ineffectiveness and irrelevance of the traditional policy sciences is precisely this Cartesian bias; the gap between the theoretical rationality of the policy sciences and the practical rationality of the practitioner. Policymakers and administrators work under the legal or organizational obligation to come up with solutions for concrete, specific issues in areas for which, mandated by their job description, they bear responsibility. For example, an administrator in a child-protection agency may have to decide either to place an at-risk child with a foster family or let it remain with its dysfunctional parent(s). A police officer may have to decide whether to break up a street brawl or trust in the powers of reason within a group of unruly youths. The obligation to act is not restricted to street-level bureaucrats, but applies with equal force to higher-level administrators. For example, the head of staff at a government ministry may have to decide how and when to present a plan for reorganization to the minister. The public prosecutor may have to decide if and how to deal with corrupt police officers. A mayor may have to decide whether or not to order the eviction of squatters at the risk of sparking civil unrest. These are situations that involve practical judgment, reflection and the bringing to bear of knowledge and experience, but above all, these are situations that require the administrator to act, to step into the situation and do something about it.

Interestingly, the emergence of the concept of 'governance' in the contemporary debate seems to lead in some cases to a renewed appreciation for the action dimension in public policy. For example, the cases of a new politics in the network society that are analysed in the first part of this book (Innes and Booher, Healey et al., Hajer), all step away from the rationalist scheme of preconceived preferences and clearly defined means to achieve these. Instead, we see practitioners of very different plumage wrestle with conflict, power, uncertainty and unpredictability. Solutions are not so much formulated as arrived at, haltingly, tentatively, through acting upon the situation at hand and through the application of practical wisdom in negotiating concrete situations. And always, there is the risk of policy failure and stagnation, as the airport case in Wagenaar and Cook (this volume) shows. Consequently, as these cases demonstrate, the role of policy analysis changes too. It is no longer about the invention of solutions *for* society; it often finds itself in the 'mud' of policy practice, trying to assist in the discovery of new policy options and the formulation of compelling arguments.

What does a policy science that takes the fundamental action orientation of policymaking (and public administration, for that matter) seriously, look like? Traditional policy science focuses on 'problems' and 'decisions'. We suggest that a reformulated, deliberative policy science takes *practices* as its unit of analysis. Practice, as Wagenaar and Cook argue in this volume, is, despite its current popularity in post-positivist policy writings, a notoriously difficult concept to grasp. Practice is more a theoretical perspective than a single concept. It is an attempt to develop a unified account of knowing and doing. It expresses the insight that knowledge, knowledge application and knowledge creation cannot be separated from action; that acting is the high road to knowing. Yet it would be wrong to see the concept of practice as merely a synonym for action. Practice theory integrates the actor, his or her beliefs and values, resources and external environment, in one 'activity system', in which social, individual and material aspects are interdependent. The focus in such activity systems is on the way the different elements *relate* to each other rather than on the elements themselves. Practice theory focuses on action as a central strategy through which the individual gains knowledge about the world. It suggests that people negotiate the world (both social and physical) by *acting* upon it. Also, the concept of practice presupposes the social. It implies that in negotiating a particular situation the actor is always aware of his or her position in a larger network of relations and obligations. People learn about the world in public, shared processes in which they test what they have learned. The way they test the relevance and validity of their knowledge in particular situations is through public discourse. The concept of practice thus stresses communication and other-directedness. And, finally, the practice concept stresses value. Actors, in interpretively moving about in their environment, articulate value in appreciating the possibilities and limitations of the situation at hand. Values tell them what is worth paying attention to and serve as compelling reasons for what to do in concrete situations.

The upshot is that the practice perspective introduces an awareness of the importance of practical judgment – *phronesis* in Aristotelian terms – in policy analysis. With this it acts as a corrective to both institutional and discourse-analytic explanations of public policy. Institutional explanations often assume a one-way influence of the institutional context upon the actor. In this sense, institutional explanations beg the question of how actors in fact organize the particulars of their institutional environment to move about in an effective and feasible manner in the concrete situation at hand. Practice theory aims to overcome the traditional actor–structure dichotomy by exploring the dialectic between the two, where, in the process of acting in a concrete situation, each brings the other into being. Practice theory also transcends discourse analysis in that it shows that the everyday actions of policy actors underlie, often in an unrecognized way, the very entities and categories that make up political narratives about contentious social issues. Moreover, as Fischer also points out in his contribution to this book, a focus on practice firmly roots interpretative analysis in the concrete objects, experiences and constraints of the world around us, thereby putting limits on what is plausible in the interpretation of policy texts and 'text analogues'.

Policy analysis is deliberative

When we talk of community in this book, we are not thinking of abstract or idealized theoretical constructs, but of living entities that can be identified in space and time. We have in mind social entities made up of people who are in one way or another engaged with their environment, both immediate and proximal. Their engagement is both fuelled and expressed in their passions and feelings about certain situations. They harbour sympathies and antipathies towards the people that make up their world. They are strongly committed to some subjects and indifferent and apathetic towards others. They see the plans and actions of their government or other actors as furthering or threatening their interests – and, in a more tacit and implicit manner, as strengthening or confounding their collective identity. Above all, they perceive and organize their world through more or less articulated value positions on a range of subjects. As a consequence, *conflict* is intrinsic to human communities. Policy issues are, almost by definition, contested. Moreover, resources of money and power are differentially distributed among the actors involved. Often these differences erupt in more or less deep-seated conflicts. Sometimes conflicts result in stalemate and policy controversies, which are immune to fact or reason (Schön and Rein 1994). Whatever reformulation of policy sciences we can come up with, both methodologically and epistemologically, it must be up to the task of understanding and furthering the interests of such real-world, conflict-ridden, living communities.

The conflictual, adversarial nature of policy communities is not just an empirical observation; it is important to be aware that it has philosophical grounding too. It is, by now, a well-accepted insight in contemporary moral philosophy that, inevitably, in the everyday concrete world we inhabit, at some point the great values begin to contradict each other. 'Value pluralism' describes the condition in which conceptions of desirable social states are plural *and* in which the realization of these conceptions mutually exclude each other. As the philosopher John Kekes puts it: 'Pluralists are committed . . . to the view that the conceptions of a good life and the values on whose realization good lives depend are plural and conditional. These conceptions and values, however, are often related in such a way, according to the pluralists, that the realization of one excludes the realization of the other' (Kekes 1993: 21). 'Conditional' here means that no value or moral code exists that is sufficiently authoritative to always override other values in case of conflict. Instead pluralists assert that every value or combination of values may be defeated by some other value or combination of values that, in the specific context, is more important (Kekes 1993: 20). Perhaps no one has expressed this inherent feature of human community better than Isaiah Berlin. 'Some among the Great Goods', as he puts it, 'cannot live together' (Berlin 1997: 11).

Value pluralism as an inescapable condition of everyday life regularly brings policymakers into situations of deep value conflict (Hajer 2002; Wagenaar 1999). Obviously, traditional policy analysis with its epistemological bias towards emotivism (the belief that values are nothing more than expressions of feeling and therefore beyond the reach of logic), and its methodological concomitant, the strict separation of fact and value, has been unable to deal with value pluralism. As a result, not only has value conflict been under-acknowledged as a regular feature of policymaking, but traditional, positivist policy analysts have developed little or no understanding of the way ordinary people, including ordinary policymakers and administrators, handle value conflict (Wagenaar 1999). The entrance into dealing with value conflict is the conditionality of values. Value pluralists, as we saw at the start of the preceding section, believe values to be conditional in that they think that the context in which values are realized determines their weight relative to one another. In fact, although value and context can be distinguished, in the everyday experience of individual policymakers or administrators, values cannot be seen apart from their context, similar to the way that, in the act of listening, the pitch and the typical sound colour of a violoncello cannot be separated. Everyday policymakers deal with value conflict through the exertion of practical judgment (Larmore 1987).

This is not the place to describe in detail all that is involved in practical judgment. In summary form, practical judgment is immediate, intuitive, concrete, interactive, pragmatic, personal and action-oriented. Moreover, practical judgment is something that comes naturally to people. It is something they do in the course of their everyday activities, usually without giving it much thought. Practical judgment is problem-oriented. It is an integral part of people's problem-solving activities, in which the joint construction of feasible problem definitions is as important as the solution of those agreed-upon problems. This interactive working on problems is relational and emotive. It involves the maintenance of relations as a form of political rationality; that is, as a way of assuring the cooperation of others when dealing with future problems. In addition, a perceptive, balanced understanding of the feelings and emotions a particular situation generates is an important element of practical judgment. Emotions function simultaneously as a mode of perception and discernment, and as a way of giving meaning to facts, events and behaviour in circumstances of uncertainty. As will be clear by now, practical judgment, contrary to received opinion, is not something that happens inside the mind of individual actors. Rather it both emerges and is accounted for in people's continuous interactions with each other. As John Forester summarizes it: 'Before the rationality of choice comes the prior practical rationality of careful attention, critical listening, setting out issues, and exploring working relationships as pragmatic aspects of problem construction' (Forester 1999: 34).

Practical judgment aims as much at good result as at proper procedure. But what counts in the end is, given the multitude of constraints that characterize most policy situations, usually not the definitive resolution of a conflict, but the discovery of a workable definition of the problem, or the temporary stabilization of a situation that is unhinged or threatens to become so, or the emergence of personal insight that allows the actor to function more effectively in the situation at hand. Concrete, everyday situations are characterized above all by what Hilary Putnam calls the 'interpenetration' of fact, value and theory. Putnam uses this phrase to emphasize, as he states, 'that the interdependence of which I speak is *not* an interdependence of elements which can always be distinguished, even notionally' (Putnam 1995: 57). To find their way in such situations, people deliberate. Such deliberation, as will now be obvious, should not be confused with the kind of systematic, principled reasoning of traditional moral philosophy. Rather, deliberative judgment emerges through collective, interactive discourse. As we saw above, telling stories and reacting to each other's stories in situations of collective action does a lot of the work of practical judgment (Forester 1999; Wagenaar 1997). As a result, practical judgment is not a one-shot affair, but on the contrary evolves slowly, often tentatively and haltingly, through mutual inquiry and mutual discourse with others.

Conclusion: the transformative work of policy analysis

In this introduction we have attempted to sketch the contours of a deliberative policy science. At the outset of the second section, we described our challenge in terms of fit; that is we outlined a policy science that helps to understand the new forms of governance that are emerging in the network society that we described in the first section. Summing up, we argue for a careful analysis of these new practices of governance, without immediately suggesting they all represent successful examples of deliberative democracy. After all, in some cases there is reason to be sceptical about any suggestion that the emergence of new loose forms equals the withering away of the state or heralds a new era of direct democracy. On the other hand, the experiments sometimes also produce remarkable results and, one may add, we are in need of new systems of governing in an era in which so many of the most pressing problems do not conform to the levels at which governmental institutions are most capable of producing effective or legitimate solutions.

What we have added in this introduction is the suggestion that it is a deliberative policy analysis that helps us to understand these problems of governance. In this, we pointed at the changing nature of policymaking in the network society that, with hindsight, seems to support some of the critical claims of the argumentative turn in policy analysis. Indeed, the emergence of deliberative forms of planning and policy analysis we see as a retreat from the Absolute. This is more than merely the observation that policymaking now operates under conditions of radical uncertainty and deep-value pluralism. The retreat from the Absolute implies the acknowledgement both on a philosophical and a pragmatic level, that the epistemic notion of certain, absolute knowledge, and its practical corollary of command and control, in concrete, everyday situations are deeply problematical. It is the insight that whatever knowledge we possess must be assessed for its relevance and usefulness in interaction with the concrete situation at hand, *and* that this ongoing process of assessment occurs in situations of intense social interaction. The capacity for practical judgment is above all a social good that is in high demand in the era of the network society. From this insight follow most of the observations and prescriptions about politics, policymaking and policy analysis we outlined above.

But, perhaps most importantly, it follows that a deliberative analysis of policy and politics implies a radically altered conceptualization of citizenship, politics and the state. Deliberative policy science sides with, as we called it in the first section, an 'enhanced' conception of democracy. Not just as a normative statement of how we would like to see the relation between citizens and the state, but also, and more importantly, as an empirical observation of the direction things take in contemporary society. Politics and problem solving have changed character and it is our task to bring out the new ways in which politics and policymaking are conducted. This, above all, is how we envision the notion of a fit between policy science and policymaking in the network society.

For policymaking it means not simply the straightforward 'inclusion' of those affected by public policy in the domain of policy formulation, decision-making and administrative implementation, but also the search for the *appropriate way* of involving the many 'others' that are affected by it (cf. Torgerson, this volume). Participation is no longer a standard solution, it has to be reinvented and will appear in many different guises. It means the creation of well-considered linkages between citizens, traditional policy institutions and the new and often unstable policymaking practices. For policy science the implication is a long-overdue retreat from its dominant self-understanding as the provider of certain, 'scientific' knowledge about quasi non-problematical policy problems to a clearly identifiable policymaking elite. Instead, a deliberative democracy and policy analysis both aim at the creation and enhancement of the possibilities of self-transformation. They aim, through direct and active participation in democratic deliberation over concrete policy problems, to develop autonomy, or a capacity for judgment (see Hajer, this volume). Autonomy and self-transformation are not only instrumentally useful in that they enhance the collective capacity for productive inquiry, but also, and perhaps above all, intrinsically valuable. As Warren puts it:

> Without the experience of argument and challenge within democratic public spheres, individuals will have little sense for what relates them to, and distinguishes them from, others; and this deprives them of an essential condition of self-development. By raising one's wants, needs and desires to the level of consciousness and by formulating them in speech, one increases one's sense of identity and autonomy – *aside from any advantages that might accrue from the substantive outcomes of collective decisions.*
> (Warren 1992: 12, emphasis added)

Clearly, this outline for a deliberative policy science and policymaking raises more questions than we can answer in these introductory remarks. Yet, we also believe that we have little choice, given the widely documented limitations of classical-modernist representative politics and the failures of centralized policymaking in the emerging network society, to move along on the road towards deliberative democracy and deliberative policy analysis. The papers in this book are so many explorations of the possibilities and limitations, the benefits and drawbacks, the prospects for and obstacles to deliberative policy analysis in the network society, and thereby shed light on its core transformative promise.

Outline of the book

Part I, 'Policy conflict and deliberation in the network society', documents and analyses several experiments with new forms of governance, in Great Britain, California and the Netherlands. In all three cases new forms of policy deliberation emerged, next to or in between existing institutional arrangements. Apart from documenting the cases, the authors seek to come up with an analytical understanding of the dynamics of conflict resolution and policy deliberation.

In the first chapter Judith Innes and David Booher analyse an array of experiments in intergovernmental cooperation and consensus-building processes in the San Francisco Bay area. Innes and Booher point out that the experiments were successful in resolving stalemates in complex and controversial public issues concerning resource allocation, infrastructure development, fiscal reform, school reform and growth management. Introducing 'collaborative dialogue' as a conceptual tool to analyse these new policymaking practices, Innes and Booher explore how what they call 'authentic dialogue' can be created. They show the changes required for this sort of collaborative policymaking endeavour. Interestingly, they do not take deadlock or conflict in the traditional policy system as their starting point, but public problems. The networks of players around such a problem are to be facilitated, in terms of staff and resources but also by developing mutual trust. So, for instance, one of the reasons why collaborative dialogue was successful in the case of the conflict-ridden water issue was that the group could hire its own staff and consultants who were answerable only to them.

Innes and Booher are well aware that collaborative dialogues are far from being the dominant approach to policymaking and discuss the many obstacles to the successful employment of such practices. Yet at the same time they show that the influence of collaborative practice should be analysed in a different way, not simply in terms of policy outcomes but in terms of restructuring the policy networks and its discourse, of the emergence of social capital and more empathic relationships among participants, of collective learning, and of increased capacity for innovative system adaptation to changing circumstances.

In the second chapter Patsy Healey, Claudio de Magalhaes, Ali Madanipour and John Pendlebury discuss 'institutional capacity building' in the city of Newcastle-upon-Tyne in the north-east of England. In particular they investigate the career of the Grainger Town Partnership, an unusual coalition of forces aiming to reconstruct and restore part of the old inner city. They show how the classical-modernist division of policy agendas into 'sectoral' concerns lacked flexibility and imagination to deal with inner-city problems. Moreover, the policy networks that built up around these sectoralized policy agendas made it very hard to break out of the established policy regimes. They analyse policy action in terms of the knowledge resources, relational resources and mobilization capabilities that actors draw upon and generate. This allows, according to Healey and her collaborators, for a better understanding of the new practices. Interestingly, they explore ways to combine both discourse analysis and an institutionalist approach. By so doing they can identify to what extent the struggle for new forms of governance is 'merely ripples on the surface of a settled modality of governance' or unsettles a whole culture of governance relations.

The chapter is also effective in rebutting any naive suggestion that we 'merely' have to readjust to a 'new reality' in which government structures have made way for new flexible forms of governance. Instead, the authors show the tensions and conflicts generated by newer 'networked' forms of policymaking and political mobilization, and illustrate how more traditionally organized municipal institutions have to readjust. They emphasize the gradual transformation that takes place, in terms of both new discourses as well as new ways of governing that is the result of such experiments.

In the third chapter, Maarten Hajer analyses the case of 'nature development' in the Netherlands. He shows the limited effectiveness of classical-modernist practices in which plans for nature conservation are first agreed upon nationally, assuming that they subsequently only have to be implemented locally. In analysing the case Hajer shows that the emerging political conflict was not related merely to the intended change of policy but at least as much to the institutional way of conducting politics. For him, this suggests that the conventional way of approaching policymaking should be reconsidered. In our age it is often policymaking that really ignites people politically. In the face of the crisis of party politics he suggests that policymaking processes gain a new, and as yet

unexamined, meaning and importance. In the days of classical-modernist politics, politicians were recognizable, people knew where politics was conducted
and by whom. In most cases people also knew what the key cleavages were,
what they wanted to get from politics and whom to approach or vote for. Yet
in the network society this is no longer that obvious. People have much more
erratic political preferences that they often become aware of only in concrete
controversies; controversies, moreover, that often relate to particular policy
initiatives. Given the fact that classical-modernist political institutions are, by
themselves, not sufficiently powerful to achieve policy change, a new agenda
emerges for policy analysis.

The case illustrates the limited effectiveness of classical-modernist political practices in dealing with the new fragmented and unanticipated political
dynamics, and documents the subsequent response from government. New 'interactive' policymaking practices were successful where traditional practices
failed. Drawing on the analysis of this success Hajer identifies new tasks for
a deliberative policy analysis. He suggests discourse analysis as a tool to help
fulfil that promise.

The answer to political conflict and value pluralism in the fragmented institutional landscape of the network society, as the authors in the first section argue,
is some form of democratic political deliberation. The three chapters in part II,
'Rethinking policy discourse', have as their common theme the obstacles that
the real world of politics and administration present to such uncoerced and open
deliberation and the political reflexivity this is supposed to promote. After all,
as we argued earlier, what we have in our mind's eye when we evoke democratic
deliberation is not some abstract, idealized theoretical construct, but real people
and communities who struggle with concrete issues in settings that are rife with
conflict and power differentials. In such settings attempts at deliberative problem solving will be marred by inequalities in political information and access,
by ingrained patterns of exclusion and marginalization, and particularly by insidious, unrecognized biases in policy rhetoric and perception. The bottom line
is that open democratic deliberation and citizen engagement, while a promising
and perhaps necessary road to take in the political-institutional landscape of
the new modernity, will be constrained from all sides by the realities of power
politics in the liberal constitutionalist state. The chapters in this section explore
the nature and extent of these constraints.

Torgerson situates the constraining influence on democratic deliberation
in the administrative-analytic complex that governs modern society. Public
administration in advanced industrial society, he argues, is above all characterized by a particular orientation (simplification of social and technical
complexity and the employment of a value-neutral, technocratic language in
the service of hierarchical control). In most societies the entrenched position

of the political-administrative elite results in a hegemonic discourse about concrete policy issues, such as environmental pollution or spatial planning, that effectively marginalizes certain groups whose lives will be affected by the former's decisions. In rare cases, enlightened administrators are able break through this discursive dominance with innovative experiments in inclusive discursive designs, but more often, even these attempts at open deliberation will result in cooptation and the stifling of alternative voices. On the basis of two cases in environmental politics, Torgerson argues for the opening up of the hegemonic space by the introduction of counter-cultural, 'carnivalesque' elements in the discourse, a theatre of the absurd, that challenge the established dynamics of power, emphasize the ambivalences of concrete problem situations against the technocratic simplifications of administrators and thus create reflective moments of policy discourse.

In addition to the constraining influence of the administrative-analytic complex, there is a more hidden obstacle to open, democratic deliberation that emanates from the taken-for-granted ways of doing things in specific societal domains. Practices interconnect intuitions, understandings, commitments and action into a meaningful, self-evident way of going about things in a particular domain. Both Wagenaar and Cook and Laws and Rein in their respective chapters show that such organized systems of action and belief powerfully shape actors' understanding of complex social and technological situations to the extent that they form their own justification and drive other ways of doing or understanding outside the sphere of what is believed to be feasible or acceptable. Their foundation in the spontaneity of people's everyday activities makes their constraining influence on open democratic deliberation particularly insidious as they, in Bourdieu's felicitous phrase, 'naturalize their own arbitrariness'. Bias understates the effect of practices upon people's understanding of the world; the term second nature would be more apposite. Practice theory goes beyond interpretation in that it stresses the *sense* (over the more cerebral *meaning*) of a situation. People who are engaged in a practice have assumed a particular social identity that they signal to their environment, and that validates what they do and say both to themselves and to the world at large.

The chapter of Wagenaar and Cook shows how practice has emerged over the last two decades as a key concept for a deliberative policy analysis. Outlining in an instructive way the variety of ways that scholars in philosophy and social theory have used the concept thus far, they employ it in their own case study. Practice, they argue, may be difficult to define, more a perspective than a concept, but in broad-brush strokes it can be seen as a patterned configuration of human activity that, in its execution, shapes and defines preferences, meanings and solutions. Using the example of the political stalemate around the expansion of Schiphol airport near Amsterdam, they show that the practices of airport managers and employees literally create the categories of the public discourse concerning the airport, thereby introducing a powerful bias in the debate that consistently marginalizes citizens and groups worried about noise, safety and pollution. Wagenaar and Cook then argue that, when properly understood, practices, instead of limiting the discourse, may function as units of reflexivity. To this end analysts and citizens must probe the problem ecology that prompted the practice, and the myriad of often arbitrary practical and moral choices that constituted it in the first place. Similarly to Torgerson they see the analyst's task as revealing the hidden ambiguity and uncertainty that is buried inside taken-for-granted policy practices and discourses, with the purpose of creating reflexive space. Practitioners, citizens and administrators may in this way cooperate in a problem-oriented, bottom-up, empowered kind of democratic deliberation on concrete issues.

The chapter of Laws and Rein contains a further elaboration of the well-known concept of a policy frame. The frame concept explains stubborn policy controversies by situating them in conflicting structures of value and belief that capture what is problematic and how to resolve the problematic situation. The chapter marks a shift in the study of frames away from framing as a strategic contest for resources towards a probing of the nature of frame shifts and the intellectual and institutional conditions of such reframing efforts. What makes frames resistant to change, the authors argue, is that they are rooted in action. This imbues them with a naturalness that resists reflection. In situations in which actors clash over conflicting understandings of a complex, uncertain situation, a frame will hold doubt at bay. But it is precisely this interplay of belief and doubt that contains the reflexive potential of frames. In an extended discussion of the problem of industrial waste disposal that was triggered by the notorious Love Canal scandal, the authors show both how the frames with which the various actors approach the problem are institutionalized in practices, and how attempting to do things differently in the face of bitter conflict or obvious policy failure opens up opportunities for constructive doubt and for attempts at reframing the situation by finding resonances with wider "figures of argument" that are available in the public sphere.

The third section, 'Foundations of deliberative policy analysis', contains three papers addressing the philosophical assumptions and professional implications of a post-empiricist, deliberative policy analysis. Their common theme is that one cannot understand the practical failings of traditional policy professionalism, nor formulate a viable alternative, without a firm grasp of the philosophical underpinnings of both approaches. Fischer's contribution is a case in point. He begins his chapter with the familiar observation that traditional policy science has failed to live up to its ambition: to contribute to an understanding, let alone amelioration, of the kind of wicked problems that confront modern society. He argues that the cause of this failure resides in the misconceived epistemological and methodological nature of traditional policy science. Locked inside a positivist image of science, traditional policy analysis, he argues, has failed to understand the socially constructed, pragmatically driven nature of scientific knowledge production, a point that is picked up and extended by Gottweis in his chapter. The facts and concepts of policy analysis, both authors argue, are 'inscribed' upon the social and natural world through practices of scientific representation. Our grasp of the objects of policy analysis, these authors conclude, rests on contextually situated, normatively driven, practical reasoning. As Yanow puts it succinctly in her chapter, the understanding of public policy 'requires local knowledge – the very mundane, but still expert understanding of, and practical reasoning about, local conditions derived from lived experience'. Policy objects, as these authors argue, are essentially contested. The representation of an issue (unemployment, global warming, genetic engineering, airport noise) *is* the issue.

The object of post-empiricist policy analysis (as Fischer calls it) is therefore not only fundamentally dispersed (no longer self-evidently located in the halls of government, but instead spread out over the communities of citizens, administrators, and executive agencies. As Gottweis has it, governing is the resultant of a 'regime of practices'), but also recast (policy analysis is, above all, concerned with the communicative, deliberative nature of political activity). All three authors in this section sketch the implications of these insights for the object and role of policy analysis. The objects of analysis, far from being unproblematic entities in the political landscape, are seen as the outcome of complex, socially patterned, processes of articulation by, and contestation between, shifting groups of actors. Policy analysis is in this sense fundamentally interpretative and reflexive. Yanow draws out what an interpretative approach implies for the role of the analyst. She demonstrates that interpretative analysis is just as systematic and methodical as traditional methods ('interpretative is not impressionistic', as she formulates it), and discusses at length the various methods that are available to the interpretative analyst. Gottweis explores the reflexive implications of post-empiricist policy analysis. Instead of assuming governability and policymaking, the complex appreciations and political judgments that constitute it must itself be posed as a problem. Second, as both Fischer and Yanow explain, in the essentially discursive and fragmented field of policymaking, the role of the analyst is not to suggest effective or efficient solutions that bring political discussions to an end. Instead its role should be to facilitate the citizen's and client's capacity for democratic deliberation and collective learning: about value and preferences, about assumptions of self and others, about mutual dependencies and power differentials, about opportunities and constraints, about the desirability of solutions and outcomes, in sum, about what it means to be an engaged citizen. In this way, these three authors, in conjunction with the other contributors to this book, give new meaning to Harold Lasswell's ideal of a 'policy science of democracy'.

Part I

Policy conflict and deliberation in the
network society

1

Collaborative policymaking: governance through dialogue

Judith E. Innes and David E. Booher

The Sacramento Water Forum, a group of contentious stakeholders from environmental organizations, business, local government and agriculture, spent five years in an intensive consensus-building process. In 1999 they agreed on a strategy and procedures for managing the limited water supply in northern California's semi-desert. Leaders in the region were sufficiently impressed to set up a similar collaborative policy dialogue around the equally volatile issues of transportation and land use in this fast-growing region. When environmental groups decided to sue the regional transportation agency for not protecting the region's air quality, the business community was ready to pull out of this nascent policy dialogue. They were stopped by a leading businessman and elected official who had been involved in the Water Forum and influenced by this way of working. He told the other business leaders in an eloquent speech, 'We have no choice. We have to stay at the table. There is no alternative.' They accused him of being 'one of them', suggesting he had crossed over to the environmentalist side. This businessman told them they were wrong, saying 'The Water Forum process transformed me. I now understand that collaboration is the only way to solve problems. I do it now in everything I do, including running my business and dealing with my suppliers, employees and customers.'[1] The business community stayed with the process and consensus building around transportation got underway.

The Water Forum is not unique. A collaborative group known as CALFED, including nineteen[2] state and federal agencies with jurisdiction over California

---

[1] Quote from interview conducted by Sarah Connick as part of a study of outcomes of water policymaking processes in 1999, funded by the University of California Water Resources Center, Centers for Water and Wildland Resources.
[2] This number keeps expanding as new agencies join.

water and dozens of competing stakeholder groups, has been at work since 1995 to resolve issues over the management of California's limited and irregular water supply. These agencies had conflicting mandates, as some regulated water quality and others parcelled out water to different constituencies. As a result they had often been at odds and seldom cooperated. By 2000 CALFED participants reached agreement on two statewide bond issues amounting to nearly $3 billion for new water-related infrastructure and environmental restoration. They created enough political capital among themselves and the stakeholders to get voters to support passage of these bonds. The group also reached agreement on controversial water-management procedures and quantities of water to be provided to different users in drought years. The group has accepted the new idea that the environment and protection of endangered species have a legitimate claim on the water supply, along with more traditional interests such as farming and urban uses. The group created innovative cooperative strategies for maximizing the availability and reliability of water for all stakeholders (Connick forthcoming; Connick and Innes 2001).

This experiment in intergovernmental cooperation has its roots in an earlier five-year consensus-building process around the management of the San Francisco Bay and Delta which produced new relationships among previously warring parties and educated them in a new form of governance (Innes and Connick 1999). The learning of those early groups was transferred to other players in other settings over time through a linked set of collaborative dialogues. While the stakeholders still at times bring lawsuits against one another or push for competing legislation, they also continue to use a collaborative approach to address and resolve water issues.

While water is the California policy arena where the most sophisticated collaborative dialogues are taking place, parallel experiments are going on in many other arenas, including fiscal reform, school reform, habitat conservation, growth management, transportation planning and planning for sustainable development. This kind of dialogue has been most common at the regional and state levels, where organized interest groups can provide representatives to sit at the table (Innes et al. 1994). At the local level in many cities around the USA citizens are coming together with local agencies in dialogues to deal with budgetary issues, community visioning (Helling 1998), and land-use planning. Around the world communities, regions and even nations are seeking collaborative ways to make policy as an alternative to confrontation, top-down decision-making, or paralysis. People in many other countries, from the nation-state down to the local community, are trying new ways to decide on public action, ways which are more inclusive of interests, more open to new options and opportunities, more broadly discursive and more personally and publicly satisfying. These often produce qualitatively different answers than do the traditional methods. They are at the leading edge of new forms of governance and deliberation

(Bryson and Crosby 1992; Fischer 2001; Forester 1999; Gualini 2001; Healey 1993, 1997, 1998; Meppem and Bourke 1999; Susskind and Field 1996).

There are reasons for the emergence of these practices at this time. We have entered the Information Age (Castells 1996). Technological change is breath-takingly rapid, information flows around the globe in days or even hours, and people from different cultures are exposed to one another as never before. We have less shared identity with our fellow citizens and less stable local commu-nities than we once did. We cannot conduct business as usual, nor can we count on shared values or objectives. Power is increasingly fragmented as globaliza-tion creates more and varied sources of power. Even the most powerful public agencies, corporations or individuals cannot produce the results they want when working alone. The terrorist attack on New York and Washington has demon-strated as nothing else before that the USA cannot address its problems alone, but it needs to work with nations around the world.

In this chapter we will outline theory to help understand how and why collab-orative policy dialogues work in practice and how they differ from traditional policymaking. We pull together key ideas from the various theory-building pieces the authors have published elsewhere and move beyond those to an overall theory for collaborative dialogue as a deliberative governance strategy (Booher and Innes 2001; Innes 1992, 1996b, 1998; Innes and Booher 1999a, 1999b, 1999d, 2000a). This theory is built in great part on a decade of research by the first author on more than a dozen in-depth case studies of consensus build-ing and collaborative dialogue in a variety of environmental management and planning arenas.[3] The chapter is also informed by twenty years of experience of the second author in developing new forms of policymaking in California. This includes more than a decade as participant, facilitator and organizer of collaborative policy processes at the state and local level on issues ranging across housing, transportation, governance, natural resources, fiscal reform and infrastructure.

Several bodies of thought also inform our theory. In particular, the work of Jürgen Habermas on the concept of communicative rationality has helped us to develop a normative concept for collaborative dialogue. This set of ideas frames conditions for discourse, speech and emancipatory knowledge (Habermas 1981). These ideas converge closely with the actual practices of successful collaborative policy dialogues as practitioners define them (Society of Profes-sionals in Dispute Resolution 1997; Susskind, McKearnon and Thomas-Larmer 1999) and theory about the transformative power of dialogue (Bush and

---

[3] These studies involved extensive in-depth interviewing of participants and observers, observation of processes and review of mountains of supporting documents, as well as review of media reports. The research inquired about the incentives for stakeholder collaboration and agreement, the nature of the processes, and the outcomes (Connick forthcoming; Connick and Innes 2001; Innes et al. 1994; Innes and Gruber 2001a).

Folger 1994; Forester 1999). The basic work of Barbara Gray on the nature and practice of collaboration informs this chapter (Gray 1991), as does recent work on dialogue – what it is like, how it works and what it accomplishes (Bohm 1996; Isaacs 1999; Yankelovich 1999). Literature in management focusing on collaborative methods of conducting business has also been influential for us (Brown and Eisenhardt 1998; Drucker 1989; Saxenian 1994; Senge 1990).

Our theory is informed by a view of the world as a complex system at the edge of chaos (Axelrod and Cohen 1999; Holland 1998; Johnson 2001; Kauffman 1995; Prigogine and Stenger 1984). Unlike periods when conditions are stable or slowly changing, rapidly changing conditions allow great creativity while bringing risk. Most importantly, they offer the opportunity to improve the system so it can be more productive, more adaptive and ultimately more sustainable. The way such a complex system can be adaptive and creative, according to these theorists, is if it is well networked so that its various components can coevolve. It must have distributed intelligence among its nodes or agents, each of which has the capacity to make choices based on their local knowledge, and there must be information flowing among these agents as well as regular feedback from its environment. We view collaborative policymaking as not just a method which can solve problems when there is conflict in the traditional policy system. It is, even more importantly, a way to establish new networks among the players in the system and increase the distribution of knowledge among these players. This includes knowledge of each other's needs and capabilities and of the dynamics of the substantive problems in society, whether in transportation, environment or housing policy. Collaborative planning, we contend, has emerged as a highly adaptive and creative form of policymaking and action in the Information Age. It is an emerging mode of governance.

Collaborative policy dialogue is far from the dominant policy discourse, nor is it suited to all policy conditions. Multiple ways of conducting planning and policy coexist uneasily in the policy world. Each of these follows different principles and entails different beliefs about reality, about what is ethical and appropriate, and about how players should or should not be involved. These forms of making policy make sense in different situations. While collaborative dialogue has probably always existed among small groups of equals trying to solve a problem, as a policymaking process applied to complex and controversial public issues including many stakeholders widely differing in knowledge and power, it remains in an experimental stage. Collaborative dialogue on a large scale requires skills, training and adherence to a set of practices that run counter to the norms of discussion to which many people are accustomed. The ability to create, manage and follow up on such processes on a large scale has emerged from the theory and the practice of alternative dispute resolution that goes back to the 1970s. This includes particularly the pathbreaking work of *Getting to Yes* (Fisher and Ury 1981), which twenty years ago laid out new principles for negotiation. The most important of these are that parties must begin with their interests rather than their positions and that they must neither give in nor insist on their own way. They must learn about each other. They must seek mutual-gain solutions that as far as possible satisfy all interests and enlarge the pie for all. They must persist in both competing and cooperating to make the negotiation produce durable results. The tension between cooperation and competition and between advocacy and inquiry is the essence of public policy collaboration.

Authentic dialogue

To achieve collaboration among players with differing interests and a history of conflict, the dialogue must be authentic, rather than rhetorical or ritualistic (Isaacs 1999). Most of us are so unaccustomed to authentic dialogue in public situations that to create and manage it typically requires the help of a professional facilitator and special training for participants. Stakeholders have been accustomed to concealing their interests and engaging in positional bargaining rather than in discursive inquiry and speculative discussion or interest-based bargaining. They tune out those with whom they assume they disagree rather than explore for common ground.

The methods for creating authentic dialogue are just beginning to be documented and analysed (Susskind, McKearnon and Thomas-Larmer 1999) to see what works, how and why. Experience of seasoned facilitators has shown that an analysis of each of the interests and of the conflicts must be done and shared among the group at the outset. The group must define its own ground rules and its own mission rather than be given these by an external authority. It must design tasks in which members have both interest and expertise (Innes et al. 1994). The facilitator must manage discussion so that participants feel comfortable and safe in saying what is on their minds even if they think others will not like it. Joint fact finding is essential to ensure that all participants agree on the nature of the problem and the conditions which affect it.

Staff of many kinds are critical to such complex dialogues – not only staff to facilitate meetings and mediate outside of meetings, but also to gather and analyse information, keep records of meetings, and prepare materials. For collaboration to work, staff must be trusted by all participants. One of the reasons the Water Forum was so successful was that the group hired its own staff and consultants who were answerable only to them. By contrast, another collaborative group we observed in transportation planning had to rely on the agency staff, who not only had an agenda different from that of the group, but controlled funds on which the participants relied. Needless to say, the participants seldom spoke their minds on many delicate issues. This was one of the main factors interfering with successful collaborative dialogue in that case (Innes and Gruber 2001a).

To be authentic, in our view, a dialogue must meet certain conditions which Habermas has laid out as prerequisites for communicative rationality (Fox and Miller 1996; Habermas 1981). Each speaker must legitimately represent the interest for which he or she claims to speak, each must speak sincerely, each must make statements that are comprehensible to the others, and each statement must be accurate. These speech conditions do not come into being automatically, but our research and practice has shown that skilled facilitators can, over time, help a group to approximate these conditions. Indeed, creating these conditions is the first priority of these professionals and their most developed skill. They can make sure each person at the table truly does speak for the interest they claim to by insisting that only recognized representatives of an interest group participate and that they routinely check back with their constituencies about what they are doing and saying. Sincerity is something individuals in the group can judge for themselves as they engage over time in face-to-face discussion and begin to know each other as people. As for comprehensibility, a good facilitator asks for clarification or examples, tries experimental rephrasing of ambiguous statements and asks for elaboration as needed. Similarly, when information is contested there are many options. In the San Francisco Estuary Project scientists, each selected by stakeholders, spent a weekend with a facilitator and decided consensually on how to measure the health of the estuary (Innes and Connick 1999). What the scientists came up with became the accepted measure, not only by those in the project, but also by state and federal regulatory agencies outside the process, in great part because of the credibility established by the method of reaching agreement. In the Water Forum, the method for getting information all could believe was to select a consultant all could agree on, who would conduct analyses, allow members to ask challenging questions about parameters, assumptions and methodology, then get revised analyses until the data were meaningful and acceptable to all. Negotiation in the USA over environmental regulations uses variations of this method (Ozawa 1991).

Authentic dialogue depends also on the group being able to follow a discussion where it leads rather than being artificially constrained by rules about what can be discussed or what cannot be changed. The group needs to be able to challenge assumptions and question the status quo. For example, in the transportation case the group was never permitted to challenge the assumption that all construction projects agreed on in the past had to be pursued, even though conditions years later suggested other priorities would make more sense. As a result many strategies were never even discussed, though they would have been far more effective in alleviating congestion than implementing the projects in the pipeline. The larger idea that transportation planning should be done on a project-by-project basis and funding allocated by formula to jurisdictions also

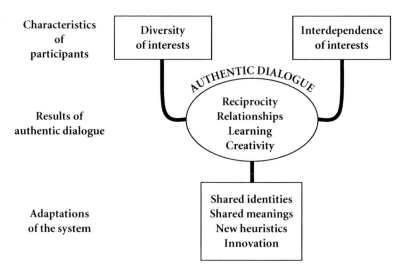

Figure 1.1 DIAD network dynamics

remained entrenched in the thinking of most transportation planners. They ignored calls from stakeholders for a strategic approach to resolving transportation problems or developing a more socially just investment approach. This insistence on the status quo kept the group trapped in the ideas, institutions and practices that led to the problems in the first place. When assumptions are challenged it can open up a discussion and generate new insights. For example, when the Water Forum was stymied in its plans for habitat conservation by requirements for paying into a federal conservation, the stalemate was broken by someone suggesting they should behave like the Boston Tea Party and refuse to pay. While they did not end up doing so, the suggestion allowed them to recognize that institutionalized arrangements are social constructions rather than real limitations and they were able to imagine and negotiate a new funding approach. It is such challenges to the norms that create adaptive governance and allow the system move to higher levels of performance.

Diversity and interdependence

Authentic dialogue can be enough to create agreements and new approaches, but without both diversity and interdependence among stakeholders (see figure 1.1), the truly significant benefits of collaborative dialogue cannot be achieved. As Habermas has argued, all interests need to be engaged in the discourse if a group is to achieve communicative rationality. This inclusiveness ensures that assumptions will be challenged by someone. Such a group, he contends, can get beyond the assumptions and acceptance of a status quo which preserves the power relations of society and blinds us to the underlying reality of the life world. Professional facilitators have learned a similar lesson in their practice: that all stakeholders should be at the table or engaged in some way in the discourse if agreements are to be durable and fully informed. Excluded stakeholders can and often do destroy agreements (Susskind, McKearnon and Thomas-Larmer 1999). Even if they are not powerful enough to do that, their exclusion may mean the group lacks some of the information those stakeholders could provide about the problem that would make the difference between an effective and ineffective strategy. Finally the exclusion of even weak stakeholders may mean an agreement will fail to garner legitimacy among the public.

Stakeholders in a policy dialogue must be *diverse* in order to take full advantage of the creativity that can come from trying to find actions that can respond to a wide set of competing interests. They must also be *interdependent* in order to achieve the kinds of results that will allow them collectively to create an adaptive learning system that can be robust and effective. The stakeholders must be aware that they cannot meet their interests working alone and that they share with others a common problem so they will continue to work together in response to change. Most voluntary collaborative processes are, in our observation, instigated and driven by a shared perception of interdependence around a problem, although this may be only vaguely articulated. For example, the Water Forum stakeholders began to explore collaboration because they concluded they all depended on a limited and interconnected set of water sources, and they understood that improvements to benefit their respective interests could not be accomplished politically without the support of the other interests (Connick forthcoming). Each had many ways to stop things from happening. Only jointly could they take positive action. Similarly, a collaborative group of transportation providers came together in the Bay Area to do transportation investment planning (Innes and Gruber 2001a). They all depended on the same pots of funds and the same transportation system. Similarly, a group of statewide stakeholders ranging across labour, business, agriculture, education and most of the major policy sectors of California formed the California Governance Consensus Project to develop fiscal and governance reform policies (http://www.csus.edu/calst/cgcp/). They were explicit that only stakeholders could join who had something they needed from others and something they could offer that others needed. At first some stakeholders did not know exactly what they had to offer each other. At the outset they often did not understand the problem well enough to know how their actions might be interdependent. For example business interests did not understand how their profits were affected by traffic congestion, and stakeholders from suburbs and inner cities did not understand how the welfare of their citizens and businesses was linked within a region.

Stakeholders begin to learn about their interdependence as they explain their own situations and needs, but they learn most about this as the group goes through the difficult tasks of agreeing on how to define and measure the problem and deciding on their shared mission. A case in point is the San Francisco Estuary Project, where the collaborative group spent two years examining all the relevant science to reach agreement on the state of the estuary. They jointly learned that land use, fisheries, biodiversity and water quality were all linked. In the Water Forum, the group spent over a year developing agreement on a mission to address two coequal objectives of meeting environmental and human needs for the water of the Lower American River. In both cases the participants learned that they each played a part in a regional resource system, that what each was doing had its impact, and that each would benefit from a healthier system. Even the property developers understood that they would not be permitted to build if the water supply was inadequate or if it would have negative impacts on fragile wetlands. And the environmentalists understood that if they agreed not to sue they could obtain the funding to restore habitat and protect fisheries. They came to recognize they were all locked together because the water supply was interconnected and because a complex system of state and federal and local agencies, and many thousands of businesses, residents and others, influenced the quality and quantity and flows of water through formal regulation, investments or failures to invest in treatment or simply thorough their actions. As group members came to understand these linkages, they were increasingly willing to seek cooperative solutions.

In a contrasting example, the regional transportation planning process we studied did not permit the players to discover their interdependence because the agency distributed funds to jurisdictions and agencies according to population-based formulae. As a result the group had neither occasion nor incentive to analyse their interrelationships, nor to understand the contribution of their pro- posed projects to the region. The expenditures did not have to be justified in terms of their contribution to solving the regional transportation problem. Indeed, the group was not working with any definition of the problem, nor of their own mission in relation to it. The group never tried to understand how the region worked as an economy nor how the transportation system affected each jurisdiction's welfare. This failure to recognize and explore interdependence was a central obstacle to collaboration. It accounts in considerable part for the lack of mutual gain outcomes in Bay Area transportation planning (Innes and Gruber 2001a, 2001b).

Not all those who have a stake in public problems are necessarily interde- pendent. Some may be able to pursue and achieve their objectives alone. Some of them may not care about the workings of the system as a whole and be able to extract what they want without collaboration, especially if they have short time horizons. But our research suggests that for the most part in complex and controversial cases of regional resource management, infrastructure planning, growth management and the like in the USA, few players are sufficiently autonomous and powerful to ignore other players.

Results of authentic dialogue among diverse, interdependent stakeholders

We have identified four categories of immediate or first-order results that authentic dialogue among diverse and interdependent stakeholders can produce: reciprocity, relationships, learning, and creativity (see figure 1.1). We have found these results in most of the dozen or so cases of comparatively productive collaborative dialogues that we have studied or participated in.[4]

Reciprocity

As participants in a collaborative dialogue develop an understanding of their interdependence, they build up reciprocal relationships that become the glue for their continuing work. One can illustrate reciprocity in the classic example of the two businessmen bidding up the price of a shipment of oranges. If they don't identify their reciprocity, one ultimately will pay a high price and the other get no oranges. If they had a collaborative dialogue they might discover that one business needs the oranges for the juice and the other for the peel. If they jointly buy the shipment, the price will be lower and each will be able to meet his needs. This example is simple, but it is far from common that this sort of reciprocity is discovered among diverse players. Axelrod similarly has shown that cooperative strategies are beneficial over time, and that players have an incentive to cooperate if they have continued relationships (Axelrod 1984).

Contrary to popular belief, what stakeholders do in these dialogues is *not* make tradeoffs. That is not what we mean by reciprocity. As we have described elsewhere (Innes and Booher 1999b) a truly collaborative discussion is typically in the form of cooperative scenario building and role playing by participants who tell the stories of what is wrong and develop alternative stories until they find the narrative of the future that is plausible and appealing to all of them.

---

[4] These include a study of thirteen cases of collaborative policymaking in environmental and growth management (Innes et al. 1994); an in-depth study of collaborative policymaking in regional transportation (Innes and Gruber 2001a, 2001b); studies of estuary management and water resource management (Connick forthcoming; Innes and Connick 1999); a study of state growth management programmes (Innes 1992). Booher has been a leader of several consensus building processes at the state level in California including the Growth Management Consensus Project (Innes et al. 1994: 71–81) and its successor projects including the California Governance Consensus Project. He works professionally managing collaborative efforts to develop state policy on growth, schools, transportation and other infrastructure, as well as on fiscal reform.

Typically in such a process players discover they can make modifications in their actions which may be of little cost to them, but of great value to another player. Many players outside these processes – such as the leadership of the groups who have representatives at the table – continue to think in terms of tradeoffs. For example in the Water Forum, after participants had collaboratively developed new water management criteria and programmes, they had to develop a list of quid pro quos for the leadership of the stakeholder organizations. The purpose was to show what each group had gained and given up so the leadership would feel their representatives had not given too much for what they had gained. The group actually had discussed few of the decisions in terms of quid pro quo, but instead they had had a cooperative discussion about options and scenarios.

Relationships

One of the most important outcomes of collaborative dialogue is that new relationships and social capital are built among players who would not ordinarily even talk to one other, much less do so constructively. When we interviewed participants in even the least productive collaborative processes, almost all of them said they valued and used the new relationships. For example, in the Estuary Project the representative from the US Corps of Engineers, which is responsible for waterway development, said he routinely began to contact the Sierra Club representative before finalizing new projects to decide if they needed to be modified to satisfy environmental concerns.

These relationships often went beyond professional contacts. Over time – and many of the processes lasted for years – the participants developed mutual understanding and sometimes personal friendships. They were able to have an empathetic understanding of why another stakeholder would take a particular view because they understood the conditions and problems other stakeholders faced and the history they had gone through. Participants learned what the issues meant to the others. They were likely to respect one another's views and believe in one another's sincerity, even while continuing to disagree. In some cases a stakeholder would even speak for the other's differing interests if the person was not present. For example, the property developer representative told the Water Forum the group could not go ahead with something that would benefit his interest because the environmental stakeholders were not there and the proposal would not meet their interests. Group members discover they are each individuals with families and hobbies, unique personalities and sincere commitments to their causes and beliefs.

Such relationships did not change stakeholders' interests, but they did change how they expressed interests and they did allow for a more respectful dialogue. They also gave members a greater incentive to seek a mutually satisfactory solution. These relationships allowed each to better hear what others said. These relationships helped people to build trust among themselves. There was more tolerance when, as in most of the cases we have studied, players also operated outside the processes to influence legislation or bring lawsuits against the interest of other players. They mostly recognized that each had to pursue their stakeholders' interests, though they hoped they could do this collaboratively. For the time being, however, participants learned to live in two worlds: the world of collaborative dialogue and the world of competition and conflict.

Learning

A third outcome of the collaborative dialogues we studied was learning. In our interviews with participants, almost all said they had learned a great deal and many said that this learning was what kept them at the table (Innes et al. 1994). Even when a stakeholder has an instrumental interest in the issue, the individual representing the stakeholder must actually *want* to attend the meetings. Meetings were well attended if there was discussion of stakeholders' interests, the problem and strategies. Meetings where long agendas and formal presentations allowed little dialogue were poorly attended. For learning to occur participants needed to be engaged in a task which they were capable of and interested in. For example, in the transportation case, the meetings where players developed scoring principles for allocating funding were well attended and interesting. All players had projects to be funded and they knew how to assess them. On the other hand, meetings where the task was to design regional system management were poorly attended because the participants did not understand or care about this task. They had no direct responsibility for it and would benefit only slightly. They were given ideas by a consultant and neither engaged in inquiry nor tried to understand the problem. The Water Forum meetings, by contrast, were engaging learning processes because participants chose the tasks and worked collaboratively with consultants to identify information they wanted and assure that its assumptions and methods were acceptable.

   Learning was a joint exercise in the productive cases as participants not only listened and asked questions of the experts but also interacted with one another around an issue. They did brainstorming and scenario building, often with different players adding pieces to build a shared story as a way of imagining various strategies and their consequences. They had small and large 'a-ha' experiences during some of the most focused sessions (Innes and Booher 1999b). This learning can be about facts, about what others think, or about how scientists see a problem, but an effective group engages at least in single-loop learning (Argyris 1993) (see figure 1.2). That is they develop a more effective way of solving their problem. For example, in the CALFED case the

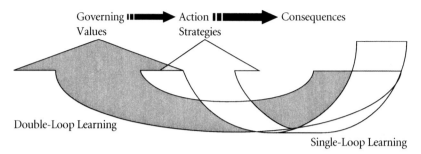

Figure 1.2 Learning in collaborative planning
Source: Argyris 1993.

group discovered they could address their shared need to improve the environment and water supply by jointly backing a bond issue to support a series of projects. They could cooperate, plan ahead for crises, develop conservation methods, share water and increase the quantity, quality and reliability of water supply.

Some problems prove intractable even after creative cooperation on new ways to solve the problem as defined. Double-loop learning may be required. In double-loop learning players rethink what they want to do in the first place, reframe the problem, or decide that they need to apply different values and reconsider their interests (Schön and Rein 1994). The California Governance Consensus Project (CGCP) came about because of double-loop learning. This was an outgrowth of earlier collaborative projects, each of which ended with a reframing of the problem and an identification of a different set of interests. The first project involved stakeholders trying to develop statewide growth management legislation. They came to agreement on many legislative provisions, but learned that without infrastructure funding, growth management could not be successful. This evolved into a second dialogue focused on development and marketing of a bond issue to support infrastructure because legal limitations on state revenue and expenditures would not allow funding from existing sources. When this bond issue failed to win legislative approval, the group evolved again (each time adding or losing stakeholders as appropriate for the task) to focus on a different problem which they had come to conclude lay at the heart of all the issues. Thus was born the CGCP, whose focus was fiscal and governance reform. This group developed agreement on a number of reforms to fiscal structure and learned through focus groups about voter attitudes to these. It disbanded when stakeholders learned that, rather than try to proceed with an all-encompassing proposal for a new statewide structure, it would be more practical for members to negotiate various parts of the proposals in smaller dialogues. They would work towards incremental changes reflecting the shared understandings they had developed in these linked collaborative dialogues. In this example of continuous double-loop learning the players changed their objectives and altered their strategy as they became more sophisticated about the problem, each other's needs, and what the public would accept under what conditions. This network of players remains highly adaptive as they continue to work on policy.

Creativity

In the effort to solve a problem or find a workable solution, tremendous creativity can be generated within a group (Johnson and Johnson 1997) when techniques like brainstorming and scenario building are used. It is curious how difficult it is for participants not just to 'think out of the box' but to be willing to put forward the half-baked ideas that can start everyone thinking. They hesitate and apologize for making things more complicated. They worry that their idea is foolish (Innes and Booher 1999b). It is even more difficult for people to challenge the status quo or even to recognize assumptions they are making. Those who manage the processes, especially if they are public agencies, may try to set boundaries on what can be discussed and limits on what can be changed. All too often the groups accept these limits and fail to find a way out of their impasses. On the other hand, once they give themselves permission to challenge the status quo and let their imaginations work, then new ideas can and do emerge. With practice, effective process management, appropriate tasks and diverse, interdependent participants, we found that groups such as the Water Forum can be routinely creative.

The Sacramento Water Forum as a model

The Sacramento Water Forum demonstrated these conditions of diversity, interdependence and authentic dialogue. This happened for a variety of reasons, but a key one was that a talented facilitator made sure everyone was heard and that issues were deeply addressed and conflicts resolved through interest-based negotiation (Connick forthcoming). The fact that the project had funding of over $1 million per year, not only for support staff but also for modelling and other research to support the dialogue, was also critical. It was a forum where challenges to the status quo were frequent and creativity was common. It was not controlled by an agency, though it was funded by the City and County of Sacramento. The funding agencies were committed to doing what participants agreed on. This project was successful also because there was a substantial incentive for the water conflicts to be resolved. Environmentalists were suing to stop water projects on the ground that they were endangering species.

The overall supply of ground and surface water was known to be interlinked and highly limited in drought years. Farmers might go out of business and the building industry might have to halt development. Forum stakeholders agreed on projects, conservation measures and habitat restoration, and altered their values to acknowledge it was legitimate for urban, environmental and agricultural interests to share in the water. They modified their views while continuing to pursue their interests, working jointly rather than separately. At the banquet held in May 2000 for 500 supporters and participants, speakers repeatedly referred to 'the Water Forum way' as their new shared model of policymaking.

How collaborative planning can result in system adaptations

During the Water Forum the participants began to change and to act differently as they did to varying degrees in the other processes we studied. This change is the most important result of collaborative planning, beyond formal agreements and new networks of players. We identified four kinds of changes over time which help a complex system turn into a complex *adaptive* system that has the capacity to learn and evolve through feedback, and distributed intelligence (see figure 1.1).

The first change is that the dialogue helps each participant to articulate his or her identity as a stakeholder and individual. Each stakeholder's identity becomes in part contingent on the identity of others as they do in a community where responsibilities and roles are simultaneously differentiated and linked together. Identity development is a critical part of the process because in the contemporary, globalized information society, individual and group identities are under challenge. In public policy many identities compete, often preventing communication, much less cooperation (Castells 1997). For example, the environmentalist whose identity as a warrior against the ravages of the capitalist system on the environment may find that this interferes with communication with the developer whose identity is wrapped up in providing quality housing. Developing and articulating linked and shared identities help to make possible the longer-term cooperation that happens in tightly knit communities.

The second change that helps the system become more adaptive and 'intelligent' is that individuals begin to develop shared meanings. As they discussed biodiversity, for example, in the San Francisco Estuary Project, participants began to see this issue in a common way; or, as they discussed drought, they developed common definitions of drought and its implications. This is a process of socially constructing concepts around which policy will be built, as stakeholders did, for example, in three states as a part of implementing state growth management programmes (Innes 1992). The dialogue speeds up a process of building shared meaning that could take years, or perhaps never happen,[5] but which is essential if the policy is to be genuinely agreed on, much less implemented. Once stakeholders have developed shared meanings, they do not have to check in with each other all the time to coordinate, but act in concert because they understand issues in parallel ways and have shared purposes. Their networked relationships give each player feedback that allows them to act more intelligently and to have a beneficial effect on the workings of the system they all share, whether it is water, transportation or ecology.

The third adaptation of the system is that the individuals in such groups may develop new heuristics. That is they may agree on, explicitly or de facto, new rules of thumb to guide their actions. They tend, for example, to use the heuristic that it is better to bring people together when there is a problem than to institute a lawsuit, push for self-interested legislation or use some other confrontational technique. The new heuristics include listening to others, treating them respectfully, looking for common interests rather than differences, and challenging assumptions. Many other heuristics about how to deal with the problem develop from a long-term collaborative process, though these are often not recognized for the significant changes they represent. These heuristics can replace the old ones that were causing the problem, or at least failing to solve it. In the paradigm where the world is machine-like and predictable, heuristics were not nearly as important as they are in complex evolving situations. It made sense in a stable conditions to try to control outcomes through top-down rule making, setting standards, and rewarding and punishing specified behaviour. Policymakers tried to design a policy machine such that when it was set it in motion it would produce specified outcomes.

Heuristics became more important as it became clearer that machine thinking does not work well today. Individuals do what makes sense to them, given the local knowledge they each have and the feedback each gets from others with whom they are networked through a communication system such as collaborative dialogue. They do so relying on the shared heuristics they have developed from collaborative dialogue. The result is not predictable because this is a self-organizing system. There is ample evidence that such a system of distributed intelligence among linked autonomous agents can produce more desirable outcomes for a complex system at the edge of chaos than a policy devised by the most brilliant analyst or powerful bureaucrat. Through multiple actors working on what they each do and know best, complex problems can be addressed effectively (Axelrod and Cohen 1999; Innes and Booher 1999c; Kelly 1994). The system cannot be controlled, but it can be made more intelligent and adaptive. Instead of assuming, for example, that regulation must be

---

[5] Hajer's story of the competition of discourses around environmental protection illustrates the importance of developing shared language and meanings (Hajer 1995).

detailed and rigid, a collaborative group usually recognizes future uncertainties and develops heuristics to deal with these. Many of them have created follow-up collaborative groups to monitor, modify and guide implementation of the principles and programme developed in the first stage. They are apt to use performance measures as a guide to self-regulated action rather than detailed rules to dictate behaviour.

Finally, what emerges from collaborative dialogue can be genuine innovation – not just creative ideas, but ideas that get turned into new practices and institutions. These often would not even be imaginable without the collaborative involvement of stakeholders and the social capital that they create. For example, in CALFED several new ways of managing water were developed. The group created a novel cooperative approach among competing stakeholders scattered around the region to collectively identify when the water levels were too low. Each provided agreed-upon observations of the level of a particular river or of the dead fish observed in a specified location. All talked by computer or telephone conferencing the day of the observation and all were able to agree within a few hours when particular channels or flows should be altered to protect the environment. In the past these decisions had been made crudely on the basis of arbitrary standards set months ahead of time. Decisions were not timely because they involved weeks of data gathering and bureaucratic decision-making on whether the regulation should start, often delayed by lawsuits. Regulations went into effect either too soon or too late and were typically followed by challenges and complaints on all sides that the process was too draconian, not draconian enough, or somehow unfair. Instead this collaborative model for managing the water flows operates in real time, is sensitive to actual conditions, and depends not on a simplistic formula but on a complex set of indicators. Because the decision is the result of a collaborative discussion by observers who represent different interests the complaints are few, even if some do not like the results. The first time this was done, some stakeholders concluded that the decision was premature and the results harmful to them. They agreed nonetheless that the process was much better than in the past and simply needed refinement. Instead of suing CALFED, those harmed rolled up their sleeves to improve it.

We found many other innovations in the collaborative dialogues we studied. One involved new ways of designating habitat and protecting species without having to limit construction across vast territory. Disputes over such designations of habitat had dragged out over years in the past while species died off. The new approach allowed a mutual-gain solution (Innes et al. 1994). In other processes we found innovations in ways of evaluating projects, sharing resources and responsibility, legislation linking together issues that had not been linked before such as housing and sales-tax revenues, and new ways of measuring crucial phenomena such as biodiversity or transportation access.

Obstacles to collaborative dialogues

Collaborative policy dialogue and collaborative action do not fit readily into the institutional arrangements for public choice and action that exist in most nations and at most levels of government. These are typically organized around hierarchical bureaucratic agencies, guided by strict mandates, and they work by applying *a priori* rules. Legislative bodies deliberate with limited time and knowledge of a problem and produce one-size-fits-all legislation. There is strict separation between public and private actors, at least in public settings. These standard policy institutions tend to categorize public participation as a separate activity for which the responsibilities of public agencies can be met with formal public hearings or advisory committees.

Collaboration is discouraged in such a conventional policymaking context. Federal and state law and practice in the USA embody expectations for both the making and implementing of policy that are often in conflict with collaboration, and policy players are unaccustomed to this approach. Collaborative policy dialogues are typically ad hoc, organized for a particular issue in a particular place and time. They involve stakeholders selected to fit the problem. They involve both public and private members in conditions of equality of discourse. This is in contrast to the conventional situation of the public responding to carefully developed proposals by public agencies, which maintain their prerogative to determine what they will explain, what information they will consider relevant and what issues can be discussed.

Collaborative dialogue, by contrast, engages scientists and agency staff with lay people who challenge analyses and assumptions, using their local knowledge which, in the dialogues, has a legitimate status. For example in the Estuary Project, fishermen told the group the bass fishery was depleted. The scientists said there was no evidence, but when they were forced to confront this assertion they did new studies and discovered the fishermen knew things they did not. Collaborative dialogues may engage representatives of federal and state agencies together in a setting where the usual hierarchical chain of command and formal communications among agency heads has to be set aside for authentic and spontaneous discussion among staff. Such dialogues involve participants in speculating about ideas that may not be legal at the time of discussion. They may pull together enough interests to effect change in the legal status quo. Legislative bodies sometimes object to collaboration as undermining their prerogatives. Public agencies may oppose or sabotage it or try to control the processes.

There are few, if any, government forums and arenas set up in most local and regional contexts in the USA where collaboration could happen easily (Dodge 1996). For example, in the USA, local governments, which make decisions on development, usually have neither incentive nor opportunity to discuss proposals with neighbouring jurisdictions. Nor do they have the chance to come up with mutually beneficial growth plans that would assure necessary services and revenues to each community and provide for needed housing and transportation in the area surrounding new development. State and federal laws not only do not encourage collaboration, they often actively interfere. For example, a federal law prevents non-governmental advocates from being regularly involved in policymaking processes with agency staff on ongoing committees.[6] Conflict of interest laws prevent the most knowledgeable and motivated stakeholders from coming to the table to help make policy if they might at some stage benefit. So-called 'pork barrel' practices of allocating funding to powerful players or jurisdictions make collaboration not only unnecessary but threatening to the whole allocation arrangement. Institutions, practices and expectations tend in general to discourage collaboration at the present time in most US policy settings. It does happen, however, in spite of these obstacles.

Alternative models of planning and policymaking

One of the obstacles that is most pervasive is the degree to which other models of policymaking are firmly institutionalized in both practice and law. We have identified four main models that are simultaneously in use in many, if not most, public policy processes in controversial or complex policy problems in the USA (Innes and Booher 2000a; Innes and Gruber 2001a, 2001b). These include the technical bureaucratic model, the political influence/pork-barrel model, the social movement model and the collaborative model (see figure 1.3). Each is useful under different conditions of diversity and interdependence among interests. Often, however, an inappropriate model is used because it is familiar and institutionalized. The technical bureaucratic model focuses on analysis, regulation and implementing stated objectives. It works best where there is neither diversity nor interdependence among interests. Technicians and bureaucracies need to respond to a single set of goals and decision-maker, and in typical practice analyses are not focused on interdependencies (though this could change with more sophisticated technology and complexity modelling). The political influence model involves a leader in allocating divisible benefits, typically projects, to powerful players and amassing power through the loyalties he or she establishes. This works well with diverse interests, but since each interest is focused on getting a piece of the pie and the political leader is busy amassing power, little or no horizontal dialogue takes place among interests. The social movement model involves one or more interests excluded

---

[6] The Federal Advisory Committee Act (Public Law No. 92-463).

	low Diversity high	
low	Technical bureaucratic *Convincing*	Political influence *Coopting*
high	Social movement *Converting*	Collaborative *Coevolving*

(left axis label: Interdependence of interests)

Figure 1.3 Four styles of planning
Source: Adapted from Innes and Booher 2000a.

by the power structure, coalescing around a vision and amassing grassroots
support to influence the decisions through protest, media attention and sheer
numbers. This method recognizes the importance of interdependence but does
not deal with the full diversity of interests. Collaboration is the model which
incorporates both high diversity and interdependence. A useful way to think
of the contrasting models is in terms of four Cs. The technical model is about
convincing policymakers through analysis of what is the right course of action. The political influence model is about *coopting* the players so they will
buy into a common course of action. The social movement model is about
converting players to a vision and course of action. The collaborative model
is about stakeholders *coevolving* to a common understanding, direction and
set of heuristics. These planning models each have their strengths, beyond
their differential ability to deal with diversity and interdependence, and each
works in a different way in practice. Each tends to be useful at a different
phase of a policymaking effort. Moreover, individuals during their careers may
move from one model to another or they may select a model depending on the
task. All the models may be at work simultaneously, sometimes in competing
ways, in a particular setting. In such cases practitioners of one approach often distrust or disdain those working in another. Aalborg planners (Flyvbjerg
1998), for example, were resentful of the political influence-based policymakers, while the latter were uninterested in the analyses the technicians produced.
Social movement planners may disdain collaborative ones because they have
'sold out', and technical planners may disdain social movement planners as
naive or unresponsive to 'neutral and scientific information' (Innes and Gruber
2001b).

The technical bureaucratic model works well in conditions of comparative
certainty where there is only one interest – in effect, where there is agreement

about the objectives and a single decision-making entity. Bureaucracy is set up to implement known policy and follow a hierarchical chain of authority. The technical analyst has come to be associated with rationality and bureaucracy. The education that planners and policy analysts in this tradition get typically ignores diverse goals and starts instead with a question about which is the best way to meet one predetermined goal. The analyst is thought of as either protected from the political arena or working for a particular advocacy perspective. Either way the analyst does not have a responsibility for diverse interests. Moreover, it follows that they are not in a position to deal with the possible interdependence among these interests.

The political influence model, so called after the classic book about Chicago and Mayor Daly of the 1950s (Banfield 1961), is not about outcomes or substantive results. Instead the objective is that powerful stakeholders and elected officials have projects and programmes for which they can claim credit. The leader then has the political legitimacy to bargain with others for resources, and a community or region can present a united front. This model maintains political peace. These projects may be given out on the basis of a personal relationship with the leader or on the basis of geographic formulas. The political influence model is a time-honoured approach in the USA for transportation, water policy, infrastructure provision and a variety of other policy arenas where benefits are both divisible and visible. This method has the strength that it deals well with a diversity of interests, although typically not with the weaker interests. It does not, however, permit discovery of interdependence. Typically deals are made one-on-one between the leader and the agency or individual. If these players were to discover their interdependence this could undermine the leader's power, which depends on everyone relying on him. In the transportation planning case the lead agency actively discouraged collaborative dialogue among the transportation providers who were the beneficiaries of the funding the agency was allocating.

The social movement model is an approach that emerges when interests are excluded from the policy process. In the USA there is typically a somewhat uneasy, even unholy, alliance between the political influence oriented players and those more in the rational technical model (Rein and White 1977). The former need the latter for legitimacy and the latter need the former to provide funding and marching orders. But the combination typically means that environmental groups, social equity interests, or even local government may not be included in the policy process. When matters are highly technical and involve sophisticated analyses, this tends also to leave out interests which cannot do their own analyses or critique the agency's studies. In this context social movement planning often emerges. Social movements are organized around a vision and bring together like-minded interests which discover that if they cannot play a part inside the policy process, they must become a political force on the outside.

An example in the transportation case was a coalition of environmental interests, social equity and environmental justice groups, and transit riders which formed to try to redirect policy through media events, advocacy analyses and packing public hearings. Social movements tend to be fixed in their idea of what the outcomes should be and use analysis in an advocacy rather than an inquiring way. The social movement approach depends on an understanding of the importance of interdependence, as it is only the strength of the coalition that gives them political clout. What the social movement approach does not do well is deal with diversity. They cannot include all interests and hold their coalition together.

It is only the collaborative model that deals both with diversity and interdependence because it needs to be inclusive and to explore interdependence in the search for solutions. It does not ignore or override interests, but seeks solutions that satisfy multiple interests. It turns out, in our observation, that it is only the collaborative model that allows for genuinely regional or other collectively beneficial solutions to complex and controversial problems in both transportation and water (Innes 1992; Innes and Gruber 2001a, 2001b). This is consistent with Ostrom's findings in dozens of cases of resource management around the world (Ostrom 1990). Those which were most collaborative and self-organizing were the ones that were most likely to produce a durable and sustainable management effort.

The collaborative model in productive cases such as the Water Forum subsumes and includes the other models, while in part transforming them. The technical planners and analysts were involved in that process, but instead of being isolated from interests or advocacy analysts, worked closely with the stakeholder group to develop information in the form the group wanted, using assumptions and parameters members understood and accepted. The political influence approach continued to swirl outside of the process, but many players began to think their chances were better of getting what they wanted inside the process. The group as a whole had more political influence than the most effective power broker. The potential for participants to work outside the process was an incentive for all to work harder to find mutually satisfactory solutions. Finally, the collaborative process brought in the social movement players, like the environmental groups fighting their battles against the dams and the damage to spawning salmon. The power these groups had amassed through their social movement gave them a genuine voice at the table. Everyone knew they could leave and that, if they did, the agreement would not survive. Collaboration is difficult and time consuming, even though it may also be engaging. It is expensive if done properly, though it may be less expensive to society than years of lawsuits or competing legislation and failures to solve public problems.

Can collaborative dialogue really make a difference?

The question that is often asked when we present this argument is about the status of agreements reached through these collaborative processes. Even if the collaboration is entirely among governmental entities the results of such dialogues do not have the legal status of decisions by legislatures or individual public agencies. Individuals participating may not be able to persuade their agencies to implement the agreements, much less to ensure that the agencies coordinate and work together to carry out action plans. In the more common case where participants are outside of government, how can they hope to achieve what they propose? The proposals of even a collaborative group that meets the criteria of inclusiveness, authentic dialogue and pragmatic task orientation are sometimes ignored, voted down or vetoed when they are placed on the desk of public officials. If this is the case, why go to the trouble of a collaborative dialogue?

This question, focusing on agreements, is grounded in the traditional policymaking paradigm and in being so it misses an essential outcome of collaborative dialogue. In the traditional view power flows up from the public to the decision-makers they select, who in turn make choices, which bureaucracies then implement. The collaborative paradigm is grounded in a recognition that this ideal version of policy does not work for controversial issues in a fragmented, rapidly changing and uncertain world. Policy decisions, no matter how they are made, are often not implemented for a wide variety of reasons, including that they turn out to be infeasible, premature or otherwise inappropriate (Bardach 1977; Pressman and Wildavsky 1979). In collaborative policymaking, agreements are only a small part of the purpose and the consequences. The real changes are more fundamental and typically longer lasting and more pervasive than agreements. These effects include (Innes and Booher 1999a) shared meaning and purpose, usable new heuristics, increased social and intellectual capital, networks among which information and feedback can flow and through which a group has power to implement many things that public agencies could not do (Booher and Innes 2001), new practices, innovations and new ways of understanding and acting. They can start changes in the direction of social, economic and political life. The processes help create a more adaptive and intelligent policy system. They can help to develop a more deliberative democracy among a wider community and increase civic engagement (Dryzek 2000; Innes and Booher 2000b). They change who participates and how. Action is generated within and around collaborative processes. Formal government increasingly becomes just one component of a much more fluid and complex system of governance.

A case in point is water policy in California. While the original agreement on a conservation and management plan for the San Francisco Estuary was not fully adopted by public agencies nor fully implemented, the ideas that emerged from dialogue are still being introduced and altering practices of communities, developers and industries abutting the estuary in ways likely to make the system more sustainable. The salinity measure agreed on as an indicator of the health of the estuary was rejected at first by the governor and state agency responsible for water flows, but by that time it was too late. The federal government and many other players had agreed this was the indicator they would trust. Ultimately the state government bowed to this consensus and released extra water into the estuary in response to movement in this indicator. The practice and principles of water management have fundamentally changed.

Elected officials do not readily give up familiar prerogatives. Stakeholders who think they have better alternatives than a negotiated agreement pursue those. But the reality is that water policymaking in California has changed for ever from what it was – a largely political influence approach with a significant component of technical bureaucratic analysis, constantly challenged by environmental social movements which could at best halt water projects, but could not do much to improve the environment. Today these players communicate and act collaboratively in deciding what to do. They have created a powerful network held together by shared heuristics about the management of water and the allocation of funding. Collaborative policymaking has become the principal model in California water policy. For example, in 2001 in two outcomes of CALFED, the state has begun to use collaborative methods to develop both a complex strategy for conjunctive use of ground and surface water and for designing the water plan for the state as a whole (McClurg 2001).[7]

Emerging, flexible, adaptive institutions

'There is nothing so hard as to change the existing order of things.'
(Machiavelli 1963)

The remarkable reality is that, despite the obstacles, collaborative practices are being put to use and even becoming the norm in some policy arenas in some regions (Fung, Karkkainen and Sabel 2001; Healey 1997). They coexist uneasily with other practices, but the concept seems to be spreading. A new sort of institution is emerging. It takes many shapes and forms, but it also has shared characteristics. It is fluid, evolving, networked, and involves dialogue and distributed intelligence. These are institutions that are defined less by hierarchies, long-term patterns of routine behaviour and structured roles, than by practices that sustain constant interaction, learning and adaptation (Healey et al. 2000).

---

[7] See http://www.waterplan.water.ca.gove/b160/indexb160.html.

To think of such a phenomenon as an institution involves a mindset different from the one that equates institutions with organizations and structures that change very little. Instead these adaptive institutions are more like the standing wave that keeps its shape while millions of molecules flow through it. This notion of institutions is informed by Giddens' concept of a symbiotic relation of structure and agency where a structure and set of patterned relations, supported by norms and values, is enacted on a daily basis by agents. Agents' actions are shaped and constrained by social structure and values but, by the same token, agents have autonomy to choose actions that strain and even break out of that structure or contradict the prevailing value system. In the process, the structure changes (Giddens 1984). In contemporary times structure changes faster than in the past and so it is harder to see, but the principle remains the same.

This postmodern adaptive institutional form can be found in many guises around the world. Examples include a cooperative, networked community sector in major US cities (Morris 1998); state dispute resolution and mediation agencies for helping address policy controversies;[8] collaborative neighbourhood-based improvement efforts such as community policing; and self-organizing local and regional collaborative planning processes bringing business and environmental interests together with community leadership to develop sustainable plans through dialogue.[9]

A powerful model for this kind of fluid institution is outlined in a handbook published by the US National League of Cities (Dodge and Montgomery 1995), which advises that strategic planning for cities is collaborative decision-making involving the full range of regional interests.

Strategic planning, they contend, develops and institutionalizes a continuing capacity to monitor change, take advantage of emerging opportunities, and blunt incipient threats. It periodically redefines a vision that is ambitious but achievable, and identifies the region's competitive niches. It actively builds partnerships with related, and even competing, regions. This volume represents an extraordinary contrast to the militant parochialism of local governments in the last fifty years in the USA. It is also noteworthy that it does not recommend regional government, but proactive collaborative governance involving public and private stakeholders and citizens.

[8] For information on these see the web site of Policy Consensus Initiative http://www.policyconsensus.org.

[9] More detailed descriptions of these examples can be found in Innes and Booher 2000a. The James Irvine Foundation has provided funding as part of their Sustainable Communities Program, to seventeen Collaborative Regional Initiatives around California which engage interests from business to environment to social equity in dealing with the regional growth issues which governmental agencies have failed to address. Information on these collaborative regional initiatives can be found at the Collaborative Regional Initiatives Network, http://www.calregions.org/civic/index.php. See also Joint Venture Silicon Valley for an example, http://www.jointventure.org.

These forms of planning and public action have become common enough that we believe they are new types of institutions. They have in common that they are collaborative, they involve stakeholders with different interests, they are self-organizing, and they are each uniquely tailored to context, opportunities and problems. These ad hoc processes have varied ways of linking back to the existing decision-making institutions, when they do. They are constantly being reinvented and evolving.

Conclusions and reflections

For collaborative dialogue to fulfil its potential as governance strategy will require the development of both practice and theory. The next evolution may be to mesh collaborative planning with the conventional institutions as, for example, the courts have done in sending cases to mediation rather than deciding them in adversarial courtrooms. City council members might emulate those in Davis, California, who set up a collaborative stakeholder process which resolved a contentious budget decision and developed a comprehensive budget strategy for the city. Institutionalizing collaborative processes may involve changing bureaucratic norms to encourage government to behave more like successful 'nimble' business today, decentralizing tasks to small groups, decreasing hierarchy and creating flexible linkages to other businesses. It may involve more radical transformation of these institutions in which the public does not have much trust. Both practitioners and theorists need to work together to recognize and understand the new practices and their appropriate uses, when and where they work, and why they do or do not.

Whatever emerges it is likely the new institutions will involve, instead of predictability, routinized responses and accountability based on inputs, creativity and new ideas, adaptive responses and accountability based on outcomes. Public agencies and bureaucrats will have to let go of the usually futile hope of controlling behaviour and outputs and participate in collaborative processes, letting them go where they will. Agencies will have to be held accountable for improving the welfare of society rather than just operating specified programmes. They will have to develop capacity for managing complex networks around the issues for which their agencies have responsibility (Kickert, Klijn and Koppenjan 1997). By the same token, the public and elected officials will have to let go of rewarding and punishing agencies based on standards, rules and prespecified outputs. They have to think in terms of performance measures that can be used by the agencies to improve their ability to meet societal goals in their own ways (Osborne and Gaebler 1992).

The new institutional forms will require the acceptance of change and evolution as normal. Society will have to reward experimentation, risk taking and new ideas rather than punish mistakes and stifle creativity. This change will require

assessing performance by exploring emergent, second-order and long-term results. It will require giving up on the idea that anyone knows the answers. It
will require public understanding that the goal of governance in complex, controversial and uncertain situations has to be to create a shared intelligence that
allows all the players acting autonomously with shared heuristics to make the
complex system into an intelligent, adaptive one.

2

Place, identity and local politics: analysing initiatives in deliberative governance

Patsy Healey, Claudio de Magalhaes, Ali Madanipour and John Pendlebury

The challenge of governance transformation

There is widespread agreement across Europe on the need for innovation in the forms and practices of contemporary governance. Within the neo-liberal discourse, this is sometimes cast as the need for 'less government' overall, justifying practices of privatization and deregulation. However, as the introduction to this book makes clear, the pressures for governance change are much more fundamental than this. They reflect both the contemporary reconfiguring of state–economy–civil-society relations and a shift in how societies and polities are understood. The challenge being experienced across Europe at the beginning of the twenty-first century is to recast governance agendas and practices around new foci and new relations. This chapter explores the micro-social relations of such transformative efforts through a particular case of 'partnership' relations to promote 'place qualities', analysed through an evaluation framework developed within the tradition of interpretative policy analysis.

Within many parts of western Europe, the organizational forms and routines of formal government have been grounded in the mid-century welfare state model (Esping-Anderson 1990). This typically divided policy agendas into 'sectors', which were concerned with the provision of services to meet universal needs (education, health and welfare), and support for economic sectors (for example agriculture, fisheries, mineral extraction, the various branches of industry). National governments took a strong role in designing and financing

This chapter draws on the study *Urban Governance, Institutional Capacity and Regenerating City Centres* funded by the ESRC (grant R000222616). Our particular thanks go to Chris Oldershaw, Grainger Town Project Director, who facilitated access to the workings of the project. Thanks also to colleagues at Chalmers University Gothenburg and KTH Stockholm for stimulating discussions on an earlier draft.

the resultant programmes. It was left to local governments to work out how to coordinate these programmes and to regulate the activities of firms and citizens, in terms of their effects on the qualities of places as living and working environments. In terms of policy relations, political representatives, officials, consultants and, increasingly, well-mobilized lobby groups took charge of providing the content of policy agendas in the different sectors, creating 'policy communities' with distinctive discourses and practices (Rhodes 1997; Vigar et al. 2000). It is these divisions, discourses and practices which now seem to trap government in modes of thinking and acting which lack the flexibility to respond to new ways of living, new ways of doing business in a globalizing context and new cultural awareness of the significance of environment and place qualities. As many now articulate, the challenge is to develop relations between the spheres of civil society, the economy and the state which are less hierarchical and less paternalist, which are sensitive to the needs and aspirations of diverse groups (and especially those who tend to get marginalized) and which have a capacity to learn from diverse knowledge resources (Amin and Thrift 1995; Moulaert 2000; Storper 1997). This means developing new foci for dividing up policy agendas, signalled by the search for different kinds of policy 'integration', as in the recent efforts towards 'joined-up' policy in the UK (Stewart et al. 1999; Wilkinson and Appelbee 1999). It also means building new connections both between government arenas and between government, citizens and businesses, the stakeholders in what happens in and to 'places' (Malbert 1998).

In this context, a significant drive of contemporary governance innovation in Britain has been towards decentralizing, from national configurations of policy agendas and relations to regional and local arenas, and towards 'area-based integration'. Within Europe as a whole, there is a great deal of contemporary 'policy talk' which emphasizes that local governments should take on the role of promoting the qualities of their places, through 'place visions', bidding for resources in terms of integrated area strategies, and developing their areas as 'learning regions', as production 'milieux' as well as environmentally benign and socially cohesive city regions (Amin and Thrift 1995; Camagni 1999; Committee for Spatial Development 1999). Within this 'talk', the normative model is of a mode of governance which is place-focused, 'open-minded' to new ideas, aware of its traditions and facilitative of the opportunities and ambitions of residents and others with a stake in a place.

These new place-focused policy rhetorics respond to many pressures. They are not just a 'romance' of the environmentalists concerned with local–global relations. There is also a firm foundation in analyses of contemporary economic dynamics (Amin and Thrift 1994; Morgan 1997; Storper 1997) and in changes in lifestyle and patterns of social polarization (Wacquant 1999). In these analyses, 'place' is understood as more than a physical locale or a collection of assets to be 'positioned' in a new geography of competing places. It refers to the congelation of meanings and experiences which accumulate around locales through the daily life experience of people living their lives and firms conducting their activities. It emphasizes an approach to the management of collective affairs which pays attention to the challenge of coexistence in shared locales (Healey 1997), while not neglecting the traditional service delivery and safety/security roles of government. However, there is no inevitability about whether shifts in governance will occur and, if they do, whether in the direction advocated. New pressures intermesh with established routines and practices in a continual process of invention and struggle (Cars et al. 2002; Imrie and Raco 1999), a 'restless search' for ways of resolving conflicting demands (Offe 1977). Breaking out of established ways of going on, the 'regimes' of the urban regime theorists (Harding 1995; Lauria 1997), is no easy shift. It is perhaps hardest in contexts where centralist, hierarchical and sectoral divisions have been most strongly embedded. Such situations not only inhibit integration of policy attention around place qualities. They also make inclusivity towards the many dimensions of civil society more difficult. The case examined in this chapter is of such a context.

Experimentation in new articulations and foci in policy agendas is widespread in Europe and North America, at all levels of government. At the local and subregional level, there are accounts of innovation in community development, spatial strategy formation, 'integrated area development', economic development strategies and environmental initiatives (Healey et al. 1997; Innes 1992; Malbert 1998). While some of these initiatives achieve a transformative goal, in that the experiment of one decade becomes the routine business of the next (e.g. many environmental recycling practices), those that succeed best seem to be those that can fit within established modes of sectoral organization or existing policy networks. Many evaluations of experiments note that, despite the excitement and mobilizing energy released by new ways of thinking and new ways of doing things, the 'mainstream' of governance activity carries on with 'business as usual' (Taylor 2000). This raises the question of the power of the 'institutional inheritance' of governance as it plays out in a locality to shape experiments and innovatory initiatives, and the potential for such experiments and initiatives to shift the discourses and practices of the 'mainstream'. In this chapter, the concepts of institutional capacity of governance and institutional capacity building are used to explore this question, exemplified in a case of a 'place-focused' governance initiative in the centre of an old industrial city.

Evaluating institutional capacity building

There is now a rapidly developing literature which argues that the quality of the social relations of a locality has an important effect on social life and business performance. As developed in the GREMI model (Camagni 1999), the objective was to find the positive qualities of *territorial innovation milieux*. Amin and Thrift use the term *institutional capacity* in order to identify these qualities. Drawing on a rich Italian literature, they argued that localities which could deliver this beneficial nexus were characterized by four factors: a plethora of civic associations, a high level of interaction among social groups, coalitions which crossed individual interests, and a strong sense of common purpose. These four factors generated a quality of 'institutional thickness', or richness, within which firms and households were embedded, and an institutional capability to mobilize to sustain supportive conditions for both (Amin and Thrift 1995: 101). Other researchers have pointed out that the four factors do not necessarily lead to the beneficial trajectories which Amin and Thrift seek, as they can be found associated with powerful local elites and with failures in economic innovation. Some qualities of institutional thickness/richness thus seem to promote economic growth and innovation. Others may be more effective at fostering particular forms of social cohesion. But while such 'cohesions' may be supportive and contribute to individual flourishing, they may also embed oppressive qualities which suppress innovation and constrain identity-formation options. Thus cohesive communities and integrated 'polities' are not desirable as such. They need to be judged by their qualities, not their existence. These ideas link to the rapidly expanding but diffuse literature focused on trust, social networks and *social capital* (Malmberg and Maskell 1997; Wilson 1997). While some authors equate social capital with culture (Fukuyama 1995), or with accumulated cultural resources (Bourdieu 1977), others contrast 'social capital' with 'human capital' and treat it more as a 'stock' of assets available within a locality (Coleman 1988; Putnam 1993).

In this chapter we develop a relational view of institutional capacity, rather than treating it as a stock of assets. It represents a force which is continually emergent, produced in the interactive contexts of its use. In previous papers, we have developed the concept of *institutional capital* (Healey 1998; Healey, de Magalhaes and Madanipour 1999). In our use of this concept, we maintain an analytical distinction between the qualities of social relations (the nature of bonds of trust and norms in the networks which link people together) and the knowledge resources which flow around and are developed through these relations. This draws on a distinction between three forms of capital which may be deployed in interactive governance contexts: intellectual capital (knowledge resources), social capital (trust and social understanding) which builds up through face-to-face encounter and political capital (the capacity to act collectively to develop local qualities and capture external attention and resources) (Innes and Booher 1999). *Institutional capacity-building* processes in local governance may thus be analysed in terms of the knowledge resources, relational resources and mobilization capabilities they draw upon and generate (Healey 1998; Healey, de Magalhaes and Madanipour 1999; Wilkinson and Appelbee 1999) (see figure 2.1).

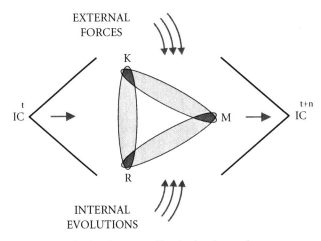

Figure 2.1 The development of institutional capacity

This approach draws upon interpretative approaches in policy analysis (Fischler 2000; Hall and Taylor 1996; Muller and Surel 1998) and communicative planning theory (Fischler 2000; Gualini 2001; Healey 1997; Innes 1995). These emphasize that meanings and actions are actively constructed in social contexts through relational dynamics. In our evaluation, we are therefore interested in the way knowledge resources and relational resources are mobilized, and how this affects the *frames of reference* or *discourses* through which meanings are arrived at and mobilized (Hajer 1995; Schön and Rein 1994), the processes by which meanings are disseminated (Latour 1987) and the relation between such discourses and the *practices* through which material actions are accomplished. The analysis of transformations in governance processes therefore needs to pay attention to continuity and change in relation to frames and discourses and in relation to practices. We thus seek to illustrate and develop into operational analysis the conception of policy analysis as a deliberative, action-oriented practice in which meanings and values are socially constructed.

Our analysis of a particular governance initiative operates at two levels. At one level, the emphasis is on the institutional capacities drawn upon and developed in and around the initiative, undertaken in terms of knowledge resources, relational resources and mobilization capacity. At a second level, we consider how far, through the flow of these resources and capacities, wider discourses which structure policy agendas and routinized practices are being reinforced or changed. Overall, we are interested in the scale and nature of change in local institutional capacity produced by a particular innovation, and the extent to which it has promoted more attention to place quality, in a more open-minded and inclusive mode of governance.

Table 2.1 *The dimensions of institutional capacity building*

Knowledge resources	The *range* of knowledge resources, explicit and tacit, systematized and experiential, to which participants have access
	The *frames* of reference which shape conceptions of issues, problems, opportunities and interventions, including conceptions of place
	The extent to which the range and frames are shared among stakeholders, *integrating* different spheres of policy development and action around place qualities
	The capacity to absorb new ideas and learn from them (*openness and learning*)
Relational resources	The *range* of stakeholders involved, in relation to the potential universe of stakeholders in the issue or in what goes on in an area
	The *morphology* of their social networks, in terms of the density (or 'thickness') of network interconnections and their 'route structure'
	The extent of *integration* of the various networks
	The location of the *power to act*, the relations of power between actors and the interaction with wider authoritative, allocative and ideological structuring forces
Mobilization capacity	The *opportunity structure*
	The institutional *arenas* used and developed by stakeholders to take advantage of opportunities
	The *repertoire* of mobilization techniques which are used to develop and sustain momentum
	The presence or absence of critical *change agents* at different stages

To operationalize our three-dimensional concept of institutional capacity building, we specified knowledge resources, relational resources and mobilization capacity into four elements. These are summarized in table 2.1.[1]

In developing our concept of knowledge resources, we draw on social constructivist conceptions of knowledge. These focus attention on formalized knowledge, tacit knowledge and experiential understanding, operating at multiple levels and in the context of specific practices, from deep structures to 'information' (Blackler, Crump and McDonald 1999; Wenger 1998). Such a focus expands and enriches the current research attention on 'policy discourses' by exploring the micro-dimensions of discourse development (Hajer 1995; Hastings 1999; Vigar et al. 2000). Drawing on an institutionalist approach to specify relational resources, we emphasize the networks or webs of relations within which governance actors are embedded. These webs may have different forms or morphologies which affect who gets access to them and their power relations. Knowledge and relational resources within a locality provide

---

[1] For a more extensive presentation of this framework, see Healey, de Magalhaes and Madanipour 1999.

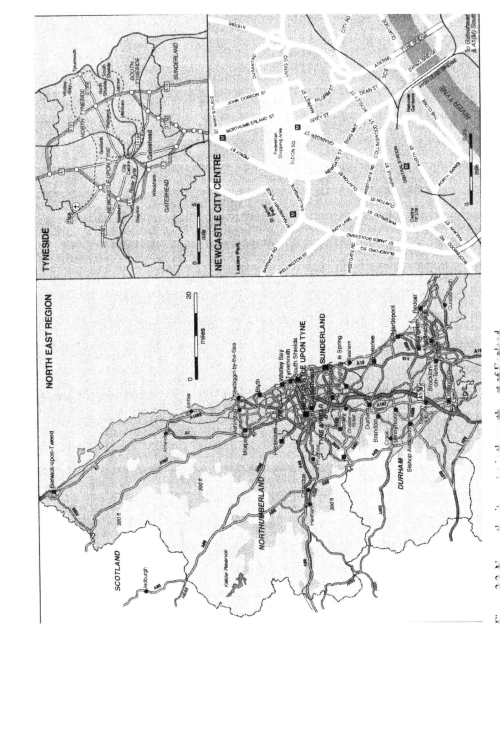

NORTH EAST REGION

SCOTLAND

Berwick-upon-Tweed

NORTHUMBERLAND

Kielder Reservoir

200 ft

200 ft

TYNE UPON TYNE

SUNDERLAND

DURHAM

Bishop Auckland

Stockton-on-Tees

Hartlepool

Darlington

0   20
miles

TYNESIDE

NORTH TYNESIDE

SOUTH TYNESIDE

SUNDERLAND

NEWCASTLE UPON TYNE

Gateshead

GATESHEAD

0   5
mile

NEWCASTLE CITY CENTRE

RIVER TYNE

TYNE BRIDGE

0   1
mile

a reservoir of capacities for urban governance initiatives. But they need to be deliberately mobilized to release their potential. We draw on Tarrow (1994) to identify dimensions of mobilization capacity. Tarrow specifies four dimensions: a political opportunity structure, the availability of 'symbolic frames' of reference around which people can mobilize (our knowledge resources), the availability of social networks which can connect the leaders and the core of a movement to its base (our relational resources), and 'repertoires' of ways of acting to achieve change. To this, we have added the significance of the arenas where mobilization takes place and the role of key change agents in initiating and managing governance innovations.

The emphasis in this evaluation is on dynamics, that is evolution through time and movements from one situation to another. In this context, visible struggles between practice customs and between practices and newly emerging discourses are of considerable significance, as they signal that some kind of destabilization is underway. However, the surface conflicts and tensions are only one dimension of the power relations of governance processes. Behind this are the more covert struggles to pursue interests or maintain positions that go on 'behind closed doors', well known in the policy analysis literature as 'the mobilization of bias'. Underpinning both the surface activities and the mobilization of bias are deeper cultural assumptions and habits, implicit but often not recognized by participants. Transformations in discourse may occur on the first level. But unless these changes penetrate into the deeper cultural level, such shifts may have only limited impact on practices. One way to identify whether significant and enduring transformations are in the making is to examine how changes on the surface are echoed in the deeper structures and vice versa, establishing a reflexive and 'circular' relationship (Dyrberg 1997). This means that micro-analysis of governance change needs to identify how much of the struggling is merely ripples on the surface of a settled modality of governance, what is shifting the parameters of established discourses and practice relations, and what is unsettling the whole culture of governance relations.

A city-centre urban regeneration partnership

The case examined in the context of this framework is a partnership set up to regenerate an area focused around the nineteenth-century core of the city centre of Newcastle, the leading city in the Tyne and Wear conurbation in the north-east of England (figure 2.2). The evaluation task was to assess how far this partnership initiative, clearly focused around an important 'geographical space' for the city, had the potential to encourage new agendas and processes of place-focused governance.

Table 2.2 *Formal government in Newcastle*

	Formal government	Special agencies* (often with business or special interest involvement)
National	Department of the Environment (Department of Environment, Transport and the Regions from 1997)	English Heritage English Partnerships
Regional and sub-regional	Government Office for the North East One NorthEast (absorbing parts of GONE and EP in 1999 Regional Assembly (prototype for a full elected regional chamber and executive)	English Partnerships (regional arm) Tyneside Training and Enterprise Council Northern Arts Tyne and Wear Urban Development Corporation (wound up 1998)
Local	Newcastle City Council (with many departments, reorganized into fewer departments in 1998)	Grainger Town Partnership (launched 1997, formal company from 1998) Other neighbourhood regeneration partnerships set up in the 1990s

Note: *Only those with a significant role in the case examined in this chapter are listed.

Figure 2.2 locates the case spatially in its region. On a broader scale, Newcastle is in the far north of England. Temporally, once a global industrial city, Newcastle and its surrounding urban areas have a 100-year history of adjusting to changing global economic conditions which have in the past undermined the traditional economic base and are now undermining the area's distinctive working-class culture. But it is also necessary to locate the case institutionally. As we argue later, the institutional relations of governance have been in considerable flux in recent years. By way of introduction, table 2.2 summarizes the key government levels and actors which appear in the case.

The initiative originated among conservation enthusiasts in Newcastle City Council, but soon linked conservation issues to those of regeneration. The Grainger Town Project, as it became known, established a new organizational arena, a Partnership Board and Executive, in a form which became very common in urban regeneration in England in the 1990s, encouraged by national and EU government. It is task oriented, and strongly influenced by the demands of its major funders, English Partnerships, the national government department responsible for urban regeneration, through the Government Office for the North

East and the City Council. It thus expresses many of the challenges and conflicting pressures in contemporary English city government, though in a context
with its own distinctive economic, political and cultural history.

The Grainger Town Project grew from within the City Council. It was initially focused around the search for ways of funding the conservation of the
deteriorating stock of what had been the grand nineteenth-century commercial
core of the city. By the mid-1990s, the area under consideration covered 30.4
hectares, mostly in offices and retail units, with slightly more than 1,000 people living within it.[2] Of 430 buildings identified in the area, 230 were listed
on the national register as being of special architectural or historic interest.
But a large part of this stock was vacant, amounting to 15,300 square metres.
As a councillor remarked in 1999, 'The central part of the town has been neglected for many years now, you can see it in the fabric of the buildings,...
I always remember walking along Clayton Street, this was about a year ago,
towards Neville Street, and I looked up and I saw a tree growing out of
the windows, and I thought, really this can't be right.'[3] However, although
the national agency concerned with historic buildings and urban complexes
(English Heritage) was enthusiastic about a conservation programme and could
provide some funding, this could never be sufficient to tackle the decline
in the commercial role of this part of the city centre. With the support of a
local business lobby group, The Newcastle Initiative (Bailey 1995), as well as
English Heritage, the project was expanded to incorporate an urban regeneration agenda. With this, it was possible to attract the interest of English Partnerships and the Government Office for the North East (see table 2.3). Funds
were also made available for a major consultancy study to devise a strategy and
delivery approach for a regeneration and conservation project.[4] This implied
a shift in both the knowledge resources drawn upon to shape the project and
the networks involved in it. One of the challenges of the project has been to
reduce the tensions and barriers between the proponents of urban conservation
and those who are seeking to find new commercial opportunities for sites and
properties.

By early 1997 these initiatives had successfully acquired a notional budget
of £120 million over six years, including £40 million from the public sector
(£25 million from English Partnerships, £11m from the national Single Regeneration Budget and smaller contributions from the city council, English Heritage
and Tyneside TEC). The remainder was anticipated contributions from the private sector. The project was launched as a formal partnership in 1997, with
a project team, a board and an executive board.[5] The director appointed by
the board later in 1997 believed in the importance of developing widespread

[2] EDAW 1996.   [3] This is taken from Healey, Madanipour and de Magalhaes 2002.
[4] EDAW 1996.   [5] It was not formalized as a legal company until 1998.

Table 2.3 *Chronology of the evolution of the Grainger Town Project*

Date	Key actors and relations	Key agendas/discourses
1989	Newcastle City Council	Conservation
1990–2	Newcastle City Council	Conservation
	English Heritage (national)	Consultancy Study: The Grainger
	The Newcastle Initiative	Town Study
	DoE (regional)	
1993–4	Newcastle City Council	Conservation
	English Heritage	
	DoE (regional) seeking funding	
	Conservation area	
	Partnership/LOTs scheme/SRB1	
1994–6	Newcastle City Council	Consultancy Study: EDAW 1996
	English Heritage	Regeneration agenda
	English Partnerships (national/	The 'European City'
	regional)	
	GONE	
	EDAW consultants	
1997	Grainger Town Partnership created	Creating the 'European City'
	Newcastle City Council	
	English Partnerships	
	The Newcastle Initiative	
	The Chamber of Commerce	
	English Heritage	
1998	As above, with the Business	Regeneration agenda
	Forum, Urban Design Panel	The 'European City'
		Co-ordination of public-sector
		activity
		Shaping market expectations
1999	GTP Partnership	Property development and investment
	Newcastle City Council	Public realm strategies
	English Partnerships	Co-ordination of public-sector
	TNI/Chamber of Commerce	activity
	English Heritage	Review of forward strategy
	Business Forum and Residents'	
	Forum	

ownership of the project among stakeholders in the area, setting up forums for both business and residents and panels for arts, culture, and urban design, as recommended by the consultants' report (see figure 2.3). Such consultative arrangements were also stressed by national government in promoting the Single Regeneration Budget programme. In this sense, they were institutional innovations 'imposed' on the local situation, reflecting a growing appreciation of the value of more 'inclusive' policymaking and implementation. But they also served important purposes with respect to widening the intellectual and social capital resources available to city-centre governance.

By 1999, over 100 people could be identified as actively involved in the project's boards, panels and forums. These included representatives of national/ regional and local government, participants from different kinds of business and business lobby groups, ranging from large companies to small firms, and some groups involved in arts promotions and urban design concerns, as well as residents. In this sense, stakeholders were drawn in from the spheres of the state, civil society and the economy to help develop, monitor and manage the project (see figure 2.4). There was a strong commitment by the executive team and some board members to open and inclusive governance practices. However, some stakeholders played a much more central role than others. Initially, some significant stakeholders were omitted, notably many small firms and most ethnic businesses, though as the project has developed these gaps have been remedied. There was no representation from the multiple 'users' of the area who were neither businesses nor residents.

Nevertheless, the project widened significantly the range of people involved in city-centre governance. However, by this time its relation with the city council itself had become ambiguous. The partnership form had been adopted primarily because the funding agencies preferred to deal with special-purpose bodies rather than provide funds directly to municipalities. This reflected thinking at both national government and EU levels. This in itself generated a tension with the city council over ownership of the project. The tension was rendered more complex by the city's political history. For many years, the city and the region as a whole had been a largely 'one-party state', dominated by Labour councillors drawn mainly from a base in trade-union politics and the poorer neighbourhoods. Their connections with new social movements, based around environmental initiatives, gender issues etc., were relatively limited, and there was an ill-developed tradition of grassroots action. The councillors' priorities were to improve housing and bring more jobs into the region, to replace those lost through the decline of the area's traditional manufacturing base, while the council's organization emphasized its role in service delivery functions, with, until 1998, separate departments for education, social services, transport, economic development, environmental health etc. Councillors and officers had assumed that commercial interests in the city centre could largely look after themselves. Conservation concerns were more an enthusiasm of officers in the planning department than a passion of councillors. There was some tradition of working in a semi-corporatist way with representatives of industry, but this primarily took the form of linkages between councillors, unionists and managers of the very large companies. Not only were these firms themselves declining in

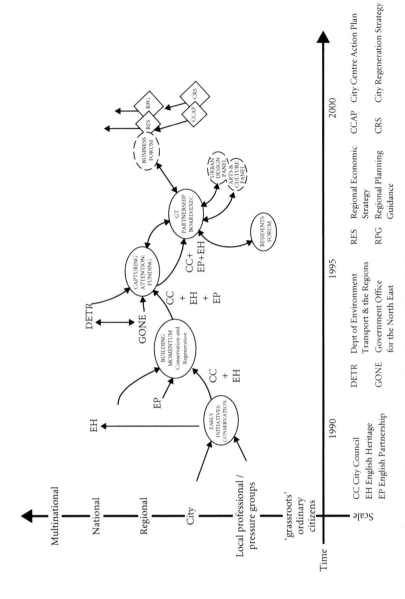

Figure 2.3 The mobilization trajectory of the Grainger Town Project

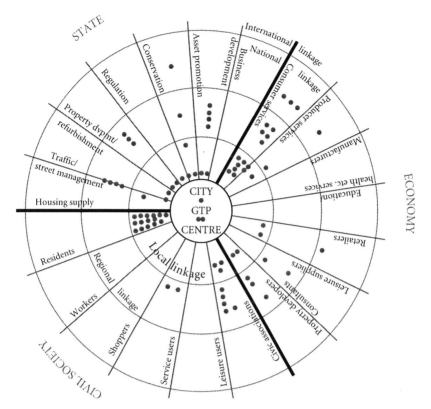

Figure 2.4 Stakeholder analysis of the participants in the Grainger Town Partnership as of 1998/9

scale or being taken over, their interests in this part of the city centre as such were relatively marginal.

Thus the city council was challenged in several ways by the initiative which had grown up within it. The project took over responsibility for property regeneration and environmental enhancement for a significant part of the council's own territory. It set up new channels of connection to business and civil society, with the potential for a different political dynamic from that which the council had developed with the disadvantaged neighbourhoods. It was answerable to several regional and national funders as well as the city council. And it focused on the quality of an area, rather than the delivery of a service. It thus challenged the council's established discourses and practices.

The city council has been under pressure to change from a number of different directions, and by the late 1990s, with new initiatives being set up at the regional level, was initiating a fundamental rearticulation of its strategic direction as well as reorganizing service delivery.[6] So far, this has not meant an easy context within which the Grainger Town Project could develop. Figure 2.3 (p. 72) summarizes the 'mobilization trajectory' of the project. From its early stages in the city council, the project built momentum and captured sufficient national attention to attract substantial funding. The partnership established as the vehicle for a multi-dimensional regeneration initiative then undertook considerable efforts to focus local attention, generating, in the forums and panels, what a city council official referred to disparagingly as a 'communicative infrastructure'. By 2000, the attention of the city council and the major funders had turned to other initiatives at the city and regional level. The project as a result was increasingly squeezed into an identity as a 'delivery arm' of the policies of English Partnership, the city council and the Government Office for the North East. In this way, its potential for widening and changing established relations between the state, the economy and civil society was contained.

The struggle for wider horizons and relations

The Grainger Town Project can thus be seen as an institutional arena within which new agendas and practices are being evolved and contested, in a situation where the institutional dynamics of the wider governance context are themselves in flux. How far has it benefited from the institutional capacities of its context? How far have new institutional capacities been developed? Are these likely to endure, or will they be swamped by the wider changes? Have they promoted a place-focus grounded in the daily life of the diverse relations which transect a city centre and a more open and inclusive style of governance? In this section, the framework outlined above is used to address these questions, drawing upon a detailed analysis of interview and documentary material relating to 1997–9, which is recorded elsewhere (Healey, Madanipour and de Magalhaes 2002). In presenting this material, the account starts with the actors and networks, the relational resources available to the project and developed within it. It then summarizes the knowledge resources which infuse the project before examining the project's mobilization capacity.

Relational resources

The project benefited from the ability of key players to access a *range* of different kinds of networks as momentum was built up for the initiative. This drew

---

[6] These pressures were coming partly from national government and from business, and could be seen as a challenge to the agenda of a people-centred focus on welfare delivery. But neighbourhood residents, especially in areas which had experienced a flow of regeneration initiatives since the early 1970s, were by the 1990s deeply critical of the council, for its paternalist and sectoral ways and for the focus of its agendas, while the quality of their lives deteriorated (see Healey 2002).

together a policy community focused around conservation issues, with good local and national linkages; the traditional business community, through the TNI and the Chamber of Commerce; the urban regeneration 'nexus', focused around the funders and the property sector; some special interest groups, including urban designers, arts and culture groups, taxi drivers, market traders, the Chinese community; and residents, for whom no previous arena had existed to meet and promote their concerns. Many of these networks spread well beyond the city, to cultural and business connections in other parts of the UK, to the rest of Europe and beyond (for example, to Hong Kong). The 'communicative infrastructure' of the initiative also added to the range of networks involved in urban governance. The focus of the project was maintained primarily on a property-regeneration agenda, linked to public-realm investments. It was through these means that key players hoped to achieve the wider social and economic agenda which had been envisaged when the momentum for the project was at its height.

The network *morphologies* displayed some web-like forms, the most notable being the TNI–Chamber relations (see figure 2.5). Here relationships were actively managed to maintain this form, particularly among the larger businesses with a long history in the city and the region. Other networks had a hierarchical form, reflected in constant reference back to a higher authority. This was clearly the case with the city council. Councillors saw the project as at the end of a chain of command which went through senior officers to the Grainger Town Executive. English Partnerships had to refer 'up' to the national level to get authority for a particular funding innovation (which was denied). The city council too tended to look upwards in its relations with central government. However, the city council was not one hierarchy but many, so that the project executive had to relate to different departments for different issues. In some instances, the project was merely a staging post on a corridor linking, say, training opportunities to training providers and training funders. In other situations, stakeholders were on their own, picking up opportunities for engagement with the project on an individual basis. For many, the project operated in a hub-and-spoke way, with agents acting either as individuals or on behalf of some group, relating directly to the organizational core of the project. This core was the most powerful nexus in relation to the project, represented by the executive board, and dominated by the project's chief executive and representatives of the city council and the main funders. But rather than working as a coherent team, this arena was where struggles over policy agendas, agency responsibility and working practices were played out. It was in effect transected by several relational networks, each with its own perception of how governance should and did operate.

There has been much discussion in the literature on networks about the significance of the 'thickness' or *integration* of networks. This refers essentially

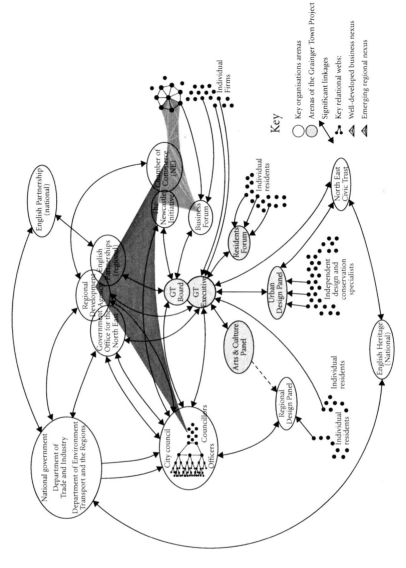

Figure 2.5 Network morphologies around the Grainger Town Project

to the number of relations which connect people to each other and the 'depth' of the bonds of linkage. It is often commented that Newcastle and the northeast of England have a strong 'density' of relationships between and within the public and private sectors. This can be seen in the weblike form of business relations. However, as noted earlier, these webs do not penetrate too well into the world of smaller and newer companies. Nor is the relation between the city council and TNI/Chamber a seamless web. Our interviewees talked of 'fences' and of a persistently problematic relationship, characterized by both lack of understanding and lack of mutual trust. Further, all three stakeholders in the economic development 'web'[7] were involved in other tranforming arenas which distracted attention away from nurturing the project. This meant that, after the initial enthusiasm, it was difficult for the project itself to generate 'nodal force' upon the relations around it. Instead, it existed on the margin of the dynamics of these wider relationships. Key actors from these networks regularly reined-in signs of autonomous action. The project thus could not develop its potential to act as a node of dense intersection between the complex relationships transecting the city centre.

This illustrates a paradox of the Newcastle governance situation. It is full of networks, as many of our interviewees commented, but they did not have within them the kind of social capital which would make them work to sustain a city-centre regeneration initiative. There was considerable goodwill towards the project and its mission. This was sustained by the multiple identities people often had, so that they could bring to the project a concern as citizens of Newcastle, or believers in cities, as well as their specific interests. But the instability in the contexts of the key players discussed above, and the continuing competition for organizational and territorial 'turf', made it difficult for this focused and integrative potential to be achieved. Functional divisions remained a problem, despite an internal reorganization in the city council in the late 1990s which sought to make the council's activities more issue focused. The traffic-management and the regeneration agendas clashed in the heart of the Grainger Town area, but by 2000 there were signs of some shifts in the traffic proposals.

Participants had no shared view of where *power* lay in this situation. Many thought it centred on the project board, that is the formal authority to which the executive reported. Others saw the power as with the executive team, the people they met at the project office, or at meetings of the forums and panels. Some people equated the project with the city council. Others saw the chief executive as in control, while some believed that control lay with the property owners and developers, since they (in the metaphor of the 'market') could hold up or facilitate the realization of the Grainger Town Project's objectives. Examined closely from the inside, however, it is difficult to avoid the conclusion

---

[7] English Partnerships, TNI/Chamber, the City Council.

that the strongest players were the main regional public sector agencies – the regional bodies and the city council. The power they exerted derived from a mixture of resource-allocating power and regulatory power. No matter how autonomous the board sought to be, these could override board decisions. For both, the project was conceived as a 'device' to 'deliver' 'their' policies. Despite all the encouragement for shared governance, it remained difficult for these government bodies to let go of their power.

In interviews and discussions, these power relations were generally personalized, with participants complaining about the behaviour of particular people and the authorities to which they were answerable. There were also instances of clear interpersonal power dynamics being played out. But underlying these surface manifestations were more complex power relations. Firstly, there were real tensions in the way the funding regimes were set up. Secondly, participants in the public sector were affected by the continual reassessment of priorities which went with this. Their links with the business sector tended to be with older firms, not the new businesses in the region. Structural forces were thus acting to shift the ground on which participants stood. Thirdly, there were deep shifts underway in the region's culture and the economy. These were strongly manifest in the city centre and had a potentially destabilizing effect on local politics. The sub-surface tensions were thus manifestations of the uneven trajectories of deeper changes, with exogenous forces perhaps most significant in the 'mobilization of bias' among institutions, while more endogenous forces moulded the power relations on the surface and shaped the detailed responses to the wider forces of social and economic change at the level of the 'deep structure'.

Thus it may be concluded that the project as an initiative suffered from an 'inheritance' of governance practices which did not encourage the kind of flexible, arm's-length agency which was envisaged as needed for the complex project it became. By 2000 there was a shift of attention of key players away from the project, which in any case was never a 'pet project' of key city council officers and councillors, but rather 'grew like Topsy' into a bid for national funding. This shift of attention produced competing arenas and competing networks. This raises questions about the long-term contribution of the wider 'communicative' governance relations built through the project. While the city council is now giving more attention to 'consumption' relations rather than its longstanding emphasis on 'production' relations, and in this context has become much more interested in the qualities of its city centre, by 2001 the Grainger Town Project was being positioned as just a part of a wider strategy,[8] the exact focus and processes of which remain as yet unclear. This provided a less conflict-ridden context for the project, but also gave it less leverage.

[8] Newcastle City Council 2000.

Knowledge resources

A broad *range* of knowledge and information was deployed by different participants in the project, covering the details of building conservation, urban design,
traffic management, business management and development, property market
and development opportunities, and experiential understanding of the way the
Grainger Town area operated at different times of day in its different parts. For
many of the policy and commercial actors, there was a shared story about the
'place' and its 'problems'. As the traditional core of the city centre, the area
had an important moral and emotive pull, as a memory and symbol of the city
and of the north-east region as a whole. But the area was primarily seen as a
place in need of attention, pulled apart by later developments to its north and
south. It was also affected by developments at a wider scale, within the region
(for example, the large out-of-town MetroCentre Project), and a shift of office
activities to Leeds, some 150 kilometres away. The Grainger Town area and its
stock were often thus conceptualized as an underutilized asset. This asset had
potential for commercial and office firms and for cultural and leisure activities.
As an historically important part of the city, it could offer a prestigious 'address', while its fine-grained morphology could promote the special qualities
of a city centre. Many residents enjoyed the ambience of city-centre life (Elliot
1999). Many people thus found themselves identifying with the area and the
project and with an array of ideas about problems and opportunities.

   Despite this common interest in the Grainger Town area, there were significant differences in the *frames* of reference which different participants used to
focus their analysis and understanding. The dominant story was that developed
over the years by the project initiators, and focused by the consultancy study
in 1996. This had boldly stated: 'Despite a generally high quality of classical
townscape, the external public realm and spaces between buildings is woe-
fully inadequate for a European regional capital of the scale and importance
of Newcastle' (EDAW 1996: para. 13). It presented the potential in terms of a
Europe of city centres with a 'café culture and an evening economy' (p. 81),
comparing the city with Sheffield, Leeds, Dublin, Glasgow and Edinburgh. It
described the area in terms of character zones and movement axes, and generated the following vision for the area:

> Grainger Town will become a dynamic and competitive location in the heart of
> the City: Grainger Town will develop its role in the regional economy, within a high
> quality environment appropriate to a major European Regional Capital. Its reputation
> for excellence will be focused on leisure, culture, the arts and entrepreneurial activity.
> Grainger Town will become a distinctive place, a safe and attractive location to work,
> live and visit.   (EDAW 1996: para. 18)

But despite the reiteration of this frame by many key actors through to 1999, it
was clear that this was neither stable nor well developed. There were different

ways of thinking about the internal structure of the area. The concept of 'European-ness' was reinterpreted, both symbolically, in terms of the images people had of idealized cities, and through direct experience of European travel, which many actors had undertaken. The project executive organized study visits to a number of other cities in the UK and elsewhere in Europe, through which participants began to see distinctive differences as well as similarities. Meanwhile, some of the less-involved participants – residents and smaller firms – had quite independent views of what the city centre and Grainger Town meant to them. The local papers and TV emphasized the 'party city' reputation the city centre had acquired, not to mention the link with Newcastle United Football Club, located in the centre of the city. The city council positioned itself uneasily among these frames and promoted some of its own. The strongest of these in practical effects was that linked to traffic management. One of the main streets in the area was to become the 'inner distributor road' in a city-centre management scheme, legitimated in the council's approved Unitary Development Plan, which guided land-use decisions. There was also uncertainty within the city council about the image of a 'European city'. It expressed the lifestyles of a new generation of mobile young professionals, challenging the traditional working class imagery of Newcastle and its culture (Wilkinson 1992). This uncertainty did little to shift the attitudes of property owners, who held on to past images of the configuration of the city centre as embodied in property values which others saw as inflated, and who were slow to recognize new market opportunities, for example the growing market for city-centre housing. This instability in frames led several key players to press the city council to develop a coherent strategic viewpoint on the city centre as a whole. This resulted in 1998 in an initiative to produce a City Centre Action Plan.

The 1996 consultancy report had argued for an integrated, area-focused approach to Grainger Town. The consultancy team had asserted the importance of a place-focus and of inclusive governance processes. The team's methods had involved extensive discussion and focus groups with different stakeholders, to help shape a coherent vision of the area. However, this momentum was followed by a two-year period while funds were acquired and project organization put in place. The boards, forums and panels associated with the project to some extent helped to bring the consultants' ideas back to active life, filling it out with all kinds of efforts by the executive to develop understanding of market conditions, conservation challenges, urban design quality and the challenges of regeneration. But this was not backed by strong and consistent support from the city council. This made it difficult to resolve the tensions between competing priorities which inevitably surfaced within the project. The most serious of these were over traffic management and public-realm qualities. There were also tensions between conservation and regeneration objectives, although key actors commented by late 1999 that considerable learning about each other's situations had taken place between the proponents of these viewpoints. Thus the *integration* of frames of reference among the stakeholders was limited.

The extent of *openness and learning* by any of the agencies involved was linked to previous experience and position within the initiative. In the mid-1990s, the regional and national players believed that the city council should become more outward-looking and strategic in its approach. The Grainger Town Project certainly promoted a learning dynamic. One of the key actors developing the momentum for the project commented in 1998: 'it's all learning curve stuff'. Others, both councillors and experts, were less prepared to see the project as a learning experience. Some spoke of it as merely another partnership, or just a 'delivery agency' for agreed policies. Other actors close to the project, however, acknowledged that it was innovative to see the new possibilities that the private sector agencies could bring to the table. For those with a private sector background, it was informative to see how the public sector worked and the checks and balances it had to go through when handling public resources. In both cases, the main achievement for most participants was the ability to see things differently, from a viewpoint they were not used to. Those who appreciated this opportunity also valued the 'communicative infrastructure' established around the project. However, there were also concerns about the flows of 'learning'. The project was praised by many of the participants as promoting a new way of doing things. It opened the regeneration process to a wider network of agencies. But it remained 'top-down' in form. Members of the board, forums and panels saw their role as advisory. They perceived a hierarchical decision process. At whichever 'level' they were, they felt that the power of decision-making lay at a higher level. At the board level, participants felt that a core of members had set the agenda beforehand. Those 'above' the board, however, saw the project as a 'delivery' tool for a particular regeneration programme, rather than an end in itself, that is, as a new way of regenerating the city. As a result, the enthusiasm expressed by many participants on becoming involved tended to ebb away as uncertainty developed as to how far they could exert an influence, a common finding in urban regeneration partnerships in England in the 1990s (Hastings 1996; M. Taylor 1995; Wolman and Page 2000). In terms of the three dimensions of power discussed at the start of this chapter, participants were aware of, but had trouble relating to, the connection between the discussions which were visible to them and behind-the-scenes governance processes.

Mobilization capacity

The tension in the flows of learning can be linked back to the way the project originated and to its relationship with the city council and the major funders. Initiated by officer enthusiasts within the city council, backed by local urban design and conservation enthusiasts, the project was developed in a top-down way as far as many stakeholders were concerned. The 'core' partners detected a favourable national and local opportunity structure for a city-centre regeneration partnership and then proceeded to enlist the support of 'minor' partners. The other stakeholders were either coopted into the structure or offered a controlled institutional space as their arena of participation. Their *opportunity structure* was therefore contingent on that created by the dominant partners. For these key players, the project was an opportunity to capture funding (the city council), or diversify into more complex regeneration situations (English Partnerships), as much as to fulfil key strategic objectives for the city centre.

The chief executive and the executive board, the core *arena* of the project, acted as 'brokers' between the dominant partners whose power lay in their control of investment resources. There was unequal access to the arenas that mattered, and the means of access to these were not entirely open or transparent, reducing the chances of a real participatory process. Increasingly, as strategic priorities for the 'core' public sector players and big businesses changed, the project risked becoming a delivery agency of a narrowly defined regeneration programme. In this context, the various participatory, consultative and decision-making structures could end up rather formal and meaningless. As of 2000, there was no significant mobilization 'from below' to secure the existence of real participation channels, despite the efforts of the project team.

The project introduced new relationships and arenas to city-centre gover-nance, in the panels and forums. But the way these *repertoires* of mobilization techniques were used related directly to access to sources of power. There was a gap between those stakeholders who could 'pull strings' and/or wield finan-cial or regulatory power and those who had to go through the official channels of participation set up by the project. For the latter, the alternative was non-participation or mobilization in opposition to the project. There was no sign of any such opposition relating to the Grainger Town Project. However, in 2000, there was a substantial mobilization of individuals and groups in opposition to the city council's plans for neighbourhood 'regeneration' (Healey 2002).

Although there were powerful *personalities* behind the history of the Grainger Town initiative, it was definitely not the creation of a single person or a group. In fact, it entered people's agendas in different ways, and sometimes only in a peripheral position. There were various change agents at different levels, with different roles and sometimes conflicting agendas. It proved difficult to command continued attention and a consistent focus even among key play-ers. Overall, the project captured a moment of opportunity, primarily linked to funding. It innovated a repertoire of new governance processes. But the context was a difficult one within which to challenge significantly established ways of doing governance. The practices of this initiative in the new 'network' gover-nance thus made few direct inroads into Newcastle's traditions of municipal government.

The micro-politics of urban governance transformation

The Grainger Town Project, when we researched it, was partway through its formal funded life. By 2001, it was 'delivering' physical changes in the look of the area, its activity mix and general ambience. It was also achieving most of its required 'outputs'. Given the substantial funding obtained for the project and the skills of the executive team, this might be expected. Our evaluative concern is with its contribution in the context of transforming urban governance relations in Newcastle, from a more paternalist and sectorally focused mode of governance to a stronger place-focus and a more open and inclusive style. Change of this kind occurs over a longer timescale and on a broader canvas than a particular initiative. Yet the objective of innovating new governance processes was inherent in the partnership form in which the project was cast and promoted by the important consultancy study of 1996, upon which the funding was based. The project executive also invested a considerable effort in widening the governance relations around the project. Our evaluation framework serves to illustrate tensions in this wider objective and the missing ingredients in the institutional situation in which the project had to work in the late 1990s. These have limited the opportunity to contribute to building new institutional capacities. As regards relational resources, the strong networks between the key players at the core of the initiative were primarily ones of convenience and mutual interest. They were characterized by a delicately handled endemic mistrust rather than open cooperation, and they were not of great breadth or richness. Many of the networks to which the project related were hublike rather than weblike, if there was any network behind a stakeholder at all. There were only limited linkages between 'families' of networks, except within the business community. Despite the qualities which the project sought to develop, the relations between the core players were tense and troubled, rather than open and trusting, owing to the conflicts over control of the initiative.

As regards knowledge resources, there was potentially access to a rich range of knowledge. However, there were only limited episodes of conscious reflection on the frames of reference which set the project parameters. Ideas and information were shared only among a penumbra of people linked to the project through various consultative forums and panels, despite considerable efforts by the project staff to broaden involvement and awareness. New ideas were injected, but a lot of effort was required to keep the whole enterprise on track as far as the core players and funders were concerned.

As regards mobilization capacity, at the supra-local level there were some structural opportunities available. However, the initiative focused on a contested territory (the various viewpoints and claims for responsibility in relation to the city centre and its management) and challenged local practices (in both the private and the public sector). Both the local and the supra-local institutional

Table 2.4 *Dimensions of power and institutional capacities*

	Relational resources	Knowledge resources	Mobilization capacity
First level of power: visible and transparent	New relationships established; new modes and styles of communication	All kinds of knowledge mobilized	Enthusiasm and commitment of many stakeholders engaged
Second level of power: 'mobilization of bias'	Shifting alliances; tensions between main actors; power of external funders	Significant filtering of ideas and agendas	Influence of new forces 'contained'; attention of key players shifts elsewhere
Third level of power: deeper structures	Major changes in economic relations, society and culture	New economic and social relations generate new knowledge and expectations	Ongoing processes of change in government–society relationships, generating new unresolved tensions

contexts were too unstable to provide it with consistent support. There were just too many arenas and too many change agents around. The capacity for collective strategic action was therefore limited.

This case at one level emphasizes the difficulties of innovating open-minded, inclusive, place-focused governance practices in local and supra-local contexts with hierarchical traditions and contemporary struggles for control over resources, policy arenas and agendas. Does this mean that an initiative which focused on place quality and which also sought to innovate new governance processes was inappropriate in such a context? This might be the conclusion if the governance context in the locality were stable. But in this case, processes of transformation were at work at several levels at once. There was a visible level of direct conflict, in public arenas and reported in the media. Behind this, all kinds of changes were going on in the organization, processes and personnel of governance. Beneath all this were deeper changes in economic geographies, property investment opportunities, socio-cultural habits and attitudes to governance. All these affected the opportunity structure available for a project such as the Grainger Town initiative. Within these changes, there were several pressures which promoted attention to place quality and which encouraged more inclusive, deliberative processes for articulating and delivering policy agendas. So struggles over discourses and practices were rumbling on at many levels and on different timescales within the governance context (see table 2.4).

The city council itself, in all its different arenas, was a central terrain across which these struggles were being played out. During 1999–2001, the pace of these struggles speeded up.[9] The opportunity for the project to affect wider governance processes related partly to its timing in the unfolding trajectory of these struggles. But the contribution of the project could also be seen as an asset for the locality as well. Its articulation of conceptions of place put qualities of place on the agenda. The various visits to other cities enlarged participants' perceptions of possibilities and potentials. These were now being developed in the city council's efforts in 1999–2000 to produce an overall 'regeneration strategy', which became known as 'Going for Growth' (Newcastle City Council 2000). The project's efforts to widen the networks involved in city-centre governance and to evolve more open and discursive forums for engagement in governance enriched the 'reservoir' of relational resources and mobilization repertoires available in the locality and expanded awareness of how governance can be done. It scattered discursive seeds and droplets of process rain in the complex shifting ground of governance. One outcome of these and other partnership initiatives in the Newcastle area has been to generate a much more articulate and demanding, if fragmented, polity among residents. Another is that council officials see the need for change. As one official commented,

> I didn't have to listen to these people before and (now) I listen to other people's ideas. That's been quite healthy really. A lively debate is a very positive sign ... also it brings in new ideas ... you've got to be able to defend your views so much more robustly and have things put in front of you that you might not have seen before. And you have to think very hard about whether you should change your views. So I think it has enriched certain things ... (Healey, Madanipour and de Magalhaes 2002)

Increasingly, the city council had been pushed into developing many more collaborative arenas in which policies and projects could be discussed and evaluated. By 2001, signs of real transformations in governance processes were being felt across the city council, though the scale and direction of these changes is as yet difficult to forecast.

Conclusions

How does this case, and the interpretative policy analysis framework used to examine it, help in examining how the institutional inheritance of governance in a locality shapes transformation processes? How does it contribute to evaluating governance initiatives in the context of transformation processes? What does it contribute to understanding governance in network societies?

Firstly, the story of the case highlights the importance of locating the micro-processes of such initiatives in their continual interaction with wider processes,

[9] See Healey 2002.

which both limit and provide opportunities for their efforts (Malbert 1998; Innes and Booher 1999b). It warns against naive expectations. It encourages more explicit attention to the particular politics of the opportunities and constraints on policy agendas and processes as they play out in place and time.

Secondly, it illustrates that the inheritance of institutional capacity is hardly a stock of assets which can be disposed of and added to by conscious attention at the visible level of power relations. It is better understood as a complex, fluid and evolving 'infrastructure', flowing at deeper levels. New elements and relations coexist, combine and shatter as they encounter older ideas and ways of going on. Understood in this way, the evidence of struggles at multiple levels of power dynamics suggests a speeding up of transformative opportunity in this case, as the congealed history of paternalist, hierarchical politics is challenged from many directions. The issue for the locality is what gets to grow in this warmer and more fluid ground. Our case shows the significant knowledge and relational resources which could be mobilized for a more open-minded and place-focused governance. It suggests that developing concepts of place-identity which have real leverage on specific policy programmes could command considerable support among stakeholders. There are also possibilities for a more inclusive governance to emerge. But releasing this capacity requires abandoning process forms which are deeply embedded in the institutional inheritance and which inhibit attention to place quality.

Thirdly, it highlights the insidious way that powerful interests outside and inside a locality can impose their agendas unless there are countervailing grassroots forces to challenge and limit their operations. In this case, the partnership form and the priorities of the funders emphasized involving stakeholders, but behind this was a business agenda concerned with overcoming the complexities of 'council politics' as much as real commitment to broadening the range of stakeholders involved in governance. The non-business stakeholders were there to supplement the pressure on the city council. Not only does this kind of funding strategy exacerbate hostile reactions to such initiatives by municipal politicians and officials, it 'crowds out' local initiative and makes key actors play a 'vertically-structured' power game, rather than being forced to rethink their relations with their grassroots supporters and develop more 'horizontal' linkages. The outcome of these kinds of power games could be to encourage a narrow transformative focus at the local level on relations with business stakeholders, reconfiguring forms of 'local corporatism'. This suggests that local authorities with more funding autonomy, less vertical dependence and a richer grass-roots politics may be much better able to help to build the kind of broadly based innovative and democratic 'territorial milieu' discussed at the start of this chapter. It also suggests that strategic actors involved in transforming urban governance contexts need to pay explicit attention not just to the agendas around which they seek to mobilize transformative efforts, but the processes through which grassroots mobilizing efforts might be given more institutional space and policy attention. This, of course, is potentially politically uncomfortable as well as time-consuming. But in the long run, the grassroots will not wait for local government, as Newcastle City Council discovered in summer 2000 when residents mobilized in vigorous and effective protests at the council's consultative failures over neighbourhood regeneration plans.

Finally, this chapter has provided a detailed 'window' on the dynamics of the governance tensions and conflicts generated by the impact of the newer 'networked' forms of policymaking and political mobilization on traditionally organized municipal councils. It suggests that transformations are rarely revolutionary events occurring at one point in time, but rather they evolve through complex interactions within which participants learn new frames of reference and evolve new policy procedures. Deliberative processes in arenas which draw in new actors, as in the Grainger Town Project initiative, have an important role in transformation because they facilitate these learning processes. But in complex networked societies, only hindsight can assess where the trajectory of transformation led.

3

A frame in the fields: policymaking and the reinvention of politics

Maarten Hajer

Could policymaking be constitutive of politics? Conventionally, policymaking is conceived of as the *result* of politics. In this view classical-modernist political institutions seek to involve people in politics via a choice of elected officials who are subsequently supposed to represent the interests of their voters, initiate policy and oversee its implementation. But what if people do not always have clear-cut identities or preferences? What if they regard 'party politics' with a certain cynicism, and are much more 'spectators' than participants (cf. Manin 1997)? Is that the end of politics? This chapter argues that this is not necessarily true. Citizens could also be seen as political activists on 'stand by' who often need to be ignited in order to become politically involved. This creates a new role for policymaking. In many cases it is a public policy initiative that triggers people to reflect on what they really value, and that motivates them to voice their concerns or wishes and become politically active themselves. Public policy, in other words, often creates a *public domain*, as a space in which people of various origins deliberate on their future as well as on their mutual interrelationships and their relationship to the government.

The idea of a network society only adds to this. Nowadays policymaking often takes place in a context where fixed political identities and stable communities always be assumed. People live their lives individually in their own networks that stretch across territorially defined boundaries, and often without explicitly seeking representation in the sphere of formal politics in the location where they happen to live. Yet the announcement of a policy intervention can change this apparent political indifference overnight. Intended policy

The author would like to thank all those who commented on this chapter, but in particular Frank Fischer and Hendrik Wagenaar for their perceptive comments on an earlier version.

interventions make people aware of what they feel attached to, thus influencing people's sense of collective identity, i.e. the awareness of what unites them and what separates them from others. To put it more pointedly: policy discourse can be *constitutive* of political identities. In effect this reverses the accepted conceptual relationship between politics and policy. It is not political communities that seek political representation in order to influence policymaking. Here it is policymaking that provides the practices in which people start to deliberate and become politically active. What is more, it is by so doing, that they first *create* political communities. This chapter shows that in a network society it is policymaking that creates a sense of community and triggers meaningful political participation. Yet these are new sorts of communities that are very much based not on shared normative beliefs but rather on the fact that their 'members' feel affected by the intended public policy programme.

This chapter analyses the case of 'nature development' in the Netherlands, a case in which a policy initiative triggered a large public protest. In analysing the case it becomes obvious that the political conflict was related not merely to the intended change of policy but at least as much to the institutional way of conducting politics. In the days of classical-modernist politics, people knew where politics was conducted and by whom. In most cases people also knew what the most important cleavages were, what they wanted to get from politics and whom to approach or vote for. In the network society this is no longer that obvious. Moreover, classical-modernist political institutions are, by themselves, not always sufficiently powerful to achieve policy change. As Torgerson (this volume) also states, this is particularly so in cases of large technical or social complexity, the kind of complexity that advanced industrial societies, and in its wake, conventional policy analysis, are reluctant to acknowledge. The case of nature development illustrates the limited effectiveness of classical-modernist political practices in dealing with these kinds of complexities and with the fragmented and unanticipated political dynamics these generate.

The role of policymaking practices as public domain raises important issues for policy analysis. This dimension of policy deliberation tends to escape the analytic gaze. Participation in policymaking is mostly discussed in the conventional language of representational politics. Consequently, it is registered as – at best – marginal manifestations of public protest against 'official' politics. The linguistic and cognitive hegemony of the representational rhetoric obscures from view the subtle democratic dimensions of these spontaneous, often innovative, bottom-up events. The argument also implies that we need to focus on a different sort of policy practice that allows for the representation of those actors that the effectiveness and legitimacy of political interventions depend on. Analytically, we need to reflect how we are to make sense of this dimension of policymaking as a 'stage' for the articulation of political conflict. If preferences shape up in interaction we need a different sort of tool that allows for such more dynamic analysis of political formation, mutual positioning and the influence of particular policy discourses. Drawing on empirical research on the experiments with new 'interactive' forms of environmental governance, this chapter suggests discourse analysis as a method that could help strengthen policy analysis in this regard.

The politics of nature: from conservation to development

Driving through the Dutch countryside one is likely to come across large bill-boards announcing major construction works. The signs do not refer to new road schemes or new rail infrastructure: they announce projects of *nature development*. Conventionally, 'nature development' refers to the development of nature into productive agricultural land, as for instance described in George Perkins Marsh's seminal study *Man and Nature* (1864). Nowadays the concept has a different meaning. At the beginning of the twenty-first century large tracts of the Dutch countryside, eventually adding up to 730,000 hectares, are to be 'given back to nature'. Land that was rationalized and modernized – first to cater for the nourishment of the Dutch population and subsequently to strengthen the competitive position of the Dutch agro-industrial sector in the international markets – is to be returned, before 2018, to its 'primeval' state. It has resulted in a slow-motion *ballet méchanique* of draglines and bulldozers, excavators and trucks. Under the direction of engineers and geomorphologists fertile topsoil is dug away to make way for wetlands or drifting sand, dikes are breached to create new lakes or 'living rivers' and at carefully chosen places dunes are opened up to allow the sea, the 'water wolf' that haunted the Dutch for centuries, back in.

The reconstruction of nature is the outcome of a major policy scheme, generally known after its main concept: the *main ecological structure* or MES. The MES refers to an interconnected network of areas of ecological importance. The official goal of the new policy is to halt the reduction of biodiversity and allow for an ecological revitalization after decades of negligence. Fuelled by widespread support for the notion of 'sustainable development' at the time (cf. Fischer and Hajer 1999), the government passed its Nature Policy Plan in 1990 (LNV 1990) and the bulldozers were lined up to take to the countryside.

The Cabinet celebrated the parliamentary endorsement of its policy of nature development as an innovative way of acting upon its commitment to the Declaration of Rio. Indeed, it was one of the few concrete policy initiatives that would act on the newly established policy goal of enhancing biodiversity. Yet to the surprise of most participants in the policy deliberations, the policy scheme ran into difficulty during implementation. What had seemed an uncontroversial plan suddenly met with fierce resistance.

One day in the early 1990s farmers erected a frame in the fields designated for redevelopment in the northern district of Gaasterland (figure 3.1). The frame,

Figure 3.1 The frame in the fields

a robust 30-foot-wide picture frame made of scaffolding poles and painted beams, stood at the edge of the fields framing the view of passers-by. Thanks to the astute sense for symbolic politics on part of the farmers the point was hard to miss: many people in the local community actually felt attached to the landscape-as-it-was.

The erection of the frame in the fields caught policymakers by surprise. Up to that moment, policy formation had been a smooth process, with experts and policymakers agreeing on the need to move beyond mere nature 'conservation'. Policymakers had invented the vocabulary of 'main ecological structure', 'networks of nature' and nature development (for a more detailed account, see below), and parliament had formally decided to fund the creation of this main ecological structure. Moreover, the policy was facilitated by the widespread societal support for sustainable development and the need to enhance biodiversity. What could the problem possibly be? The farmers in the region were well aware that their agricultural practices were not economically viable. They knew that things were going to change: the supply- and growth-oriented policies of the European Union were under siege and without the accompanying subsidy schemes it was hard to see how they could survive economically. Hence their 'strategic interests' could not be with mere continuation of the current practice. Yet in Gaasterland some 75 per cent of the local population opposed the plans for nature development (Keulartz, Swart and van der Windt 2000: 59).

The limits to classical-modernist practices of policymaking

The policy conflict marked by the frame in the fields was not merely based on different notions of beauty of the Dutch rural landscape. In actual fact it brought out in the open the limits of the classical-modernist practices of politics and policymaking, more in particular the institutionalized format in which societal interests get represented. There are at least three dimensions to this: (1) the reliance on a stable but small set of actors when it comes to preparing policy plans combined with the assumption of a smooth implementation of any well-considered plan; (2) the difficulty in dealing with seemingly 'erratic' policy preferences; and (3) the new role for policymaking practices under conditions of reflexive modernity.

The frame in the fields first of all confronted government with the limited effectiveness of its traditional strategies of 'conceive–decide–implement' in a network society. Top-down implementation strategies faltered on local protests. Protests in plural, because in several other regions similar concerns were raised soon after Gaasterland.[1] The protests were not anticipated in the predominant neo-corporatist practices of consultation at the national level. These practices of consultation did include farmer organizations yet centrally organized policy deliberations no longer guarantee a reliable representation of the feelings of the various 'constituencies' just as the farmer organizations no longer have the authority to control their alleged constituencies.

The second dimension to the institutional crisis concerned the nature of the protests. The frame in the fields showed that environmental policy should not be regarded as a fixed programme for ecological improvement that 'only' needs to be implemented, that politics was not merely a matter of doing 'more' or 'less' for the environment (cf. also Fischer and Hajer 1999). Of course, we have known for a long time that implementation of apparently sound ideas often poses new and often unanticipated difficulties (Pressman and Wildavsky 1979). Yet in a network society the limited scope of the traditional analysis becomes problematic. Compared to the times of Pressman and Wildavsky the problem of implementation is far less a matter of instrumentality and the complexities of coordination. It was quite literally a confrontation with different ways of framing the problem on the part of the variety of actors.

As it happened, one of the principal narrators of contemporary Dutch history, Geert Mak, had settled in Gaasterland for a year to write an account of the changing Dutch countryside. Inevitably he encountered the policy of nature development. He observed the particular attitude towards the landscape. For many local people the landscape was not merely 'out there', it was part of their identity:

> The government wanted to magically transform 150,000 hectares of agricultural land into 'strategic green projects' by the year 2020. Near the Dutch rivers summer dikes had to be stabbed to give space to riverine forests and squishy wetlands. To the North,

---

[1] Interestingly, the symbolic icon of the frame in the fields made a political career as well, emerging in several other places where the main ecological structure was to be implemented such as in Helenaveen.

polders would become lakes again, and elsewhere meadows would be given back to the forest, the heath and the barren sand ... Most farmers that I knew saw it as a capitulation, a total comedown, even craziness. Fine agricultural land, reclaimed from the water and the barren sand with sweat and determination by their fathers and grandfathers – and sometimes even by themselves – had to be brought back into its primary state – whatever that might have been.

'This is not nature, this is negligence,' they said. Some farmers feared for their succession since farmhouses located near the nature plans were now eternally doomed. Moreover, in the villages the unrest spread, since cafés, churches and voluntary associations could not live off goose and wetland flora. And tourists would stay for a few months only. (Mak 1994: 120, author's translation)

For the government 'nature development' might have been an innovative way of acting upon the Declaration of Rio – something everybody would agree to, yet for the local communities 'nature development' meant first of all a denial of their identity. To them the existing landscape told the proud story of generations of farmers. Their fathers and grandfathers had first reclaimed the land, had then found ways to make the land productive, constantly applying the latest ideas to enhance the efficiency of agricultural production. They had been part of a concerted effort to nourish the Dutch population with its own products. In that sense the landscape had its own particular functional and cultural-historical significance. Hence to them the landscape was everything but a *tabula rasa*. It was not a mere 'surface' waiting for a new plan; the landscape was loaded with meaning and signifiers, stories and achievements.

In this sense, the implementation was not held up because of a lack of efficiency. The protest of the farmers addressed the alleged lack of concern for the complicated problems that the contemporary rural communities faced: why was the government willing to spend millions on new nature but did not have a coherent strategy to address the problems of the rural communities? These included a lack of jobs – which was often blamed on the various restrictions that had been imposed on economic development in their regions already. Allowing nature to have its way appeared but a further confinement of their freedom.

Moreover, it was not simply addressing the plans to create new wetlands but encompassed the alleged 'denial' of what was meaningful to them, the sudden 'devaluation' of their 'lived' environment (cf. also MacNaghten and Urry 1998). In the eyes of the farmers the plan for nature development indicated a lack of appreciation for the labour of previous generations, indeed for their way of life.

Yet it is the third dimension to the limits of the classical-modernist that is most far-reaching in its repercussions: it shows the importance of concrete policy-making practices for political representation and deliberation under conditions of reflexive modernity. It is this aspect that we will address at some length below. Policy implementation, a longtime concern of policy analysis, seems to have acquired a new significance in society. It is no longer merely about the execution of political decisions, it nowadays is often *constitutive* of politics. To explain this idea, let us first turn back to the case.

The case of nature development: the government's response

Following the erection of the frame in the fields, the government changed strategy. Several evaluation studies had indicated the poor implementation record of the policy of nature development (cf. Berkel, Bosch and Clausman 1994). In many cases this was due to local protests. Thus far the government had relied on sectoral strategies for implementation. These made way for a broader, 'area-oriented' policy approach to regional development. Moreover, the new practices were to be 'interactive' (LNV/VROM 1992). They allowed local people to bring other concerns to the fore that did not immediately relate to nature development. A couple of years later the introduction of new interactive policymaking practices and the broadening of the agenda could be shown to have been an effective way of improving the implementation record (cf. LNV/IPO 1999).[2]

Interactive policymaking practices are common in the sphere of environmental politics nowadays. The frustration with the limited effectiveness of more hierarchical 'top-down' policymaking practices of the past has been felt in many different polities, and hence much environmental policymaking now includes various forms of 'policy dialogues' (cf. Hajer and Kesselring 1999; Jänicke 1996; Lafferty and Meadowcroft 1996). These interactive practices differ from the familiar participatory practices in terms of the moment and focus of engagement: interactive policymaking practices are typically employed *before* a formal political decision has been made. As such the new interactive policymaking practices signify a shift away from the 'first generation' of environmental policymaking practices. In the first generation practices public or stakeholder involvement took place 'end-of-pipe' (i.e. *after* policymakers and politicians had basically achieved a consensus around a particular plan). Now this participation shifts to the early phases of policymaking. The second-generation practices are often promoted as 'open' alternatives to the previously 'closed' policymaking practices. The emergence of the interactive practices signals an explicit recognition of the plurality of legitimate interests and concerns on the part of the government.

Interactive practices operate with a more open definition of the problem to be solved. Policymaking moves away from a purely 'sectoral' orientation towards an integrated or 'area-oriented' approach, allowing for other concerns to be taken into account as well. There are plenty of examples in which these new

---

[2] New problems with the implementation have occurred since then, but that is another matter that does not speak to the core theme of this chapter.

practices achieved 'win–win' solutions that the classical-modernist practices were unable to generate (cf. Healey et al. and Innes and Booher, both this volume). In the case of nature development in Gaasterland the broader area-oriented approach to rural development resulted in the elaboration of a new scheme, in which nature development was combined with other uses of the land (cf. Keulartz, Swart and van der Windt 2000: 60–61).

All of this is now well understood. Yet we can also infer some more profound changes in the meaning of policymaking practices. The frame in the fields was the symbolic representation of a new type of politics that calls for deliberation and legitimacy in new locations. It did not merely concern the *content* of policy-making but the *practices of policymaking* as well. The subsequent introduction of interactive policymaking marked the attempt to readjust the practices of governing. It is here that the story enhances our understanding of governance in the network society.

Policymaking and the creation of political community

Governmental interventions are commonly judged in terms of their capacity for effective problem solving and generating legitimacy. The quality of policymaking is then judged in terms of these two criteria. In our society policymaking rapidly acquires a third quality, which constitutes a third way to judge the quality of decision-making. Considering the evolution of the case of nature development we can see how public policymaking in that case de facto functioned as a *stage for reflection* on the preferred future of a particular region. It was a public policy initiative that led people to reflect on what they actually valued, who they were, where they came from and where (if anywhere) they wanted to go to collectively. Public policy, in other words, functioned as *public domain*, as a space in which people of various origins deliberated on their future as well as on their mutual interrelationships and their relationship to the government.

This of course potentially creates some friction with the idea of representative democracy. After all, protests emerge rather late, often after a formal decision has been taken. Yet at the same time the concerns that are brought to the fore are often new and in themselves legitimate. Here the 'design' of the policy process is at stake. My argument, then, is that in the context of the network society (Castells 1996, 1997) or what others would call a post-traditional society (e.g. Beck, Giddens and Lash 1994) *it is likely that it is the confrontation with a particular policy programme that first provides the shared basis for discussion, that first brings together the range of individuals in a particular region.* It is the flip side of the diminishing grip of political parties on political voice. Whereas the political themes in the postwar era got a fair representation via political parties, we now see a growing discrepancy between the world of political parties and the widely diverse politics of the network society. Yet this idea that the

protests and discussions that are initiated by policy initiatives are the flip side
of the crisis of party politics should not be misunderstood as a purely negative
thing. There is no reason to talk of 'crisis' here. Yet at the same time it is clear
that there is a problem of institutional design that needs to be addressed.

The quality of public policy practices as a public domain, as a stage for
joint reflection and deliberation, calls for explicit attention. Policy discourse
then is *constitutive* of a region or, to be more precise, of political community.
The case of the frame in the fields can be used to elaborate this third aspect
of policymaking in the network society. In terms of political geography, rural
regions are non-existent. Rural areas by no means constitute coherent 'communities'. It does not make sense to see the existing administrative boundaries as
marking different communities. The same holds true for cities, in which people
themselves decide to which communities they want to belong, irrespective of
politico-administrative boundaries, Areas are composed of a great variety of
people and actors that participate in a range of networks, the shape of which is,
each time, determined by the interests and activities of a particular individual
(Hajer 2000a; Hajer and Reijndorp 2001). In the case of nature development
the rural areas are much better approached as a set of actors that happen to share
a particular space but operate within separate but partly overlapping networks
of social activity. Indeed, in most cases there is no appropriate governmental
level to debate issues of common interest: problems rarely fit the pre-given
administrative boundaries. By implication, the standing political institutions
(the city council, the provincial parliament, etc.) do not necessarily match the
territorial scale at which citizens would like to discuss a given issue. Hence, if
a problem comes up, politics is first of all a matter of finding and defining the
appropriate setting in which to stage the discursive exchange. These 'sites' of
discursive exchange have an influence on what can be said meaningfully and
with influence. A discussion in the back room of the local pub is not the same as
a meeting at the Town Hall. Obviously, different actors will have different ideas
about the ideal setting, as settings of course also come with different rights and
rules about who is allowed to take the floor, etc.

Characteristic for the network society is the fact that the problems that people
get worked up about often have no obvious 'fit' with an existing council of
territorial politics. If problems do happen to match a given level, we constantly
see how (new) political actors introduce other spaces for debate. These 'new
political spaces' are essential for the creation of political communities (cf.
Hajer 2002). In these times of constitutional politics, political practices, in other
words, first have to be (re)invented. Consequently, *communities do not pre-date
politics, politics leads to the formation of communities.* Depending on the issues
that have this potential, the territorial scale might differ. This, of course, turns
the theories of politics upside down: the established thinking focuses on the
issue of how to represent a (given) community and how to come to a fixed

system of legitimate decision-making on policies (cf. Manin 1997). Here we see how policymaking leads to the creation of communities that *for themselves* have to determine what constitutes a legitimate decision in a particular instance (cf. also Dryzek 1999). Politics is about defining what is a legitimate political institution. This is what governance in the network society is also about.

What sort of community is this? Taking nature development as our example, the regions within which nature development was to take place typically included an array of interests. Looking closely, there was no coherent community at all. The people living in the area included farmers, commuters to urban centres, retired couples looking for a peaceful environment, local families, people from outside but depending on the local economy, people active in the recreational economy at the weekend but living elsewhere during the week, second-home owners, squatters of old brick works, people with an administrative address in the city but residing permanently in recreational dwellings, etc. It was the looming threat of 'nature development' that brought this erratic group of actors together. Here nature development serves as an example of a policy initiative that was perceived to be a threat to a much-liked state of affairs, although no actor was – until then – actively protecting that state of affairs. There was no pre-given community to resist the plans; it was the policy programme that created what can be aptly described as a *community of fate* (van Gunsteren 1998): a group of actors that, because they are all affected by a policy plan, develop a sense of shared interest. Once this community of fate had constituted itself, the frame in the fields could result. Hence policymaking created a community of fate composed of people that might never have perceived themselves to be part of the same community before.[3] It is a policy programme that triggers shared preferences by actors who recognize a bond because they are all potentially affected by it. It is policymaking that creates the basis for politics, for the development of a collective deliberation on a collectively preferred future.

There is empirical support for this assertion of a new meaning of policymaking. In a recent study Thissen and Droogleever Fortuijn (1998) investigated social cohesion in Dutch rural areas. They started from the presumption that rural areas were slowly dying. According to this popular narrative, schools and shops are forced to close, and the once strong and coherent communities dissolve as families with children move elsewhere. To see if this community life had indeed disappeared the researchers investigated the level of membership of all sorts of associations. Contrary to their expectations the level of membership had actually increased in many places. Yet as they looked into the type of

---

[3] Another case illustrates this in a more extreme way. The controversial decision of the Dutch government to build a railway for freight transport from Rotterdam to the German hinterland led to public protests. In the course of this, a community of fate emerged that followed the projected railway track, cutting through all sorts of administrative, religious and social divisions.

memberships it came out that many of the new associations had been founded as a response to certain policy measures: protests against the construction of a road, mobilization for (maintaining) certain social and cultural facilities.

Here policymaking meets the new dynamics of political activity. Elaborating on Giddens' 'life politics' (Giddens 1991) or Beck's notion of 'subpolitics' (Beck 1992, 1999) we can see a new style of political involvement in which people combine individual lifestyle choices and an at best latent interest in 'party politics' with the capacity for very sharp and focused but at the same time discontinuous political activity. In reflexive modernity many people are 'politicians on stand-by' for whom one push on a red button is enough for them to become fully engaged in fierce and focused political battle.

The central point here is of course that this changes the meaning of policy-making practices. The above leads to the conclusion that policymaking itself leads to a reinvention of politics. Some will be reminded of Theodore Lowi's dictum that 'policies determine politics' (Lowi 1972: 299) and wonder what is new. Yet Lowi was actually engaged in a different project. As Barbara Nelson has pointed out, Lowi argued that 'different types of policies embody different types of relationships between individuals, groups, and the state and thus are characterized by different politics' (Nelson 1996: 567). Lowi saw it as his task to develop a taxonomy of the various 'problem types'. This is of course a rather different endeavour. For me the point is that political activity develops a new dynamics in a reflexive modernity. In this policymaking initiatives are often the match that ignites often short but intense bursts of political activity and the practices within which policymaking is conducted develop a new meaning.

Hence the new area-oriented and interactive policymaking that followed the frame in the fields should not simply be understood as innovative as it facili-tated the implementation of the agreed upon policy of nature development. In addition to that we should appreciate the meaning of such new practices for the development of a notion of democratic governance.

The new practices of governance that are emerging in the wake of the failure of classical-modernist politics create a secondary reality of politics. It is a complicated form of politics hidden in the shadow of the well-established ex-isting political institutions. The reinvention of politics relates to the general cul-tural process of individualization and de-traditionalization (Beck 1999; Beck, Giddens and Lash 1994). Yet policymaking itself fulfils a more central role in this reinvention than has been appreciated so far. Politics emerges in new places, with new actors that do not even qualify as single-issue actors. After all, it is a policy initiative that can suddenly call their hibernation to an end, just as it is most likely the policy initiative that forms the glue that holds them together. Once the threat is gone, or some acceptable deal has been struck, the community of fate will fade away as a coherent political actor (although it is probably fair to say that, once it has existed, it can be resurrected more easily).

This new way of looking at policymaking constitutes a challenge for the analysis of policymaking and politics. Drawing on the abstract concept of re-flexive modernization as put forward by Ulrich Beck, one might even argue that the failure to recognize the significance of these processes of policy-induced deliberation will erode the legitimacy of politics, whereas the active attempt to seek to incorporate these processes might precisely enhance the legitimacy of politics.

New forms of governance as challenge for policy analysis

The new role of policymaking practices raises fundamental issues for policy analysis. How are we to make sense of this dimension of policymaking as a 'stage' for the articulation of political conflict? Given the fact that experiments with new 'interactive' forms of governance can be observed widely, how do we approach these processes?

Interactive policymaking practices are a contested terrain. On the one hand there is no reason to see them as necessarily contributing to a more democratic and more open form of policymaking. Indeed, they might just as well lead to a Foucaultian 'subjectivization'. We know since early studies such as Amy (1987b) on related topics such as mediation, such policy practices tend to imply a strong coopting effect: concessions might be made, but the dam/road/airport gets built. On the other hand they might function as 'public domain', as practices that have the potential to create the equally Foucaultian notion of heterotopic, non-representative spaces within which the power-effects in discourse mutually cancel out one another, new knowledge is created and new identities and com-mitments are found and defined (Foucault 1986). These are very much questions that merit further theoretical discussion as well as empirical investigation.

In terms of theory, interactive policymaking can be analysed as a practice that partly shapes the process of preference formation of various stakeholders. This concern for interaction as preference formation is typical for deliberative democratic theory (cf. e.g. Benhabib 1996b) but might run counter to the more immediate concerns of policymakers.

It suggests that policy analysis should not be confined to the determination of the criteria that make the interactive policymaking practices function as consensus-making devices. If the idea of a changing topography of politics holds, then interactive policymaking practices should not simply be analysed with goals of effective implementation in mind. They should also be analysed and indeed appreciated as sites for the articulation of conflict and difference, as a place of social and cultural contestation (cf. Mouffe 1996). Now that political parties have lost their centrality policymaking practices might become more important in this regard. Seen in this light policy analysis should once more increase its effort to understand the interaction in interactive policymaking practices in terms of how they might help people to recognize an element of what they see as worth striving for, standing for and/or living for. Here the notion of deliberative policy analysis aptly describes what needs doing.

Of course, policy analysis cannot be about the articulation of conflict and contestation alone. It will always have to aim for the facilitation of collective decision-making. Yet in light of the above, it seems inevitable that we address more seriously the 'third dimension' of policymaking, the one in which we address value pluralism or issues of identity and difference. To understand how people develop what we may call 'identities of shared preference' through deliberation is a new question for research. In such cases people actually reposition their distinct preferences in terms of the deliberation generated in interactive policymaking practices.

At the same time there is no reason to assume that this discourse of inclusion will always work. Sometimes people might develop an identity precisely because they disagree with what they hear. But how are *conflicts of value pluralism and identity* dealt with in the new practices of governance? We know a great deal about values in public policy but now we need to know more about how policy practices are also constitutive of values and identities. Although the public policy literature has paid attention to the way in which issues of identity feature in public policy (most notably Schram 1993; Torgerson 1985, 1999a; Yanow 1993, 1996), the issue of the interactive explication of identities as a separate element of a policy science of democracy has not been an explicit theme (but cf. e.g. Guba and Lincoln 1989).

Writing in much more general terms, Castells has suggested three forms of – collective – identity building: (1) a *legitimizing identity* where dominant institutions make certain 'identity offers'; (2) *identities of resistance* that emerge as a response to processes of stigmatization, using categorizations that run counter to the dominant patterns of allocation of meaning in society; (3) *project identities* where particular social actors construct a new identity and thus challenge the prevailing patterns of allocation of meaning (Castells 1997: 8). In this, 'identities of resistance' may develop themselves into 'project identities' as the communities that form around a particular identity of resistance become 'subjects' by challenging the prevailing symbolic order in a given social field. The quality of interactive policymaking practices could be assessed in these terms.

Applied to the case of the frame in the fields, the top-down imposition of the 'main ecological structure' on various regions resulted in the almost spontaneous emergence of identities of resistance. The subsequent introduction of interactive practices, then, led to a transformation of these identities of resistance into project identities. This was not merely a matter of making new 'identity offers' available, but was the product of the interaction in the practice of policymaking.

Policy analysis should enhance its appreciation of how the opportunities for interpretation and opportunities for identification are created in policy deliberation. If done well, they in turn lead to the development of particular shared 'scripts' as to how to proceed on the part of actors that engage in the process (Swidler 1995: 38).

By paying particular attention to the aspect of *identity formation* (what is it that motivates people to speak up?) policy analysis would pick up an old theme already characteristic for Lasswell's 'contextual' policy science. As Torgerson observed a long time ago, this contextual orientation could be understood to include a 'quest for identity'

> during which individuals 'loosen the bound of the culture into which they are born by becoming aware of it...' The process is one, alternately, of 'breaking through current stereotypes' and 'articulating key symbols of identity'... Disclosing a perhaps forgotten past and projecting a potential future, the elaboration of a developmental construct, in particular, involves analysts in a 're-definition of identity'. (Torgerson 1985: 250)

An important difference with the Lasswellian approach is that we might nowadays be less convinced that the policymaker is automatically the 'agent of change'. The shift from government to governance should go hand in hand with the appreciation of a whole new range of non-state actors that are actively mediating these new processes of policymaking (cf. the contributions of Innes and Booher and Healey et al., this volume). Lasswell also held a very ambivalent view of the role of public debate in this and again that is something up for reconsideration.

The study of identity formation would link up policy analysis to wider political concerns; more in particular the politics of recognition as promoted by political theorists such as Honneth (1992), Taylor (1994) or Gutman (1994). It would give new meaning to the old commitment to a policy science of democracy, taking the examination of the level of democracy beyond the dimensions of franchise (referring to the number of participants) and scope (referring to the domains that are brought under democratic control).

Methods of a new policy analysis

This strand of research will have considerable methodological implications. If preferences and identities are constructed through interaction we must approach it as a dynamic process. A useful starting point for such an analysis is the pioneering work on identity in public policy as done by Yanow (1993, 1996). It opened new routes to understanding public policies both as 'expressive' and as instrumental solutions to particular problems. Yanow's idea that 'interpretative modes of policy analysis seek to identify both the specific meanings, intended and made, of specific policies and how those meanings are communicated and variously interpreted' (1996: 222) lends itself for application to the study of interactive policymaking and more general governance. Drawing on her work we can also seek to analyse the discourse produced in these practices for the 'identity stories', 'communities of interpretation' or what I would call discourse coalitions. Yet on top of that we will have to put more emphasis on the *dynamics* of policymaking and political preference. If preferences shape up in interaction we need a different set of tools that allow for such a more dynamic analysis of political formation, mutual positioning and the influence of particular policy discourses.

Likewise, it seems inevitable that we move beyond the examination of the direct sphere of policymaking. This, too, will have methodological repercussions. If we want to find the communities of interpretation that must be allowed to have their say, we cannot confine our research to the direct sphere of policymaking. One needs to get to those people that *should* be included but might, as yet, be unidentified. In terms of method we should explore ways to identify themes that could mobilize these new groups. Here discourse analysis could be helpful (see below), but one could also envisage using more anthropological research techniques as we would need to get a better sense for the concerns of various communities in their own terms. Ethnographies are a possible tool to map life worlds and identity stories separate from policymaking practices.[4] A third methodological inspiration might come from the knowledge accumulated in research on social movements. In recent years it has become common wisdom in the policy sciences to appreciate social movements and individual citizens as a valuable source of 'local knowledge' that enhances the knowledge produced by more formalized policymaking practices (Fischer, this volume; Wynne 1996; Yanow 1996 and this volume). To that extent we have, as Eyerman and Jamison (1991) put it, recognized the importance of social movements as 'cognitive praxis' (see also Jamison 2002). Yet once the issue of identity is taken seriously, we must reconsider the way in which this local knowledge is mobilized. In what institutional practices do these engagements take place? What is the effect of this instrumentalization of the knowledge of movements? What is, in more abstract terms, the effect of the transfer of the cultural into the political? Which meaning gets lost in the process of translation as policymakers seek to integrate local knowledge into their more complex knowledge systems? Here the fact that the policy sciences tend to conceptualize their reality from the policymaking concerns outwards may sometimes impair their insights. The alternative is to look also from the outside in. Eyerman and Jamison, for instance, focus their work on the actual creation and recreation of 'interpretative frameworks' (1998: 19). Their critique on 'mainstream social movement literature'

---

[4] A nice example thereof can be found in de Haan (1998). In the context of an exploration of the possible urbanization of Rotterdam to the southern rural area, an ethnographer reconstructed the 'signs in the landscape' in order to get to the identity formations present in the area.

is that it moves too quickly from very abstract frames to the actual imposition of frames on individuals.

Policy analysis might have to reconsider some of its inclinations in a similar way. We know a great deal about how nominally democratic practices can be impaired by all sorts of organizational choices (e.g. Hajer 1995; Torgerson 1985) yet what conceptual knowledge have we generated in the policy sciences about groups that *might* engage but do not? What do we actually know about the processes of adjustment to engagement in policymaking discourse on the part of social movements or individual citizens, i.e. what do we know about the exclusionary effects of the culture or indeed the discourse of policymaking (cf. Torgerson, this volume)? Critical policy analysts might all agree that we want a 'critical dialogue' based on claims, concerns and issues put forth by various societal groups (e.g. Guba and Lincoln 1989) but one may wonder if we really have the conceptual tools to facilitate these dialogues. The features of the network society may require us to rethink standard rules of procedure here (see also Hajer 2002).

Discourse analysis as tool of a deliberative policy analysis

It is obvious that we need better methods to disentangle policy conflicts. And also to understand why classical-modernist practices sometimes fail to produce intended results. The case of nature development can be used to explain the way in which discourse analysis could be employed.

Drawing on earlier work (cf. Hajer 1995, 2000b), we might interpret the events in the case of nature development in terms of changing discourse coalitions, which shape up in an identifiable set of policy practices. Analytically we can distinguish three distinct elements to such an analysis. Firstly, the study of the *terms* of policy discourse, i.e. the (new) vocabularies, story lines and generative metaphors, the implicated division of labour and the various 'positionings' for the actors and stakeholders involved; secondly, the formation of particular discourse coalitions around these story lines; and, thirdly, the analysis of the particular institutional *practices* in which discourses are produced. The case of nature development can then be examined (1) as a shift in *the terms of policy discourse*, (2) in relation to the formation of alternative discourse coalitions and (3) in terms of the particular *institutional practices* in which the discursive conflicts are played out.

Terms of policy discourse

Any discourse analysis aims to show how language shapes reality. Yet under this common denominator discourse analysis hides a variety of approaches. Some focus much more on the analysis of linguistic elements, while others would include the study of the institutional practices within which discourse is

Table 3.1 *Three layers in policy discourse, with illustrations from nature development*

Layers	Examples from the 'nature development' case
1. Analysis of *story lines, myths and metaphors*: (crisp) generative statements that bring together previously unrelated elements of reality and thus facilitate coalition formation	• Creating a 'network of nature' • The threatened extinction of the otter is illustrative of the state of nature • The myth of the Oostvaardersplassen
2. Analysis of *policy vocabularies*: sets of concepts structuring a particular policy, consciously developed by policymakers	• 'main ecological structure', 'target types', 'ecological corridors', 'nature development areas'
3. Analysis of *epistemic figures*: certain rules of formation that underpin theories/policies but that are 'not formulated in their own right'	• 'networks', 'infrastructure', 'investment in nature' (1990s) • previous examples: 'pollution', 'limits' (1970s)

produced as well. My approach is based in the latter tradition. Analytically, we can distinguish various aspects of policy discourses. I start off by examining the *terms of policy discourse*. Drawing on Bill Connolly, 'terms' thus are understood as 'institutionalized structures of meaning that channel political thought and action in certain directions' (Connolly 1983: 1). I here reserve the concept of 'terms of discourse' to refer to the ways in which the biases are structured in textual utterances. This analysis can help us to understand the initial stability of the policy discourse of nature development.

The move from nature conservation to nature development is an example of the way in which institutional bias can be structured into text. Once people made the conceptual move from conservation to development a whole set of new options for policymaking emerged. Yet we can refine the analysis of the formative power of utterances in policymaking by introducing an analytical distinction of *three layers* in policy discourses that together make up the terms of policy discourse (see table 3.1).

The first layer consists of the story lines, metaphors and particular myths that help sustain the societal support for particular policy programmes. Story lines are defined as (crisp) generative statements that bring together previously unrelated elements of reality. The main function of story lines is that these short narratives help people to fit their bit of knowledge, experience or expertise into the larger jigsaw of a policy debate. The idea that 'the best way to take care of nature is by creating a *network of nature'* is an example of a story line in the case of nature development. This type of story line allows for shared orientations and is an important factor in the formation of a supporting coalition. Story lines often carry metaphors: linguistic devices that convey understanding through comparison. Metaphors such as 'network of nature' are vehicles for the discursive reduction of complexity, allowing people to communicate over complex policy issues. Myth, then, brings coherence by explaining why things cohere: a 'constitutive myth' explains cohesion by narrating a foundational event, a 'dystopian myth' makes people cohere to avoid a catastrophe.

A story line that helps to explain the influence of nature development was the threat of the otter becoming extinct in the Netherlands. Dr André van der Zande, the policymaker who is often regarded to be the architect of the concept of main ecological structure, recalls how the Dutch Minister of Agriculture at the time kept asking if the state of nature was indeed as grim as many people projected. Pointing at the threatened otter, the much loved water animal, van der Zande had to agree.[5] The otter thus functioned as 'emblem' (cf. Hajer 1995: 19–20) for the wider problem of nature conservation and thus facilitated a shift to a new, more encompassing policy approach.

Yet the 'career' of the language of nature development was not only based in the political recognition of the need to do more. It was facilitated by a constitutive myth. This was the saga of the 'Oostvaardersplassen' that policymakers kept retelling in interviews. The Oostvaardersplassen refers to a large wetland area that emerged, allegedly quasi-spontaneously, in the course of the creation of the new Flevopolder in the Netherlands. The endlessly reiterated story is that, as the drainage initially was ineffective, the area 'overnight' became one of the breeding areas for a great variety of migratory birds. In the story line this is supposed to have caused a 'cognitive shift': apparently it is possible actually to *create* nature! The insight was loved by policymakers: suddenly it became apparent that one does not have to restrict oneself to conserving 'what is left' of nature. And, if nature has a capacity to regenerate itself, then nature policy might explore new routes! If we create a larger 'network' of interrelated reserves, nature might indeed be able to recover. What makes it a constitutive myth is that it is constantly told and retold as if the relevant actors actually collectively experienced this 'gestalt switch'. It brought together the coalition sustaining nature development but reduced a much more complex genealogy of the approach at the same time.

A second layer comprises concrete *policy vocabularies*. This refers to sets of concepts structuring a particular policy, consciously developed by policymakers. In the case of nature development it comprised terms like 'main ecological

---

[5] Dr A. van der Zande cited by A. Schreuder, 'Pionieren in een plantenbak', *NRC Handelsblad*, 2 September 2000, p. Z4.

structure', 'target types' (in nature), 'ecological corridors' and 'nature development areas', as well as concepts borrowed from science such as 'natural balance' and 'biotopes'. These terms structured the white papers and codetermined what was a legitimate policy action and what was not.

It can be shown that the new policy vocabulary was supported/legitimized by a particular scientific theory. It drew on ecological and biological research that had determined which 'biotopes' were characteristic for nature in the last interglacial era (cf. Keulartz 1999). Moreover, nature was conceived not merely in terms of 'species' but as biotopes. The ideal was to restore (some of) 'nature-as-it-was', bringing back wild animals in order to restore the 'natural balance' lost in the era of agro-industrial dominance. Once they were lifted out of the scientific debate and were included in the policy vocabulary the terms gained a new meaning.

The third layer focuses on the formative power of *epistemic* notions in policy programmes. Drawing loosely on Foucault (1970) – who was trying to catch a different and far bigger sort of fish – epistemic notions refer to a regularity in the thinking of a particular period, structuring the understanding of reality without actors necessarily being aware of it. Epistemic notions resemble a 'state of mind', or what Foucault called a 'positive unconscious' of knowledge: certain rules of formation that underpin theories/policies but that are 'not formulated in their own right' (Foucault 1970: xi).

Nature development is structured by two concepts that structure thought and action. First and foremost it is the concept of 'network' that provides the main organizing principle. The move from nature conservation to nature development was made possible by this concept: instead of protecting the 'remaining islands' of natural beauty, nature policy became a matter of creating a network by creating the 'missing links', the so called 'ecological corridors'. 'Networks' are of course also a metaphor yet not all metaphors have an epistemic quality: this is only the case if they are among the principal vehicles for our understanding of the contemporary world. 'Network' most certainly is one of the most central metaphors for our understanding of reality. The power of this concept transgresses sectoral boundaries (see the introduction).

The second epistemic notion in the discourse of nature development is the concept of 'infrastructure'. This concept emerged as an epistemic notion in many countries during the 1990s (cf. Luke 1999; WRR 1999). Initially, it referred to the 'hard' infrastructure of road, rail and fibre networks. Yet nature conservation policy was affected as well. As Luke observed for the United States, in the 1990s new forms of eco-knowledge emerged that facilitated an 'infrastructuralization' of the earth's ecologies (Luke 1999: 110). Seeing nature as infrastructure creates new meanings that take the discourse on nature beyond the sphere of morality. Talking about nature as infrastructure creates a link to the importance of nature as amenity (which is essentially a functional idea), but also allows for an engineering approach to nature. If nature is seen as infrastructure, we can also make the move from mere conservation to the actual creation of new (and better?) nature. Moreover, having freed nature from its heavy moral meanings it also becomes possible to talk about 'green compensation' for investments in more traditional infrastructure elsewhere.

Each policy discourse comes with its own power effects as it shapes the knowing and telling one can do meaningfully (cf. Hajer 1995: 100). Yet discourses are not static and do not exert power by themselves. The question is how discourses are taken up in a *process of mutual positioning*: the ways in which actors intersubjectively create and transform political conflicts using language. Whether they like it or not, actors are positioned by the language of nature development, either unintentionally or actively.

Positioning is not merely a matter of cornering one's opponents in concrete discursive exchanges. The power of policy discourse is also a matter of routinizing a particular 'parlance of governance', of excluding or marginalizing alternative ways of seeing. Yet in other cases positioning might be an unintended side effect.

Discourse coalitions

Yet the analysis of the terms of discourse alone does not suffice to explain why the classical-modernist policymakers were caught by surprise by the frame in the fields. In addition to that, one should analyse the coalition of actors that supported the policy-discourse of nature development, including several NGOs. Shared story lines were (1) the idea of creating a 'network of nature', robust enough to be self-sustaining, and (2) the idea of 'investing in nature' that nature development implied. In order to achieve the goals of nature development, additional agricultural land had to be bought and restyled to become nature while existing nature reserves were to be (re)connected. In that sense nature development was a remarkably successful act of reframing (cf. Laws and Rein, this volume).

The discourse coalition linked up two previously unconnected policy domains, nature conservation and economic development. It was made explicit by a Dutch environmental NGO, Natuurmonumenten. It sought to strengthen the politics of nature development by explicitly arguing that the high investments in 'economic' infrastructure should be matched by investments in 'ecological' infrastructure. Subsequently, they were criticized by other actors within the environmental movement for implicitly legitimizing the controversial investments in more 'hard' infrastructure. It implied a 'hitching on' to the dominant frame of its time (Schön and Rein 1994), the development of road and rail infrastructure but, as the critics might have pointed out, this obviously has effects on what can be said meaningfully.

The discourse coalition was based on the assumption that resource exploitation and nature policy could be reconciled in the projects of nature development. 'Every dumper that leaves the area helps to create more nature', a sign explains at the edge of a site of nature development in the riverbed of the River Waal.[6] And so the digging up of clay and gravel – essential resources for the building industry – was seen as a case of creating nature. Linking a 'weak' policy field (nature conservation) to a 'strong' ally like economic development was seen as a major boost for the policy programme. But still, the government had not identified the stakeholders that might be opposed to this plan.

Practices

Rules and structures are not only immanent in language; it is also relevant to examine the settings in which discourse gets produced. The third element of a discourse analysis therefore consists of the analysis of the institutional *practices* in which the discoursing takes place and conflicts are played out. In this respect nature development can be related to institutional practices from within the national Ministry of Agriculture. The very strong institutional interlinkages between research and policymaking were important. Several organizations belonging to the former Dienst Landbouwkundig Onderzoek (Division for Agricultural Research, DLO) monopolized knowledge generation and had a direct link to policy development. This direct link between science and policy facilitated a swift 'discourse institutionalization' (the translation of new discursive insights into enduring policy practices).

This institutional success imposed discursive constraints on the policymaking domain (see Wagenaar and Cook, this volume). Ecology became the language that would discipline the debate on the politics of nature (cf. Keulartz 1999). Perceiving themselves as a policy elite, the nature developers had all the characteristics of a powerful 'epistemic community' (Haas 1990): they shared both cognitive and normative convictions and were committed to implement the MES to the best of their capacities, adding as many square metres of 'reference nature' as possible.[7]

Ecologists did not merely act as scientists, they were effectively 'co-producers' of policy. They conceived the policy vocabulary of nature development with a good sense of the needs and concerns of the policymaker in mind. Apart from the central concept of 'main ecological structure' it comprised concepts such as 'target types' (in nature), 'ecological corridors', and 'nature development areas'. This catered for the policymakers' wish to monitor the effectiveness of policy interventions. On an operational level, the policy

---

[6] Nature development at the Millingerwaard, exit at Kekerdom.
[7] They literally had photo images of 'reference nature' that were to be matched by reality.

vocabulary of nature development made policy measurable. It allowed for questions such as: How many acres have been transformed into nature? How many target types have returned? How many connections have been established? (For an illustration, cf. LNV/IPO 1999: 15.)

The discourse coalition was in fact much broader than this policy elite. As shown above, national environmental NGOs with a policy orientation such as WWF-Netherlands and Natuurmonumenten also started to employ the discourse of nature development. They were stimulated to do so as their spending power had increased with the stunning rise in their memberships. Natuurmonumenten in particular had considerable funds and the discourse of nature development gave them the incentive to buy agricultural land and transform this into new nature. The inclusion of environmental NGOs working on the national level only served to stabilize the discourse coalition. Hence the policy was developed within established practices of consultation at the national level. If one would stick to the classical-modernist assumption of a *matrouchka* system of government, a successful policy then subsequently just needed to be implemented. The failure to act upon the new reality of a network society, in which both local governments as well as citizen initiatives do not automatically respect rules and policies from a higher level, helps to explain why the conflict over the implicit choices in nature development did not arise until the implementation phase.

However innovative the idea for nature development might have been, and however well tuned to the demands of policymakers, institutionally it had strong overtones of traditional top-down policy planning. The MES was conceived as a 'national policy plan' and was agreed upon by the national parliament.[8] Having gained official policy status, it had to be implemented at the regional level. Local communities, however, had difficulty with the superimposition of 'new nature' on their lived environments. Conceptually innovative, it was based on a limited range of institutional practices. The traditional policymaking practices did not provide the appropriate 'communities of practice' (Wenger 1998) to facilitate the restructuring of the countryside.

The subsequent reframing that occurred with the erection of the frame in the fields exposed the hidden bias in classical-modernist institutions of policymaking.

Conclusion and outlook

The frame in the fields and the subsequent success of the more inclusive area-oriented strategy suggest that policymaking can function as a public 'stage' where deliberation on goals and means can and indeed does take place. In the new modernity these 'interactive' policymaking practices will play an important

---

[8] For an analysis of the Dutch tradition of policy planning, cf. Hajer 1995, chapter 5.

role as acting upon interdependence and organizing collaboration will be essential for effective policymaking in the network society. Classical-modernist institutions will have to readjust in order to prevent end-of-pipe deadlocks. Yet this is by no means easy. After all, how can potential stakeholders be roped into an early and extended policy deliberation if time and again it is a very concrete threat that arouses political controversy, not the abstract discussion on the change from 'nature conservation' to 'nature development'. Since these concrete threats will often materialize during implementation, end-of-pipe conflicts are here to stay. Yet doubtless much controversy can be avoided by allowing for more flexibility in that stage.

In light of the findings of this chapter, policy analysis seems to have a triple task. First of all, renewing its methods so as to be able to understand the complex ways in which meaning is hidden in policymaking discourse and thus be able to anticipate political controversies. Secondly, to analyse the variety of experiments with collaborative planning, interactive policymaking and consensus dialogues in order to understand the ways in which these practices can help remedy the problems of the classical-modernist institutions and enhance the capacity of actors to interact and communicate in a way that is both effective and perceived as legitimate by all the participants (of course, in the awareness that institutional change is slow and classical-modernist institutions will dominate the policy scene in the years to come). Thirdly, it should renew its effort to deliver on Lasswell's call for a policy science of democracy by showing how these new interactive practices might actually fulfil a role in renewing democratic governance in a new modernity. It suggests that a deliberative policy analysis must be strong in detailed empirical research just as it must strengthen its ties with political theory, in particular with those theorists who are interested in grounding theory on empirical work themselves (cf. e.g. Fung and Wright 2001). This time that relationship could be much more balanced than previously, as it is not merely policy analysis that can learn from political theory. This chapter has shown that it is in the mundane world of policymaking that the rules of politics are rewritten and politics is being reinvented.

Part II

Rethinking policy discourse

4

Democracy through policy discourse

Douglas Torgerson

The word *policy* has acquired such strong technocratic overtones that the idea of pursuing democracy through policy discourse may seem puzzling, if not inherently contradictory. Of the *polis* family of words, policy occupies the middle position in a threesome – located somewhere between *politics* and *police*. Here the latter term needs to be understood not in its narrow contemporary meaning, however, but in the early modern sense of social control and regulation (see Heidenheimer 1986; cf. Foucault 1991a). In the latter half of the twentieth century, policy took on much of the old sense of police, though with a new, distinctly technocratic accent. Policy came to be viewed as something that was – or should be – removed from politics (see Torgerson 1986a).

This essay, nonetheless, pictures policy discourse as a potential means of democratization. The prospect is that democracy might be enhanced not against or in spite of policy discourse, but through it. For, with the advent of reflexive policy discourse, it becomes increasingly possible to contest the meaning of policy and draw it into closer association with politics – particularly a democratic politics at odds with technocratic policy discourse. The prospect of democratic policy discourse becomes conceivable.

Any potential for democratization has to depend on much more, of course, than a change in policy discourse. The potential depends on context. We thus find ourselves returning to what Harold D. Lasswell, when advancing a policy focus in the social sciences, long ago stressed as central. Lasswell emphasized the importance of a deliberate project of contextual orientation, whereby inquirers would continuously question, test and revise the images of 'self-in-context' that, whether explicit or implicit, inescapably guide action and inquiry (see Torgerson 1985). Such a deliberate process of contextual orientation is in principle never concluded, but is continuously open to new information, insights and emerging events.

A major feature of a project of contextual orientation is the elaboration of developmental constructs, necessarily tentative images of past trends and future prospects. The prospects can be either desirable or undesirable, and the point of identifying them can be either to promote or inhibit their realization. The elaboration of a developmental construct is necessarily inconclusive, but is itself also part of the emergence of future events, necessarily implicated in the overall context of inquiry and action.

Any of the many ways of characterizing emerging developments can be understood as developmental constructs. Looking to the past, both Marx's diagnosis of the contradictory character of capitalist development and Weber's assessment of the rationalization of the modern world can, for example, be understood in these terms. In the contemporary period, there has been a proliferation of names meant to capture key features of past trends and future prospects – e.g. organizational society, consumer society, limits to growth, sustainable development, late capitalism, postmodernity, disciplinary society, risk society, reflexive modernization, globalization. Despite the differences among them, such ideas do not necessarily exclude one another; they often overlap, even as they focus attention differently.

The current idea of a network society[1] is helpful in drawing attention to often neglected patterns of complex social interaction in policy processes. This complexity is typically obscured by images of policy and administration that focus on linear lines of authoritative command and give paramount status to the sovereign state. Despite the persisting strength of traditional imagery, this status was actually eclipsed long ago (Torgerson, 1990). Even as the modern state emerged as a distinct institution, its apparently paramount significance was already attenuated by the simultaneous emergence in the social structure of a larger complex of administrative institutions. As the significance of this larger complex became clearer, traditional images of administration centring on the state had to contend with new images of technocratic management framed by a systems metaphor.

With the idea of a network society, there is a shift from an older notion of government to a newer concept of governance. There is, however, now a further question raised by the idea of a network society. Is governance just another name for technocratic systems management, or is something qualitatively different involved? Does governance in this new network context, that is, accentuate policy or politics?

Technocracy presupposes a rational administrative sphere capable of monitoring and regulating social systems efficiently and effectively through complex

[1] See the editors' Introduction in the present volume.

patterns of input, output and feedback. Even though traditional lines of administrative authority give way in this conception, a basically oligarchical pattern is preserved. The administrative sphere, the privileged domain of policy discourse, holds sway over the larger society. By drawing attention to complex patterns of interaction that extend the policy process beyond officialdom, however, the idea of a network society has the ability to throw into question the oligarchical presuppositions guiding technocratic policy discourse.

A contextual orientation informed by the network idea has a capacity, in particular, to focus on interchanges between the administrative sphere and the public sphere of civil society. This focus suggests at least the promise of inquiry and action proceeding in a way that serves to undermine oligarchical relationships. Considered in this way, the move from government to governance does not have to end in a technocratic cul de sac, but instead suggests a potential for democratization through democratic policy discourse. With such an eventuality, governance would be associated not only with policy, but also with politics.

Democracy and policy discourse

The idea of democracy here departs from the liberal democratic image, in which a public interest is formulated by a representative legislature whose purposes are then given effect by an administrative apparatus. This sense of democracy has generally been all too comfortable with a quiescent public and technocratic governance, too comfortable generally with continuingly oligarchical features in modern society. Here democratization is instead viewed in the sense of a citizenry becoming actively engaged in discourses that enter into the very process of governance (see, e.g., Dryzek 1990b, 2000; Fraser 1992).

The traditional liberal democratic image arose from a concern to insulate governance from the irrationalities of a mass public. Even John Stuart Mill, often regarded as an early champion of participatory democracy, was careful when proposing his 'rational democracy' to shield the governmental process from public intrusions (Mill 1835: 195, 1865; cf. Pateman 1971: ch. 1). In more recent times, this same kind of concern was evident in liberal democratic reactions to newly emerging social movements. These were seen as disrupting social order by challenging the apparently happy consensus of the postwar world. So many new demands confronted liberal democratic systems that democracy itself seemed endangered by *too much democracy* (Crozier, Huntington and Watanuki 1975).

Although discursive democracy departs from liberal democracy by unequivocally championing an active citizenry (Dryzek 1990b, 2000), there sometimes remains an ironic continuity. 'Discourses do not govern.' So Jürgen Habermas bluntly states (1992: 452), even as he promotes an active sphere of public discourse that would include the voices of new social movements. For Habermas, a rational society depends on such a public sphere, but there seems to be something about the policy process, as he conceives it, that deflects direct public involvement.[2]

In the case of John Dryzek, there is emphatic concern about the irrationalities of liberal democracy and its administrative apparatus. For him, there is no reason in principle why citizens could not become directly involved in the policy process, but there is a significant reason for them not to do so. Dryzek is concerned about a potential for cooptation – the possibility that democratic social forces might be neutralized by too close an association with officialdom. Contrary to Mill, he worries that the irrationalities of a supposedly rational policy process could undermine the very potential for rationality in public discourse.[3]

This potential depends on what Dryzek calls 'discursive designs' (1987b, 1990a), communicative spaces designed to allow for an open and level playing field of discussion while checking the tendency of participants to manipulate one another for the sake of strategic advantage. For Dryzek, these communicative spaces have particular potential in the unofficial domain of civil society. Indeed, one of his associates, David Schlosberg (1999), has recently shown how a communicative network in civil society can become a discursive design writ large.

What connection between policy discourse and public discourse should proponents of discursive democracy regard as possible and desirable? In promoting discursive democracy, Dryzek is reluctant to associate discursive designs with officialdom. He fears, in effect, that mobilizations of bias in this context usually undermine the potential for any semblance of communicative rationality. In his view, we thus find a potentially rational public discourse at odds with a typically irrational policy discourse that is practised in official circles. Nonetheless, Dryzek does acknowledge, in two respects, a potential for discursive designs in the context of public policy: (1) he explicitly identifies the prospect for at least a partial realization of discursive designs in some official settings, and (2) he conceives unofficial discourse in civil society as part of an expanded policy process.

If the policy process is thus part of a larger social network, governance cannot be limited to official circles. The boundary between public discourse and policy discourse then becomes a matter of contention, and the promotion of discursive democracy becomes a possibility. As boundary disputes are played out, it is

---

[2] This corresponds to Habermas' (1984/87) bifurcation of system and life world; but see also Habermas 1996: 440–441. For further discussion of this point, see Torgerson 1999b: 9–11, 171 n. 43.

[3] See Dryzek 1996b: 151–154, 1996c, 1996d: 115–121. For further discussion, see Torgerson 1999b: 9–10, 140–141.

possible that public discourse will effect a change in the established terms of policy discourse. Of course, there is no guaranteed outcome. Another possibility is that public discourse will be constrained and homogenized by the idiom of officialdom.

Discursive democracy here anticipates the development of a dissident policy professionalism to help to counter prevailing mobilizations of bias in the policy process and to change the prevailing order of policy discourse.[4] The very possibility of posing this prospect arises now because of an incipient change in policy discourse, a tendency for it to become reflexive. Reflexive policy discourse is at odds with technocratic inclinations to ignore and diminish discursive dimensions of the policy process. By drawing attention to these dimensions, a reflexive moment in policy discourse accentuates the political character of *policy*. Such a reflexive moment enhances critical awareness of the absence of communicative spaces for free and equal discussion, thereby offering support to a key goal of dissident policy professionalism: that of reversing the order of policy discourse from a technocratic to a democratic pattern. Thought through, the implicit logic of reflexive policy discourse involves a challenge to established power dynamics.

Here we move beyond the functional matters that preoccupy technocratic policy discourse. We enter a domain of constitutive politics that questions the very form of the established policy process and its relationship to advanced industrial society. It is in this context that we find a clear connection, moreover, between public discourse and reflexive tendencies in policy discourse. It is here that the challenge posed by new social movements – environmental, aboriginal, feminist – to established power happens to coincide with the aspirations of dissident policy professionalism to foster a democratic mode of policy discourse.

The ambivalent potential of reflexive policy discourse: Berger revisited

Reflexive policy discourse is not a happy ending, but a point of departure that offers a prospect of democratization. Some might be tempted to overstate this prospect, others to discount it. This very vacillation, however, suggests something obvious: the potential is ambivalent. This ambivalent potential can be seen in the context of discursive designs, particularly when these serve as points of intersection between public discourse and policy discourse.

Critics of discursive designs in the policy process generally divide into two camps – conventional and radical. The conventional viewpoint proceeds from technocratic presuppositions and sees discursive designs in the policy process as being impractical, incapable of reaching conclusions efficiently, opening the

---

[4] See Dryzek 1994: 188; also 1990a. For further discussion, see Torgerson 1999b: 140–141.

door to irrelevant distractions that are inimical to rational analysis. The radical viewpoint, in contrast, sees discursive designs in the policy process as cooptive devices that serve to domesticate dissident voices while reinforcing the powers that typically dominate the policy process.

For proponents of discursive designs in the policy process, the Canadian case of the Berger Inquiry remains the outstanding example (see Berger 1977; Dryzek 1982; Gamble 1979; Torgerson 1996). Although held in the mid-1970s, the Berger Inquiry remains an intriguing and instructive case. The inquiry, commissioned by the federal government of Canada, centred on the social and environmental implications of an industry proposal to construct a natural gas pipeline from Prudoe Bay in Alaska south through the Mackenzie River valley in order to reach markets in Canada and the United States. However, the head of the commission, Mr Justice Thomas Berger, interpreted his mandate – violated it in the view of critics – to involve a comprehensive consideration of development options in northern Canada.

In addition to giving his inquiry a broad focus, Berger not only allowed but actively and systematically encouraged the participation of actors typically marginalized in deliberations over northern policy in Canada. Although accustomed to having their voices heard only in the domain of public discourse, these marginalized actors became central to the policy discourse of the Berger Inquiry. In particular, Berger saw to it that aboriginal peoples and environmentalists had the opportunity to engage in the formal hearings on an equal footing with advocates of the industry proposal. This meant intervenor funding and, perhaps just as importantly, a requirement for the full disclosure of relevant information by all parties to the inquiry.

The inquiry thus became a forum not only for policy professionals, but also for dissident professionals, who worked on behalf of aboriginal peoples to expose conventional biases in agenda-setting, problem definition and epistemology (Torgerson 1996). By designing the inquiry to enhance open discourse on a level playing field, of course, Berger himself already presented a challenge to the technocratic orientation. This challenge became especially evident beyond the scope of the formal hearings and in the context of a series of community inquiries, during which Berger visited all major Canadian cities and all the potentially affected towns and settlements in the north. A key principle of the community hearings was that Canada's official languages, English and French, were not privileged; all participants had the right to testify in their own language. The community hearings became a significant social phenomenon in the Canadian north, broadcast on radio through the Northern Service of the Canadian Broadcasting Corporation. According to Berger, moreover, the community hearings were particularly decisive in the presentation of aboriginal viewpoints:

No academic treatise or discussion, formal representation of the claims of native people by native organizations and their leaders, could offer as compelling and vivid a picture of the goals and aspirations of native people as their own testimony. In no other way could we have discovered the depth of feeling regarding past wrongs and future hopes, and the determination of native people to assert their collective identity... (Berger 1977: vol. 2, 228)

The Berger Inquiry demonstrates that discursive designs in the policy process have a potentiality at times to at least approach communicative rationality and fairness. Policy professionals, representing industry, found themselves confronted by dissident professionals, who probed and challenged the conventional assumptions upon which the pipeline proposal was based. The inquiry was further opened, decisively on Berger's account, by inviting aboriginal people to speak for themselves. Notably, they did so in a way that was not limited to rational argument, but included their own stories, poetry and songs. These bore witness to an experience of the north not as a frontier to conquer, but as a loved place shaping the lives and identities of people who called it home.

Even proponents of discursive designs nonetheless have their doubts. Is Berger all there is? If so, does this not demonstrate that discursive designs really do lack feasibility or are fated to degenerate into cooptive exercises? Certainly, Berger was something of an anomaly, and even during the course of the inquiry one well-informed observer commented that it was something that the federal government would not allow to happen again (Dosman 1975: 217). But Berger is, of course, not all there is. Indeed, even within Canada, the experience of the Berger Inquiry has influenced the shape and conduct of numerous inquiries (see Salter and Salco 1981; Torgerson 1980: ch. 7, 1996: 288–289). In the particular political context of the Canadian north, moreover, the experience of the inquiry significantly concentrated and accelerated emerging trends towards the aboriginal assertion of self-determination (Abele 1983; Caloren 1978). The policy discourse of the Berger Inquiry amplified – in a new context – themes that were becoming salient in the wider domain of public discourse. Policy discourse and public discourse entered into a new, reciprocal relationship. After Berger, things could no longer remain the same.

It is thus a mistake to think of the potential of discursive designs as something somehow inherent in the model itself. Rather, discursive designs unavoidably emerge from contexts of power such that a discursive design in the policy process has an ambivalent potential that depends on power structures and alignments. The institutionalization of a discursive design also has the potential to influence the power context from which it emerges and may, indeed, be opposed because of this. Both the feasibility of discursive designs and their cooptive tendencies thus need to be considered in terms of the power relationships found in particular settings.

The Berger Inquiry emerged in a context in which new social movements were having an impact on public discourse, giving dramatic new attention to environmental concerns and the interests of aboriginal peoples. In this context, technocratic voices began to ring hollow and even at times met resistance within administrative agencies. Berger's innovations can thus be viewed as a particular expression of a changing focus in the theory and practice of policy discourse.

Policy discourse in the looking glass

Policy discourse has begun to look itself in the mirror, so to speak, to take account of itself as a form of discourse. There is much explicit talk of story lines and narrative policy analysis, of policy as text, of differing policy rhetorics; of metaphors, ambiguities and contextual meanings in policy language.[5] But this reflexive encounter remains constrained in grasping the significance of policy discourse. For there is something remarkable that has generally escaped much explicit notice, perhaps because it is simply too obvious. Like the purloined letter, it is hidden in plain sight.

Policy discourse ironically deflects attention from itself as discourse, from its own communicative character. With its rationalistic imagery, policy discourse appeals to the domain of the mind and its proper authority, implicitly repeating the key gesture Francis Bacon made in his early celebration of instrumental rationality (Bacon 1960[1620]: 7). Appearing detached from mundane confusion and error, policy discourse typically projects itself as being for experts alone, a narrowly bounded and focused technocratic enterprise. The epistemological touchstone of the enterprise is nominally science, but is actually scientism – the extra-scientific doctrine which holds that science is the sole source of legitimate knowledge.

On these grounds, the ineluctable vagaries and complexities of human communication are pictured as little more than peripheral inconveniences. Deliberation and decision are typically portrayed as matters of analysis in a domain of pure reason. Oblivious to itself, policy discourse is to be practised in constricted circles, concerned with the orderly governance and continuing development of advanced industrial society.

Technocratic policy discourse typically assumes a stable, objective world that can be codified and controlled through a neutral language. This 'objectivist ideal' was already noted by Laurence Tribe in an early critique. He stressed that this objectivism was accompanied by a type of codification employing an

---

[5] See, e.g., the editors' Introduction in Fischer and Forester 1993; Garvin and Eyles 1997; Hajer 1995 and this volume; Kaplan 1993; Roe 1994; Schram 1993; Swaffield 1998; Throgmorton 1991; Yanow 1993. For a remarkable earlier discussion, see Archibald 1980.

'antiseptic terminology' that reinforced an image of neutrality and tended to deaden moral sensibility: 'To facilitate detached thought and impersonal deliberation, what more plausible path could there be than to employ a bloodless idiom, one as drained as possible of all emotion?' (Tribe 1972: 97–98). The ideals of objectivism and linguistic neutrality here seem pleasantly joined together, but this apparently happy marriage has been disrupted by a growing awareness that both the conduct and the subject-matter of policy inquiry are enveloped by language.

'We talk of policy problems with words.' Deborah Stone (1997: 137) thus draws attention to policy discourse by quietly stating the obvious; she also states the not so obvious, however, when she indicates that there is no escape from discourse through numbers, for these operate 'exactly like metaphors' (p. 165): 'To count is to form a category by emphasizing some feature instead of others.... To count as unemployed only people who have looked for work in the past month ... excludes from the unemployed people who desperately want to work but are unable or too discouraged to pound the pavement.' The inescapable vagaries of discursive practice have not allowed policy experts to establish a reign of rationality, but have instead drawn them into a 'politics of expertise' (Fischer 1990, 1993; cf. Peterse 1995), in which the terms and practices of discourse become matters of contention.

Policy professionalism promotes rules of legitimate policy discourse that, at least implicitly, set it off from other discursive practices that might help to identify and resolve public problems. If a democratic citizenry has a role, it is conceived here as one that is set apart from policy discourse, located in that broad domain of public discourse where emotionalism and irrationality can be tolerated and discounted because they do not intrude into the rational domain of the policy analyst. The very term 'policy analysis' (Lindblom 1958; Melzner 1976: 1–2 n. 1; cf. Heidenheimer 1986) has suggested an impenetrable world of expertise, setting analysis off against the objective world that it was to analyse. This sharp demarcation has of course raised concerns about the relationship between policy experts and others, especially the citizens of a democratic society. Even if it remained unstated, what was especially perplexing, both methodologically and politically, was how there could be any meaningful communication.

By speaking of policy *discourse*, we begin to frame the policy world in a decisively new way, clearly locating both analysts and citizens in a communicative context that allows the potential for interchange, challenge and mutual learning. This is not to eliminate important differences – even divergent understandings – but it is to abandon sterile abstractions and invidious distinctions, thereby opening a conceptual door to the enhanced participation of citizens *with* experts in policy discourse. To focus attention on policy discourse is to anticipate democratic possibilities – potential changes in the way citizens, as well as experts, might 'talk policy'. Who is to talk policy, with whom, under what conditions, to what effect and purpose? With these questions clearly posed, we are in a position to consider appropriate roles for expertise without being mystified by the idea that serious policy deliberations must inevitably remain a closed world, restricted to official domains of administrative organizations and the state – i.e., the administrative sphere.[6]

In a mirror everything is the same, but reversed. Similarly, reflexive policy discourse suggests the possibility of turning things around. Heralding scientism, technocratic policy discourse pictures a world of rational experts managing a mass society made up of people who are preferably quiescent, democratic citizens in name only. The expert mind, conceived on an image of pure reason, here screens out attention to discursive relationships. Reflexive policy discourse brings these relationships clearly into view and suggests the possibility of reversing them, of creating a world in which citizens speak and experts listen.

Imagine the world turned around so that policy discourse is a central preoccupation of citizens while experts are on the outside looking in. Although fantastic, this reversed image serves to bring into view the possibility of a closer relationship between policy discourse and the sphere of public discourse. This does not mean that the two necessarily become the same, but we are placed in a better position to understand and strengthen precise connections as part of a project of enhancing democracy.

Democracy and the policy orientation: the loyal opposition

Policy discourse, deflecting attention from itself as discourse, has typically employed a technocratic idiom tending to obscure and deny democratic potentialities. In this regard, policy discourse has generally repeated a pattern set by nineteenth-century positivism (see Torgerson 1986a: 34–36). When Lasswell advanced his proposal for a policy focus in the social sciences, however, this was not the idea. By instead accenting a democratic potential, he implicitly raised the prospect of a reversal in the older pattern.[7]

During the Second World War and throughout the postwar period, Lasswell still maintained the progressive promise of harmony between science and democracy. It was thus that he sought to promote the policy sciences of democracy. In a world where anti-democratic forces loomed large, Lasswell focused on the problem of promoting order and rationality in a manner that was consistent with democratic values. In this context, his primary concern was the protection and promotion of liberal democracy, but it is noteworthy that his project

---

[6] On the concept of the administrative sphere, see Torgerson 1990, 1999b: 8–12.
[7] This discussion of Lasswell and related figures is based on Torgerson 1985, 1995. Detailed documentation may be found in those sources.

still contained accents derived from the participatory hopes earlier advanced by John Dewey.

Progressive faith in the union of science and democracy had been seriously thrown into doubt during the First World War and its aftermath. Concerned about the propagandistic manipulation of public opinion, Walter Lippmann in particular came to link his progressive goals to circles of expertise immunized from the irrationalities of mass society. Although not denying the importance of expertise, Dewey responded by warning of an oligarchy of experts and stressing the need for the education of a public capable of assessing experts and contributing intelligently to deliberations on public affairs: 'The essential need ... is the improvement of the methods and conditions of debate, discussion and persuasion. That is *the* problem of the public' (Dewey 1927: 365; cf. Dewey 1922).

Lasswell's project for the policy sciences of democracy was, as he explicitly acknowledged, a development from Deweyan pragmatism. Although Lasswell was an early student of propaganda – focusing especially on the experience of the First World War – he saw a potential for the enlightenment of public opinion. With Dewey and against Lippmann, he came to speak explicitly of 'democracy through public opinion', arguing that democracy needed a 'new way to talk'. The social scientific policy professional would act in the role of a 'clarifier' to dispel the effects of ignorance and propaganda and thereby enhance the quality of public debate (Lasswell 1941: ch. 7; cf. Lasswell 1926). This task would require the development of a professional identity through a process of critical contextual orientation.

By casting policy professionals as clarifiers for the citizenry, Lasswell promoted a form of policy professionalism that, he hoped, would counter tendencies toward oligarchy and bureaucratism. Here he followed not only the lead of Dewey, but also that of Charles Merriam, who had explicitly called for reliance on 'the insight and judgment of the citizens' (Merriam 1931: 178–180). For Lasswell, the principle of critical contextual orientation is thus to extend beyond a professional domain to include the citizenry. Significantly, moreover, this is to be accomplished in a way that is emphatically discursive: through the development of *a new way to talk*.

What is key in this process for Lasswell is that policy professionals enhance the rationality of citizens by providing them with a contextual map that offers a clear, critical understanding of the social process. This idea was long central to his thinking, and it was only near the end of his career that he recognized the problem that disagreements among social science professionals would require not one map for adequate orientation, but a plurality of maps.

Given the prevalence of technocratic tendencies in policy theory and practice, Lasswell's contribution may be counted as part of a 'loyal opposition' that challenges conventional policy professionalism while basically accepting the institutional context that sustains it. Also following the lead of Deweyan pragmatism, Charles Lindblom struck another oppositional note by directly rejecting technocratic rationalism and giving a key role to 'ordinary knowledge' (Lindblom and Cohen 1979; cf. Braybrooke and Lindblom 1970: 18–19). Similarly, Aaron Wildavsky indicated that 'speaking truth to power remains the ideal of analysts who hope they have the truth' (Wildavsky 1979: 12). But he also pointed to a problem: 'the truth they have to tell is not necessarily in them, nor in their clients, but in what these cerebral prestidigitators often profess most to despise, their give and take with others' (p. 405). It is thus that Wildavsky can promote a possibility of 'citizens as analysts' – or, what is more to the point, the possibility of citizens as participants in policy discourse (Wildavsky 1979: ch. 11; cf. Forester 1985).

Dissident policy professionalism: the recognition of bias

The relationship between experts and citizens has now emerged as an even more significant concern for a dissident policy professionalism that goes beyond the loyal opposition. Dissident policy theorists and practitioners, sharply critical of the conventional reliance on expertise, have sought to explore the possibility of bringing citizens as well as experts into the policy process in a manner that not only influences the functioning of the process but also reshapes it. Here there is a politics of expertise, in other words, that is not only functional, but also constitutive – potentially transformative.[8]

Explicit calls for the democratization of policy discourse through enhanced participation (e.g. Durning 1993; Fischer 1992; Kathlene and Martin 1991) typically proceed with a rationale that is threefold: (1) the inclusion of citizens is promoted in the name of democracy in order to counter technocratic tendencies, either of direct expert rule or – what is usually more to the point – of experts mobilized for other oligarchical interests; (2) the inclusion of citizens is promoted in the name of a communicative rationality that would counter mobilizations of bias in the policy process (cf. Bachrach and Baratz 1970); (3) participation educates and empowers people as citizens.

Dissident policy professionalism here, however, not only aims at improving the education and activity of a generalized citizenry, but recognizes and responds to a diverse range of particular social movements, such as environmentalism and feminism, which currently animate civil society and have come to exert an influence on the policy process – especially in regard to the way agendas are set, how problems are defined and what constitutes relevant and legitimate policy knowledge. The tendency is thus to reinforce changes in agenda-setting,

---

[8] For discussions of dissident policy professionalism, see Torgerson 1997, 1999b: chs. 4, 7; cf. 1986a, 1995. On the distinction between functional and constitutive politics, see Torgerson 1999b: 17–18, 131–154.

problem-definition and epistemology through the inclusion of diverse, typically marginalized, perspectives (see Torgerson 1997, 1999b: ch. 4).

The administrative sphere of advanced industrial society has been the central domain of conventional policy discourse, but dissident policy professionalism distances itself from officialdom as a privileged locus of policy reason. This move both recognizes and reinforces change to the contested boundaries of policy discourse and anticipates enhanced rationality through policy dialogue. The conventional lines of discourse within the administrative sphere implicitly deny this potential through attachment to a monological ideal of administrative rationality.

The promotion of policy dialogue arises not only from a democratic commitment, but also from concern about the irrationalities of advanced industrial society – dysfunctions that particularly arise from its incapacity to cope adequately with complexity (see Williams and Matheny 1995). Ecological irrationalities provide a key example of a kind of complexity that industrialism has been reluctant to recognize. As a case in point, attempts to define and solve environmental problems one at a time often give rise to the phenomenon of problem displacement.

Here a problem is not solved but simply transferred elsewhere in terms of time, space or medium. It is possible to delay facing a problem, thereby buying time, as in the temporary storage of nuclear wastes in the absence of a way to dispose of them permanently. Similarly, environmental impacts can be transferred in space, as with dispersed acid-rain effects that have arisen from tall industrial smokestacks built in the conviction that 'dilution is the solution to pollution'. Impacts can also be transferred across media – air, water and land – as an official of the US Environmental Protection Agency once observed: 'somewhere in the country, toxic metals are being removed from the air, transferred to the waste water stream, removed again via water pollution controls, converted to sludge, shipped to an incinerator and returned to the air' (quoted in Dryzek 1987a: 429). Dryzek has offered an image that strikingly portrays both the particular character of problem displacement and the larger challenge of complexity (Dryzek 1987c: 20): 'Imagine an inflated balloon as representing the sum of our ecological problems. Any solution to a particular one may be likened to sticking one's finger into the balloon. If we get displacement rather than solution, the balloon will expand by an equal volume at some other point(s).' The neglect of complexity, however, is not a matter of some momentary lapse but part of a larger orientation of the administrative sphere. As Herbert Simon (1976: 82) has stressed, 'devious consequences' have to be ignored. The potential for administrative rationality depends on the adequacy of a grossly simplified image of the context of action. This simplification is accomplished, Simon argued in association with his colleague James March, by 'uncertainty absorption', a systematic filtering of communication through official channels and technical vocabularies (March and Simon 1958: 164–165).

Guided by an objectivist ideal, technocratic policy discourse shares with the administrative sphere generally 'a rational, goal directed image' (Gowler and Legge 1983: 198) that constrains while it legitimates. The idiom, that is, serves to absorb uncertainty through a grammar and vocabulary – a linguistic structure – that keeps to well-worn pathways which are clichéd, stereotyped, normal. Through its serious, rationalistic tone, conventional policy discourse projects an implicit image of itself as necessary and normal, something all right-thinking people – i.e. all but the weak minded and emotional – will take for granted.

In this rather solemn and tedious context, a joke might be helpful in revealing this discourse in all the ridiculousness of its irrational rationality. Let us consider for a moment, then, a fanciful device known as the 'systematic buzz phrase projector'.[9] This device employs a lexicon of 30 words, arrayed in three columns of 10 words each:

Column 1	*Column 2*	*Column 3*
0. integrated	0. management	0. options
1. total	1. organizational	1. flexibility
2. systematized	2. monitored	2. capability
3. parallel	3. reciprocal	3. mobility
4. functional	4. digital	4. programming
5. responsive	5. logistical	5. concept
6. optional	6. transitional	6. time phase
7. synchronized	7. incremental	7. projection
8. compatible	8. third-generation	8. hardware
9. balanced	9. policy	9. contingency

The projector serves as a handy tool for generating phrases appropriate for official and professional communication. To generate a needed buzz phrase, one simply picks any three-digit number and lists the three corresponding words from the lexicon. This can be done in a completely random way, but since our particular interest here involves policy, let us keep the middle digit constant at 9 and consider a few possibilities:

090: integrated policy options
493: functional policy mobility
597: responsive policy projection
792: synchronized policy capability
994: balanced policy programming

[9] The buzz phrase projector was reportedly devised by a retired official of the US Public Health Service, Philip Broughton (see Gloin 1989: M2).

Phrases like these implicitly testify to the rationality of the conventional policy world. However, this rational image can be sustained only so long as the language of this world is taken seriously and viewed as necessary and normal. When a joke reveals the arbitrary, ridiculous character of this language, the prevailing rationality is exposed as something irrational and is suddenly made into a figure of fun.

As a member of the loyal opposition, March himself seems to have recognized something irrational and ridiculous about the uncertainty absorption of rationalistic discourse. He has even promoted his own kind of loyal opposition. Administrative rationalism is so constraining, he argues, that rationality itself depends on the creative potential of a 'technology of foolishness' able to entertain divergent perspectives and ideas. For March, however, there should be care not to loosen constraints too much; he calls for a responsible foolishness, one that is 'serious' and 'appropriate' (March 1989a: 181, 1989b; cf. Torgerson 1993, 1996: 287–288).

What looms large here is the figure of the fool who, as in Shakespeare's *King Lear*, pokes fun at the powerful (cf. Kolakowski 1969; Torgerson 1992). In doing so, however, the fool obliquely bears witness to unwelcome insights that test the limits of what may properly and safely be said. In the contemporary administrative sphere, uncommon insight becomes the aim of exercises in creative problem solving, as with the 'provocative rearrangement' (de Bono 1977: 129) in the 'reversal method' where 'one takes things as they are and then turns them round, inside out, upside down, back to front'. Sometimes such reversal may appear 'utterly ridiculous', but this is inconsequential because 'it is just as useful to practice being ridiculous as to practice reversal' (pp. 125–126). Here we have an example of a technology of foolishness. But what if the results of the exercise are not only ridiculous but also come to pose a threat to the legitimacy of established power?

The loyal fool remains a member of the king's court, ultimately bound by its propriety. The figure of the fool, though, is but a shrunken residue from the carnivalesque tradition that pervaded medieval Europe and, in the account of Mikhail Bakhtin, created a world outside the dour domains of officialdom, a world with another language and another logic (Bakhtin 1968: 11): 'All the symbols of the carnival idiom are filled . . . with a sense of the gay relativity of prevailing truths and authorities. We find here a characteristic logic, the peculiar logic of the "inside out" (*à l'envers*), of the "turnabout", of continual shifting from top to bottom, from front to rear, of numerous parodies and travesties, humiliations, profanations, comic crownings and uncrownings.'

The proposal for a technology of foolishness clearly hearkens back not only to the figure of court fool, but also to the language and logic of the carnivalesque. When employed in the administrative sphere, carnivalesque language and logic generate unconventional perspectives that promise to enhance creative problem solving in the face of complexity. There is, however, also the problem that the carnivalesque idiom might provoke unwelcome insights that could expose established power as irrational rationality, thus placing on display an emperor without clothes. The loyal opposition, particularly in the case of March, resists going this far. Dissident professionalism, however, is willing to take this step as a necessary aspect of action and inquiry that both promotes democracy and attempts to cope with complexity.

The best bet for coping with complexity, according to Dryzek, is a communicative rationality that challenges the irrational rationality of conventional policy discourse and the administrative sphere (Dryzek 1987a, 1987c; cf. Torgerson 1999b: 137–138). To this end, diverse interests and perspectives need to be voiced on problematic situations in the context of discursive designs. Proposals advanced by figures of the loyal opposition – such as Lasswell, Lindblom, Wildavsky and March – often approximate this idea. These figures recognize limits to rationalism in the administrative sphere, and their proposals would clearly bring an element of reflexivity to policy discourse. At times, they even show an inclination to connect policy discourse with public discourse. The loyal opposition, however, typically avoids what dissident policy professionalism tends to endorse: challenges to established power.

Public discourse and policy discourse: the case of the Clayoquot Sound scientific panel

Public discourse and policy discourse often intersect, as we have seen, in the context of discursive designs. There is thus a need for research into actual experiences with discursive designs in the policy process, neither to praise them as open communicative forums nor to denounce them as inevitable tools of cooptation, but to examine the ambivalent potential they exhibit as they interact with contexts of power. One relevant case involves events in Canada surrounding the Clayoquot Sound controversy, particularly the move of the provincial government in British Columbia to establish a scientific panel in order to help resolve disputes over forestry policy.[10]

In the course of the 1990s, logging practices in British Columbia became a matter of public discourse that involved significant international controversy. The region of Clayoquot Sound on Vancouver Island was a particular focus of concern and became the site of many efforts to protect its significant areas of

---

[10] On the case of Clayoquot Sound, see Abrams 2000; Burney 1996; Friends of Clayoquot Sound, 1998; Hatch 1994; Nuu-Chah-Nulth Tribal Council 1990; Scientific Panel 1995a, 1995b, 1995c, 1995d; Smith 1997. Also see Magnusson and Shaw 2002. The account here relies, in addition, on a series of interviews with key informants conducted in Victoria and Tofino, British Columbia, in April 2000.

temperate rainforest from intensive logging, particularly from clear cutting. In the course of these efforts, public and policy discourse – as in the case with Berger – entered into a new, reciprocal relationship.

There were various official and unofficial discursive designs, committees and panels established to discuss ways to change forestry practices. Yet there was also a turn toward civil disobedience: blockades of logging roads, mass protests and mass arrests. This civil disobedience did not put an end to discourse, however, but can itself be counted as a discursive move that threw into question the legitimacy of established frameworks and practices of discourse, an exclamation point of dissent against an uneven field of discourse (Burney 1996). In fact, civil disobedience played its part in a congruence of events giving rise to remarkable developments in policy discourse.

After much public opposition to the clear cutting of ancient forests and many failed efforts to find consensus through negotiation, the provincial government attempted to impose a policy decision by fiat. It was this particular gambit that provoked dramatic public protests by environmentalists, leading to the largest mass arrest in Canadian history, as well as determined opposition from the First Nations of the area, collectively known as the Nuu-Chah-Nulth. In retreating from its decision, the provincial government took the route of creating a 'scientific panel' of experts to determine world-class forestry guidelines for Clayoquot Sound. This move initially was greeted by considerable scepticism by many who viewed the formation of the scientific panel as a typical technocratic effort to quell dissent while maintaining established patterns of power.

Things, however, did not turn out as expected. No one now claims that the scientific panel was a technocratic cover-up. The criticism instead is that the recommendations of the panel, although accepted by the provincial government, have not been fully implemented. Indeed, the focus of conflict has now shifted to the question of implementation. Even here, what we witness is not a situation in which laudable recommendations have dropped into an institutional vacuum, never to be heard of again. For the advent of the scientific panel came in the context of wider institutional changes in Clayoquot Sound that have placed the interests and perspectives of First Nations, local communities and environmentalists in a new position (Abrams 2000). Their position has been dramatically strengthened in relation to the collaborative conjunction of industry and government that earlier exercised almost exclusive control over forestry policy in British Columbia (Wilson 1998). The big question in current public and policy discourse is why the model of institutional and policy change in Clayoquot Sound should not be applied throughout the province's forestry sector. Determined to see no repetition of the loss of control they experienced in Clayoquot Sound, officials are indeed at pains to stress the uniqueness of the situation there.

How did the institutional and policy changes in Clayoquot Sound come about? The short answer is that the opposition to established logging practices demonstrated an obstructive potential that could not be ignored (cf. Offe 1972). In the early 1990s, the potential for obstruction took the form of civil disobedience – particularly roadblocks on logging roads – culminating in 1993 with mass arrests. For most of this period there was a working alliance between environmental groups and the First Nations of the area, the Nuu-Chah-Nulth. Their paths later divided, however, after a Nuu-Chah-Nulth success in court that demonstrated the obstructive potential of land claims. The First Nations subsequently pressed ahead with court actions while negotiating successfully with the provincial government for a role in forestry management. By the time the scientific panel was formed, it proved politically impossible to ignore aboriginal and environmental perspectives. The scientific panel consisted not only of scientists and conventional experts, but also of several representatives of the First Nations, who exerted a significant impact on the panel. A Nuu-Chah-Nulth chief, in fact, became co-chair of the panel. As it developed, the scientific panel thus incorporated diverse perspectives, including that of traditional ecological knowledge.

In the policy world of advanced industrial society the very phrase 'scientific panel' clearly makes a scientistic appeal: let us abandon political conflict, the message goes, so as to base policy decisions on hard, authoritative knowledge that no rational person can dispute. Of course, there were many scientists and scientifically trained experts on the panel. The epistemological criteria of the scientific panel, however, could not be restricted to scientism. Representatives of the First Nations insisted that they had their own experts on the forests in Clayoquot Sound: chiefs and elders whose traditional ecological knowledge merited recognition and respect.

Such a claim for the relevance and validity of traditional ecological knowledge is clearly at odds with scientism and the conventional outlook of many scientists and policy experts. The idea was nonetheless accepted, and a panel process emerged in which there was substantial mutual learning between perspectives that might well have been thought diametrically opposed and thoroughly incompatible. The panel concluded that an 'integration of scientific and traditional knowledge' was 'essential' for the development of forestry standards able to 'ensure sustainable ecosystem management' (Scientific Panel 1995a: 17). In developing a holistic approach to forestry policy, moreover, the panel was significantly influenced by a key concept of the Nuu-Chah-Nulth: *hishuk ish ts'awalk* ('everything is one'). The overall orientation of the panel, indeed, produced a key conceptual innovation in reframing the forestry problem in Clayoquot Sound. Previous policy proceeded from the question of what should be cut down, but the panel's approach turned this question around to instead ask what should *not* be cut down. The previous framing of the problem focused attention on criteria of economic efficiency, but the newly posed question gave prominence to concerns about ecological integrity.

The success of the panel members in bridging often divergent orientations was a result of serious work to develop common understandings, particularly including efforts by First Nations representatives to educate other members of the panel about their outlook. It is notable, however, that the other members turned out to be receptive. This was not simply a matter of good luck, but reflected the context of power at the time. Government officials responsible for setting up the panel were concerned that it be publicly accepted as legitimate. What was not needed was criticism either by the First Nations or by environmentalists. Thus, although environmentalists had no official representation on the panel, there were informal consultations between government officials and environmentalists about potential panel members. This process appears to have been important in adding to the panel certain scientists who were determined that their expertise not be coopted and whose participation on the panel enhanced the capacity of panel members for respectful communication and understanding.

In Clayoquot Sound, we witness the emergence of a discursive design in the policy process that, influenced by patterns of public discourse, has exerted a clear impact on forestry policy. The policy direction set by the scientific panel has also been carried on by a larger, emerging set of institutions. Finally, the entire experience in Clayoquot Sound now serves as a point of contention in public and policy discourse. Is the model necessarily unique to Clayoquot Sound or does it set a pattern for forestry policy throughout the province? That is to say, this discursive design has been significant in terms of both functional and constitutive politics.

As we have noted, this was also the case with the Berger Inquiry. Not only was there an impact on a particular policy decision, but there was also an impetus to a significant reshaping of political relationships in Canada's north. Here public involvement in policy discourse animated a larger public discourse and helped to institutionalize a continuing space for it (see Torgerson 1996: 288–289).

Like the case of the Berger Inquiry, the case of the Clayoquot Sound scientific panel thus offers a key lesson about reflexive policy discourse. Its democratic potential cannot be assessed simply by reference to particular successes or failures in the domain of functional politics. Attention must turn, rather, to a larger political and historical context of forces that, though perhaps largely continuous over time, are also subject to change. This is the domain of constitutive politics where diverse powers contend to promote or inhibit democratization. The potential of reflexive policy discourse – and its relationship to public discourse – resides in the role it comes to play in that ambivalent drama.

Reversing the order of policy discourse

The very idea of discourse presupposes order, a cultural space bounded and stable enough to make both agreements and disagreements possible.[11] Persistent regularities and limits no doubt typically order and bound discursive practices, establishing a scope and limit to possible actions that eludes the awareness of the actors themselves and sets the point of departure for any change. To the extent that a particular order of discourse depends on a surreptitious mode of operation, change is introduced whenever the order is itself brought to attention. The advent of reflexivity thus signals an incipient change in policy discourse. The change points beyond politics at the level of normal system functioning toward a constitutive politics that brings into question the established dynamics of power.

Parties to a discursive contest must have significant commonalities as well as differences if they are even to achieve any meaningful disagreement. Contention, nonetheless, can also throw into question the order of discourse itself, to the extent that it can be made a focus of attention: 'boundaries are border wars waiting to happen', Stone (1997: 379) has aptly argued: 'At every boundary, there is a dilemma of classifications: who or what belongs on each side? In policy politics, these dilemmas evoke intense passions because the classifications confer advantages and disadvantages, rewards and penalties, permissions and restrictions, or power and powerlessness.'

Policy discourse has historically developed with a form shaped by particular alignments of power, but this form does not exclude the possibility of transformation. To assume otherwise would simply be to reinforce prevailing

---

[11] Two starkly contrasting images of discourse are relevant here, one of utopia and one of prison: the Habermasian utopia of communicative rationality that privileges argument, in contrast to the prison image that arises from formalism and structuralism and persists in poststructuralism. Neither image deserves to be enshrined, but each possesses methodological significance in supplying a needed perspective. The notion of a communicative utopia of argument may appear naive against the image of the discursive prison. In the latter, discourse is pictured as a set of constraints that not only limits the possibility of what can be said – of how language can be used – but that also constructs the very identities of the participants. Those who imagine themselves as possessing and freely using language are themselves portrayed as artefacts of language (see Eagleton 1983; Hawkes 1977; Jameson 1972; Rorty 1983. See also Dreyfus and Rabinow 1983; Fraser 1989: ch. 1; Hajer 1995: ch. 2; Laclau and Mouffe 1985; Seidel 1985). At the same time, any attempt to argue directly against the principle of a communicative utopia finds itself to be at odds (qua argument) with its own unavoidable presuppositions. (See Habermas 1970a, 1970b, 1979, 1990; see also Benhabib 1990; McCarthy 1978: ch. 4.2; Young 1990.) In promoting a reversal of policy discourse, dissident policy professionalism cannot dispense with the utopian image of communicative rationality. However, even this ideal – as it enshrines a pure discourse – cannot stand without question; for it overstates the capabilities of the straightforward statement to the detriment of more diverse and supple discursive practices. Concern with the proper conduct of argument does imply a critique of mobilized bias, but a fixation on reasoned argumentation and its rules risks deflecting attention from the tilt unequal powers can give to an apparently level playing field (cf. Dunn 1993; MacRae 1993).

alignments of power by conjuring up an unalterable order with fixed regularities and boundaries, lending policy discourse a clear and unequivocal identity just at the moment its order has become a matter of questioning and contention in the politics of expertise.

The order of policy discourse comes more clearly into view when its discursive character is recognized through a reflexive move. What emerges at this point is the potential for change. Making policy discourse a focus of attention is already to introduce a change by making explicit its form as discourse. What further becomes evident is that the form – in denying its own status as discourse – confronts exigencies of discursive practice with which it is ill suited to cope.

The established order of policy discourse – its boundaries and identity – is not the only possible form. Policy discourse has been shaped, and continues to be shaped, in an historical context of political contention and social conflict, involving different interests, diverse perspectives, unequal powers. A democratic prospect lies in the potential of changing this form, of challenging and expanding the prevailing boundaries of policy discourse.

In order to understand the democratic prospect in policy discourse, we need to consider more precisely how the prevailing order of policy discourse is constituted and circumscribed. To this end, we can identify four dimensions of discursive practice and consider how each of these changes as we shift from technocratic to reflexive orientations: (i) codification, (ii) institutionalization, (iii) participation, (iv) conceptualization.

(i) *Codification.* Technocratic policy discourse seeks to formulate a code through which to control an objective world. In such codification, the agent would in principle be removed from discursive practices; the mind would simply assert its authority through abstract formulas, controlling a world in which it did not participate. The language would be transparent, devoid of rhetorical gestures; it would be the neutral idiom Hobbes celebrated (though did not himself employ). In reflexive policy discourse, however, agents enter into discussion with one another, shaping their identities and constituting a shared discursive world. Faced with the biases characteristic of what often passes for policy reason, reflexive policy discourse finds it has an immediate task in encouraging argumentative practices. Encouraging argument is not only constructive, though, but also critical. The task of making argument possible cannot be accomplished through argument alone, simply through a mutual testing of claims; for what is absent is the level playing field that this requires. Levelling the ground requires gestures able to reveal how even an apparently neutral language ('antiseptic', as Tribe puts it)[12] implicitly involves surreptitious relations of power.

---

[12] See above, p. 121.

Reflexive policy discourse points beyond the oligarchic monologue of officialdom to the prospect of democratic policy discourse. This discourse risks becoming less of a dialogue than another monologue, however, to the extent that it is restricted to the genre of argument and its privileging of straightforward meaning. It is thus that Bakhtin has stressed the challenge that the polyphonic idiom of the carnivalesque poses to officialdom (Bakhtin 1968: 5–6). There is something 'impermissibly naïve' about the unequivocal use of a word; genuine rationality, he suggests, cannot endure rigidity (Bakhtin 1981: 278; 1968: 121–123). Conflicting arguments do not by themselves provide the diversity of voices needed to expose the naive uniformity of a discussion. Iris Marion Young similarly points to the limitations of rational argument and highlights the importance of other genres such as 'chants, music, song, dancing' (Young 1987: 75; cf. Dryzek 1996a). Notably, however, she does not make her case by chanting, singing, or dancing, but by engaging in argument – making explicit claims and giving explicit reasons. The point this suggests is that there may be some justified privilege to argumentation, though not the unquestionable status of a trump card.

(ii) *Institutionalization.* A code is itself, of course, already both an institution and part of a larger institutional context. The idiom of technocratic policy discourse fits with a larger range of oligarchic institutions – economic, social, governmental. As it employs a different idiom, however, reflexive policy discourse anticipates a space of communication that involves a different set of institutions. An unavoidable point of departure is the existing ensemble of institutions that constitutes the administrative sphere of advanced industrial society. This is the central focus and home domain of technocratic discourse. Concerned that the potential of discursive designs is sharply attenuated in this domain, Dryzek directs the focus of democratic forces towards civil society. Spheres of public discourse in this realm can provide an institutional context, he claims, that is vital to democratization. Locating discursive designs strictly in civil society, however, would divide policy discourse from public discourse just at the moment when reflexivity in policy discourse allows us to imagine and begin promoting stronger connections. The development of such connections would certainly come with no guarantee. Their potential is ambivalent – and would depend on a larger context of changing power relations – but they at least signal the possibility of changes in the administrative sphere that would seem necessary for any robust realization of discursive democracy.

(iii) *Participation.* Who participates in policy discourse? The message ultimately implicit in technocratic policy discourse is paradoxical: no one. Policy is a matter of mind rather than discussion; to possess objective knowledge means that there is no need for debate. The authority of the analytic monologue ultimately stems from the province of the self-sufficient, rational mind. The message of policy discourse here is that communication in a mundane world remains something peripheral, non-essential. To the extent that policy experts actually do find themselves communicating, the circle of discussion is to be tightly drawn around the experts themselves, except to the extent perhaps that they speak to clients through simplified summaries of their findings. Reflexive policy discourse, in contrast, turns things around to make problems of communication central. Who speaks, who hears, who listens? What is the principle of inclusion and exclusion? With such questions, the idea of a charmed circle of rationality is thrown into question. A politics of expertise comes to the fore, and there is a blurring of the line that separates the policy discourse of experts from the public discourse of citizens. In this context, the rationale for participatory expertise is not simply one of levelling the playing field of discussion on policy matters, but also of countering the kind of bias that typically emerges from the interests and perspectives of expert circles (see Lovins 1977; Majone 1989: 5–6; Otway 1992).

(iv) *Conceptualization.* By drawing attention to itself, reflexive policy discourse already contains a conceptual innovation that breaks with technocratic fixations. Shifting away from the old paradigm of mind, policy discourse enters the fallible, all-too-human world of communication (cf. Benhabib 1986). With expert bias challenged, there is an unsettling of the technocratic orientation at the levels of agenda setting, problem definition, and epistemology. The ideal of communicative rationality, with its promise of a level playing field for discussion, opens the door to diverse interests and perspectives capable of creative reversals – to the employment of a technology of foolishness that may or may not be responsible in the sense of being kind to established power. It is precisely here, however, that a problem arises in the privilege that communicative rationality would give to the genre of argumentation. To allow for conflicting arguments is not the same as to allow for the fullness of voices diverging from the explicit language of reason. Expressing things that cannot be directly stated in the idiom of explicit argument may, indeed, prove a crucial moment in reshaping the conceptual framework that guides policy deliberations.

Democratic policy discourse: a question of power

Initiatives tending to reverse the order of policy discourse are sure to meet with resistance from established power. How to understand this resistance and how to deal with it, though, are far from certain. It often appears that established policy regimes possess, as if by some kind of magic, a panoply of defence mechanisms that systematically block significant change along these lines. In the case of any policy dispute, however, we can expect a diverse range of specific interests to weigh against such change – interests involving particular economic concerns, matters of convention and institutional privilege, personal rivalries, social status, epistemological criteria and ideological fixations, to name just some. In different cases, conflicting interests are likely to line up differently, even to alter their alignments over time. Thus, although a systems metaphor can provide insights into the dynamics of power (e.g., Bachrach and Baratz 1970; Offe 1972), it is by no means clear that the established order of policy discourse is maintained by the unalterable imperatives of a system. In concrete cases, we encounter a multiplicity of interests, perspectives and interactions that, even though they may often confirm prevailing power alignments, also hold out the possibility of unforeseen convergences and fortuitous surprises.

Certainly, in the cases of the Berger Inquiry and the Clayoquot Sound scientific panel, we encounter such surprises. Cases of this kind might be dismissed out of hand as mere anomalies in an otherwise fixed system. However, such a dismissal would enshrine a theoretical position at the expense of denying practical vicissitudes and the results of inquiry. As we have seen, it is in looking to particular cases that we are able to uncover an ambivalent potential in the reflexive moment of policy discourse. Reflexivity in policy discourse is of course not the same as the democratization of policy discourse, but a moment that opens up the potential for democratic policy discourse. Generally speaking, even with a reflexive turn, that potential remains more likely to be frustrated than realized.

Once definite steps toward democratization are taken, indeed, frustration still remains quite likely. What are now needed in terms of the agenda of inquiry are, however, not *ex cathedra* pronouncements about things that are inevitable, but concrete case studies of discursive designs in the policy process that attempt to determine *how* a democratic potential is at times largely achieved and *how* this potential tends much more usually to be frustrated. What is needed, beyond that, is contextual sensitivity in inquiry that locates particular experiences with policy discourse in relation to other political developments, especially in an historical context embracing a clearly oligarchical past and a potentially democratic future. It is only by virtue of such contextual orientation that inquiry can avoid the common preoccupation with functional issues that threatens to obscure the larger drama of constitutive politics and the historical potential to reconfigure the relationship between public discourse and policy discourse. In terms of democratic practice, though, no general rule of procedure is available, except perhaps avoiding too much reliance on theoretical presuppositions that neglect the promises, risks and challenges contained in the ambivalences of concrete situations.

Technocracy is not what it used to be. Technocratic style and imagery are often still able to suggest a claim of some crediblity, bolstering the notion that policy professionalism and the order it defends are necessarily rational and right. The claim, however, does not have the strength it once did, some half a century ago, when it could largely go unquestioned. That was before the rise of new social movements and the emergence of a dissident policy professionalism, a time when the politics of expertise seldom entered the focus of public discourse to reveal disputes among experts. Now the claim is becoming rather threadbare as conventional reason is thrown into question by previously marginalized interests and perspectives.

Technocratic discourse is now liable to be exposed not as the voice of reason, but as a device serving irrational and illegitimate power. Public participation in policy discourse is now more difficult to oppose. No longer can liberal democratic notions easily resist demands for democratic participation in policy discourse. Just as significantly, old spectres of popular irrationality and social chaos lose much of their credibility when technocracy can be portrayed as contributing to the dysfunctions of industrialism. Suggesting an irrationality in the administrative sphere and initiating a reflexive moment, indeed, even the loyal opposition indicates a democratic potential in policy discourse that may prove difficult to contain.

The democratic potential is to change the terms, conditions and meaning of policy discourse, bringing it into a closer relationship with public discourse. This potential can effectively promote democratization, however, only by breaking free of prevailing constraints, and that depends on strong democratic tendencies emerging in a larger context. The idea of a network society helps to bring such a contextual possibility into focus by placing the accent on connection rather than separation. Indeed, the idea suggests emerging patterns of social interaction that challenge conventional boundaries. With such a challenge, the privilege of a neatly bounded domain of policy discourse is put at risk.

If governance in a network society is cast in terms that accentuate policy over politics, democratic potentials are obscured while technocratic patterns are reinforced. Democracy cannot dispense with democratic politics, and the democratization of a network society requires a constitutive politics. In such a constitutive politics, emerging patterns of interaction would involve not only functional cooperation, coordination and problem solving, but also democratic action that confronted and challenged oligarchical relationships, defining them as *the* central problem in public discourse and demanding a further democratization of policy discourse.

Democratic policy discourse adds new dimensions to the policy process – e.g. questions of identity, culture, aesthetics, history – that serve to connect *policy* with *politics*. The significance of reason and argument are redefined, as is the very notion of what are to count as policy problems and solutions. Along with the promotion of a level playing field for argument, we at times encounter new genres of communication – poetry, dance, song, the laughter of the carnivalesque – that expose the typical biases of conventional policy discourse. It is crucial, however, that these discursive innovations be understood not narrowly, but in their full political significance, as involving a realignment of power among policy actors, the inauguration of new forms of democratic practice and the general promise of enhancing democracy through policy discourse.

5

Understanding policy practices: action, dialectic and deliberation in policy analysis

Hendrik Wagenaar and S. D. Noam Cook

Introduction: the modernist legacy in policy analysis

From its inception in August Comte's positive social philosophy, policy analysis has been a vanguard of the modernist project, the pervasive cultural programme characteristic of the western world, to take rational, scientific control over the social and physical environment and shape it according to a preconceived ideal.[1] One of the cornerstones of the modernist programme in public policy and social reform, specifically, is the opposition between theory and action. From Charles Merriam to Harold Lasswell's policy sciences, via the rational choice theorists to the progenitors of the public choice doctrine, the aim of policy analysis has been to bring the unstable, ideology-driven and conflict-ridden world of politics under the rule of rational, scientifically derived knowledge. To see this traditional approach to policy analysis – and the critique that we develop in this chapter – in the intellectual currents of our age, it is important to be aware

The authors would like to thank Thomas Schwandt for his perceptive comments, in a summer long e-mail exchange, about practice in the context of modernism, and Maarten Hajer for his careful reading of an earlier version of this chapter.

[1] Modernity is, of course, a notoriously slippery concept, but we understand it here as an all-encompassing economic-political-scientific-cultural movement that has its roots in the scientific enlightenment, the political revolutionary upheavals of the late eighteenth century, and the industrial revolution of the early nineteenth century. Conceptually, the diverse manifestations of modernity are united by a pervasive individualism and a quest for mastery of one's natural and social environment (Wagner 2001).

   Modernity in this sense is above all a reflexive moment, a philosophical assumption for the social sciences to exist at all. When it is reified into an alleged empirical characteristic of social life, modernity descends into modernism (*ibid.*). As Berman (1988), one of the foremost theorists of modernity states it: '[T]he whole point of modernism is to clear the decks of all these entanglements [historical, social] so that the self and the world can be created anew.' Policy analysis is but one manifestation of modernity in this sense.

that the theory/action dichotomy is not just a belief or a doctrine that one can adopt or abandon at will. Instead it is an element of a broad cultural institution; a self-evident, habitual and tenacious understanding of the way we ought to relate to the world around us, that informs our opinions, values and self-image.

This stance, as a seemingly self-evident positioning of ourselves as human actors towards the world (and because of its many unexpected intellectual ramifications, there is no avoiding of some philosophical context here), is almost wholly and unrecognizedly couched in epistemological terms. Mastering an aspect of the world is in the modernist tradition seen to be synonymous with *knowing* it (Taylor 1995a).[2] One of the implications of this primacy of the epistemological is that that we habitually partition the world in self-evident, taken-for-granted dichotomies: autonomous actors and an independent reality; sovereign individuals and the communities of which they choose to be a part; facts as the correct representation of an independent reality and values as emotionally driven, information-empty preferences for one thing or another. Thus, in the modernist framework, the practical and the epistemological go hand in hand. Knowledge is reduced to *technē*, the making of a product or state of affairs that can be precisely specified by the maker in advance of making it (Dunne 1993). The aim of policy analysis as such a technical enterprise is to eliminate the ambiguity, uncertainty and unpredictability of the everyday world, by bringing it under the command of general, systematic, means–end, foundational knowledge (Dunne 1993; Schwandt 2000a; Taylor 1995b). It is believed that the careful application of nomological knowledge to ever more sectors of society will result in the progressive improvement of social conditions and the gradual elimination of disease, want and social unrest. In this modernist scheme, action is supposed to follow logically and automatically from knowledge; any other action is taken to be at best intuitive and at worst blind. More significantly, the notion of action as an appendix to knowledge has resulted in an almost total neglect of its central role in the way in which humans understand and value their world.[3]

This chapter argues for a new recognition of the place of action in politics and policy analysis. By this we mean not simply that policy analysis should be expanded to take action into account, but that the primacy of the epistemological in policy analysis should be overcome. This amounts to no less than a different stance towards the world of policymaking; a stance that is exemplified

---

[2] Taylor sees the emphasis on theory in practical affairs as a 'pervasive feature of modern intellectual culture', and calls it 'the primacy of the epistemological: the tendency to think out the question of what something *is* in terms of how it is *known*' (Taylor 1995a: 34, emphases in original).

[3] There have always been important counter voices to this dominant paradigm. Most notably Charles Lindblom and his student Aaron Wildavsky, who not only recognized the limits of scientific knowledge in public decision-making, but also pointed to an alternative, more interactive and democratic way of collective action (Lindblom and Cohen 1979; Wildavsky 1979). Yet these have hardly affected the self-image of policy analysis as a profession and branch of applied social science.

by the concept of *practice*. We will argue that practice, in which the concept of action is embedded, is not just the executive arm of rational knowledge, but instead is a way of engaging with the world in its own right; a way of moving about that is much more attuned to the pluralistic, open-ended, moral-political character of the everyday world. Practice, we argue, is an important and distinct dimension of politics, with its own logic (pragmatic, purposeful), its own standards of knowing (interpretative, holistic, more know-how than know-that), its own orientation towards the world (interactive, moral, emotional), and its own image of society (as a constellation of interdependent communities). Practice is part and parcel of a distinct form of reason – *phronesis* or practical reason – that cannot be wholly or effectively displaced by scientific, technical reason. We will argue that the taken-for-granted hierarchy of knowing and acting is fallacious, and explore the implications of this contention for our understanding of public policy and policy analysis.

The emergence of practice in contemporary policy theory

It is for these reasons that we believe that one of the most important developments in contemporary policy theory has been the budding recognition that practice plays a key role in the formation and discourse of public policy. One of the earliest statements of the role of practice and action in public policy is to be found in Martin Rein's theory of policy frames. Formulated as an explanation for the 'puzzling persistence of stubborn, intractable policy controversies' that proved to be immune to scientific evidence, Rein describes policymaking as being caught in 'frames'. In a formulation that, as we will see later, comes remarkably close to the concept of practice we wish to develop here, Rein describes frames as 'structures of thought, of evidence, of action, and hence of interests and of values' (Rein 1983b: 96). In his further exploration of the concept he takes pains to explicate the particular role of action in frames. Frames are not exhaustively defined by their cognitive component; they are more than theoretical perspectives. In fact, Rein goes on to argue, we only know that we are dealing with a frame once we know what actions a policy actor favours. As he states: 'It is not so much that a frame provides an individual with a prescription for action but rather that once we have a prescription for action, we can discover the implicit frame organizing the action and integrating theory, activities, interests, purposes, facts, and values' (p. 99). In his later writings with Donald Schön he takes the action component of framing even further. Instead of just being 'preferences', however well defined or understood by the actor, action, in truly pragmatic fashion, becomes a mode of understanding and grappling with a world of difficult and contentious policy situations. An actor, Rein and Schön state, 'converses with materials', thereby 'taking account of the constraints and possibilities inherent in the situation', and 'observes the effects of her moves as she reformulates both her problem and her solutions' (Schön and Rein 1994: 169).

More recently, Hajer, in his well-known analysis of environmental policy, defines discourse as an 'ensemble' of ideas and concepts that are 'produced, reproduced, and transformed in a particular set of practices' (Hajer 1995: 44). 'Discourse then', as he argues there, 'is seen as internally related to the social practices in which it is produced.' Accordingly, Hajer discusses 'tree-health surveys', 'excursions' and 'awareness campaigns' as examples of practices that were instrumental in the 'creation of an image of (environmental) damage' (pp. 202–214). Wagenaar, in a study of public administrators, locates practice in everyday work. Through a reconstruction of the view from the shop floor he shows that the world that policymakers and administrators face is concrete, open-ended, action-oriented, conflict-ridden, unpredictable and urgent. From this perspective these practitioners tell stories to negotiate the contingencies and dilemmas of the situations that confront them in their everyday working lives. For these practitioners narrative functions as a form of practical judgment (Wagenaar 1997). Similarly, Forester discusses planning practice as the lived experience of concrete planners in their city offices. Collective storytelling functions as a kind of practical deliberation for them (Forester 1993b). Finally, Fischer and Forester, in their landmark *Argumentative Turn*, take pains to depict policy arguments not as mere linguistics, 'sales talk' as they call it, but as practical accomplishments themselves, forged in the day-to-day struggle of policymakers, planners and administrators with concrete, ambiguous, tenacious, practical problems (Fischer and Forester 1993; see also editors' Introduction, this volume).

Thus, while more and more authors have become sensitive to the role of practice in planning and politics, such examples also indicate that there is little agreement about the nature of a practice and its role in policymaking and policy discourse. So far, the concept of practice means different things to different people. What is a practice, for example? Going by his examples, Hajer sees practices as distinct techniques or organizational routines.[4] Rein in his early writings talks of 'action-preferences', by which he means general strategies for solving public problems, such as a preference for income transfers versus a preference for active labour market policies as respective solutions to the problem of poverty. In their later work, however, Rein and Schön embed their understanding of policy practices in a fully developed pragmatist theory of practical design. Forester, finally, seems to think of practice in terms of practical judgment and deliberative rationality.

Another unresolved issue concerns the relation between policy practice and policy discourse. While the early Rein thinks of practices as flowing more or less unproblematically from the narrative representation of a policy problem, Hajer thinks of practices as *determining* problem setting, and, alluding to Foucault's

---

[4] Although in more recent work his concept of practice has moved more towards the practical ecology that we will discuss in this chapter.

concept of '*disciplines*', uses the equivocal phrase 'internal relation' to describe the relation of discourse to practice. Wagenaar, meanwhile, more or less tends to equate practice with narrative (once actors succeed in formulating a good story about an intractable, contentious policy issue, for example, they have, for all practical purposes, reached closure about the issue).

Also, none of the authors is very explicit about the role of policy practices in policy analysis. For example, how do we analyse practices to understand the formation and implementation of public policy? What is the added value of the analysis of practices for policy analysis over and above explanations couched in institutional terms? Is practice analysis just another tool in the analyst's toolbox, or does it represent something more fundamental, such as a changed perspective on the role of the analyst? What is the relationship in this respect between the practice perspective and the new modernity in politics and policy?

What explains the lack of agreement among these authors about the nature of practice? We believe they are, if nothing else, struggling with the pervasiveness of the modernist stance toward knowledge, action and the world of public policy. Each of these authors pulls at a different thread (organizational routine, narrative, practical judgment, language) in an attempt to unravel the tightly woven modernist fabric of their field. In this chapter we discuss such questions as those above in a more systematic way. The argument in this chapter rests on two closely related claims: (1) Practice is a distinct dimension of public policy. By distinct we mean that it is elementary, that it is a building block of any concerted human activity, both individual and collective, and that it cannot be reduced to anything else. To avoid any misunderstanding as early as possible, we do not treat practice as mere doing (although action is a central component of it, as we will see later), but 'a phenomenon *sui generis* that has its own unique moral and cognitive demands' (Schwandt, personal communication); (2) Practice, indeed, is the major way by which human beings negotiate the world. In fact, the concept of practice highlights the interactive, context-bound character of our activities and accomplishments in the world. Practice, accordingly, is part of the way we conduct our lives as members of a society (Schwandt 2000b: 217). To continue a point made before, it is this interactive, context-oriented nature of practice, the 'continuous interaction, the gradual achievement, the constant give-and-take' as Wenger puts it (Wenger 1998: 53), that lifts the concept of practice above mere doing, and elevates it to a central position in a democratic, pragmatic, problem-oriented policy analysis.

What is practice?

It is an understatement to say that the concept of practice is elusive. All too often it seems an archetypical example of what in discourse-analytic jargon is called an 'empty signifier', a suggestive term that functions as a projection screen for everyone's private meanings. Instead of a clearly defined term it is better to think of practice as a family of related meanings. Without being exhaustive, the following uses of the term can be encountered in the literature[5]:

- Practice as mere doing, as in the traditional Comtean distinction of a realm of doing versus a realm of thinking. The term 'realm' is apposite here, as Comte believed that a wall existed – and, it must be added, *should* exist – between the world of practical men and the world of theorists. Labour, Comte's term for the realm of action, is blind, lacking in imagination and prone to be swayed by 'disturbances' (Lenzer 1975: xli). The products of labour are therefore by definition fleeting or 'temporal'. Thought, or 'theory' in Comte's phrase, is analytical, universal and, in his conception of a positive philosophy, aimed at discovering the timeless laws of nature and society. It is difficult to underestimate the impact on policy analysis of this doctrinaire hierarchical ordering of thinking over doing. In particular it has defined to this very day the relationship between the analyst and his or her object: policies and citizens. By favouring thinking over doing it inserted into policy analysis a normative stance of the inquiring subject towards the object of inquiry, whereby the first must be detached and analytic, while the latter is seen as inert, pre-existing and manipulable. We will return to this later.
- Comte's distinction is, in a way, a vulgarized, heavily ideological version of a more universal theme that runs though the whole of western philosophy from Aristotle to Charles Taylor. Its original statement is Aristotle's distinction between two broad and distinct realms of human activity, two modes of reason and action that he indicates with the terms *technē* and *phronesis*.[6] *Technē*, or technical reason, can best be understood as a craft. According to Aristotle it involves making (*poiēsis*), while *phronesis* or practical wisdom is broader and proceeds by acting. The difference is particularly significant with respect to the rightness of the actor's actions, and, by implication, his relation to his endeavour. Rightness in the case of technical reason is more or less exhaustively defined in terms of the quality of the product it generates. The qualities of a good shoe, for example, can be specified in advance, and, after the shoe has been produced, assessed with precision. Technical rightness is thus contained within the produced object. It does not exceed it (Bostock 2000: 81). Rightness in the case of practical reason, on the other hand, is broader. It not only involves other people, but also the specific circumstances of the situation at hand. *Phronesis* occurs in a communal space, with others,

---

[5] For a much more extended discussion of the concept of practice in western philosophy, see Dunne, 1993.

[6] The distinction here mentioned is a distinction within the broad realm of practical reason. Comte has, in fact, little to say about practical reason, and, in Aristotelian terms, assimilates all social action to the realm of theoretical reason. Theoretical reason involves the ability to deduce conclusively from premises, and the ability to grasp the premises or first premises from which the deduction must start (Bostock 2000: 75).

to realize 'excellences' that are constitutive of that community (Dunne 1993: 10). Consequently, the standards of rightness, the ability to act in the right way, and the outcome of one's actions, are closely tied to one's character, to one's excellence as a person, much more so than the skills that make up *technē*. Several twentieth-century thinkers, such as Gadamer and Arendt, have elaborated upon Aristotle's distinction in their work. Arendt, for example, has applied this distinction specifically to the political (i.e. public life). On the one hand, she argues, there is labour: repetitious, blind (not guided by a *telos*), manual, reproducing the necessities of life. On the other there is work: purposeful, resourceful, rising above the imperatives of nature and aimed at mastery and the creation of things of lasting value. *Animal laborens* versus *Homo faber* (Arendt 1958: 82; Dunne 1993: 400).

- Practice as *habitus*. With the concept of *habitus* Bourdieu tries to transcend another modernist opposition in social theory, that between structuralism and individualism. According to Bourdieu human activity is neither constituted (as in structuralist or crude institutionalist theories of political action) nor constitutive (as in ethnomethodology), but both at the same time. To this end he asks us to be sensitive to the role of (spontaneous) action in the way we are in the world. In a wonderfully evocative example he explains what he means:

> You need only think of the of the impulsive decision made by the tennis player who runs up to the net, to understand that it has nothing in common with the learned construction that the coach, after analysis, draws up in order to explain it and deduce communicable lessons from it. The conditions of rational calculation are practically never given in practice: time is limited, information is restricted, etc. And yet, agents *do* do, much more often than if they were behaving randomly, 'the only thing to do'. This is because, following the intuitions of a 'logic of practice' which is the product of a lasting exposure to conditions similar to those in which they are placed, they anticipate the necessity immanent in the way of the world.
>
> (Bourdieu 1990: 11)

Thus, although action is purposeful and effective, it is not, in essence, rule-driven or the product of conscious reflection. Instead, human actors move about in a field of dispositions that function as generative schemes that, while durable, leave room for improvisation and contingency. *Habitus* is a 'structured space of possibilities defined by the intersection of material conditions and fields of operation' (Postone, LiPuma and Calhoun 1993: 4). Other theorists besides Bourdieu have emphasized the continuity of actor and in-stitution, for example Giddens in his structuration theory (Giddens 1984), or Polanyi in his concept of tacit knowledge (Polanyi 1958, 1966), but few have done this with such an articulated understanding of the role of action in the constitution of the social world. Thus, to sum up: *habitus* (and related con-cepts) emphasizes two important aspects of practice: (1) the primacy of (spontaneous) action as a social phenomenon *sui generis*, with its own logic, origins, and demands, purposeful, but not reducible to the following of rules, (2) the dialectic between actor and context, in which the social order is constantly reproduced in the course of acting in and upon it.

• Practices as a particular configuration of human activity. The classic definition is from MacIntyre, who states that:

> By a 'practice' I am going to mean any coherent and complex form of socially established cooperative human activity through which goods internal to that form of activity are realized in the course of trying to achieve those standards of excellence which are appropriate to, and partially definitive of, that form of activity, with the result that human powers to achieve excellence, and human conceptions of the ends and goods involved are systematically extended. Tic-tac-toe is not an example of a practice in this sense, nor is throwing a football with skill; but the game of football is, and so is chess. Bricklaying is not a practice; architecture is . . . Thus the range of practices is wide: arts, sciences, games, politics in the Aristotelian sense, the making and sustaining of families, all fall under the concept.
>
> (MacIntyre 1981: 187)

MacIntyre's definition has been criticized for being too restrictive and too internally homogeneous (Tamanaha 1997: 170), but for our purposes it is more important to emphasize the strengths of his definition. First, by seeing a practice as a socially established form of cooperative activity, it cannot be confused with an institution. Institutions may contain reified or codified elements of practices, they may support practices, but they are nevertheless distinct in that institutions are empty without the practices that sustain them. Also, practices in this sense are not the same as organizational routines or standard operating procedures (Allison and Zelikow 1999; Turner 1994). Although a practice may have standardized or routine elements, engaging in a practice involves a considerable amount of practical on-the-spot judgment (Cook 1982). Practices are only partly defined, and as MacIntyre makes clear, entering upon a practice means to define the practice.

• Practices as constitutive meanings. Practices in this sense are linguistic-performative configurations that constitute social realities. From Charles Taylor comes the example of the term 'bargaining'. To be meaningful the word 'bargaining' must be rooted in a set of activities, conventions, mutual relations, and standards of rightness that a particular society understands as belonging to bargaining. As Taylor puts it: 'the realities here are practices; and these cannot be identified in abstraction from the language we use to describe them, or invoke them, or carry them out' (Taylor 1977: 17). The constitutive perspective on practice highlights several things: First, practice is broader than an institutionalized configuration of cooperative activity. Such dispersed practices as greeting, accepting a gift, or keeping the proper physical distance from someone in a public space, are also practices. Second, practices in this wider sense are public. That is, understanding or knowing does not take place exclusively in the mind, but is inescapably a public process. Knowing and understanding therefore are not exclusively subjective but also inescapably objective phenomena, not only mental but also social. People learn about the world in public, shared processes in which they test what they have learned. The way they test is through public discourse, of which narrative is an intrinsic part. Jeff Coulter puts the central question very well when he says: '[T]he problem being posed is not mentalistic in form . . . but social – organizational (e.g. how – on the basis of what culturally available reasonings and presuppositions – do members actually avow and ascribe mental predicates to one another?)' (Coulter 1979: 37).

Third, and for policy analytic purposes perhaps most important, buried in the practice concept there resides a sophisticated argument about the interconnectedness of language and action. Briefly put, practices and the language we employ to describe practices bring each other into being. Terms such as 'greeting' or 'cursing' only make sense when the users of these terms are intimately familiar with the practices they describe. But, conversely, the practices could not exist without a vocabulary to describe or discuss them *in situ*. There is no simple one-way dependence here. As Taylor concludes: 'We can speak of mutual dependence if we like, but really what this points up is the artificiality of the distinction between social reality and the language of description of that social reality. The language is constitutive of the reality, is essential to its being the kind of reality it is' (Taylor 1977: 117). It is this nexus of language and activity that is the object of the sociolinguistic analysis of practice (Gee 1990; Schiffrin 1994; Wagenaar and Hartendorp 2000).

• Practice as a theory of action or an 'activity system'. Lave, one of the originators of this approach, describes practice or activity theory as an attempt to deal with the problem of context. While it is by now a common and well-accepted insight that human action is indexical, that is situated in a material and social world, much less attention has been given to the conceptualization of the relations between the persons acting and the surrounding world (Lave 1988: 5). In general, this relation is described either in deterministic terms (context as a rigid container that causes human behaviour, yet is untouched by the influence of human actions), or in subjectivistic terms (the ethnomethodological view of contexts as interpersonal constructions, that arise out of human interaction). Lave has summarized this dilemma with the happy phrase that: 'One has system without individual experience, the other experience without system' (p. 150).

To resolve the dilemma between determinism and subjectivism, Lave and her collaborators think of context as a 'social world constituted in relations with persons acting' (Lave 1993: 5). Actors and their world stand in a purposeful, dialectical relationship with each other. In trying to solve problems that come up in the course of their everyday work, they improvise with the material, social, and experiential resources at hand. Dialectical means here that problem and solution are not given, but bring each other into being in the process of acting upon the world. Lave again puts this well when, commenting upon the way that housewives moved about in a supermarket, she says that 'the problem was defined by the answer at the same time an answer developed during the problem, and that both took form *in action* in a particular, culturally structured setting, the supermarket' (Lave 1988: 2).

There is more than an echo of Dewey here. This understanding of practice as a form of purposeful, flexible engagement with the world is clearly inspired by Dewey's notion of 'inquiry'. Dewey saw 'inquiry' not as a kind of cognitive, analytic reflection upon the world, but as a kind of active extension of what one knows beyond the immediate situation. His aim is to develop a unified account of doing and knowing in which inquiry is ongoing action in and upon a situation that has become indeterminate by some sort of blockage or opportunity. As a result routine action becomes interrupted and this blockage or opportunity precipitates mental and communicative processes that involve a simultaneous restructuring of the initiating situation, the corresponding activity or inquiry, and the resulting closure. Inquiry, or practice in our terms, is thus always transformative. This is why Dewey often calls it 'productive' inquiry. The result of inquiry is a kind of closure. A situation that is indeterminate has become whole again, at least temporarily (Dewey 1920; see also Burke 1994; Strauss 1993).

A number of implications follow from this approach to practice that need to be emphasized. First, this conception of inquiry is a clear instance of the general antidualism of Dewey's position. With his use of the term 'situation' he puts forward an ecological view of the relation of an actor and his environment. According to Dewey there exists a strong continuity between actor and environment. Actors are not distinct objects, but form with their environment a 'living system': 'a dynamic system incorporating both organismic and environmental elements, with some sort of built-in impetus towards self-maintenance' (Burke 1994: 27). The Deweyan heritage can be found in Engeström's concept of an activity system, in Wenger's concept of a 'community of practice', and in Vickers' notion of an 'appreciative system' (Engeström 1993; Vickers 1995; Wenger 1998). Practices are thus not just a patterned fabric of activities, but also contain the spaces and artefacts that are necessary to fulfil the practice (for example, the practice of teaching requires a classroom, a blackboard and textbooks, Elmore 1996). Second, it is important to observe that this conversation with the world involves engagement with the task at hand and active participation in the community that forms the social setting of the activity in question. This implies that practice involves the whole person instead of a disengaged actor who receives information or acquires knowledge about pre-existing objects (Lave and Wenger, 1991). Engaging in practice implies that the actor's identity is involved, but, to avoid misunderstanding at this point, identity should not be understood in its familiar subjective meaning but in a social sense. That is, we define our identity in terms of our experiences with membership in various groups (Wenger 1998: 146).

We do not intend to 'choose' from among these different approaches to practice. All of them, even the by now discredited Comtean approach, highlight some aspects of practice that are underemphasized in the other approaches. In addition, the different approaches emphasize the variety of practices that analysts will encounter in their analysis of public policy. Moreover each of these perspectives goes after different analytic fish. For someone who is interested in the tacit dimensions of government bureaucracies it might useful to think of practices as a form of know-how. On the other hand, for someone who tries to explain the tenacity of certain policy discourses it might be more useful to think of practice as institutionalized configurations of human activity. For these reasons we want to approach the concept of practice more open-endedly as part of a theoretical perspective, an understanding of the way people negotiate in a structured and meaningful way the challenges they encounter in life's course. Describing a number of interrelated concepts that, taken together, constitute the perspective will outline such an approach. Practice then entails: action, community, situatedness, criteria, standards, warrants, knowing, dialectic, discourse, emotions and values. In the remainder of this section we will briefly comment upon on each of these interrelated elements of practice.

- *Action.* This is the core element of any conception of practice. People negotiate the world (both social and physical) by *acting* upon it, or more accurately, interacting with it. The centrality of action is what distinguishes the practice approach from the traditional rational perspective on knowledge and policy formation. The philosophical, epistemological and disciplinary implications of the primacy of action are sufficiently far-reaching that we will not try to describe them exhaustively in the limited space of this chapter. We wish to mention two that are particularly relevant to the policy analyst. First, by focusing on action as our entrance into the world we distance ourselves from some deeply embedded intellectual reflexes concerning the relation between thought and action. For example, according to the received Cartesian view of knowledge actors acquire knowledge of the world through 'reason and the use of concepts that are freed as much as possible from the fallibilities of our senses or the exigencies of given situations' (Cook and Brown 1999: 384). Action, on the other hand, has its own epistemological demands. For example, action is about flow, smoothness, economy of movement, timeliness, spontaneity and continuity. Standards of rightness are pragmatic, evaluative and aesthetic. Action must lead to a resolution, or at least containment, of a 'situation' (in the Deweyan sense), but the quality of the resolution or containment is intimately tied up with the evaluative-aesthetic dimension of the performance. The central 'epistemic' issues are: 'Does it work?' and 'Is it done well?' Think of swimming in a pool. To be called swimming at all, it must fulfil certain technical criteria. Everything else is called by another name: paddling; splashing about.

Second, action, again contrary to the dominant rational belief, is not explicitly goal-oriented. Instead it is triggered, holistically, by 'situations', everyday situations that because of some external or internal shift of events have suddenly become indeterminate and urgent (in either a positive or a negative way, presenting itself respectively as an opportunity or a constraint to the actor) and therefore require some sort of intervention by the actor. Think, for example, of Lave's shoppers navigating a supermarket. For both situations no algorithm or blueprint exists, both require a considerable amount of improvisation, yet the actor is generally not at a loss. The situation both enables and constrains. It signals to the actor that certain actions are called for, but also that certain conventions, commitments, physical obstacles, normative beliefs, procedures or rules have to be taken into account. The actor, the situation at hand and the wider context form a unified whole, a sort of ecology or activity system, that gets activated by the impetus to act. In swimming across a pool, buying groceries, or assessing eligibility for welfare, the actions engaged in unify problem and solution. The situation in this sense is grasped holistically. By engaging in ongoing action the actor discovers what needs to be done, how it needs to be done, and what counts as right or wrong, feasible or infeasible resolutions. In this sense action is spontaneous *and* purposeful.

- *Community.* Acting, thus, is never random. While behaviour can be random or mindless, when we attribute meaning, direction or disposition to it, behaviour becomes action. Likewise, when action draws its meaning from a community, action becomes practice. Cook and Brown illustrate these distinctions with the following example: 'In the simplest case, if Vance's knee jerks, that is behavior. When Vance raps his knee with a physician's hammer to check his reflexes, it is behavior that has meaning, and thus is what we call action. If his physician raps his knee as part of an exam, it is practice. This is because the meaning of her action comes from the organized context of her training and ongoing work in medicine...' (Cook and Brown 1999: 387).

The social, therefore, is central to practice, but the communal dimension of practice pulls in two different directions. First, action, in this sense, as opposed to *technē*, emerges with and is aimed at a network of relationships. This gives practice, as opposed to technical reason, an intrinsic indeterminacy. Working with people and social relations places severe limits upon the extent of mastery over one's domain of activity. Effect becomes a matter of influence over others as Dunne (1993) observes, or, in terms of democratic theory, reasoned deliberation, of which outcome and success are usually hard to predict. This is no academic matter, as the law of unintended consequences in public policy derives from this inherent characteristic of action. Assessing in advance the effects of one's actions and the meaning they will have for a particular group has bedevilled policymakers since time immemorial (Wagenaar 1995). People at the receiving end of policy tend to elude *technē*.

However, the social situatedness of practice does not just place limits upon action, it also structures it. Practice implies that one's action always points towards one's position in a larger network of relations, conventions and obligations, i.e. the various communities from which its meaning is drawn (and within which instances of practice are subject to evaluation). In the context of practice theory the concept of 'community' describes the social configurations in which the aspirations, values, purposes and standards are formulated that identify some activities as worthwhile, and by which some activities distinguish themselves as meaningful or competent.[7] The ongoing assessment by an actor of his social and professional standing and the continuing adaptations he has to make to maintain it in such a community of obligations, are what unites the practical and the moral in practice (see especially, Vickers 1995). This 'other-regarding' (Forester 1999: 46) suggests that good practice is inherently dialogical and interactive. To be effective in practice implies that actors must be willing to understand and be influenced by the point of view of other members of their community. To sum up, action, as practice, means active participation in a community (Lave and Wenger 1991; Wenger 1998). Practice theory transcends in this way the dichotomy between individual and community. Good practice is not just an individual achievement. A practice is also a way to transform the historical, cognitive, emotional and experiential capital of a particular community in purposeful collective action. (For an example from urban planning, see Healy et. al., this volume.)

Yet, not all practice, no matter how creative or ingenuous, is automatically good practice. Actors can be focused on a narrow community whose standards conflict with those of other or wider communities. Or actors might not be aware of the negative unintended consequences their practices have for other groups. For example, the wider public often considers the practices of

---

[7] The social foundation of practical judgment is a common theme in fields as diverse as organizational theory and the history of science. Wenger applies the term 'community of practice' to capture the communal basis of everyday judgment (Wenger 1998: 5). Cook has used the term 'cultural context' in a similar fashion (Cook 1982). Cook and Yanow, meanwhile, speak of organizations as cultures that function in this way (Cook and Yanow 1993). Also Kuhn's notion of 'disciplinary matrix' and Vickers' 'appreciative system' are likewise relevant parallels (Kuhn 1977; Vickers 1995).

policymakers or public administrators, while they abide by the standards of
their own professional community, narrow-minded or even wrong-headed.
Or practices might be embedded in a misguided or harmful policy design.
No matter how heroic the actions of individual members of the community
of practitioners who succeed in making the policy work against all odds, the
aggregate result may be a policy that is detrimental to society. It is at this point
that the policy analyst may be useful by broadening the dialogical character of
the original practice, for example by introducing the standards of different or
broader communities, or by introducing important moral-political constraints
that have a bearing on the situation at hand.

- *Knowing.* In the received view of policy analysis all knowledge is of one
kind: formal, codified, inert, and easily communicable over groups and organizations. This understanding of knowledge is subject to the widespread
confusion of knowledge with information. Knowledge seen this way can be
stored, transmitted, applied, coded, and even, in a general sense of the word,
quantified, as in the expression 'a shortage of knowledge'. Also, in keeping with this understanding, knowledge is generally seen as an individual
attribute, as some kind of personal feat or possession. In understanding practice, we find it valuable to draw a clear distinction between 'information' and
'knowledge'. A simple example will illustrate what we mean. Information
can indeed be stored in various media, such as books, newspapers or computers. Knowledge, as distinct from information, however, requires knowers.
Knowledge is always in one way or another embodied in people. The intrinsic embodiment of knowledge implies that knowledge, like the people who
know it, is not by its nature inert or static, but tied to action. Indeed, what
people know gives form and direction to what they do. That is, what is known
can be embodied in action. We mark the distinction between what is known
in the sense of what is 'held in memory' and what is 'embodied in action'
by the terms *knowledge* and *knowing*, respectively (Cook and Brown 1999).
Following this, we treat knowing as the epistemic dimension of action – or,
in the context of a given community, as the epistemic dimension of practice.
With this last point, we touch again on the social dimension of action noted
above. Differently put, with respect to practice knowing is always situated in
communities.
- *Dialectic.* Knowing as a dimension of practice is inherently improvisational.
That is, knowledge is rarely applied in a literal sense or as a template for
action. Engaging in a practice may involve routine elements, but it is never
completely formulaic. Practice is not a matter of implementing an algorithm.
Problems and their solutions are not natural entities that are hardwired into reality. Instead they are fundamentally equivocal, made up of particulars 'that
could have been otherwise'. From the perspective of actors, problems and
their solutions emerge because they, the actors, must constantly negotiate

the details of the everyday world. Such details – from problems and solutions to opportunities and constraints – often entail considerable ambiguity and indeterminacy. This aspect of practice disaccords with the urge towards standardization and uniformity that is so characteristic of contemporary organizations, both in the private and the public sector. We do not mean to argue that standardization is useless, but merely that it only tells one part of the story of organizational practice. Every task, either ordinary or exceptional, requires that we determine whether a standardized routine should be applied or not, and if so, we have to decide how to apply it. Time and again, ethnographic observation of work in organizations shows that standard solutions work because they are balanced by the improvisations that are a common part of the practices of experienced workers (Kusterer 1978; Orr 1996). Routines are often optical illusions. This subtle, difficult-to-capture aspect of everyday work is frequently overlooked in the literature on organizations.

However, just as action and practice are not random, neither is the improvisation that carries them forward. Based on earlier experiences, a veteran practitioner can recognize a situation at hand as having a familiar meaning, being a particular kind of problem, constituting a proper solution, etc. By registering the effect of his assessment of the situation at hand through intervening in the situation, the practitioner also assesses the success or failure of his action. In this way, a reciprocal, dialectical relation exists between problems and solutions. This is a relationship in which the different elements are mutually constitutive, or as Lave puts it, in which 'its component elements are created, are brought into being, only in conjunction with one another' (Lave 1988: 146).

- *Criteria, standards and warrants* are as much part of practices as problems and solutions, or, more neutrally, possibilities and instrumentalities. The following illustrates the distinctions we wish to draw among criteria, standards and warrants. A criterion, like a measuring stick, is a means of assessing the relative position of something along a given dimension. A standard is a generally agreed upon position on that measuring stick that distinguishes 'enough' or 'sufficient' from 'too little' or 'too much'. Warrants are reasons that can be given to justify an explicit or implicit claim that this particular dimension and this particular position on it are relevant to the situation at hand. In dealing with concrete situations, criteria, standards and warrants are often intermingled. When a Dutch welfare official, for example, complains that her client demonstrates 'an insufficient sense of responsibility', all three are at play (Wagenaar 1997). The official uses 'sense of responsibility' as a criterion for assessing the client. She places her client below an informal standard on that 'scale'. And she expects people to meet this standard because she finds adequate basis or warrant for doing so – here in the Dutch Welfare Act, which states that clients are expected to 'demonstrate a sufficient sense of responsibility' in providing for their own income. Warrants are thus more deeply rooted than criteria and standards. They suggest both a practical grasp of some moral end or *eudaimonia*, and a more or less substantial theory of the causal or intentional relation between this end and the particulars that are relevant to the practice at hand. For example, the responsibility clause in the Dutch Welfare Act is itself grounded in a generally agreed upon understanding of the value of responsibility, and why it is an important value. (For example, because we feel that a relationship exists between the possession of a sense of responsibility and other valued traits such as a sufficiently ingrained work ethos and the willingness and ability to provide for oneself and one's family.)

To assess the rightness or feasibility of a particular action, practitioners employ criteria, standards and warrants that are part of a particular community or communities within which that practice must function. These criteria, standards and warrants are local, open and instrumental. That is, a reciprocal relation exists between the concrete situation and the relevant criteria, standards and warrants. Even general criteria, such as sense of responsibility, will always have to be applied to the concrete situation at hand. This means that to a certain extent criteria, standards and warrants are flexible and negotiable, as indeed they must be to be effective at all. This negotiability extends to various aspects of the criterion–standard–warrant configuration. For example, someone might argue that the welfare official's standard of responsibility is too harsh, or that her standard on the responsibility 'scale' is too high. Likewise, others might challenge her application of the 'scale' itself by questioning the relevance of the criterion of 'responsibility' in this particular situation (e.g. the client, might be mentally incapable of mustering the desired 'sense of responsibility'). In short, the ongoing 'dialogue' within the environment in which practice takes place may prompt reflection concerning the relevance or usefulness of the criteria, standards or warrants that are employed in a given situation, and even suggest a more or less thorough revision of them. We shouldn't overextend this point, however: in many cases criteria, standards and warrants are experienced as self-evident and routine. Likewise, they do not apply just to solutions but also to problems. On the basis of generally accepted criteria, standards or warrants, certain situations are recognized as within the horizon of the possible or feasible while others are relegated to the background as irresolvable, irrelevant or unimportant.

- *Emotion.* In the Cartesian–Comtean worldview passion is the enemy of reason. Knowledge is seen as particularly vulnerable to the distorting power of emotions. One of the main purposes of Comte's influential positivist epistemology was to insulate the intellect from the sway of emotions, or 'the sentiments' as he called them. In the practice perspective, on the other hand, emotion is not only considered an inevitable accompaniment of action, but, more importantly, as a necessary element of perception. What exactly is the role of *emotion* in practice? First, to be able to act there must be a reason to act. That is, action requires engagement. Certain situations must be sufficiently meaningful or important to merit the risk and effort of active involvement. It is difficult to separate cause and effect here, but one sure signal that a particular situation is sufficiently important to the actor is when it is invested with emotion. This is perhaps so obvious that it tends to be overlooked. Emotions, both positive and negative, can tell us what we truly value, which aspects of the world call for our attention and energy to attain or avoid certain circumstances.

Second, and just as importantly, emotion is a prerequisite, or better, an integral element of, perception. Feelings, however inarticulate or ambiguous, can act as markers in given situations by signalling that something is the matter that requires our attention. When the welfare worker that Wagenaar (1997) describes says that her client gives her a 'creepy feeling', she signals that something is not quite right in the situation although she is still unable to articulate analytically or cognitively what exactly is the matter. Also, just as reason helps dampen the hard edge of emotions (as when we rein in our anger at a child by reasoning that he is too young to appreciate the consequences of what he has done), affect can help reason see things in a fuller perspective. Perception, as Martha Nussbaum observed, is 'both cognitive and affective at the same time' (Nussbaum 1990). And as John Forester compellingly describes, emotional sensitivity works together with technical knowledge as a mode of practical response (Forester 1999: 54). Emotions are not merely corollaries of the 'real' work of technical analysis or objective decision-making. Instead, in practice, each is complementary to the other. This can be seen in practice, for example, where moral attentiveness and technical expertise merge to yield a practical judgment that is attentive to the detail and the demands of a given situation (Cook 1982). Conversely, treating a client as an emotive being – for example, by recognizing and respecting his or her emotional state – can mark the difference between effective practice and ineffective bumbling. Nor is effective and responsible practice aided by ignoring one's own emotional cues. Thus, the strength and direction of the emotions that are displayed in a contested policy situation can reveal the meaning and importance that issues have to the participants. In a similar way emotions can tell the analyst something about the feasibility of the solutions that are being suggested. Emotions are the guideposts on the road to practical judgment.

- *Values.* The search for problems and solutions in practice situations is also guided by values. We have noted above the role of aesthetic values as a formative element of practice, but obviously other values such as moral, political and social values are important too. Like emotions, values tell us what is worth paying attention to, and often the two go hand in hand. Values also serve as reasons for what we do in concrete situations (Putnam 1985). This is not mere legitimating-after-the-fact, but instead an integral part of the way that actors negotiate their standing in the communities of which they are members, in society at large. The stories practitioners tell, as we will see, are full of so-called 'contextualization cues', implicit references to carefully chosen aspects of the wider context that suggest to the listener how to perceive and assess the storyteller. Values or appreciations literally accompany every step in the 'recognition of problem–action–knowing' nexus of a given practice. One implication of this recognition is that ethics, for example, is not a special province or adjunct to practice, but rather is part and parcel of it. Differently put: in the realm of practice the epistemological is continuous with the axiological. That is, what we value informs our acquisition and deployment of what we know.

• *Discourse*. Finally, actors negotiate practice by telling *stories* about their and other people's actions within the various elements of their community. The relation between practice and discourse is subtle and complex. In broad-brush strokes it is fair to say that discourse is a key vehicle by which the practical, active negotiating of reality takes place. By constructing stories with others, actors make sense, to themselves and others, of their actions (Cook and Brown 1999; Orr 1996; Wagenaar 1997).

Stories, however, are not merely representations of actions and consequences; they are also performative and generative. As a form of discourse, by telling stories, actors simultaneously shape, grasp and legitimate both their actions and the situations that give rise to them. Research in sociolinguistics has demonstrated that actors actively select and integrate elements from the context into their stories. By placing various 'contextualization cues' in their stories, actors shape the listener's expectations about how to perceive and appreciate the situation they describe (Gee 1990; Gumperz 1982; Wagenaar and Hartendorp 2000). Thus, the meaning of a story in a given context emerges from an interplay between text and context that is actively managed by the actor/teller in interaction with the 'listeners' in a given context. 'Context', meanwhile, should not be seen as a permanent or static entity. It is not a stable set of constraints or a fixed body of knowledge in which actors find the materials from which they construct their stories. Actors do not operate in a fixed figure-ground relationship that automatically promotes some facts to the status of 'relevant situation' and relegates others to a more or less unrecognized background. Rather, in a reflexive relationship between knowledge, situation and text, actors shape their environment. They discover what is situation and what context by telling stories about it, or, more exactly, by negotiating the appropriateness and meaning of the stories with listeners and/or other storytellers. This is another example of the fundamentally reciprocal relationship in situations of practice among actor, knowledge and environment. As the sociolinguist Barbara Schiffrin puts it, from the perspective of actors engaging in a practice it is not easy to distinguish between 'what is said of the situation' from 'the situation in which it is said' (Schiffrin 1994).

Thus, the concept of practice entails action, community, situatedness, criteria, standards, warrants, knowing, dialectic, discourse, emotions and values. In the following section we will present a case that exemplifies the centrality of practice as we have outlined it.

Case study: the expansion of Schiphol airport[8]

In January 1999 the Dutch Ministry of Transport formed a participative, democratic forum called the Temporary Platform Deliberation Schiphol (TOPS). TOPS brought together environmental NGOs, employers' organizations, unions, organizations representing the airport and the airline industry, along with local and provincial governments of communities bordering the airport. Officially TOPS was a major element of a deliberative effort to develop a new 'strategic' policy concerning the expansion of the Dutch national airport. Unofficially the government and the airport tried to avoid long and bitter legal procedures by the environmental movement over the expansion. Although created by the Ministry of Transport, TOPS operated independently of the national government. The ministry did not have a seat on it. The role of TOPS was to advise the government about a 'measured' growth of air traffic in the Netherlands, the outlines of such a policy had been formulated in the 1995 White Paper on the airport.[9] By creating a 'space to exchange ideas in a constructive manner' TOPS' mission was to translate the general principles of the White Paper into feasible operational rules (*PKB* 1993–1995; Schiphol 1999).

However, TOPS' career as a deliberative forum for working out the enduring dilemmas of airport expansion was short-lived. In less than a year after its promising start the environmental NGOs angrily abandoned TOPS. The occasion for the break-up was the following. One of the environmental NGOs involved in TOPS had participated in a meeting with the National Aviation Service (Rijksluchtvaartdienst), the aviation arm of the Ministry of Transport. During the meeting it became clear that the RLD and Schiphol were preparing long-range plans that widely exceeded the environmental norms that were agreed to in the White Paper and subsequently affirmed by the court. The NGOs concluded that the government was not serious about environmentally based limits to growth and decided to abandon TOPS. Moreover, the government had

[8] The following case is based on thesis research by Jacco Kuyt, one of Wagenaar's students, and on Wagenaar's interviews with actors involved in the airport controversy.

[9] *Planologische Kernbeslissing Schiphol en Omgeving*, or *PKB*.

indicated that it wanted to set long-range environmental norms before TOPS could formulate its advice. The Minister of Transport expressed her regrets. TOPS continued to exist, but lost a large part of its legitimacy with the exit of the representatives of the environmental movement. What happened?

Beginning around 1990, the expansion of the airport became one of the most contested and longstanding policy issues in the Netherlands. The airport, which handled about 44 million passengers in 2000, is sandwiched between a number of densely populated urban areas. To the north-east it borders Amsterdam, in the south-west Hoofddorp, a fast-growing residential and business community, and to the north-west lies the historic town of Haarlem with its agglomeration of wealthy suburbs. Since the early 1990s the government has chosen a policy of ecological modernization regarding the airport. This policy, known as the 'dual objective', was laid down in a series of position papers and planning decisions culminating in the 1995 White Paper. This document formulates the main objectives for the airport expansion, establishes zoning guidelines for the airport area, and sets standards for noise, pollution and safety. The dual objective was stated as follows: 'The government chooses for reinforcement of the mainport function of Schiphol airport *and* for the improvement of the quality of the living environment in the area surrounding the airport.' The paper made the construction of a, contested, fifth runway possible. At the same time it bound the airport to very strict long-range environmental limits. Beyond 2003 pollution, air quality and safety were not to fall below, and noise levels should even improve upon, 1990 levels. The dual objective represented a difficult political compromise. As usual, the operational question of how to arrive at this ambitious goal was not spelled out in the White Paper.

Not surprisingly the stalemate around Schiphol has led to diverging explanations. The most common one is in the pluralist liberal democratic mode. Several powerful actors with 'diverse interests and unequal influence' have been struggling for control over the future of Dutch aviation. The successive decisions regarding airport expansion do not represent an optimal rational choice, but are the result of conflict, compromise and confusion (Allison and Zelikow 1999: 295). The success of the airport in realizing its parochial interest is explained by that fact that it has succeeded in aligning itself with the most powerful players in the game, the Dutch government, the prime minister, and the RLD (the National Aviation Service). The NGO is convinced, for example, that the airport authority was never serious about TOPS and used it to buy time. Although TOPS was deliberately designed so that it could act independently of the government, the airport throughout the discussions in TOPS kept an exit option open through its connections with the RLD. Also, the airport, the government and a small industry of economic consultants were untiring in their efforts to point out the expected benefits of airport expansion in terms of job growth, attracting foreign businesses, and GDP growth. This explanation fits two powerful frames of contemporary political doctrine: liberal constitutionalism, in which politics is seen as the aggregation and reconciliation of predetermined interests under the guidance of a set of neutral rules (legally mandated planning procedures, court proceedings, constitutional rules), and welfare economics, where the net benefit of airport expansion is thought to be sufficient to compensate for the costs of environmental degradation and reduced safety in the vicinity of the airport (Bobrow and Dryzek 1987: 34; Dryzek 2000).

The Schiphol case has also been the subject of a number of discourse-analytic studies. As might be expected, the studies concluded that the public debate around Schiphol was structured according to a number of underlying narrative frames. Abma, for example, has reconstructed the 'narrative infrastructure' of the airport debate. It consists of two opposing grand stories, an economic growth and an environmental story, that, according to her, keep the participants captive in a linguistic cage. The success of the airport in realizing its objectives is explained by the fact that it inhabits the dominant economic frame, dominant because it fits national tradition, as opposed to its opponents' much weaker environmental frame (Abma 2001; see also van Eeten 1999). These studies are imaginative attempts to transcend traditional pluralist explanations by showing the extent to which these are shaped by the linguistic practices of the relevant actors. Yet these discourse-analytic analyses are not without problems themselves. The studies accept the categories of the political debate about the airport as a given. Differently put, the reconstructed story lines are probably valid representations of the ongoing debate, but the analysis gives short shrift to the generative function of policy narratives. This kind of discourse-analytic analysis gives us no insight into the semantic-technological processes that 'produce' the conceptual demarcations that have characterized the airport debate (Gottweis, this volume).

Representation springs from intervention. The exclusive focus on the argumentative dimension in the Schiphol controversy instils a linguistic bias in the analysis. This obscures the practical reality of the everyday lives of thousands of airport employees, the locus of the subtle dialectic between the technical interventions that define their daily jobs and the societal consequences that haunt the public debate about airport expansion. Deliberation is always located in specific organizations and practices that generate tangible social experiences about the problems at hand. The Schiphol debate is a perfect example of this. While the policy initiatives followed each other in rapid succession, and while the parties involved argued their case in the TOPS forum, unrecognized and only partly understood by those outside the airport authority, the very nature of the Schiphol controversy, and the ensuing policy debate, was driven by a number of powerful practices. These included unquestioned routines and conventional ways of doing things that were part and parcel of the everyday operational fabric of business as usual at the airport. The narrative 'fixations' that both Abma and van Eeten observe are ultimately rooted in the obviousness, the customariness, the taken-for-granted character, of the activities that together constitute the airport's business as usual. By way of example we will discuss in more detail one of these practices: the so-called 'mainport strategy'.

The airport authority began to formulate this strategy in the late 1980s. At its core is the expansion of the volume of passengers and cargo at the airport. To this end traffic flows to and from the airport need to be structured according to the familiar hub-and-spoke system. 'A "mainport" is a major hub for air, road and rail traffic carrying both passengers and cargo. Another feature of a mainport is its concentration of commercial enterprises which depend on one or more of these forms of transport' (*PKB* 1993: 2).[10] 'Hubbing' was used by airlines in the USA to improve aircraft occupancy levels in the deregulated environment of the late 1970s. The European airlines were quick to embrace this change in business strategy, with the added twist that the national airports became the hubs in their network of flight routes (Bouwens and Dierikx 1996: 361). Governments accepted this trend as a *fait accompli*. The 1995 White Paper, for example, accepts the mainport strategy as a major element of its policy goals.

From the mainport strategy flowed a series of practice implications supported by a particular policy vocabulary and a number of story lines (Hajer 1995). To become a 'knot' in the traffic flows to and from the airport, Schiphol had to supply a number of attractive 'products'. In particular it requires appealing 'transfer', 'traffic' and 'location' products. To this end it needs to do three things:

• to increase the attractiveness of Schiphol as an intercontinental gateway and European traffic hub;
• to stimulate the flow of passengers and cargo to the Netherlands to reinforce its international distribution function;
• to create a well-endowed airport area with all necessary facilities.

But products require production factors. At this point the airport's activities reveal the practical logic of the mainport strategy. The airport authority realized that it had relatively limited influence over its 'location product', a combination of ease of access, attractiveness as a business location and environmental and touristic quality. Schiphol is constrained by a relatively small home market, and it is 'less than centrally located' in Europe.[11] But transfer and traffic products *are* under control of the airport. The airport needed to 'supply sufficient

[10] The close link between the government and the airport is reflected in the fact that this White Paper is also published in a cover of the 'N.V. Luchthaven Schiphol'.
[11] This statement must be considered strategic rhetoric. Already in the early 1970s the airport, realizing that its location at the edge of Europe was ideal for goods coming from Japan or the USA, had invested heavily in cargo facilities.

capacity, particularly at peak hours' and 'to maintain and where possible reinforce its transfer qualities'. Sufficient capacity is determined by a number
of 'quality standards' such as MCT (minimum connecting time) and MTT
(maximum transfer time). To attain needed capacity the airport needs to expand
its 'core production factor', its system of runways. To sum up: Schiphol's business strategy to develop its role as a mainport requires it to enlarge its traffic
flows by increasing the number and length of its runways. That is, one of the
most contested issues in the airport debate, namely the addition of a fifth runway,
is a direct consequence of the mainport strategy and its associated practices.

The mainport strategy spawned a series of practices that must be seen as practical implementations of the main strategy itself. For example, the practice of
designing the airport as a city changed the very idea of an airport. 'Airports came
to look more and more like air cities, with shopping malls, office parks, hotels,
cinemas, casinos, and nearby industrial parks' (Bouwens and Dierikx 1996:
364). Taken together these practical innovations paid off in an unprecedented
growth of the number of passengers, many of whom are transit passengers.[12]
In addition the airport expanded its cargo-handling capacity. Already in the
1960s it had invested heavily in enlarged warehousing capacity, but to bolster
the mainport strategy it now developed a unique practice of customs clearing.
Overseas goods for which the Netherlands was not the final destination didn't
have to be cleared by Dutch customs but were transported by road to the final destination, where customs clearing took place. This innovation, known
as 'trucking', made cargo transfer via Schiphol airport so easy that it resulted
in a surge in intercontinental air cargo. Between 1967, when the system was
developed, and 1977, cargo volume almost tripled.[13]

But what about the 'dual objective' of regulated growth and improvement
of the living environment? In the 1995 PKB it was stated with considerable
prescience that 'the core of the problem is to find a balance between these
claims'. Yet by 2001 the deliberative platform for doing so had broken down.
The government had been forced by public outrage to impose fines upon the

---

[12] Between 1988 and 2000 the number of passengers that used Schiphol airport more than tripled
(from 14.5 million 44 million). Part of this increase reflects the worldwide growth in air traffic
in this period, but another part is the result of autonomous growth of the airport itself. In the
same period the number of passengers that flew through the three London airports, for example,
less than doubled (from 59 million to 110 million). As a result in 1996 Schiphol airport ranked
highest among European airports in the percentage of passengers that were transfer passengers
(44 per cent, as opposed to 43 for the secondly ranked Frankfurt airport, and 34 for London
Heathrow). In terms of the number of passengers it is the fourth busiest airport in Europe (after
London Heathrow, Frankfurt and Paris Charles de Gaulle). It rates consistently in the top three
of international business surveys about airport quality and its concept of the 'airport city' is now
an export product (the Schiphol Airport Authority has redesigned the international terminal at
Kennedy Airport).

[13] From 108,782 in 1967 to 274,396 tons in 1977. The figure for 1995 is almost a million tons
(Bouwens and Dierikx 1996).

airport for exceeding the annual ceiling of flight movements. (Nevertheless the public continues to sense that the airport regularly violates agreements over flight paths and gets away with it.) Government and environmental NGOs were at odds about the system for measuring aircraft noise and safety.[14] Parliament was backtracking on its commitment to the airport's planned flotation. And the government wanted to overhaul the 1995 *PKB* with a new Aviation Act, but was heavily criticized by a number of independent advisory bodies about the lack of arguments for the environmental claims in the Act.

The case shows that the practices that emerged in the implementation of the mainport business strategy interfered with public deliberation about airport expansion. Although the everyday practice of running the airport's business and the public debate about the future of the airport took place in separate spheres, the first exerted a subtle but decisive influence over the second. Each of the practices entailed its own solutions, and highly successful ones at that, to practical problems that arose from the mainport strategy. Out of the public eye, often in a highly technical and arcane realm of 'mainport thresholds', MCT's, and '26 L_{Aeq} night zones', the everyday practices of the thousands of airport employees brought into being the very categories that dominated the public debate. Directly or indirectly, their practices created the policy categories such as noise contours, flight-level ceilings or *PKB* risk norms with which the government actors and NGOs were grappling. In this way, the everyday experiences of the community of airport employees, managers and the administrators of the RLD, the National Aviation Service, shaped the public issue of airport expansion. The day-to-day practical experiences of these 'acting agents' (Bourdieu 1990: 13) created a huge artefact that established itself in the lives of the surrounding communities and in the political landscape of the Netherlands; an artefact that itself engaged and conditioned the responses of citizens and political authorities. The airport as it developed in the middle of communities that were themselves expanding became a huge boundary object (Wenger 1998), mediating between the goals and aspirations that were enacted in the airport's practices, and the needs and desires of its neighbouring communities. Thus, Schiphol as artefact and symbol in the debate on the future of aviation in the Netherlands, and as an organizing principle for the policies of successive governments, is not so much

---

[14] The noise pollution debate is extremely complicated, partly because of its technical nature, partly because of the complexities of measuring a phenomenon (noise pollution) that combines objective and subjective factors. The main points of contention are that the current measure has a cut-off point at 65 decibels. This means that all noise below this level is not registered. With the increase in the number of less-noisy planes, that may imply that considerable noise levels around the 65 dB cut-off point go undetected. Also, the number and location of measuring devices is now questioned. It is argued that they are too close to the airport, and quite a few in less-populous areas, thereby artificially 'shrinking' the area affected by noise pollution. Both the airport and the government have been very reluctant so far to increase the number of measuring points.

a preconceived preference, a pluralist public debate or a fixed parameter of regional planning procedures, but instead the result of the network of practices that has given rise to it and whose products shape and condition the possibilities and constraints of affected citizens and communities.

Obviously, practices constrain as much as they create. The constraining aspect of the network of practices that enact the mainport strategy manifests itself in different ways. First, in the inability or unwillingness (or both) of the airport managers and RLD administrators to imagine a limit to growth. The logic of the mainport practices dictated continuous growth. This led these actors to subjugate the political and legal environmental limits to their long-term growth projections. Although these actors were willing to consider environmental constraints, they needed to be adaptable to the realization of the mainport strategy.

Second, the constraining influence of the mainport practices is most exerted in the policy narratives that surround it. The mainport practices are supported by a positive and a negative story line. Both story lines are about economic growth or decline. For example, a section of the White Paper called 'Economic benefits for the whole country' opens with the sentence: 'Schiphol is an important pillar of the Dutch economy and is extremely important for Holland's competitive position in Europe'. The White Paper goes on to argue that in 1993 Schiphol airport accounted for 1.75 per cent of Dutch GNP. A successful implementation of the mainport strategy is believed to result in a projected 2.8 per cent increase in GNP by 2015. Moreover, in that same period the number of people who are directly or indirectly employed in the aviation industry is expected to grow from 75,000 to 126,000. The purpose of the negative story line, meanwhile, is to suggest that the nation really has no choice in the matter. To maintain the airport at its current capacity would have dire consequences. Jobs would disappear, economic decline of '1–1.5 per cent of net national income' would set in. In the stark language of the report: 'In the absence of an airport with a mainport status the Netherlands would have to give up a substantial part of its share in the world's economic markets. Schiphol would sink down the ranks of Europe's best and largest airports to a far less important position.'[15]

The relation here between practice and narrative is complex. On the one hand, the example shows that the narrative supports the practices. The economic narrative is not an autonomous 'infrastructure' but instead springs forth from a series of practices (typically unrecognized by both the general public and members of parliament) that are connected with the mainport strategy. The

---

[15] In a perhaps unrecognized nod to the arbitrariness of the mainport practice, the government's White Paper supplies another, more emotional story line in addition to the narrative of economic growth and decline. Historical reasons why Schiphol needs to become a mainport are also given: 'Furthermore, it's the government's belief that the Netherlands, as a nation of traders, cannot do without an international airport with links all over the world for the benefit of national and international enterprises.'

story bolsters the tacit, unaccounted choices that have defined the mainport strategy. Or, more precisely perhaps, practice and narrative, as Hajer (1995) also observed in the field of environmental modernization, form an ensemble that powerfully shapes the beliefs, standards and arguments that organize the debate about airport expansion.

On the other hand, the public has no inkling of the story's foundation in the network of everyday practices that surround the airport. For them the story, and its conceptual categories, is indeed an autonomous reality. The effect has been that the debate over airport expansion became more and more detached from this practical reality. The debate became a symbolic reality *sui generis*: an autonomous rhetorical space littered with linguistic and visual icons ('dual objectives', 'measured growth', 'balancing airport expansion with environmental quality', or the well known, amoeba-shaped 'noise contours') that politically defined the airport's outer limits. As a result the public (and to a large extent the government itself) discovered time and again that they were simply behind the facts. This resulted in an accumulation of policy adjustments, new planning procedures, reformulations of caps on the annual number of flights or CO_2 levels (which were violated by the airport before the ink on the agreements had dried), endless rounds of negotiations between the multitude of parties involved, and a government that is wavering between clamping down on the continuing violations and following a policy of toleration in the name of economic progress. Few people in the Netherlands nowadays understand the complexities of the Schiphol case, and relations between the government and the airport on one side and environmentalists on the other have been badly damaged to the extent that the latter are determined to resist any further expansion of the airport.[16]

Practices as units of reflexivity

What is the role of practice in policy analysis? What techniques are available to study practices in their natural ecology: the everyday working environment of 'practitioners' of various sorts? How does the inclusion of practice in the analytic arsenal change the stance of the analyst, both towards his analytic object and towards the public at large? Is it really sufficient for the analyst to be sensitive to the practical, everyday aspects of problem setting and policy implementation to allow him or her to step down from the modernist, expert, command-and-control attitude towards public problems? And finally, how does a practice-oriented policy analysis relate to the large changes in the political-institutional landscape of modern governance. To what extent does the inclusion

---

[16] As one of the parliamentarians complained in one of the many debates about Schiphol: 'I want to note that it is really not that simple any more for a humble member of parliament to understand what it is that we are doing here.' He continues to ascribe this to the complexities of the case and to the large number of actors who are involved. (In Bouwens and Dierikx 1996: 391.)

of practice in the analysis of public policy result in *deliberative policy analysis*, as the editors of this book call it? For, as the Schiphol airport case makes clear, practices seem above all to have an insidious constraining effect on public discourse. How then can the inclusion of such practices in the analytic enterprise lead to the kind of authentic, non-coercive and critically reflexive discourse that is a prerequisite for genuine deliberative democracy (Dryzek 2000)? These questions will be discussed in the final two sections of this chapter.

Practices cannot simply be read from the surface of the world. It is not enough to point to a series of routine activities and declare it a practice. (For example, Schiphol airport's trucking system, or the its use of the Kosten unit for aircraft noise measurement.) Even if we could trace the effects of these organizational routines upon, for example, the discourse on airport expansion, we still would have a superficial and misleading understanding of the role of these practices in problem setting and policy implementation. More seriously, such superficial understanding would hamper the policy analyst in understanding his or her role in what the editors in the introduction to this book call the network society.

The Schiphol case shows that in such ambiguous institutional environments, practices can act both as creator of form and substance and as institutional drag. In the course of designing novel solutions to concrete, practical issues, practitioners, the people on the shop floor, literally bring new realities into being. We deliberately use the phrase 'realities' as the public is unaware of the equivocal, confusing character of the problem situation as it initially presented itself to the actors, and likewise of the tentative quality of the original solutions. It has no insight into the original set of constraints that defined the problem for the practitioner (i.e. the relatively arbitrary judgments that partitioned the problem ecology as dimly perceived configuration of blockage and opportunity, into signal and noise). Similarly the public is unaware of the norms and criteria that are embedded in the practical solutions that have been discarded and accepted in the original process of inquiry. The public is particularly unaware, although it might have an unarticulated intimation of it, of the moral dimension of such practices. The genesis of any practice is littered with countless choices of which elements in the original problem situation to emphasize and which to neglect, which elements from earlier practices to incorporate and which to discard (practices themselves are often repositories of older practices), from which related practices to borrow in the solution of a problem, which consequences to take seriously and which to take for granted, and how in general to define what is relevant foreground and irrelevant background in the first place (Kahne and Schwartz 1978). All of these choices, some of which are made deliberately, while some follow logically and automatically from earlier choices, have a moral dimension. They imply a distribution of costs and benefits to a public that may at the time be only dimly perceived by the practitioner.

The public, for its part, experiences such practices as actual entities or procedures, the hardware of social reality. They are unaware of their constructed nature. Efficacy and repeated performance tend to confirm this (at least seemingly) concrete status for the public and the practitioner alike. But, as we have seen, this transformation of practical solution into social objects powerfully shapes and constrains the discourse on policy issues. This framing through practice prevents the emergence of a level playing field in the public debates about policy issues. It prevents the needs, aspirations and capacities of some actors from coming to the fore, while it stimulates and advances those of others. A policy practice is in this sense an important public act that legitimates some problems, solutions and experiences as appropriate for public action, while marginalizing others (Reich 1988: 142). For example, on an experiential level aircraft noise is a subjective unpleasant sensation, an acoustic overload caused by too many flight movements in given flight paths. Its appearance as a public problem subject to political debate, however, is driven by the practice of making 'scientific' measurements of aircraft noise and plotting analytical projections of noise contours. It is these measurements and plottings then, not the subjective experience, that determines the nature of the problem qua policy problem. Where a particular practice comes to dominate, it defines the moral-political landscape while pushing other experiences or possibilities out of the debate. The force of habit and convention exiles these experiences to beyond the horizon of what is politically acceptable or legitimate, or, in the ultimate case, even imaginable. The seemingly self-evident, objective nature of such policy practices simply robs many important and perfectly legitimate human experiences of the possibility of gaining standing in the political arena. However, as we will show later, a careful analysis of policy practices also opens up possibilities for change and deliberation.

The upshot of the preceding paragraphs is that a deep knowledge of the assumptions and pragmatics that underlie the activity systems of the main actors in a policy issue is one of the prerequisites for the analyst who aspires to a reformed and effective role in the new modernity of contemporary politics. Policy analysis in the context of modern governance requires that we bring the person back in. The analyst needs an inside understanding of the formal and tacit knowledge that informs actors' daily activities. A lack of understanding of the practices of policy actors, in the sense of a thick description of what it takes for the actor to be an experienced practitioner, would keep the analyst from understanding the pragmatic roots of contested policy situations. People solve problems by employing their commonsense rationality, their *phronesis*; even when they 'apply' general knowledge, since general knowledge can never exhaustively cover the contingencies of concrete situations. As the evaluation theorist Thomas Schwandt puts it, in words that are just as relevant to policy analysis as they are to evaluation research: 'The contingency, situational specificity, inherent openness, and ambiguity of evaluating cannot be eliminated, reduced, or made more manageable by having the "right" kind of technical knowledge' (Schwandt 2000b: 218). In the final analysis policy controversies may often be rooted less in a lack of formal knowledge (although we do not deny of course the contribution of scientifically obtained knowledge to our understanding of social and technological issues), and more in the moral-political interactions of ordinary people struggling with the concrete, practical face of social and technical issues. General knowledge can abet but never replace practical judgment.

Thick description requires techniques. Examples are discourse analysis (for example, the contextual analysis that helped Wagenaar and Hartendorp to visualize and decipher a welfare administrator's practical judgment in delivering welfare to the homeless (Wagenaar and Hartendorp 2000)), or ethnographic field research (such as the research on the practices of Schiphol to establish itself as a mainport). These are important and necessary tools for the policy analyst as they help him or her to visualize and reconstruct the micro-sociology of a particular practice. We want to emphasize that there are no short cuts to this work. To get at the way that ordinary people who implement a policy or feel its effects understand and assess the world, the analyst must interpretatively reconstruct their point of view. One has to describe and interpret the concrete, temporal and presumptive knowledge the actor evokes to find his way through the practical contingencies of concrete 'situations' (Jonsen and Toulmin 1988; Schwandt 2000a: 227). Or in the spirit of Dewey, one has to travel the practical ecology that the actor is simultaneously immersed in and that one shapes in the course of engaging in a practice. Political anthropology is thus a minimum requirement for policy analysis in the new modernity.

But techniques alone are not enough. They are useful for providing the participants in a policy process with insight into the pragmatic logic of their role in the policy programme, and to lay bare the assumptions and implicit moral choices that underlie their practices. However, a focus fixed on technique would once again place the analyst in an instrumental role with respect to the actors. Techniques are no substitute for grappling, in their own terms, with the ambiguities and uncertainties, the give-and-take and hard work, of democratic deliberation, which is required to bring about the above-mentioned 'possibilities for constructive change'. What the redefined role of the analyst in the network society amounts to is, above all, a *stance*. That stance needs to be authentic, critical, participative, reflexive and pragmatic.

Governance, the practice perspective and democratic deliberation

The practice perspective in policy analysis implies not only a change in the level (micro versus macro) or in direction of analysis (bottom-up instead of top-down), but, much wider and more profound, a parallel change in analytic focus and in the stance towards political actors, those officials, administrators and citizens who through their actions and interests populate public life. The practice perspective in policy analysis recasts the traditional object of analysis – policy formulation, implementation and policy effects – in dialectic terms. Practice, as we have argued, is never merely instrumental, even given its pragmatic orientation. Instead, it always entails an overall judgment, taking into account various aspects of the situation, both the 'objective' and the personal. Policy as a practical achievement implies, in the words of Lave and Wenger, 'the relational interdependency of agency and world, [of] activity, meaning, cognition, learning, and knowing' (Lave and Wenger 1991: 50). Practice originates in engagement, a sense of currency and urgency about a particular lived-in situation. The valuations and assessments that are entailed in that engagement, that make a situation stand out as meriting practical attention in the first place, go on to infuse the whole problem–assessment–action configuration with a specific moral character. Thus, the practical orientation of a policy actor inevitably is also itself rife with moral implications. The actor is never a detached observer. One's practice rests on one's conduct. How the actor relates to others in the proximate and distal policy environment, and how he or she wants others to see him or her, are inescapable concerns of effective practice (Dunne 1993: 358). For example, how a problem is solved, how it affects other people, will have consequences for the individual's standing, both in the immediate community of colleagues and peers, and in the wider environment of citizens, agencies, adversarial groups and the media. Also, as we saw in the NGO's indignation about being 'betrayed' by the airport authority, a two-way relationship exists between engagement and affect. Engagement both generates and requires feelings and emotions. The discernment that policy actors need in order to judge what is valuable, to assess what is feasible and to determine what needs to be kept in perspective, requires a certain emotional sensitivity to complement any technical competence he or she may possess (Forester 1999: 52). Effectiveness in public policy is the synthesis of the evaluative and the practical.

Also, the moral and emotional dimensions of practice are closely related. Policy actors engage each other on the basis of their assessments of the other's sincerity and trustworthiness. When they feel that this has been violated (as the environmental NGO did), they may withdraw from further interaction. The socially situated character of practice, finally, suggests that engaging in practice entails the formation and definition of identity. Who we are, in our own eyes and in those of others, rests in part on the way we negotiate our identities and membership in our communities. This means that all politics is to a greater or lesser extent identity politics. Political engagement can be a form of personal transformation (Arendt 1958).

Obviously all this changes the analyst's relation towards policy actors. In the introduction to this chapter we described the traditional, rational approach to policy analysis as a manifestation of the modernist project. In this tradition, problems (such as homelessness, juvenile delinquency, airport expansion, flood threats) are 'objects' to be controlled through the implementation of rationally designed (in the sense of clear teleological connections between means and ends) policies. With policymakers, the analyst shares an instrumental, managerial attitude towards his object; improvement or amelioration of the problem at hand is effected through control over the conditions that determine the problem. The analyst's contribution consists of an assessment of the particular configuration of conditions that have led to the problem, an assessment of the best possible means or most feasible legal procedures towards improvement of the problem, and an evaluation of the results of the policy intervention. The added value of the analyst resides, so the modernist would have it, in his detached stance towards the 'object' of analysis, and his mastery of special methods to arrive at reliable and certain knowledge. The analyst's aim is to arrive at problem diagnoses and policy solutions that have an objective and universal value. Above all, the problem definition must be insulated from obvious value positions. The purpose of rational policy analysis is, thus, to transcend the contested arena of politics as usual.

With hindsight it has become clear that the modernist, technological approach to policy analysis has depended upon the taken-for-granted institutional environment of the hierarchical administrative state. As the editors argued in the Introduction to this book, the social and institutional environment that sustained traditional, rational policy analysis is undergoing irreversible changes. In the 'new modernity' of public policy, the analyst works in highly contested situations of policy controversy, where discourses clash. Traditional hierarchic institutions of government see their steering capacity in these situations curtailed, as they have to share power with shifting networks of private, semi-private and transnational organizations (Mayntz 1999). There is often little recourse to the arbitration of scientific knowledge because the parties involved mobilize the research towards their particular aims. In such situations trust erodes, emotions run high and positions harden because people feel that their interests and identities are at stake. Often the complexities of an issue are such that almost no one has a synoptic understanding of it, while external events, technological developments or the unintended consequences of earlier solutions keep the problem evolving continuously (Sabel, Fung and Karkkainen 2001). In such situations of institutional ambiguity, political deliberation requires that new ways of political problem solving, new political practices, have to be negotiated among a wide range of actors. As the phrase goes, government has been transformed into governance.

A practice-oriented approach to policy analysis, on the other hand, approaches problems, people and policies interactively and deliberatively. Policy 'problems' do not emerge in the analyst's field of vision through 'objectification', but are treated as both situated in and the products of collective practical problem setting and problem solving. Policy problems are located in concrete settings with respect to which the normative judgments are made that give rise to a sense that something is amiss in the first place. Policy problems are thus tied to the concrete experience of situated people. In this sense, policy problems are indexical: their meaning depends upon the setting in which they arise. But policy problems are also enacted. They unfold through the practices of particular communities. Policy problems are thus constituted in the complex detail of local situations, endowed with meaning, tied in with people's position in their communities and their communities' relation with the wider environment, and continuously unfolding in the enactment of concrete practices.

Practice-oriented policy analysis contributes a different vocabulary from this, a vocabulary that points to a different ontology of abiding values and commitments. In the neutral language of traditional, modernist policy analysis, the pragmatic, value-laden, affective world of the practitioner makes little sense. In such language we cannot capture the way that people who are immersed in deep conflict understand their disagreements or arrive at agreements, as they obviously do (Cook 1994; Wagenaar 1999). Problem solving in the practice paradigm is not manipulation of preconceived variables, but more the discovery of preferences, position and identity; it is finding out where one stands in relation to the problem at hand, what we value in this particular situation, who we are in relation to the others who are involved in the issue. Success is not measured in terms of the one best solution, that is in terms of a position on a set of hard, preferably quantitative, criteria, but rather, as Taylor observed, in terms of transitions. Is it possible, we need to ask, given a particular social problem, to move to a different situation that, although perhaps not optimal, is perceived by the parties involved as a gain in value and/or understanding, while the reverse does not hold (Taylor 1995a: 51)? In this light, practice-oriented policy analysis is indeed much more than a set of techniques, or a shift in perspective. In many ways practice-oriented policy analysis amounts to an emancipation of language, particularly since the modernist vocabulary in which we habitually discuss social issues tends to make the language of practice seem inferior.

Finally, a particularly valuable implication of a focus on practice for policy analysis is that practices function as units of reflexivity. This reflexivity must, first of all, be understood here in the double meaning of Giddens' mental reflectivity (Giddens 1984) and Beck's unintended consequences (Beck 1999: 109). In the first meaning the analysis of policy practices helps the analyst and the audience reflect on the foundations, consequences and problems of policy processes in the changed institutional landscape of the new modernity. In the second meaning it points to the unintended consequences of policies, as mediated by the practices that constitute them. Both suggest that we be more mindful of the limitations of concerted collective action and alert to the presuppositions about it. But we note a third meaning of reflexivity that ties the other two to the microlevel of *phronesis*. Both Giddens and Beck locate their reflexivity in a macro-sociological level. Theirs is a world without individual actors.[17] Yet one of the characteristics of the practice perspective is precisely that it reintroduces the acting person in the policy process. By locating 'policy' in the everyday world of concrete practical judgment, practice theory collapses such traditional dichotomies as that between individual and environment. Policymaking in this view is not a top-down, technical-administrative event that affects to a greater or lesser extent the lives of ordinary people. Rather it is, to quote Thomas Schwandt once again, 'a moral-political undertaking unfolding in the temporal world of everyday actions and corrigible opinions' (Schwandt 2000a: 227). Reflexivity, in this third sense, makes us aware of the ambiguous, open-ended, and mutually constructed character of political reality. By questioning the taken-for-granted, and often tacit, constellations of aspirations, constraints and judgments that define, in practical terms, both problems and solutions, it makes the obviousness and 'normalcy' of practical solutions problematic. Practical reflexivity opens up the black box of the practical ecology of everyday policy actors.

Practical reflexivity also connects actors and solutions to democratic politics. As policy originates and is sustained by practices, and practice, as we saw, involves people's values, emotions and sense of identity, the analytic stance is, compared with the command and control stance of the rational approach, a much more level playing field. In the new modernity good policy analysis requires greater inclusion of the voices and actions of a large variety of actors. This is a different way of describing active democratic participation. It is a view of democratic policymaking as local, concrete and deliberative. The analyst is positioned close to the points of action, in no small part by engaging local actors' intimate knowledge of the complexities of the situation. The practice-oriented analyst looks to ordinary people in addressing social problems in cooperation with other political, civic and corporate actors. But stimulating democratic engagement is only one side of the story. At the same time the practice-oriented policy analyst needs to establish lines of accountability and communication between these local deliberative efforts and higher political units (Fung and Wright 2001). By helping social actors to deliberate in a more open, more authentic and less coercive way about how felt problems can be addressed, the practice-oriented analyst becomes the servant of a genuine pluralistic and reflexively deliberative democracy.

---

[17] See, for example, Beck 1999: 50: '[Risks] differ from pre-industrial natural disasters by their origin in decision-making, which is of course conducted never by individuals but by entire organizations and political groups.'

6

Reframing practice

David Laws and Martin Rein

How should we behave when 'the business isn't what it used to be'? In a rough and ready way, this is the question that Maarten Hajer and Hendrik Wagenaar raise in the Introduction to this volume. They argue that the business of policymaking has changed. Policy issues are characterized by radical forms of uncertainty and an 'awareness of the unwareness' they generate; the institutions that used to guarantee stability and security are less effective in this role and may become sources of uncertainty themselves; difference plays a more prominent role in policymaking, as whatever consensus on values could be assumed as a base for political community and public policy has eroded. Society is diverse in ways that come into play directly in the policymaking process. Policymaking begins from these diverse roots and community is as often the outcome as the origin of policymaking.

In this chapter we discuss the implications these developments have for reframing as an aspect of governance, political action and policymaking. We examine reframing as one of the ways in which the synthesis these processes demand can occur. This is important because of the role frames play in policy beliefs. Reframing is more prominent in the kind of period that Hajer and Wagenaar describe, whether this is a transitional period or, as they suggest, a new era in which uncertainty and instability will endure as distinguishing features of many policy domains. These developments heighten the significance of reframing, if only because they multiply the incidence and raise the stakes of frame conflicts and the controversies that ensue. These developments contribute to a shift that was already underway in the study of framing, away from the notions of a strategic contest for resources and into a situation that puts more significance on the cognitive role of frames and the ongoing problem of making sense that characterizes reframing efforts in policymaking.

172

The central theme of this chapter is that the scope for reframing is strongest when the ideas, concepts and theories that reframing draws on derive from the experience, understanding and active involvement of actors in concrete social situations. The 'felt needs and experienced ... sufferings of the agents involved' animate the process and ground it in a stubborn persistence that leads, over time, to an increased capability to act effectively that involves adjustments in actions that spill over into a reframing of beliefs (Fay 1976: 96).

This combination of persistence and capability derives from two sources: learning from one's own experiences and diffusion across local domains. Action is tied to the experiential world of others. This tie has two dimensions: a loose network grounded in the practice worries of actors in broadly similar but also quite different privatizations (such as race and family), and practice worries that are shared with more distant actors such as public health professionals, scientists, public health officials and representatives of industry. These networks comprise relations based on a shared system of beliefs and relationships that cross belief systems and are based on a commitment to take action on a particular issue. Together these networks of actors constitute a social practice that defines the broad structure of democratic governance in primary social institutions. This broader conceptual view of governance and networks is a central theme of the editors of this volume. This chapter is a contribution to this broader vision. We try to disentangle two cases of frame stability and reframing in the field of environmental policy and practice.

We begin with a brief overview of the role frames play in the world of public policy. We then turn to two cases. In the first case primary reframing of policy and practice has largely not occurred, despite increasing doubt about the veracity and utility of the frame as a guide to action. The second case provides an account of an extended controversy in which environmental justice emerged as a viable policy frame. In the conclusions we offer some rationales for why reframing occurred in one case but not the other.

An interpretation of policy frames

Frames and framing have been used in a variety of ways. This contributes to the apparent popularity of the concept, but can interfere with understanding what it is we talk about when we speak of frames and (re)framing.[1] Our use of frames is guided by the idea that they serve as a basis for both discussion and action. We treat framing as a particular way of representing knowledge, and as the reliance on (and development of) interpretative schemas that bound and order a chaotic situation, facilitate interpretation and provide a guide for doing and acting.

---

[1] For a review of four different ways of viewing frames see Rein and Schön (1996).

In everyday language we may think of framing a poem, a constitution, or a bust from marble. We also use frame to refer to the structure we infer when we observe a stable building whose underlying structure is not visible. We may also call to mind the way a picture frame arrests our attention to context and focuses it on what is inside the frame. The more general phenomenon then is that of distinguishing between what demands attention and what can be neglected, and of giving stable shape by providing structure, even when that structure cannot be directly observed.

We are concerned here with the use and importance of frames in policymaking and use frames to note a special type of story that focuses attention and provides stability and structure by narrating a problem-centred discourse as it evolves over time.[2] Actors express *beliefs* through these normative-prescriptive stories that interpret an uncertain, problematic, or controversial situation into a policy problem that names the phenomenon and implies a course of action. These problems mediate the interaction between groups and the interplay between thought and action in policymaking. They define the boundary between evidence and noise, and shape views about what counts as progress. The stories wed fact and value into belief about how to act. This gives policy frames their interpretative character and highlights the unity between fact and value and the interplay between thought and doing that are broad characteristics of policy frames (Rein and Gamson 1999). The problem-centred character of the discourse holds whether we are talking about a situation in which there is a dominant frame or one of frame pluralism in which multiple frames coexist and paralyse a policy domain by inhibiting agreement on a course of action. Most policy environments can be described in terms of either dominance or pluralism. Both situations are open to change over time, through the development of a change in the definition of the problematic situation or in the course of action that should be followed.

Our emphasis on reframing changes the inflection from treating frames as stable objects or tools used by actors to command action and influence the distribution of resources to viewing frames as systems of belief that intertwine with identity and social action. This approach shifts attention from the *contest* among conflicting frames to the *interplay* between belief and doubt within a frame viewed as a struggle that generates efforts to make sense of a changing situation and to coordinate action.

Recognizing this struggle of identity and belief within a frame is a first step in connecting the themes of governance, political action and policymaking with insights of the work of Goffman, who argued that framing is a response to the

---

[2] Here we thank Frank Fischer for a thoughtful clarification. The connection between frames and stories is not at all self-evident. It becomes clear only when you refer to a particular kind of story, often not accessible, that makes explicit the implicit organization that structures perception and action.

problems encountered in everyday life by everyday citizens seeking to make sense of the world they inhabit. His description of the process is insightful.

> I assume that when individuals attend to any current situation, they face the question: 'What is going on here?' Whether asked explicitly, as in times of confusion and doubt, or tacitly, during occasions of usual certitude, the question is put and the answer to it is presumed by the way the individual then proceeds to get on with the affairs at hand.   (Goffman 1974: 8)

We are concerned with the problem individuals face in such circumstances and the competencies they bring to the moment or develop in it. Our analysis highlights a critical moment in policymaking that is often obscured by attention to the strategic interplay between groups. Controversies include such moments of doubt when accepted stories are challenged or events upset conventional accounts and an indeterminate situation arises that requires interpretation. The loss of stability that occurs at this moment can be unsettling, or even threatening, particularly when the stakes are high. The multiple levels at which these controversies play out in interorganizational fields of action make it difficult to sort out how practices and institutional arrangements provide access to doubt. The rush to restore control is generated not only by the 'irritation of doubt' but also by the opportunities for reshaping the distribution of influence and resources among groups involved in a policymaking process.[3]

Goffman's examples are drawn from the experience of people coping with the problems in everyday living. We want to show that this process also captures the dynamics in which policymaking can change through reframing. We suggest that the dynamics through which belief and doubt generate change and reframing are not well understood in the field of policymaking. These moments of doubt are precisely the moments when systems are open to new insights, ideas and behaviour. The strategic incentives to use such openings as opportunities to gain control combine with the cognitive tendencies to remove the irritation of doubt to make scarce those moments in which doubt is available and something new is really possible. This scarcity also raises concerns about how such opportunities are handled when they are available.[4]

We want to suggest that at least two distinct processes are at play in the dynamics of reframing. First there is the need to 'fix belief', which over time gives rise to opposition and then to formal challenges of the dominant frame. This oppositional politics is, of course, quite varied, but in our narrative community-based initiatives are one place that 'opens the space' for challenges grounded in the everyday experience of citizens, i.e. the world that Goffman is describing. But this process often occurs in many different places, contributing to the

---

[3] The phrase is Dewey's. Responses can include taking no action if the problem can be shown to be just part of 'the way things are'.
[4] We refer to doubt in the sense Dewey used it as the state that motivates inquiry.

spread of interest in decentralized decision processes both at the national level and in deliberative local democracy. Such processes open the possibility of learning from the experience of others coping with similar problems in different contexts, as well as learning from actions organized explicitly to challenge dominant policy positions.

At the same time, we see that conventional policy is continuously 'adapting' to local challenges as online, personal, experiences introduce doubts about whether conventional policy provides a good account of the problematic situation and the action that is appropriate to it. Initially such policy adaptation does not lead to reframing, but simply provides a way to cope with the unwanted challenges. But adaptation can have unintended effects as cumulative adaptations yield a redefinition of the problem and the action required to address it. This is a rough sketch of our understanding of the process of reframing in the two cases we describe: one characterized by the fixation of belief and the second by a complicated process of doubt, challenge, adaptation and reframing.

In the first case, a longstanding frame has resisted efforts to call it into question. Here we are concerned with what produces stability in the face of critique and the ability of a frame to resist reflection. In the second case a dramatic reframing does occur, but the effort takes over twenty years.

Frames and reframing in practice

Michel van Eeten's story of the Green Heart provides a clear illustration of the narrative character of frames. In his book *Dialogues of the Deaf* he describes how the policy frame of the 'Green Heart', or, more clearly, the frame set by the cognates of Green Heart and Randstad, developed in Dutch spatial planning (van Eeten 1999). The Green Heart tells an authoritative story about the importance of the less developed green region that lies inside the urban ring (or Randstad) formed by Amsterdam, Leiden, the Hague, Rotterdam and Utrecht. This Green Heart is the pump that maintains the vitality of the urban ring. Since the name was first coined in the 1930s by Albert Plesman, an airline executive, who looked at the western Netherlands from the air and saw an urban ring with an open heart, the image of the Green Heart has resonated with the concerns and aspirations of planners who feared spreading urbanization would take over the countryside. The frame lent itself easily to the demands of planning and policymaking. It told a story about what the problem was – the threat of spontaneous uncontrolled development – and what should be done about it – keep the Green Heart open.[5]

Over time, as van Eeten describes it, this narrative has penetrated policymaking and culture in the Netherlands.

---

[5] This is an important point because it highlights the strategic role played by the 'triad' consisting of practitioners in the policy process, and not only the importance of research.

Planners *see* the open center as the heart that keeps the urbanized areas alive and vital . . . Many . . . take pride in having been able to keep this green area . . . open and free from massive urbanization . . . No longer just a planning concept, the Green Heart has entered Dutch parlance as the very name of the area in question. For most people, the region *is* the Green Heart.[6]

As such, the Green Heart frame has shaped public policy, limiting the sovereignty of communities in the Green Heart to developing and securing funding for projects that 'aim to reinforce the green qualities of the Green Heart'.

Recently, doubt has begun to intermingle with commitment. People speak of the Green Heart as an idea that they still depend on even as they recognize signs of its 'infirmity'.[7] Critics have begun to question the veracity and usefulness of the Green Heart more directly. Some argue that the Green Heart holds up an unattainable goal (keeping all development out) that has begun to jeopardize the spatial quality of the region.[8] Others argue that commitment to the Green Heart blocks new ways of looking at the relationship between urban regions and green space that are more responsive to contemporary conditions and needs. Still others see the Green Heart as a fiction that persists in the plans and imaginations of policymakers and politicians, but is at odds with the facts.[9] Such a fiction is 'unacceptable as a basis for national policy' (van Eeten 1999: 98).

The ability to point to facts at odds with the frame has not made serious inroads into the dominance of the Green Heart, however. It still appears to hold tenaciously to its prominence in spatial planning and popular discussion. The strength of its grip in the face of mounting evidence is a new distinctive feature in our account of reframing that is as yet unexplained.

The Green Heart's grasp may be due to its 'continuing capacity' to convey an authoritative story 'in ways that neither its critiques nor its so-called alternatives have yet been able to' (van Eeten 1999: 102). Alternative frames such as the 'Ladder Metropolis', 'Green Archipelago' and 'Green Metropolis' fail to offer as compelling an image of the problem or as clear a programme of action. In the absence of a viable alternative, belief in the Green Heart may simply remain more attractive than the prospect of open-ended doubt associated with giving it up. The apparent tenacity with which planners and policymakers cling to the Green Heart may fall in between the kind of 'will to believe' that a

---

[6] Van Eeten 1999: 94–95, emphasis added.

[7] 'Good scientists, then depend on learning to depend on ideas while assessing their dependability: Feyerabend, for instance, speaks of a "principle of tenacity" to capture the rules of thumb and heuristics by which a scientist determines to maintain a certain belief despite indication of its infirmity' (Sabel 1993: 91).

[8] This kind of jeopardy argument is discussed in Hirschman 1991.

[9] The arguments show that the Green Heart 'has no firm boundaries', 'does not form a homogeneous unity', 'is scarcely green', is 'not so open', and that the 'Randstad does not exist'. See van Eeten 1999: 99–101 for a review of these critiques.

prudent scientist will display by learning to depend on ('even visibly flawed') ideas while she assesses their dependability and the tenacity Peirce spoke of, in which the will to believe dominates experience and pushes aside contradictory evidence and alternative perspectives.[10] The Green Heart may simply offer a belief that, at the margin, has always been more attractive than the vulnerability and irritation of doubt.

This account appears incomplete, however, if we consider what the critics do when they present new evidence in an effort to raise questions about the Green Heart. Does it accurately describe the relationship between urban areas and green space in the western Netherlands? Does it continue to guide action in a way that makes sense? In calling the Green Heart into question, they ask planners, policymakers, and citizens to *reflect on* the frame. This, in turn, raises the question, 'What is it that must be reflected upon?' To the extent that it has really penetrated policymaking and culture and guided action, the Green Heart is no longer just a name. The frame is constituted in an interdependent body of intuitions, categories, commitments and actions that is best categorized as a practice.

Pierre Bourdieu's account of practice helps us to understand why the Green Heart might resist reflection.[11] Bourdieu isolates the salient characteristics of

[10] The first formulation draws on Charles Sabel's (1993) rendering of the role tenacity plays in the development of science (see note 7 above). Peirce gave a somewhat different account of tenacity in 'The Fixation of Belief':

> If the settlement of opinion is the sole subject of inquiry, and if belief is of the nature of habit, why should we not attain the desired end by taking any answer to a question which we may fancy and constantly reiterating it to ourselves, dwelling on all which may conduce to that belief and learning to turn with contempt and hatred from anything which might disturb it? . . . I have often known this system to be deliberately adopted. Still oftener, the instinctive dislike of an undecided state of mind, exaggerated into a vague dread of doubt, makes men cling spasmodically to the view they already take. The man feels that, if he only holds to his belief without wavering, it will be entirely satisfactory. Nor can it be denied that a steady and immovable faith yields great peace of mind . . . And in many cases it may well be that the pleasure he derives from his calm faith overbalances any inconveniences resulting from its deceptive character . . . A man may go through life, systematically keeping out of view all that might cause a change in his opinions, and if he only succeeds . . . I do not see what can be said against his doing so. It would be an egotistical impertinence to object that his procedure is irrational, for that only amounts to saying that his method of settling belief is not ours. He does not propose to himself to be rational, and, indeed, will often talk with scorn of man's weak and illusive reason . . . But this method of fixing belief, which may be called the method of tenacity, will be unable to hold its ground in practice. The social impulse is against it. The man who adopts it will find that other men think different from him, and it will be apt to occur to him, in some saner moment, that their opinions are quite as good as his own, and this will shake his confidence in his belief. His conception, that another man's thought or sentiment may be equivalent to one's own is a distinctly new step, and a highly important one . . . Unless we make ourselves hermits, we shall necessarily influence each other's opinions, so that the problem becomes how to fix belief, not in the individual merely but in the community. (In Houser and Kloesel 1992: 115–116)

[11] In this analysis, we draw on the work of Pierre Bourdieu (1977) and an analysis of his work by Brubaker (1993).

professional and scientific practices like spatial planning as 'embedded in institutions and embodied in dispositions' understood as habits of thought reinforced by institutional norms and rules and a history of socialization. His organizing theme is practitioners' need to act in concrete situations. They must think not only about the nature of a social problem, but also about the practical steps that follow from understanding. This requires 'a familiarity with the familiar environment' – 'like a fish in water' – in which action is to occur.

Practice is built on these taken-for-granted assumptions that provide a self-evident foundation on which action can proceed. *Doubt* about these implicit beliefs would inhibit the spontaneity that action in concrete situations requires. Moreover, these self-evident habits and dispositions 'naturalize their own arbitrariness' (Bourdieu 1977: 164). A distinctive feature of practice is the way it limits and constrains both thought and action through the development of a 'sense of reality' in which the natural and the social worlds correspond. This crucial dimension of practice defines what is discussable, what is realistic, what is natural, without the recognition of the arbitrary foundations on which these judgments are based.

Now consider the difficulties this raises for the kind of reflection the critics call for when they ask for others to 'stop and think' about the Green Heart. They are trying to open a kind of ideal Socratic dialogue, in which participants draw out and make explicit the taken-for-granted assumptions, principles and values, compare them with evidence, and resolve conflicts in a higher-order discourse. But practice as Bourdieu describes it resists such reflection because thinking is intimately tied to doing. Even ideas, theories and frames like the Green Heart make actionability a central ideal. The taken-for-granted, the self-evident and the unconscious are essential for doing in concrete situations. Practice is regulated through the institutionalization of these habits of thought. They generate action 'in an unconscious, unintentional manner ... a spontaneity with neither consciousness or will'. This insight about the nature of practice is intuitively self-evident when applied to skilled activities such as riding a bike or playing a musical instrument but it extends to spatial planning, policymaking and even, in Brubaker's argument, to social theory.

We have added a new idea that amends our account of reframing. In addition to narrating a relationship between a view of the problem and a sense of what should be done that responds to the doubt in uncertain situations, frames become institutionalized in habits of thought and action, in *practices*. This expression of a frame in practice that completes a reframing effort by making the tie to action enduring and tangible also insulates a frame from reflection. This highlights a tension that Bourdieu suggests is central to our ability to retain the creative potential immanent in practice, avoid determinism and become, to some degree, authors of our actions. We rely on frames, but must find ways to manage the relation they create with our disposition to act. Reframing demands a 'second move' – an effort to turn analysis back on itself and 'step back and gain distance from these dispositions'. Through reflexive analysis, 'which teaches that we are the ones who endow the situation with part of the potency it has over us', we can learn to 'alter our perception of the situation and thereby our reaction to it'. 'Failing [such] an analysis of such subtle determinations that work themselves out through dispositions,' frames stagnate and we become 'accessor[ies] to the unconsciousness of the action of dispositions, which is itself the accomplice of determinism' (Bourdieu and Wacquant 1992: 136).

In examining the story of the Green Heart we took the origin of the frame as a response to doubt for granted. We accepted that, at some point, there was a doubtful situation in which the story the Green Heart told established itself because of the sense it conveyed of what the problem was and the concreteness of the actions it proposed for addressing this problem. We turn now to a story in which the problem of origins and the persistent influence it can have is explicit.

From NIMBY to community health partnerships

This second, more complex, case of reframing has unfolded since the late 1970s in the USA The story begins where the story of the Green Heart ends – with increasing uncertainty and doubt. To understand the origins of the environmental justice frame we have to place it in an evolutionary context that played out over almost a quarter of a century. The outcome of this reframing effort has been the establishment of environmental justice as a category of policy practice that is embraced by government and local groups concerned about the threats that environmental hazards pose to health. This reframing effort has been completed with the very kind of translation into practice that we suggest insulates the Green Heart from reflection. Here we see that the same tie to practice that insulates also provides the thick overlapping relationships in which the kind of reflexivity that is essential for reframing can develop.

The controversy that occurred at Love Canal near Niagara Falls in New York State is a good place to start our account. First, Love Canal was perhaps the most prominent of a series of controversies that opened questions about environmental hazards in American society and triggered the development of an initial generation of 'toxics' policies. Second, Love Canal provides a vivid illustration of the local experience and institutional dynamics that have figured prominently throughout the reframing process.

The controversy opened when local news reports focused attention on hazardous wastes that Hooker Chemical Company had buried on a parcel of land before selling it to the local board of education. An abandoned canal that ran through the site had been used as a dumping ground by Hooker before they covered it and sold the land.[12] The local news reports opened questions about the cause of health effects experienced by residents who lived in the housing projects that abutted the canal, particularly among the mothers whose children attended the school that had been built on the site. These residents began to ask why their children had epilepsy or couldn't seem to stay focused at school. They started to look for causes when a woman miscarried or a child had birth defects. Pregnant women and couples contemplating conception just worried.

The common experience among the residents was a threat that opened doubt in a physical, tangible and immediate way. 'The night was very warm and humid and the air was stagnant. On a night like that the smell of Love Canal is hard to describe. It's all around you. It's as though it were about to envelop you and smother you' (Gibbs 1982: 25). The experience of this threat disrupted the unity of the stories that families told to make sense of their lives and orient themselves with respect to the past and future.

> You have bought, hook, line, and sinker, the 'American Dream'. You and your spouse have invested all of your resources and bought your first home. You are the proud parents of a young child to whom you want to give the best that you can provide. You would do anything to protect your child from harm. Your life has never been 'wonderful' as a working-class family, living from paycheck to paycheck, but you're happy. Then something happens. You learn that there is a hazardous waste site a short distance from your home. No one knows quite what is buried in that site, but it is believed that the site may pose some level of danger to your community. Your first response is fear. As you look at your child, you feel this in your gut. You have a desperate need for answers to the many questions now running through your mind. Has my child been harmed? Is his asthma (or constant ear aches or skin rash) caused by the chemicals? Will he suffer later as a result of exposure to this contamination? You want to hug your child but resist because you do not want to communicate your fears to him. You look at your home, which always gave you such a sense of security. Now it feels like a trap, a threat, a place that could be poisoning you and your family. It has become a liability instead of an asset. You look to your spouse for comfort and help. But your spouse feels helpless. He does not understand the problem. He feels inadequate because he does not have enough money to move the family. He feels as though he has failed to protect his family.   (Gibbs 1994: 327–328)

This opened Goffman's question, 'What is going on here?' in a very tangible way. A lot was riding on the answer for the residents of Love Canal. They *needed*

---

[12] The Love Canal was named after its principal proponent, William T. Love. Love wanted to connect the upper and lower Niagara rivers and use the flow for power generation. The project was started but never completed. Hooker Chemical Company purchased the abandoned canal at public auction in 1920 and used it to dispose of industrial wastes including benzene and dioxin until 1953, when it sold the site to the local board of education for one dollar, with a stipulation in the deed that Hooker would not be responsible for any health effects associated with the chemicals buried on the site. Soon after the sale, residential neighbourhoods were constructed in the area surrounding the site and a school built on the site itself (Gibbs 1982: 3).

to name what was happening to them and figure out what to do about it to restore continuity to their lives. They tried to frame the situation by asking questions in the context of their families and extending this to asking questions of, and then with, their neighbours.[13] Their efforts originated in the first-hand experience of doubt and uncertainty and extended this common world of experience into political action.

The effort to understand health effects drew neighbours at Love Canal into contact with one another. Through these conversations they developed a sense that 'something had gone wrong' and 'something ha[d] to change'.[14] The common experience of a threat to health in the family provided a basis for interaction in which doubt emerged in concert with a disposition to act. Door-to-door conversations began to suggest patterns that demanded attention even if they could not be named or explained.[15] The assembly of these stories allowed the neighbours to express their discontent in a way that created an 'exigency for agreement' (Wagner 1994: 274). Public officials had to respond.

Yet, in many ways, interaction with public officials only heightened the sense that something was wrong. This is not because the officials dismissed local concerns, but because of what unfolded when administrative practice came into contact with the immediate emotional quality and moral force of the local experience of threat. The Love Canal residents brought 'the authority of mother – who can condemn mothers? – it is a tool we have. Our crying brings the moral issues to the table. And when the public sees our children it brings a concrete

---

[13] The physicality of doubt extended to the social process of talking with others about their stories. When Lois Gibbs first went door to door with her petition she confronted doubt in this personal, physical way.

> I had heard that a lot of the residents near the school had been upset about the chemicals for the past couple of years. I thought they might help me. I had never done anything like this, however, and I was frightened. I was afraid a lot of doors would be slammed in my face, that people would think I was some crazy fanatic. But I decided to do it anyway. I went to 99th and Wheatfield and knocked on my first door. There was no answer. I just stood there, not knowing what to do. It was an unusually warm June day and I was perspiring. I thought: *What am I doing here? I must be crazy. People are going to think I am. Go home you fool.* And that's just what I did. (Gibbs 1982: 12–13)

[14] Boltanksi and Thevenot describe these 'critical moments' as follows. 'The starting situation is something like the following: People, involved in ordinary relationships, who are doing things together – let us say in politics, work, unionism – and who have to coordinate their actions, realize that something is going wrong; that they cannot get along any more; that something has to change' (1999: 359).

[15] As I proceeded down 99th Street, I developed a set speech. I would tell people what I wanted. But the speech wasn't all that necessary. It seemed as though every home on 99th Street had someone with an illness. One family had a young daughter with arthritis. They couldn't understand why she had it at her age. Another daughter had had a miscarriage ... I continued going door-to-door. I heard more. The more I heard the more frightened I became. The problem involved much more than the 99th Street School. The entire community seemed to be sick.' (Gibbs 1982: 15)

moral dimension to our experience – they are not an abstract statistic' (Gibbs in Krauss 1993: 113). Interaction with public officials demonstrated just how incompatible this 'concrete dimension' was with the categories of public admin- istration. Public officials were drawn into the immediacy of the events and the familial settings in which they were experienced when they went into residents' homes to test for chemicals and draw their blood. They tried to demonstrate concern by providing advice about such issues as whether residents should eat food from their gardens and where they should and shouldn't let their children play. At the same time, the health officials analysed the residents' experience from within the context of a practice (with all the 'intuitions and embedded dispositions' this involves) that was at odds with residents' approach to making sense of the situation and figuring out when and how to act. The health officials looked at the situation on a chemical-by-chemical basis and applied statistical methods to avoid reporting effects where none existed.[16] They started with cate- gories defined by policy and scanned events for statistically significant patterns. Anything that didn't fit into these categories had a difficult time making its way into their practice. They emphasized monitoring and regulatory enforcement as actions. These commitments mediated their approach to Goffman's question, 'What is going on here?'

The residents' perspective, on the other hand, was anchored and punctuated by their experience of a threat, their growing sense of uncertainty and their solidarity around the contention that something needed to be done. They acted from a foundation in which basic relationships had been disrupted. Some wor- ried about their ability to care for their children. Others wondered whether they should still try to conceive. The uncertainty merely heightened the perception of the threat.[17]

These fears and concerns resonated with public officials.[18] Residents ac- knowledged the responsibilities public officials faced. Yet the groups could not frame a context for interaction in which they could make sense to each other or interpret the problem in terms they could share. The disjuncture they experienced is clear in Lois Gibbs' description of an early public meeting.

> The health department tried to explain its studies. [They] had done liver tests and blood analyses . . . They were relieved they didn't find what they had feared: leukemia or even very low or fluctuating white blood cell counts . . . But the health department still wouldn't say that the neighborhood was safe. Nor could they tell anyone what to do . . . [They] were telling us, 'Don't eat out of your gardens! Don't go in your

---

[16] See Ozonoff's (1994) discussion of the historical roots of statistical procedures used in health impact assessment.
[17] As Bob Dylan captured in *Masters of War* when he described 'the worst fear, that's ever been hurled' as 'the fear to bring children into this world'.
[18] This held early in the controversy. Later the divergent experiences and practices contributed to the alienation and distrust that permeated all interactions as the conflict escalated.

backyard! Don't even go in your basement.' It was at this point [they] did something incredibly stupid. Even today I can't imagine what they had in mind. Maybe they thought they were being honest and open. They gave out air sample results for individual homes. The results were in the form of a written list of chemicals – chloroform, benzene, toluene, trichlorethylene, tetrachlorethylene. Next to the names were some numbers. But the numbers had no meaning. People stood there looking at the numbers, knowing nothing of what they meant, but suspecting the worst. One woman, divorced with three sick children, looked at the piece of paper with numbers and started crying ... 'No wonder my children are sick. Am I going to die? What's going to happen to my children?'   (Gibbs 1982: 35)[19]

The situation was clearly a common one, clearly one that demanded attention, but the officials and residents could not find a way to make their disagreements meaningful. In this situation, action inflamed doubt. As the residents escalated their efforts, government agencies were compelled to take action. The first action they took was to evacuate pregnant women and children under two, two groups they designated as 'vulnerable'. For many residents this only deepened the shadow of doubt. If expectant mothers and young children were threatened, many wondered, what about other family members? From within the context of the family, the government action called the future into question: 'My daughter is three, why is she safe?' 'If pregnant women are being evacuated, is it OK for my wife to conceive?' 'I've been pregnant for five months already, is my child at risk?'

Everyone kept trying to make sense of the uncertain situation in which they found themselves. Residents conducted their own surveys and developed their own theories about how to link cause and effect in a pattern that made sense. The state continued to do tests. The residents compiled stories. The state held hearings. The residents led visitors on tours to smell the threat and see the barren yards and black ooze. The state put together a secret blue-ribbon panel to assess the risk to health. Recommendations that looked responsible to public officials shocked residents.[20] Technical logic and common sense would not

---

[19] At other times the disparity in outlooks surfaced in a conflict between the technical logic and common sense, as in the following interaction.

> Frank Rovers ... was on stage to explain the remedial construction plan. He was the engineer who had drawn it up ... 'Wait a minute,' I said, 'What about the underground streams?' He said they would be taken care of and gave me a technical explanation I couldn't understand. 'Excuse me,' I replied, 'I'm just a dumb housewife. I'm not an expert. You're the expert. I'm just going to use a little common sense. You will have underground streams running through the canal beneath those pipelines. The chemicals will get out. There's no way they are going to go into your pipe. They will be under it. Now how do you take care of that?' He answered with some more incomprehensible engineering terms. (Gibbs 1982: 31)

[20] We began talking about women who wanted to have children. Why had nothing been done? Why was he ignoring the problem? He said it was a policy decision, that there was nothing he could do. He could only make recommendations. I asked Axelrod what his recommendation was. He

come together. The disparity between frames contributed to the escalation of the controversy that peaked in December 1979 when two EPA staff who came to explain the results of chromosome tests were taken hostage.

Doubt was opened at Love Canal, but there was no reframing. Residents and public officials could never agree on what the problem was or what to do about it. Even the seeming agreement on a course of action (a government financed relocation of all families) that resolved the proximal conflict was rooted in disagreement and misunderstanding. The official justification for the buyout – mental anguish – conflicted with the residents' belief that this step was necessary because of a pressing threat to their health. The problem terrain remained contested and action was an adjustment intended to stabilize the situation and push unresolved questions to the side. The controversy spilled over into the broader policy debate, however, where it contributed to the instability and conflict that persisted for over twenty years.

Federal and state policymakers responded quickly to frame a policy response to the doubt that was opened at Love Canal and similar sites around the country.[21] A package of legislation offered a diagnosis of the problem – substandard, sometimes illegal, practices for handling and disposing of hazardous wastes – and a programme of action organized around the notion of responsible management.[22] This programme accepted waste as an unavoidable byproduct of industrial society. One of the organizing principles for the Massachusetts Hazardous Waste Facility Site Safety Council, for example, was that 'Massachusetts citizens should be prepared to assume risks for activities

---

wouldn't say at first, but I kept prodding and pushing. Finally, he said he had recommended against relocation for women who were contemplating pregnancy. I was shocked . . . A health commissioner who knew the miscarriage rate was far above normal, who knew the first trimester of pregnancy was the most delicate time, refused to recommend relocation for those who wished to have more children. (Gibbs 1982: 135)

[21] Love Canal is a revealing and important case. It was by no means unique, however. It was preceded by the highly publicized explosion of a chemical plant in Seveso, Italy that distributed environmental hazards over a broad area. Times Beach, MI, and Woburn, MA, were other prominent controversies. Many small controversies had a similar character. In 1981, for instance, an electrical failure caused a fire and contaminated a state office building in Binghamton, NY, with PCB-laden soot. This case displays many of the characteristics we are describing in Love Canal, including concerns about the continuity of family life. 'You know, I want to get married and have children, but how will I know my babies will be okay? Someone told me not to worry because they now have good detection techniques and you can abort. But what about the next one? I can't do that too many times' (Lois Whitmore in Clarke 1989: 4–5). Clarke's account of the office building controversy provides a vivid sense of many of the experiences that follow an incident of contamination.

[22] It had begun with the 1976 Resource Conservation and Recovery Act. The Comprehensive Environmental Liability Response Act (commonly known as Superfund), passed as Love Canal was being resolved, addressed the need to clean up existing contaminated sites. The commitments in this package of legislation framed the problem as an issue of responsible management that could be addressed through the development of management protocols and the organization of remediation efforts. Both provisions demanded new capacity for waste disposal.

from which we benefit, rather than exporting those risks.' In this context, social responsibility implied the need to manage hazardous materials in a chain of custody that stretched 'from the cradle to the grave' and to create the legal and financial capacity (a 'Superfund') to clean up the legacy of waste buried at sites like Love Canal around the country.

Tighter management would catch the wastes that were slipping out of the industrial stream through mistakes, accidents and outright criminal activity. Clean up would also generate wastes. Both commitments converged on a third element that was necessary to complete the frame – the development of new capacity to dispose of hazardous wastes. Siting the facilities that would provide this capacity became a priority for national and state government. This created an imperative for policy action and, at the same time, a leverage point that would force proponents of the new frame to interact with local groups interested in toxics and health.

State governments were given the responsibility for siting these new facilities. The 1986 SARA amendments to CERCLA forced states to estimate demand for hazardous waste disposal and take steps to provide supply to meet that demand. The amendments stipulated that no remediation actions under Superfund would be undertaken in states that could not 'provide assurances' that they will 'have adequate capacity for the destruction, treatment or secure disposition of all hazardous wastes that are reasonably expected to be generated within the State' during a twenty-year planning horizon set by the Act (Massachusetts Hazardous Waste Facility Site Safety Council 1987: 12).

These responsibilities were taken seriously at the state level. In Massachusetts, the agency in charge noted that

> [f]inding sites for new hazardous waste treatment and disposal facilities is one of the most challenging problems facing society today. For years, we have been careless about disposal of hazardous waste, and this carelessness has led to environmental disasters, such as Love Canal. In response, both state and federal governments have imposed strict controls on the handling, transport, and disposal of hazardous wastes. Although these regulations have forced unsafe facilities to close, they also have increased the amount of waste that must be processed in off-site facilities. Consequently, legal disposal facilities have become scarce in many regions, and developers must find new sites.
>
> (Massachusetts Hazardous Waste Facility Site Safety Council 1987: 2)

Policymakers and analysts emphasized that the alternatives to siting and operating new facilities were grim: 'the waste must still go somewhere: to existing, increasingly expensive and overburdened sites ... or sometimes to organized-crime fronts, midnight dumpers, or the kind of company that has a driver open the stopcock and drop waste along two hundred miles of rural road across a dozen counties (a real case in 1978 in North Carolina)' (Popper 1991: 13).

Siting these facilities proved to be a more intractable problem than expected, however. A consistent counterpoint of local opposition disrupted the efforts of these state agencies and of private proponents. Drawing on the experiences like Love Canal that highlighted the risks associated with living in proximity to industrial wastes and a loose network of support, local activists delayed, and in many cases derailed, efforts to site new hazardous waste facilities or replace existing ones. In Massachusetts, despite a substantial investment in a new policy programme, not one facility for managing or disposing of hazardous waste was sited in over a decade.[23] Save Our Country in East Liverpool, Ohio held off Chemical Waste Management's effort to build a hazardous waste incinerator for nine years. Mothers of East Los Angeles blocked construction of the Vernon hazardous waste incinerator. In New York City, the Community Alliance for the Environment (CAFÉ), an environmental group that brought together the Latino and Hasidic communities, marched across the Williamsburg Bridge to meet the Lower East Side Community Health and Environment (LECHE) and CAFÉ con LECHE helped defeat a waste incinerator proposed for the Brooklyn Navy Yard.

Interaction in these settings repeated the interplay between the *familial* context in which doubt was experienced and the administrative categories in which action was discussed. Cora Tucker's account of a public meeting illustrates the family resemblance these interactions bore to the conversations at Love Canal.

> So when they first called me a hysterical housewife I used to get very upset and go home and cry ... I've learned that's a tactic men use to keep us in our place. So when they started the stuff on toxic waste ... I went back and a guy gets up and says, 'We have a whole room full of hysterical housewives today, we men need to get prepared.' I said. ' You're exactly right. We're hysterical and when it come to matters of life and death, especially mine, I get hysterical.' And I said, 'If men don't get hysterical, there's something wrong with them.' From then on, they stopped calling us hysterical housewives.   (Cora Tucker in Krauss 1993: 112–113)

Many of the protests and local controversies that constitute the reframing effort share this characteristic origin. Tucker, a mother-turned-activist from Virginia, describes the roots of protest in the forensic activities of mothers: 'It's not that I don't think women are smarter than men [she laughs] but I think that we are at home with the kids all day long ... If Johnny gets a cough and Mary gets a cough we try to discover the problem' (Krauss 1994: 260). Aurora Castillo of

---

[23]   The most obvious criticism of the Process established by M.G.L. c. 21D for the siting of hazardous waste facilities is that, in the ten years since the enactment of the statute, no hazardous waste facility has been sited under it. Continuing along this path would be environmentally and economically dangerous ... Chapter 21D ... has proven to be unsatisfactory to project proponent, local communities, regulators, and environmentalists. It has forced everyone who has participated in the Siting Process to spend substantial time, money, energy, and resources needlessly. (Massachusetts Siting Policy Task Force 1990: 1)

the Mothers of East Los Angeles (MELA), the group that successfully fought
the siting of the Vernon hazardous waste incinerator, describes a similar tie
between threats to the family and activism. 'We were compelled to unite, because the future quality of life for our children is being threatened. And we've
been fighting every which way. You know, if one of [her] children's safety
is jeopardized, the mother turns into a lioness' (Aurora Castillo in Guitierrez
1994 : 223). Responsible management offered two ways to address this local
opposition. In some states, policymakers saw local protest as a threat to the
community and an abrogation of the collective sense of responsibility that was
necessary to address social problems such as hazardous wastes. 'Look...at me,
myself, and mine. We're losing a sense of community responsibility. There are
certain things we generate – waste, traffic, and so on – and we have a collective
responsibility to deal with these things' (Piller 1991: 159–160).[24] These actors
characterized local opposition as NIMBY (Not In My Back Yard) to highlight
the shortsighted and sectarian reasoning they saw in local protests that tried to
push the costs on to someone else and contributed to the continuation of such
practices as midnight dumping. Such actions demanded a preemptive response
that would override local control and create the authority to respond responsibly
and serve broader social needs. This interpretation was expressed tangibly in
state legislation that provided mechanisms for overriding local control of land-
use decisions for facilities involved in managing and disposing of hazardous
wastes.[25]

The second approach tried to capture local opposition in terms of its rationality. The problem with waste facilities was the way the costs and benefits
were distributed. A small community was asked to absorb most of the cost of
managing wastes while a much broader community enjoyed the benefits.[26] The
way out of this dilemma was to share the benefits through the negotiation of
compensation packages that would address local concerns and make facilities
attractive. The analysis that led to Massachusetts' policy captures this approach.

> Most local residents oppose the construction of hazardous waste facilities out of self-
> interest. They perceive that the local benefits from such facilities, such as increased
> tax revenues and new jobs, are outweighed by the local costs, such as health and
> environmental risks, noise, congestion, and reduced property values. In theory, if
> the benefits obtained by the community from the project are increased so that they

[24] Cited in Wheeler (1994: 245 n. 4). Piller is quoting Ray Brady, an analyst for the Association
of Bay Area Governments in San Francisco, CA.
[25] Sixteen of the twenty-five states that had hazardous waste facility siting statutes in the early 1980s
contained provisions to override local authorities on siting decisions. States such as Connecticut
and Florida permitted local communities to make initial decisions, but provided for state level
review and preemption of these local choices. Maryland held that the state level review provided
sufficient protection and preempted all local control. Minnesota and New Jersey preempted local
control, but provided a substantial role for local input into the siting process (Tarlock 1984).
[26] The analysis closely followed Mancur Olson's (1965) *Logic of Collective Action*.

offset the residual social costs, the community should no longer have any incentive to oppose. Indeed, if the benefits to the community are large enough, it might actually desire the facility.   (Bacow and Milkey 1982: 275)

This diagnosis suggested that what was needed was a bargaining process in which side payments could be negotiated to correct the skewed distribution. The 'incentives approach' to siting sought to open bargaining by creating legal scope for the negotiation of compensation and a procedural framework for bargaining.[27]

Neither approach succeeded. As local protests thrived, they drew on and contributed to a growing competence and interconnectedness. This process was episodic and disjointed. It proceeded in fits and starts and along over-lapping lines of action and critique. Common elements became accessible as local stories were shared and accumulated experience was analysed to in-form action in subsequent controversies.[28] Central elements of the Love Canal controversy – fears about threats to health, concerns about the ability to con-ceive and raise healthy children, the social costs (high divorce rates, disruption of local community) of living under environmental threat, an awareness of

---

[27] The Massachusetts Hazardous Waste Facility Siting Act was, at the time it was passed in 1980, the best example of this policy frame. It (1) provided for a legal right for developers to construct hazardous waste disposal facilities on any land zoned for industrial use providing they fulfilled all permitting requirements and completed a negotiated or arbitrated siting agreement with the host community; (2) allowed local communities to exclude these facilities only in situations where they could show special risks; (3) provided potential 'host communities' with technical assistance grants so that they could be proficient partners in the negotiation; (4) established arbitration as a clear default in the event of negotiation deadlock; and (5) provided a means to compensate abutting communities (Bacow and Milkey 1982: 279; see also Laws and Susskind 1991). Other states established similar statutes about this time. Bacow and Milkey summarize these efforts as follows:

> Connecticut allows the host community to choose between receiving compensation through a set statutory formula or negotiating a package of incentives with the developer. North Carolina allows local communities to assess an annual licensing fee based on the costs incurred as a result of the facility's existence. Ohio establishes a dispute resolution mech-anism called an 'adjudication hearing,' which includes the developer, affected individuals, and officials of the state, county, and local governments.

[28] The interdependent emergence of the frame and networks of actors is an important theme that we will make reference to but do not stress. The general outlines of this process are consistent with the analysis of policymaking in a network society that Hajer and Wagenaar provide in the Introduction to this volume. The interactions and development of competencies drew on and contributed to the development of networks. This played out at multiple levels and scales: women going door to door in their neighbourhood to ask about sick children; Latino, Hasidic, and Slavic community organizations cooperating to protest against an incinerator and then extending this interaction to cooperation on a study of childhood asthma in Brooklyn; or the forty organizations that are tied together in the Southwest Network for Economic and Environmental Justice (SNEEJ). Recently these networks have begun to span the boundaries that defined earlier protests. This perspective also helps to explain the significance of acts as simple as Lois Gibbs visiting Warren County or the support provided by the Citizens' Clearinghouse for Hazardous Wastes.

the uncertain implications of chronic low-level exposure to a mix of environmental hazards, and the central role of women – emerged as themes in this narrative.

Over time these protests began to challenge not just individual proposals, but the policy frame itself. They found a limited pluralism within the dominance of the prevailing policy frame that permitted distinct overlapping challenges. In any situation one or more of these threads was usually available. We trace three challenges that addressed distinct aspects of the policy frame and each required an adjustment. Over time these challenges and adjustments have accreted in a reframing. The relationship among these challenges, that prospered as broader themes developed out of and continued to develop through local expression, is one of the distinctive characteristics of the development of environmental justice.

The first challenge responded to the characterization of local protest as a self-interested action – NIMBY. The NIMBY characterization was problematic for local groups because it undercut the force of their protests and, in their view, distorted what they were trying to say. Their intention was not to shift the burdens to someone else's backyard. Activists made up alternative slogans to combat the force of the NIMBY accusation. 'BANANA' (Build Absolutely Nothing Anywhere Near Anything) and 'NOPE' (Not On Planet Earth) were coined to set local resistance in a new light. 'Not In Anybody's Backyard' was more successful in drawing attention to the character of local objections and available alternatives for policy development.

> The second assumption underlying the NIMBY position suggests that these facilities are socially desirable and, as a public good, should be placed somewhere, just not in my backyard. It is here, on the public good assumption, that tension appears to be growing. On one side are state officials, project sponsors, waste generators, and many national environmental organizations, such as the Conservation Foundation and the National Wildlife Federation, who accept the premise that these facilities are needed. On the other is a growing grassroots environmental populism ostensibly demanding that no new facilities be provided for until industry and government are committed to a level of source reduction that goes well beyond the process, recycling, and waste stream modifications now being pushed by state waste management hierarchies.
>
> (Heiman 1990: 359)

Not In Anybody's Backyard inverted the framing that cast policy as responsible action and local protest as an attempt to shirk broader responsibilities. It told a story in which local resistance was not a site-specific objection, but a critique of the mapping that wed production to waste and both to well-being. Activists pointed out that *they* were acting *responsibly* by demonstrating that no one should be asked to absorb the uncertain costs of living with waste when alternative strategies that might shift the balance between waste and production remained unexplored.

As fantastical as this challenge sounded initially, the ability to point to prac-tical alternatives such as source reduction made it accessible to policy. An adjustment in the action context emerged in a second generation of policies that embraced source reduction and pollution prevention as part of the programme of responsible action and highlighted the importance of demonstrating need.[29] In Massachusetts, activists, public officials and industry all supported the de-velopment of a toxics use reduction programme that focused specifically on the development of practical steps that would reduce the volume of wastes.

The second challenge emerged from local protests such as the 1982 effort to halt the development of a hazardous waste site in Warren County, North Carolina. The state government had acquired a site in rural Ashton to dispose of thousands of tons of PCB-laden soils that had been contaminated by illegal dumping of hazardous waste. The case looked like a textbook example of the need for responsible management expressed in federal and state policy. Faced with high costs created by limited disposal options, a local waste company and an out-of-state trucking firm were indicted for opening the stopcocks on their trucks and dumping 30,000 gallons of PCB-contaminated fluid along 270 miles of road in fourteen counties in North Carolina (Geiser and Waneck 1994: 50). The state was trying to act responsibly by cleaning up the mess created by this 'midnight dumping' and providing a safe outlet for hazardous wastes produced in North Carolina.

Over five hundred people were arrested for (unsuccessfully) trying to stop trucks from entering the Warren County site. Among those arrested were Reverend Benjamin Chavis Jr, executive director of the United Church of Christ's Commission for Racial Justice, Dr Joseph Lowery of the Southern Christian Leadership Conference, and US Congressman Walter Fauntroy of Washington DC (Grossman 1994: 276). These participants looked at the situ-ation in Warren County in a new way. They drew on an established analytic vocabulary and addressed the question, 'What is going on here?' by fitting the local controversy in a broader setting that highlighted the recurrent pattern. Again, they demonstrated that it was not the isolated incident but the broader pattern that was at issue. In Warren County they recognized the pattern of Jim Crow they had been fighting for a long time in the South.[30]

---

[29] The reforms proposed when the Massachusetts statute was revisited in 1987 were lauded for their efforts in this direction: 'We wholeheartedly agree with your policy to prefer waste minimization and source reduction as the most environmentally sound means of dealing with hazardous waste' (O'Donnell 1987: 1).

[30] 'Jim Crow' refers to a pattern of formal and informal segregation in southern states that began in the late 1890s 'when southern states began systematically to codify (or strengthen) in law and state constitutional provisions the subordinate position of African Americans in society. Most of these legal steps were aimed at separating the races in public spaces (public schools, parks, accommodations, and transportation) and preventing adult black males from exercising the right to vote' (Davis n.d.: 1). The term itself derives from a stock character in minstrel shows (ibid.).

> [T]he residuals of Jim Crow housing and unfair industrial and land use policies are still with us. African Americans and other people of color are burdened with more than their share of toxic waste dumps, landfills, incinerators, lead smelters, dirty air and drinking water, and other forms of pollution that threaten their health in their homes.   (Lewis 1993: vii–viii)

Dr Charles E. Cobb, then director of the United Church of Christ's Commission for Racial Justice articulated the imperative civil rights activists saw:

> We must move in a swift and determined manner to stop yet another breach of civil rights. We cannot allow this national trend to continue. If it means that every jail in this country must be filled, then I say let it be. The depositing of toxic wastes within the black community is no less than attempted genocide.   (In Bullard 1990: 37)

The struggle for environmental protection merged with the struggle for civil rights.

> The struggle for civil rights instilled in many of us the dream that through disciplined, non-violent action we could transform this nation into . . . a community of peace, justice and brotherhood . . . In the 1980s, similar moral imperatives emerged around the quest for environmental justice . . . Just as African Americans and others mobilized to protest the evils of segregation and discrimination, they have now mobilized to protest unjust public policies, discriminatory facility-siting practices, unequal protection, and other forms of environmental racism.
> (Lewis 1993: pp. vii–viii)

The civil rights experience supplied new categories in which to try to analyse these controversies. This highlighted patterns of discrimination in the distribution of environmental hazards. The selection of the Warren County site, for instance, seemed more readily explained in terms of who lived there – Ashton and Warren County were primarily (63.7 per cent) African-American – than in terms of the physical characteristics of the site.[31] Hitching on to the established vocabulary of discrimination enhanced the critical force of the emerging narrative.

The civil rights activists brought resources and an organizational base that helped to develop this analysis. The United Church of Christ's Commission for Racial Justice sponsored an influential study that provided statistical confirmation of the correlation between waste, race and income.[32] The Commission's

---

[31] 'The site at Ashton was not even scientifically the most suitable. The water table . . . is only 5–10 feet below the surface, and the residents of the community derive all of their drinking water from local wells' (Geiser and Waneck 1994: 51).

[32] The study found that, for commercial hazardous waste facilities: (1) 'race proved to be the most significant among variables tested . . . This represented a consistent national pattern'; (2) communities with the greatest number of commercial hazardous waste facilities had the highest composition of ethnic residents'; (3) for 'uncontrolled toxic waste sites' like Love Canal 'three out of five black and Hispanic Americans lived in communities with one or more

standing as a religious and civil rights organization gave the study prominence and credibility.[33] This analysis told a story about *unfair burdens* that captured the feeling of piling-on that communities felt when they were asked to host new facilities and looked around to see that they already bore many of the risks and uncertainties associated with the industrial waste.

Hitching-on led to renaming the problem. Reverend Chavis came up with the new name as he was getting ready to present the Commission's report in a talk at the National Press Club. 'As I was trying to figure out how I could adequately describe what was going on it came to me – environmental racism. That's when I coined the term. To me, that's what it is.' Chavis' definition tied pollution and civil rights together:

> [Environmental racism] is the deliberate targeting of people-of-color communities for toxic waste facilities and the official sanctioning of a life-threatening presence of poisons and pollutants in people-of-color communities. It is also manifested in the history of excluding people of color from the leadership of the environmental movement.
> (In Di Chiro 1998: 110)

The analysis of discrimination produced a double hitching-on that created a tie back to local protests. If discrimination was what was at issue, then siting decisions could be challenged under the Equal Protection Clause of the Fourteenth Amendment and Title VI of the Civil Rights Act.[34] The claim of discrimination also directly challenged the existing policy frame of responsible management

---

uncontrolled toxic waste sites'; and (4) 'blacks were heavily over-represented in the populations of metropolitan areas with the largest number of uncontrolled toxic waste sites' (Grossman 1994: 277).

[33] The Commission was the civil rights arm of a major Protestant denomination that had been working since it was founded in 1963 on issues including voter registration, educational access and racial violence.

[34] Title VI of Civil Rights Act of 1964 reads: 'No person in the United States shall, on the ground of race, color, or national origin be excluded from participation in, be denied the benefits of, or be subjected to discrimination under any program or activity receiving Federal financial assistance.' In a landmark case brought under the Equal Protection clause, *Bean v. Southwestern Waste Management Corporation*, a solid-waste disposal facility was challenged as discriminatorily sited because the facility was to be put next to a predominantly African-American public school. The case ultimately failed to meet the strict standard of discriminatory intent, but it ignited the use of demographic data in analysing the distributional fairness of facility siting (*Bean v. Southwestern Waste Management Corp.*, 482 F. Supp. 673 (S.D. Tex. 1979). Aff'd without opinon, 782 F. 2d 1038 (5th Cir. 1986)). A solid-waste facility siting was also challenged as environmentally discriminatory in *Chester Residents Concerned for Quality Living v. Seif*. In this case, the residents of the predominantly African-American community of Chester, PA, raised allegations of discriminatory siting practices against the State of Pennsylvania Department of Environmental Protection for issuing a waste facility operating permit in the community. The community residents received injunctive relief from the District Court that was overturned by the Court of Appeals. The case eventually made it to the US Supreme Court, where a brief on the case declared it moot after the state DEP revoked the original permit (*Chester Residents Concerned for Quality Living v. Seif.* 132 F 3d 925 (1997)).

Title VI claims have been more successful in part because they are administered by the EPA, which has chosen discriminatory impact as a standard (Sandweiss 1998: 49).

as implausible. Action could not be socially responsible when it produced (or reproduced) patterns of discrimination and unfair burdens that fell on those who were already disadvantaged. The response that decisions about what to do with race followed an economic logic rather than one of racial discrimination did little to blunt the force of the environmental racism critique.[35]

This body of experience, intuitions and challenges was formalized into a positive doctrine at the First National People of Color Environmental Leadership Summit in October 1991. This summit codified environmental justice as an alternative to responsible management. The representatives who attended elaborated a set of 'Principles of Environmental Justice' that gave shape to what they were looking for. Among the seventeen principles they demanded:

- [that] public policy be based on mutual respect and justice for all people, free from any form of discrimination or bias;
- the cessation of the production of all toxins, hazardous wastes and radioactive materials;
- [affirmation of] the fundamental right to political, economic, cultural, and environmental self-determination of all peoples;
- [protection of] the rights of victims of environmental injustice to receive full compensation and reparations for damages.
  (Grossman 1994: 274–275)

The alternative frame had an almost immediate effect on policy. In 1992 the US EPA issued its own report, *Environmental Equity: Reducing Risk for all*

---

[35] Bacow (1993: 43) summarizes the counter-argument.

> Policies and decisions that may be interpreted as racially motivated may be the predictable consequence of the economic incentives faced by both facility developers and potential host communities. While racial consideration cannot be ruled out (especially on behalf of public officials), the motivation of facility developers is almost exclusively economic. This poses a vexing problem, because it would be easier to influence the distribution of landfills and incinerators if siting decisions were based on race rather than economics. In an ideal world in which social costs were fully priced and accounted for, waste facilities would be located in places that minimized the sum of their economic and social costs. Because the benefits derived from most waste facilities are not likely to vary substantially from location to location, social and economic costs will mostly determine location patterns.

Bullard's response is characteristic.

> No single segment of society should have a monopoly on a clean environment. Nevertheless, some individuals, neighborhoods, and communities are forced to bear the brunt of the nation's pollution problem. Blacks, the working class, and the poor are impacted disproportionately by industrial toxins, dirty air and drinking water, and the location of noxious facilities such as landfills, incinerators, and hazardous-waste treatment and disposal facilities . . . The roots of institutional racism are deep and difficult to eliminate. Even in today's society, racism influences where a person lives, works, and plays. Racism also influences the likelihood of exposure to environmental toxins . . . If the United States is to achieve environmental equity, the environment in urban ghettos, barrios, reservations, and rural 'poverty pockets' must be given the same protection as the environment in the suburbs. (Bullard 1993: 29–30, 34)

Communities, which acknowledged the broad argument about unfair burdens directly: 'Racial minority and low-income populations experience higher than average exposures to selected air pollutants, hazardous waste facilities, contaminated fish, and agricultural pesticides in the workplace' (US EPA 1992: 12). In 1994, President Clinton signed Executive Order 12898, 'Federal Actions to Address Environmental Justice in Minority Populations and Low-Income Populations', which also embraced the concept of unfair burdens. The Order directed federal agencies to 'make achieving environmental justice part of [their] mission by identifying and addressing, as appropriate, *disproportionately high* and adverse human health or environmental effects of its programs, policies, and activities on minority populations and low-income populations' (Clinton 1994: 1). Clinton's order gave agencies the mandate to introduce categories of race, income, and distribution into their practice at all levels. This emphasis aligned with the Federal Environmental Justice Act introduced in the US Congress in 1992 that focused on ensuring equal protection and non-discrimination in the implementation and enforcement of environmental laws and regulations. Environmental justice offices were created within the US EPA, other federal agencies and some state governments.

Many of these early steps have been criticized as thin.[36] As might be expected from looking at cases such as the Green Heart, adjustment in practice, which must confront the 'habits of thought reinforced by institutional norms and rules', has been more difficult. At the US EPA, the translation from organizational commitment to administrative practice has been led by regional offices, the central office has focused on preparing organizational guidance for implementing environmental justice. The documentation that is available emphasizes commitments to meaningful involvement of affected communities, defines review processes and articulates commitments to take race and class into consideration in the full range of administrative activities from employment, education and outreach to data management, enforcement and grant-making. In Region One (New England) the commitment takes the form of pledges to ensure that 'program managers and staff have access to the information and analytical

---

[36] For example, Sandweiss (1998: 48; cf. US EPA n.d.) notes that

> [t]o date the procedural remedies offered by the Clinton administration do not appear to offer much in the way of substantive changes in environmental policy. Despite EPA Administrator Browner's claim that her agency is committed to giving people access to the decision-making process about what happens in their communities and neighborhoods, the performance of the interagency Working Group on Environmental Justice, established by Executive Order 12898, has demonstrated otherwise. Just three weeks prior to the deadline for the submission of its proposed environmental justice strategy, the working group held its first public meeting . . . Panelists were unprepared for engaging in substantive dialogue, offering little more than platitudes to activists demanding answers to serious problems. Moreover when the . . . recommendations were finally presented . . . they were acknowledged to be more 'consciousness-raising than prescriptive,' focusing on 'options' as opposed to 'action plans.'

support necessary to successfully identify, evaluate, and resolve EJ issues in the Region New England', to '[m]aximize the use of EPA's statutory authority and practical influence to protect public health and the environment in a manner that openly addresses EJ', and to consider 'EJ principles ... among the factors ... in establishing enforcement priorities and targeting enforcement actions' (Varney 2001). In practice, this commitment receives tangible expression in an effort to develop mapping procedures that identify the kind of correlations between race, income and environmental hazards that were used in the United Churches of Christ Study to identify areas where environmental justice is a concern.[37]

The third challenge evolved directly out of the experience at Love Canal, both conceptually and organizationally. The evacuation of the families did not exhaust the commitment of residents to pursue the doubts that had been opened. Local activists felt their involvement had 'brought a new awareness to the world of what can happen if toxic, hazardous wastes are buried in the earth – our earth, not industry's earth' (Gibbs 1982: 172). Their experience led them to seek interaction with 'people in communities, with government officials, with anyone who will listen, explaining what happened at Love Canal and how it can be avoided elsewhere ...' This commitment led them to transform the Love Canal Homeowners Association into 'a National Citizens' Clearinghouse for Hazardous Waste problems ... to work directly with communities, individuals, and small municipalities to assist them at the local level with information to fight industry and move government to resolve their problems' (Gibbs 1982: 172–173). The Citizens' Clearinghouse for Hazardous Waste (now the Center for Health, Environment, and Justice) has helped to enhance the force and extend the interpretation of local experience over the duration of the reframing process. It has provided an organizational locus for the experience of mothers and other activists, and helped develop this into an increasingly explicit challenge of the institutionalized habits of thought and action – the practices – that have shaped the policy response.

The challenge developed coherence, force and a vocabulary as experiences at Love Canal were replayed in other locations and tied together through a loose but effective interorganizational network. Each proposal to site a new waste facility, expand an existing one, or estimate the risk of buried wastes brought concerns about health into sharp focus. Repetition clarified the gulf that divided

---

[37] This 'mapping strategy' is one of five strategies outlined in Region One's 'Environmental Justice Action Plan for Fiscal Years 2001 and 2002'. The other strategies address 'communication', 'external stakeholder engagement', 'organizational engagement' and 'training' (EPA, Region One: 2001). The goal of the mapping strategy is to create a computer-based tool that can support a ranking based on a 'statistical method for determining (a) reference value' (ibid., p. 10). The available documentation suggests that the mapping and ranking will give prominence to the minority and income status of 'block groups' (ibid.). The specificity and definitive discriminations that this mapping procedure will provide contrast with the more general or procedural commitments that characterize the other strategies and can be expected to fit more easily into established organizational practices.

the local experience of health threats from the procedures used to assess them. It deepened perceptions that uncertainty was not an isolated experience, but part of living with low-level chronic exposure to multiple chemicals. These interactions highlighted the failure of existing institutions and practices to make sense of this experience and began to provide a vocabulary that activitists could use to challenge central tenets of policy. Steven Lester of the Citizens' Clearinghouse for Hazardous Wastes describes the blindness (or disregard) that activists saw in institutional practices:

> Neurological disease, reproductive disorder, and respiratory illnesses are frequently concentrated in communities with ... environmentally hazardous facilities. Community activists ... have documented a higher incidence of childhood leukemia, heart defects, and miscarriages in communities with a proximity to hazardous waste sites ... Many of the health effects of industrial pollutants have not been tested and evaluated thoroughly. Less than 10 percent of the chemicals in the workplace have been adequately tested for carcinogeneity. Moreover, almost no research is conducted on the cumulative effects of chemical exposure ... Scientists and epidemiologists ... actually know very little about the health effects of exposure to combinations of chemicals at low levels.
> (In Novotony 1994: 139)

These repeated encounters bred familiarity with the moral epistemology of risk embedded in technical administrative practices. These procedures failed to engage the experience that activists were trying to bring to the policy debate. They focused on cancer, for instance, and discounted or disregarded the concerns about asthma, rashes and reproductive disorders that local activists stressed. Responsible management assumed that the risks associated with exposure from a waste facility were well enough understood to be estimated ahead of time. Yet as CCHW and other organizations pointed out:

> We do not know with any accuracy or certainty what health or environmental problems will result from low level exposure to toxic substances and we know even less about exposure to mixtures of chemicals. It is presumptuous to assume that we can control or manage exposure in the face of these uncertainties ... The scientists who carry out risk assessments are often well aware of all the uncertainty (the problems of extrapolating from animals to humans or from adult male workers to the general population, the unknown shape of the curve in extrapolating from high dose to low dose ... the degree of variability among humans in response to chemicals). However when these risk assessments are provided to others, the limitations of the process are ignored and the numbers are treated as truth or hard science rather than guesses ... The greatest failure of risk assessment is that the experts have begun to believe that their numbers are more valid than the facts and conditions of a real-life situation.
> (Gibbs 1994: 332)

This challenged a central tenet of the siting frame: that people would be willing to trade off environmental risks against other benefits if given the opportunity. Proponents pointed out that

Society tolerates these choices [about risk] in many other cases. We permit people to engage in risky work for economic gain, although we try to regulate workplace hazards and environmental risks . . . With the exception of drug use, we impose almost no limitations on the pursuit of risky recreational activity. People smoke, drink, skydive, and eat high-fat foods and often contend they have a constitutional right to do so. So it is difficult to conclude that it is somehow unfair or immoral to permit people to trade off environmental risk for economic gain, provided the choice is informed.   (Bacow 1993: 46)

Yet if risks were not well understood, these tradeoffs could not be made in an informed way. Nor did people jump at the chance to trade off hosting a facility against other benefits when the opportunity was offered. The desirable tradeoffs that were to facilitate the completion of the responsible management frame did not look as attractive (or voluntary) as anticipated to the local communities. From their perspective these tradeoffs were dominated not by bargaining that improved welfare, but by the contrast between

who is being asked to take the risk and who is getting the benefit . . . [R]isk assessments are 'the risks that someone else has chosen for you to take.' What is a life worth is the burning question, but equally important is whose life . . . These debates over risks usually are not occurring in communities where highly educated and affluent people live. People who are more affluent can choose to move out of a contaminated community . . . whereas working class and lower income families have no realistic choices. Consequently, the people who are most often asked (or told) to bear the risks of a polluting industry [or] facility often have little ability to escape the poisons. As a result, the use of risk assessments is seen by many as a part of societal racism and classism. They are used to justify victimizing poor communities or communities of color.
                                                                  (Gibbs 1994: 329–330)

The development of these critiques was important in prompting an adjustment in policy in the domain of health assessment. The most interesting aspects of this adjustment developed in communities in which protests were supplemented by experiments in environmental health assessment that brought local organizations into discussion and cooperation with public officials and experts. The experience in the Greenpoint-Williamsburg neighbourhood in Brooklyn, NY, provides a good illustration.

El Puente, a Latino community organization, had first been drawn into the environmental arena to protest against the presence of waste disposal facilities in the community. They cooperated in these protests with the United Jewish Organizations. Later these two groups, together with the Polish and Slavic Center worked together on a research and intervention programme that explored the link between pollution and childhood asthma.[38] El Puente has developed

---

[38] The reframing of organizational goals in community based organizations such as El Puente to include environmental considerations has been a prominent characteristic of the broader

this competence and, since 1995, its staff have performed six community health surveys with the assistance of Community Information and Epidemiological Technologies, a non-profit organization (Corburn 2001: 20). These studies have met traditional standards well enough for El Puente to publish its findings in the *American Journal of Public Health*. At the same time El Puente's work has challenged the institutionalized habits in environmental and risk assessment by asserting '(a) community ownership of both the information and the research process; (b) the premise that research will lead to action for the benefit of the community; and (c) the weaving of research into a process of community reflection and learning' (Corburn 2001: 20). The organization has received funding to 'act as the principal investigator for an expanded four-year asthma study, which will include physicians from Woodhull Medical and Mental Health Center, and the New York University School of Medicine, Department of Environmental Medicine' (Corburn 2001: 23).

The cooperation in Brooklyn was not an isolated occurrence. A recent meeting of the National Environmental Justice Advisory Council (NEJAC, the chief EJ advisory body to the US EPA) highlighted similar programmes across the USA. The Southern California Environmental Health Partnership Institute is a collaboration among community representatives, local health care providers

reframing effort. Many of these organizations did not see environment as part of their core concerns and only came to do so through repeated interaction over environmental health issues. The description by Frances Lucerna, one of the founders of El Puente, of her experience suggests the character of this reframing.

There's a moment where this convergence of wellness and environment [happens]. I remember my own personal feeling ... I was here one evening ... and we were sitting around and my mother walked in and she had a bag and in these she had these foil wrapping and in there she had her herbs. She had *ruda* and *mananilla*. She had brought it for me, *menta* you know ... Here we were at the table and young people start saying, 'ay mira, ruda' and 'you know what my grandmother uses that for? She puts it in her tea' ... and before you know it there was this big circle of young people and facilitators all kind of exchanging these stories in a very animated way about these herbs ... And all of a sudden as I was sitting there something really started to open up. In terms of what could possibly happen here, what needed to happen ... [I]t led to the idea of the environment and wellness ... I made the connection. For me it merged there. And finding consistency in terms of the campaigns we did around measles and lead screening and all of the work we had been doing. (In Penchaszadeh 1998: 81)

This sense of development is also clear in the summary of a young member of El Puente's staff:

I have to say that all of this started with the Toxic Avengers ... And it was really the young people that started ... Then came the environmental justice team, the work that we did, WEPA (Williamsburg Environmental Preservation Activists), the Outreachers, and now I hear CHE (Community Health and Environment). It's important that the young people still get that. How important it is that they have a say in what is going on in their community and also that they know about what is going on. I think that when I grew up here, I didn't know anything that was going on. It was Toxic Avengers that taught me: did you know Radiac was here all these years? And I was like, 'WHAT? Are you kidding?' So that's why it's important for them to be doing this work and making sure that communities like that are not going to stay quiet. (Delia Montalvo in Penchaszadeh 1998: 20) and university researchers organized to 'educate community members and health care providers', 'promote adoption of pollution prevention measures' and 'establish a community-based strategy for reducing community and worker exposure to environmental pollutants' (NEJAC 2000: 62). The Rural Coalition: The Community-Responsive Partners for Environmental Health is working to develop and implement a 'partnership model' to develop 'collaborative projects to achieve measurable results in identifying, preventing, and mitigating exposures' in Sumter County, AL, and El Paso, TX (p. 62).

These programmes recognize to some extent that environmental justice can also be understood as a question of how you behave in the face of uncertainty, rather than how you distribute externalities. They start with the experience of the community and try to fit it into an intelligible frame and involve affected communities in this interpretative process.

Many of the discussions at a recent NEJAC meeting in Atlanta focused on how to organize programmes of 'community-based health research' that would involve local groups in the assessment of health effects and the identification of sources of exposure. In discussions of these pilot programmes and review of other experiences, participants at this meeting began to reconsider central commitments in health and risk assessment. In doing so they appear to be constituting the beginnings or a more substantial reframing of practice than can be observed in other domains of adjustments to the challenge posed by environmental justice. Among the revisions that participants discussed was the need to change the way health assessment is practised:

> [W]e have to find a way to talk to communities about what we can and cannot do in a better way. This should be different from the risk assessor coming in and calculating risk, or saying that they cannot calculate it ... scientists and policymakers have to be more helpful to communities, or they will lose credibility ... (a 'federal stakeholder' in NEJAC 2000, V: 51)

> I think that an overall conclusion of this committee is not only the fact that there is a need for greater research, particularly research that understands and links the relationship between environmental causes of disease and health disparities in minority low income communities, but that this kind of research needs to be done in a different way.   (Charles Lee in NEJAC 2000, II: 34)

The participants acknowledged the role that local groups can play as partners rather than subjects in research:

> [S]ome of the best ideas for doing research really arise from the community because they are in a much better position than the researchers are to understand what the real issues are.   (Patrick Kinney in NEJAC 2000, II: 59)

They also acknowledged that their knowledge had limits that might come into play when making choices about when and how to act:

I think there's still value to research. However, I think we should take certain precautionary steps applying the precautionary principle to certain public policies where
we reached those limits of science. It's important for us to stop and intervene in those
problems that are happening in the community and understand that there is another
principle out there that we from the environmental justice movement put forward.
That's self-determination.   (Carlos Porras in NEJAC 2000, II: 18)

They reflected on core commitments such as peer review:

Who are your peers? I mean, if they're community-based partners, you need
community-based folks doing the review. And we know that. But then getting a
common understanding between reviewers about what's good science and what's
good community-based research is also a challenge.
                                          (Jon Kerner in NEJAC 2000, II: 11)

Finally they explored ways to link the development of knowledge about health
effects more closely to efforts to take action.

I would suggest that one of the things that we might want to consider is how do we
begin to combine our expertise so that when we look at a community we can begin to
understand what are some of the things that in a community partnership we can begin
to treat, even if it's the symptoms, that begin to improve the health of the community
as we try and understand what those triggers are.
                                     (Hal Zenick, in NEJAC 2000, II: 27–28)

The changes that are being contemplated in these discussions provide the clearest evidence of reframing as a reflection on institutional habits of thought. The
process is still ongoing and may or may not have impacts proportional to the
level of reflection that seems to be underway. At the same time, it is clear that
those who participate in health assessment have begun to take account of the
history of challenges in terms of the implications it would have for the reorganization of their practice. This is the step that could never be broached in the Green
Heart case and appears to be only marginal in other aspects of environmental
justice reframing.

Reframing in practice

The narrative above is rich in detail about a series of changes that generated
a reframing of policy about hazardous waste over a twenty-five-year period in
the USA. No one set out to reframe policy, nor was the alternative clear to its
advocates at the beginning of the contest. Indeed the notion of a frame contest
does not appear appropriate here. But policy and the terms in which action is
discussed clearly have changed. Reframing developed out of interaction around
a set of problems.

We want to say something about the dynamics of reframing that is faithful to these events, but captures generalizable insights about the generative processes that contribute to reframing. Our starting point is Goffman's stress on the doubt that individuals confront in making sense of the problematic situations they confront in everyday life. Peirce, Dewey and the pragmatist school draw on similar insights, but in an effort to understand science and policy. Goffman stresses the doubt that individuals confront in making sense of the reality they experience. The pragmatic school stresses the tenacity of beliefs that fill the void that doubt generates around the disposition to act. Thus they stress belief characterized by tenacity and the role of doubt in a process of continuous change. Connecting these central ideas is the notion that conventions of belief are continuously challenged by personal experience and organized groups, but that these processes, in turn, promote ad hoc adjustments that try to abate the challenges in order to maintain the continuity of beliefs.

In the real world of lives and policy, people do change their minds. Even the most intractable policy debates can lead to reframing. The management of waste and attitudes toward toxics clearly have changed over the interval from Love Canal to the present. This process can be succinctly captured drawing on the ideas sketched above. Our case can be best summarized first as an experience of uncertainty and doubt about what was happening in Love Canal that produced perverse health effects which were difficult to understand. Public policy was challenged at least three times in the story that followed Love Canal. Each of these challenges produced an adjustment in action. The first challenge confronted the belief that waste is a necessary part of economic and social life and that the policy question was how to manage waste responsibly. The second challenge hitched on to the developed vocabulary of civil rights and externalities to define the situation as a problem of unfair burdens and environmental racism. The third challenge stressed the inherent uncertainty that characterized the experience of communities and the inability of established scientific practices to tame or stabilize the doubt entailed in the experience of families living with pollution.

The new practices highlighted by the first challenge were easily accommodated as an additional step in the dominant frame of responsible management. A second generation of policies simply listed this as a prerequisite for any effort to site new waste management and disposal facilities. No deep reconsideration of beliefs was necessary, nor was real tenacity necessary to maintain the continuity of the policy beliefs. The second challenge was more disruptive. The charges of unfair burdens and environmental racism and the demands for environmental justice that were articulated by activists demanded explicit acknowledgement and adjustment in prevailing policy practices. This adjustment is clearest in new administrative guidelines. The adjustments in practice have been ad hoc and have delayed any rethinking of any of the central commitments in the dominant policy frame. The third challenge, which most clearly sustained doubt, has produced the deepest reflection on the foundation of practice and reconsideration of action strategies.

We have presented these as distinct challenges. In practice they overlapped organizationally and conceptually. These overlaps were important in maintaining continuity and vitality in the reframing effort. One thread or more was generally available in a local setting. The process of hitching on to broader national initiatives also contributed to the continuity and vitality of these challenges. In addition to civil rights, these efforts hitched on less directly to a growing interest in participatory and deliberative democracy. A distinctive characteristic of the EJ story is that hitching on was always balanced by close ties with local experience. The challenges, shingled together by the overlaps and marginal adjustments in the policy arena, accumulated as an embrace of reframing, probably without conscious recognition of the extensive implications this had for practice.

The protests were underpinned by the emotional experience of threat and doubt that created a level of commitment at the local level that can only be described as tenacity. The experience of environmental threats had an immediate emotional character that gave moral force to the commitment and claims of local activists. The fact that relationships in the family – the care of children, the ability to conceive – were perceived to be threatened enhanced this experience. The experience of threat was heightened by the disconnection that residents felt between their experience and concerns and the administrative procedures of public health and environmental protection.

Repetition permitted the development of the themes that characterized early experiences at Love Canal and the capabilities clearly to articulate criticisms and to identify practical alternatives. This was only possible because of the tenacity of local opposition. Many local groups sustained their efforts over years. This tenacity had a particular character. It was not solely a tenacity of conviction, in many cases it expressed doubt. Even as they identified patterns of discrimination and alternative practices that they preferred, these groups managed to keep Goffman's question, 'What is going on here?', open in the policy conversation. This contributed to a degree of openness that, however small, was important for the evolution of the environmental justice frame.

Another prominent characteristic of the broader process was the continuity provided by agents and networks. The grassroots initiatives, in particular, were linked in a loose network that permitted the exchange of ideas and strategies and the sharing of experience. Because of these networks local protests were not isolated incidents, but were linked in a way that contributed to the recognition of broader patterns and sustained the sense that each individual protest was part of a larger conversation.

The significance of these ties becomes clear if we consider the case in light of the elements of the kind of 'learning by monitoring' system that Sabel (1994) has described. Learning becomes possible when a series of one-off exchanges is transformed into a continuous discussion; when the status quo is persistently perturbed, either because it is inherently uncertain or unstable or because it is consistently upset by the actors involved; and when actors become involved in a joint exploration of the limits of understanding and of common ends that prompts a reconsideration on the part of the actors involved of 'views of self, the world, and interests arising from both' (Sabel 1994: 138–139; 144–145). Such an ongoing pattern of joint and several redefinition in light of an emerging understanding of the world is what constitutes learning in this context. It also meets with our definition of reframing.

In the environmental justice case, the repeated character of the local controversies, together with the loose but effective ties between events, created a continuous discussion out of a series of discrete events. A mix of factors knitted these local events into something more continuous. First, recurrent themes that arose in case after case. The personal quality of the threat, the concerns about children and the horizon of uncertainty that the controversies brought into view, all contributed to the sense that each local event was part of a broader pattern. The central role that women played also provided a point of solidarity that tied individual controversies together. The loose but effective network provided support and also provided continuity across these distinct experiences and in the terms that were used to discuss them. It also provided a context in which to repeat stories so that common themes emerged in a way that was accessible to the actors involved.

The status quo was persistently perturbed. For the local activists, and perhaps for others, this was because of the constitutive uncertainties that characterized their situation. They operated with a developed appreciation for the uncertain implications of chronic exposure to a variety of environmental insults. They recognized health effects as a kind of canary in the coal mine that signalled the need for precaution, rather than conclusive evidence of a known pattern. The emerging health practices that respond to these concerns begin with this uncertain situation. For the advocates of the responsible management frame, the status quo was perturbed by the actions of local opponents. They did not face a single stratagem, but always a pattern of protest that drew on local themes and capabilities. This added uncertainty to the ongoing disruption of the frame.

By challenging the expression of the responsible management frame and the assumptions and commitments it expressed, the parties involved consistently, if unwillingly, explored the limits of understanding. These limits were clearly felt by residents. They experienced this in the mismatch between their experience and administrative processes and in the increasingly explicit critique they developed of the epistemology of risk. And they did their best to acquaint others with the emotional force associated with brushing up against those limits. The public officials and industry representatives involved experienced the limits of their understanding in their inability to craft a successful siting policy. They continually had to confront adversaries to whom they could not make themselves understandable.

The interactions that played out in these local controversies triggered an ongoing redefinition of the sense of the problem and, through this, of actors' understanding of their roles and of what an acceptable course of action would be. This was certainly more explicit for proponents of projects who had to confront the emotional experience of residents, but it also applied to activists who suddenly found themselves confronting patterns of discrimination in what looked like cases of environmental risk. The relationships that are being considered under the rubric of health partnerships reflect a reconsideration of self and of relationships to other (previously antagonistic) actors. The interdependence, recognition of the importance of trust and developing sense of the problem that have been gained demonstrate the kind of learning that these patterns of interaction have produced.

The remarkable thing is that this kind of learning could develop out of conditions of such antagonism. Siting disputes, as a rule, are not cordial affairs. People have something at stake. One of the most instructive elements of the learning-by-monitoring framework is that it suggests how learning could develop out of even antagonistic relationships where a background of uncertainty highlights interdependence in repeat interactions.

We have explored the dynamics of reframing by examining two cases in which important aspects of the reframing process came into play. In particular, these examples highlight the importance of practice. Reframing emerged out of concrete situated interactions. It drew on the vitality of the settings and the level of commitment they triggered, even as other characteristics of practice consistently raised problems for the actors involved. Where the reframing has been the most dramatic, as in the case of the community health partnerships, it was preceded by episodes of practice in which traditional roles were suspended. Think of the patterns of practice that have developed in Brooklyn. These prior moments of practice appear to have provided the 'liminal spaces' that set the stage for reframing. Cobb (2001) suggests that as 'these moments occur in the contexts of a relationship, they alter the relationship, as well as the space in which that relationship resides, the relational container, the "between space" where personal identities are inextricably intertwined and overlapping'.[39] In our terms they open the way for reflection and reframing.

---

[39] Cobb (2001: 5–6) defines liminal spaces as the 'between' spaces, of relationships, of meaning. She describes her study in terms that resonate with the kind of study of reframing we are proposing as 'an ethnography of "how" evolution occurs in the negotiation process; it is my attempt to describe both the management of relational *thresholds* (between-spaces) as well as the thresholds where new meaning, new ways of sense making begin to materialize but are not yet realized'.

This chapter suggests the need for a more detailed understanding and account of the pragmatics of the liminal spaces and other moments that influence the development of public discourse. This form of microanalysis can shed additional light on the processes by which disputes are opened and resolved and practices are reframed in a complex society.

Part III

Foundations of deliberative policy analysis

7

Beyond empiricism: policy analysis as deliberative practice

Frank Fischer

Why has policy science failed to generate a significant body of knowledge capable of playing a significant role in solving the pressing social and economic problems that confront modern urban-industrial societies? An important part of the answer can be traced to discredited, but often still operative, empiricist epistemological assumptions. Drawing on newer developments in epistemology and the sociology of science, the discussion outlines a postempiricist conception of policy science designed to address the multidimensional complexity of social reality. As a discursive orientation grounded in particular reason, the approach situates empirical inquiry in a broader deliberative, interpretative framework. More than just an epistemological alternative, the postempiricist approach is offered as a better description of what social scientists actually do in practice. The chapter closes with a brief discussion of the implications of the approach for both a socially relevant policy curriculum and deliberative governance.

The social sciences emerged in the main as an effort to develop a rigorous empirical science patterned after the methods of physics and the natural sciences. Today all but a few diehards are willing to admit that this 'positivist' programme has failed to pay off on its promises (Giddens 1995; Lemert 1995; Wallerstein 1996). The social sciences neither have developed anything vaguely resembling the promised causal, predictive 'science' of society, nor has their subfield, the policy sciences, been able to provide indisputably effective solutions to pressing social and economic problems (Baumol 1991; deLeon 1988).

The recognition of these shortcomings, however, has not meant that all of the positivist inclinations that gave rise to the initial efforts to create a causal

This chapter is a revised version of a paper that was published in *Policy Studies Journal*, 26(1): 129–146.

science of society have vanished. While it is common for mainstream social scientists to argue that their post-positivist critics pick on a straw man – that no modern-day social scientists would recognize themselves in the caricature – the criticism misses the mark on two fronts. First, positivist-oriented social and political research remains very much alive in important quarters, rational choice theory being the most important example. Indeed rational choice, especially as borrowed from or practised by economics, is clearly on the ascendancy. It now constitutes one of the most popular theoretical orientations in political science and sociology.

Equally important is the second point. Although few describe themselves as positivists in traditional terms, many of positivism's basic tenets are still well embedded in both our research practices and institutional decision processes. Emphasis on an empirical conceptualization of reality, at the expense of the normative sides of social life, coupled with neo-positivist concepts of objectivity, the separation of facts and values and value neutrality, are still very much the kinds of things that social scientists are expected to take seriously in one form or another. They are not only the sorts of things that graduate students at most of the leading universities are compelled to acknowledge, if not respect – they still reflect the sort of understanding of social science that is explicitly or implicitly on offer to the public. Moreover, it represents the kind of empiricist language that the funders of social science research look for in the grant applications they consider. To believe that such practices have no effect on the way social scientists look at the world is to fail to understand the sociology of social science. Most troublesome, though, these positivist residuals continue to impede the effort to get on with the pressing task of developing the alternative post-positivist practices that better speak to what are the broader needs of contemporary social policy. Even if we were to adopt the view that the empiricist practices of positivism need no longer be taken seriously, we would still be left with the task of articulating the alternative conception of social and political knowledge that should replace it. It is to this task that the present discussion seeks to contribute.

Those who have recognized and acknowledged the failures of policy analysis have spelled it out in different ways. In policy studies, one of the most important approaches has been to speak of the search for a 'value-critical' policy science capable of generating 'usable knowledge'. Or, stated more concretely, these scholars have asked: How can we keep the endless flow of research reports from gathering dust in the file cabinet? Writers such as Rein (1976), Lindblom and Cohen (1979), Forester (1993b), Dryzek (1990b) and Fischer (1995) have devoted considerable thought to the question of what a socially relevant post-positivist alternative might look like.

None of these writers argues that the social sciences have had no impact on public issues. To the contrary, the influence of social science is everywhere to be found in contemporary political discourse. But the role has been more to *stimulate* the political processes of policy deliberation than to provide answers or solutions to the problems facing modern societies. While such deliberation is generally acknowledged to be important to effective policy development, this 'enlightenment function' is not the analytic mission the policy sciences have set for themselves (Weiss 1990). More ambitiously, the policy sciences have traditionally dedicated themselves to the development of methods and practices designed to *settle* rather than stimulate debates. Here I shall argue that this traditional understanding of the policy-analytic role represents an epistemological misunderstanding of the relation of knowledge to politics. Further, I argue that the continued reliance on the narrow methodological perspective that informs this orientation hinders the field's ability to do what it can – and should – do: improve the quality of policy argumentation in public deliberation.

To this end, the chapter proceeds in four parts. The first part briefly identifies the problematic epistemological features of empiricist practices. Next is outlined the theoretical origins of the search for a 'post-positivist' or 'postempiricist' approach to social science generally.[1] Thirdly, it examines more explicitly the postempiricist alternative. Such social science is based on a turn from the dominant emphasis on rigorous empirical proof and verification to a discursive, contextual understanding of social knowledge and the interpretative methods basic to acquiring it. Instead of merely suggesting postempiricism as an alternative epistemological orientation, this 'argumentative turn' is offered as a better description of what social scientists already do (Fischer and Forester 1993). Finally, drawing these strands together, section four examines the more concrete implications of the approach for policy inquiry. Rather than altogether rejecting the empirical methods of the social sciences, the chapter argues that the issue is how to situate them within the context of normative concerns that give their findings meaning. It concludes with a discussion of the implications of a postempiricist policy analysis for the practice of deliberative governance.

Mainstream policy analysis: empiricism and its technocratic practices

Neo-positivism supplies the empiricist ideals of the social and policy sciences (Hawkesworth 1988). Positivism, a theory of knowledge initially put forth to explain the concepts and methods of the physical and natural sciences, lives on

---

[1] There is no standard definition of 'postempiricism' or 'post-positivism'. Most fundamentally, it is grounded in the idea that reality exists, but can never be fully understood or explained, given both the multiplicity of causes and effects and the problem of social meaning. Objectivity can serve as an ideal, but requires a critical community of interpreters. Critical of empiricism, it emphasizes the social construction of theory and concepts, and qualitative approaches to the discovery of knowledge (Guba 1990). McCarthy (1978) has defined the task of developing a post-positivist methodology of social inquiry as figuring out how to combine the practice of political and social theory with the methodological rigour of modern science.

in modified form as 'neo-positivism', a term designed to acknowledge various reforms and correctives in the theory and practice of positivism. It undergirds the contemporary pursuit in the social sciences for a body of knowledge empirically organized as replicable causal generalizations (Fay 1975). Most easily identified as the principles spelled out, both explicitly and tacitly, in the research methodology textbook, this 'empiricist' orientation emphasizes empirical research designs, the use of sampling techniques and data gathering procedures, the quantitative measurement of outcomes and the development of causal models with predictive power (Bobrow and Dryzek 1987; Miller 1991). Sliding over or ignoring the normative sides of inquiry, such an orientation is manifested in policy analysis through quasi-experimental research designs, multiple regression analysis, survey research, input–output studies, cost–benefit analysis, operations research, mathematical simulation models, forecasting, and systems analysis (Putt and Springer 1989; Sylvia, Meier and Gunn 1991).

As leading empiricists such as Sabatier and Jenkins-Smith (1993: 231) and Hofferbert (1990) argue, the only reliable approach to knowledge accumulation is empirical falsification through objective hypothesis-testing of rigorously formulated causal generalizations. The goal is to generate a body of empirical generalizations capable of explaining behaviour across social and historical contexts, whether communities, societies or cultures, independently of specific times, places or circumstances. Not only are such propositions essential to social and political explanation, they are seen to make possible effective solutions to societal problems. Such propositions are said to supply the cornerstones of both theoretical progress and successful policy interventions.

Underlying this effort is a fundamental positivist principle emphasizing the need to separate facts from values, the principle of the 'fact–value dichotomy' (Bernstein 1976; Proctor 1991). According to the most rigorous interpretation of the principle, empirical research is to proceed independently of normative context or implications. Because only empirically based causal knowledge can qualify social science as a genuine 'scientific' endeavour, social scientists are instructed to eschew normative orientations and to limit their research investigations to empirical or 'factual' phenomena. Even though adherence to this 'fact–value dichotomy' varies considerably in the conduct of actual research, at the methodological level the separation still reigns in the social sciences. To be judged as methodologically valid, empirical research must at least officially pay its respects to the principle (Fischer 1980).

In the policy sciences the attempt to separate facts and values has facilitated a technocratic form of policy analysis that emphasizes the efficiency and effectiveness of means to achieve politically established goals. Much of policy analysis, in this respect, has sought to translate inherently normative political and social issues into technically defined ends to be pursued through administrative means. In an effort to sidestep goal–value conflicts typically associated with policy issues, economic and social problems are interpreted as issues in need of improved management and programme design; their solutions are to be found in the technical applications of the policy sciences (Amy 1987a). Often associated with this orientation has been a belief in the superiority of scientific decision-making. Reflecting a subtle antipathy towards democratic processes, terms such as 'pressures' and 'expedient adjustments' are used to denigrate pluralistic policymaking. If politics doesn't fit into the methodological scheme, then politics is the problem. Some have even argued that the political system itself must be changed to better accommodate policy analysis (Heineman et al. 1990).

In the face of limited empirical successes, empiricists have had to give some ground. Although they continue to stress rigorous empirical research as the long-run solution to their failures, they have had to retreat from their more ambitious efforts (Peters 1998). Today their goal is more typically stated as aiming for propositions that are at least *theoretically* provable at some future point in time. An argument propped up by the promise of computer advances, it serves to keep the original epistemology in tack. But the modification misses the point, as postempiricists are quick to point out. The failure to make such scientific progress is more fundamentally rooted in the empiricist's misunderstanding of the nature of the *social* rather than in a lack of empirical rigour. As we shall see, it is a misunderstanding lodged in the very concept of a generalizable, neutral objectivity that empiricists seek to reaffirm and more intensively apply.

Postempiricism: theoretical foundations

The postempiricist challenge is rooted in developments in the natural sciences, the history and sociology of science and contemporary cultural studies. With regard to the natural sciences, the advent of quantum mechanics and chaos theory in physics and evolutionary theory in the biological sciences have led growing numbers of scientists to reject the Parmenidean worldview in favour of the Heraclitean conception of flux (Toulmin 1990).[2] In short, the traditional understanding of the *physical* world as a stable or fixed entity is no longer adequate. For neo-positivist empiricists, this poses a fundamental problem: they lose its firm epistemological anchor.

On the heels of these discoveries arrived new historical and sociological observations about the nature of scientific practices. From these postempiricist studies we have learned that both the origins and practices of modern science

---

[2] Such research has also led some physicists to argue that the explanation of the behaviour of a particle depends in significant part on the vantage point from which it is observed (Galison 1997). That is, in explaining important aspects of the physical world, *where* you stand can influence *what* you see. Relatedly, chaos theory has demonstrated that an infinitesimal change in any part of a system can trigger a transformation of the system at large (Gleick 1987; Kelllert 1993).

are rooted as much in social and historical considerations as they are in the disinterested pursuit of truth. Historical studies of science, for example, have shown the origins of positivist epistemology to be a response to the ways in which the Reformation and the religious wars of the fifteenth and sixteenth centuries destroyed the foundations of certainty, dictated up to that time by the Church (Wagner 1995). In an effort to establish a new basis for the determination of truth, which could serve as a new foundation for social stability, Descartes and his followers sought to anchor knowledge to the confirmation of empirical experience.

Revealing the interplay of these social and technical concerns, critical historians of science have not only shown how what we call knowledge is socially conditioned, but also how other historical periods have defined knowledge in quite different ways. In short, having emerged to address problems in a specific socio-historical context, neo-positivist epistemology is not necessarily relevant to all other contexts. That is, it should *not* be taken as a universal grounding for scientific practice as a whole. Its historical role in the development of modern industrial society and its contemporary technocratic variant, postindustrial society, in no way offsets the point. Rather, it demonstrates how a particular conception of knowledge can condition or mediate the very shape of societal development.

Cultural analysts have extended these studies to show the way in which social science has been dominated by specific conceptions of race, class and gender. Particularly important in this respect have been feminist studies of epistemology which show the ways in which both the theory and practice of scientific research has often been shaped by the masculine worldview (Fox-Keller 1985). Similarly, cultural theorists have shown how western understandings of science and technological progress have often ignored or neglected non-western understandings of social relations and their implications for appropriate development strategies (Wallerstein 1996: 51–57).

Beyond the historical and cultural dimensions, sociological investigation has shown the elements of empirical inquiry – from observation and hypothesis formation through data collection and explanation – to be grounded in the theoretical assumptions of the socio-cultural practices through which they are developed (Rouse 1987). Detailed scrutiny of research practices turns up something quite at odds with the conventional view of the lone, disinterested scientist in the laboratory struggling to uncover the objective laws of nature (Knorr-Cetina and Mulkay 1983; Latour and Woolgar 1979). Time and time again sociological research has documented the extent to which science is as much a socio-cultural activity as a technical enterprise. Indeed, full understanding of scientific findings is impossible without the socio-cultural settings which give them purpose and meaning. From Woolgar (1988) and Collins (1985) to Foucault (1980) and Latour (1987), scientific inquiry is recognized as a social practice contextually mediated through symbolic means.[3] Its knowledge emerges as a socio-technical construction set in ongoing specific historical and linguisitic contexts of conjecture and refutation (Gottweis 1998). Scientific accounts have to be understood as explanations proffered by a specific community of inquirers situated in particular places and times.

None of this means that science, whether physical or social, should not be taken seriously. It means rather that the thing we call science has to be understood as a more subtle interaction between physical and social factors. Whatever constitutes scientific truth at any particular time has to be seen as more than the product of empirically confirmed experiments and tests. Such truths are better described as scientific *interpretations* or *beliefs* based on an amalgam of technical and social judgments. In some cases, the technical judgments are more decisive than in others, but both technical and social considerations are always involved (with the mix between the two remaining a question to be empirically examined case by case). Influenced by many more factors than the mere pursuit of truth, such claims have to be understood as the relative product of a community of practitioners who establish the evidential criteria and guide the research processes through which truth claims are decided. The communities that render these opinions, as historical and sociological analysis makes clear, constitute hierarchies of practitioners organized in significant part around their own internal power structures, interests and status claims (Kuhn 1970).

Such studies also help us to recognize that scientific communities are not the only bodies capable of making judgments about the same reality. From competing perspectives, alternative groups grounded in other forms of rationality can make valid judgments about the same phenomena. Historically, the determination of whose rationality prevails has largely been decided by those wielding the most influence or power. Invariably these determinations are subject to future challenges and new technical findings have always played an important role in such confrontations. But their role has generally been mediated by changing beliefs. Contrary to the official story, new findings alone have seldom been decisive from the outset. The advance of knowledge, in short, cannot be understood as a linear process driven by the better experiment.

---

[3] From such investigations we have come to see the degree to which the application of scientific methods to particular problems involves social and practical judgments. The model form of the experiment, for example, proves to be more than a matter of applying a causal research design to a given reality. As often as not, as Latour has shown, reality is discovered to be fitted to the empirical instrument. In some cases, scientists get their results by identifying and organizing those parts of reality that are amenable to the research design. In other cases, they go beyond such selection processes to restructure the social context (Rouse 1987). Given such considerations, a proper assessment of research results has to go beyond an appraisal of empirical data to an examination of the practical judgments that shape both the instrument and the object. Although such judgments structure and guide the research process, they are almost never part of the research paper. The formal write-up of the results is organized to conform to the official judgment-free logic of science.

From this perspective, facts, in the natural as well as the social world, depend upon underlying assumptions and meanings. What is taken to be a fact is in effect the decision of a particular community of inquirers who work within a set of theoretical presuppositions to which they subscribe. Customarily, of course, we simply accept a particular view of the world; the presuppositions that undergird it seldom come into play. This makes it possible, at least most of the time, to treat large parts of the world as natural and given. While such an organization of reality facilitates communication and understanding between social actors, it cannot serve as an adequate basis for social research. Beyond seeking to explain a 'given' reality, social science must also attempt to explain how social groups construct their own understandings of that reality. Not only do such constructions constitute the most basic level of social action, their implications are fundamental to an understanding of the processes of social change, without which we would have little need for social science. The failures of social science can in significant part be attributed to the neglect of these subjective processes.

Nowhere are the implications of this critique more important than in the study of politics and public policy. As the network of presupposed assumptions underlying social and political propositions are reflections of particular social arrangements, the assumptions are themselves influenced by politics and power. Not only is one of the basic goals of politics to change an existing reality, much of what is important in the struggle turns on the socio-political determination of the assumptions that define it. As many scholars have made clear, policy politics is itself about establishing definitions of and assigning meaning to social problems (Edelman 1988; Gusfield 1981). Thus, the effort to exclude meaning and values from the work of the policy analyst cuts the very heart out of political inquiry. Empiricism, in its search for such objective generalizations, has sought to detach itself from the very social contexts that can give its data meaning.

Seen in this light, empirical findings can at best be relevant only to the particular socio-historical understanding of reality from which they are abstracted. Moreover, empiricism's attempt empirically to fix a given set of social and political arrangements tends to reify a particular reality. By neglecting or diverting attention from the struggles to challenge and change such arrangements, social science – wittingly or unwittingly – serves as much to provide ideological support for a configuration of power as it does to explain it.

Both the interpretative nature of the social object and the meaning of the empirical findings themselves render neo-positivist science an easy target for those who wish to dispute the validity of specific experiments or object to particular claims. At best, such research can offer a rigorous and persuasive argument for accepting a conclusion. But such an argument cannot prove the issue. Those who dispute a claim can easily find problems in the myriad social and technical interpretations and assumptions embedded in both the research design and practice. Nowhere is this more obvious than in the endless confrontations over the validity of claims made by environmental scientists. Such disputes have given rise to a full-scale politics of 'counter-expertise' (Fischer 1995). Working with the *same* findings, groups on both sides of an issue easily construct their own alternative interpretations of the evidence.

This is not to say that it is never worth carrying out an empirical test. The post-positivist objective is not to reject the scientific project altogether, but to recognize the need properly to understand what we are doing when we engage in any form of research. Postempiricism, in this respect, can be explained as an attempt to understand and reconstruct that which we are already doing when we engage in scientific inquiry. Recognizing reality to be a social construction, the focus necessarily shifts to the nature of situational context and to the discursive processes which shape the construction. We turn at this point more specifically to the alternative understanding.

Postempiricism: from proof to discourse

In view of this sociology of scientific practices, postempiricism focuses on science's *account* of reality rather than on reality itself. Which is not to argue there are no real and separate objects of inquiry independent of the investigators. It is not the objects or their properties per se, but rather the vocabularies and concepts used to know and represent them that are socially constructed by human beings. Scientific accounts are produced by observers with different ideational frameworks, types of educational training, research experiences, perceptual capacities etc. The goal is to understand how these varying cognitive elements interact to discursively shape that which comes to be taken as knowledge. Toward this end, postempiricism's reconstruction of the scientific process is founded on a 'coherence' theory of reality that emphasizes the finite and temporally bounded character of knowledge (Brown 1977; Stockman 1983).

In contrast to correspondence theory, which sees scientific concepts as direct referents of reality, coherence theory addresses the indeterminacy of empirical propositions.[4] Seeking to describe a world that is richer and more complex

---

[4] On the 'correspondence theory' of truth see Lincoln and Guba (1985: 22). As they put it, 'The scientist . . . can capture the external facts of the world in propositions that are true if they correspond to the facts and false if they do not. Science is idealistically a linguistic system in which true propositions are in one-to-one relation to facts, including facts that are not directly observed because they involve hidden entities and/or properties, or past events or far distant events.' The truth of a proposition is established through deduction, following upon certain assumptions. Rational choice theory, based on 'given' assumptions about rational action, is the most rigorous contemporary representative of this 'hypothetico-deductive model' of explanation. 'Coherence theory', by contrast, judges the truth of a proposition in terms of its fit (or coherence) with experience as a whole. Unlike correspondence theory, coherence theory insists on investigating and rendering judgments on the 'givens'. A classical example of a coherence concept of reality is Marx's analysis of the concept 'commodity'. Following Hegel, he provides an analysis of the social roots, meaning and role of the term as it is situated in the larger context of capitalism.

than the empiricist theories constructed to explain it, coherence theory seeks to capture and incorporate the multiplicity of theoretical perspectives and explanations that bear on a particular event or phenomenon. To use Toulmin's (1982: 113) words, postempiricist coherence theory seeks to bring to bear 'the range and scope of interpretative standpoints that have won a place'. Alongside quantitative analysis, the postempiricist orientation includes the historical, comparative, philosophical and phenomenological perspectives. Quantitative empirical research, in the process, loses its privileged claim among modes of inquiry. While it remains an important component of theory construction, it no longer offers the crucial test.

Given the perspectival nature of the categories through which social and political phenomena are observed, knowledge of a social object or phenomenon emerges from a discursive interaction – or dialectical clash – of competing interpretations. Whereas consensus for the empiricist is inductively anchored to the reproduction of empirical tests and statistical confirmation, consensus under postempiricism is approached through the discursive construction of a synthesis of competing views (Danziger 1995). For postempiricists, the empirical data is turned into knowledge through interpretative interaction with other perspectives. Only by examining such data through conflicting frameworks can the presuppositions that give it meaning be uncovered. For the postempiricist, the crucial debates in politics are seldom over data per se, but rather over the underlying assumptions that organize them. Such deliberations produce new understandings in a process better framed as a 'learned conversation' than the pursuit of empirical proof. Emphasis shifts from the narrow concerns of empirical-analytic theory to the development of 'a rich perspective' on human affairs (Toulmin 1990: 27).

Knowledge, in this evolving conversation, is more accurately understood as consensually 'accepted belief' than as proof or demonstration (Paller 1989). Such beliefs emerge through an interpretative forging of theoretical assumptions, analytical criteria and empirical tests discursively warranted by scholarly communities (Laudan 1977). With one decisive exception, this description is consistent with the neo-postempiricist understanding of the process. Instead of understanding these beliefs as the empirical outcomes of intersubjectively reliable tests, the postempiricist sees them as the product of a chain of interpretative judgments, both social and technical, arrived at by researchers in particular times and places (Bernstein 1983). From this perspective, social scientific theories can be understood as assemblages of theoretical presuppositions, empirical data, research practices, interpretative judgments, voices and social strategies (DeLeuze and Guatani 1988). One of the primary strengths of a theory, in this respect, is its ability to establish discursive connections and contrive equivalences between otherwise disparate elements, as well incorporating new components.

While the methodological principles of a postempiricist social science can-not be as firmly fixed as those of neo-positivism, such research does not lack rigour. In many ways, the adoption of a multimethodological approach opens the door to a more subtle and complex form of rigour. Instead of narrowly concentrating on the rules of research design and statistical analysis (which too often passes for empirical rigour), the postempiricist framework involves the exercise of a multimethodological range of intellectual criteria, both qualitative and quantitative. Basic is the recognition that an epistemology which defines knowledge and rationality in terms of technique, be it logical deduction or em-pirical falsification, is simply too narrow to encompass the multiple forms of reason manifested in scientific practices. The interpretative judgments that are characteristic of every phase of scientific investigation, as well as the cumula-tive weighing of evidence and argument, are too rich and varied to be captured by the rules governing inductive or deductive logic (Collins 1992). For this reason, postempiricism substitutes the formal logic of neo-positivism with the informal deliberative framework of practical reason.[5]

Formal logic is thus too confining for a methodology that needs to mean-ingfully combine quantitative and qualitative orientations into a new method-ological configuration. We turn at this point to the postempiricist alternative emphasizing informal logic and practical discourse.

Practical reason as reasoning-in-context

The postempiricist alternative is grounded in the recognition that the formal models of deductive and inductive reason misrepresent both the scientific and practical modes of reason. As Scriven (1987) writes, 'the classical models of reasoning provide inadequate and in fact seriously misleading accounts of most practical and academic reasoning – the reasoning of the kitchen, surgery and workshop, the law courts, paddock, office and battlefield; and of the disciplines'.

---

[5] It is important to note that in recent years some attention has been given to these qualitative con-cerns. For example, a number of leading empiricists have begun to concede ground to qualitative methods. In particular, the work of King, Koehane and Verba (1994) has generated a good deal of discussion. Given that quantitative social scientists have long denied or denigrated the validity of qualitative methods, interpretative theorists have some reason for optimism. But it can only be a qualified optimism. While acknowledging qualitative methods, authors such as King et al. have sought only to incorporate them on terms amenable to the logic of empiricist research. That is, qualitative research has to be designed and conducted in such a way as to render its results empirically testable. While qualitative research can indeed serve as a corrective or a corroborative perspective for the mainstream project and its problems, the approach offered by King, Koehane and Verba misunderstands qualitative research. More than just another way of collecting data, such interpretative research, as we have seen, rests on an altogether different epistemological understanding of social reality and its construction. To the degree that social constructivism accurately conceptualizes social explanation, this attempt to neo-positivize qualitative research only reproduces the very problems it has set out to solve. These new efforts, as such, are best understood as one more effort to patch up the cracks in a troubled enterprise.

Nor is most of such reason best interpreted as an *incomplete* version of the deductive reasoning of logic or mathematics, long the standard interpretation of social scientific explanation. They are more appropriately conceptualized as forms of informal logic with their own rules and procedures. In pursuit of an alternative methodological framework, postempiricists have returned to the Aristotelian conception of *phronesis*, or the informal logic of practical reason.

Informal logic, designed to probe both the incompleteness and imprecision of existing knowledge, reconceptualizes our understanding of evidence and verification in investigations that have been either neglected or mistreated by formal logics (Scriven 1987). Countering social science's emphasis on generalizations, informal logic probes the argument-as-given rather than attempting to fit or reconstruct it into the abstracted, confining frameworks of deduction and induction. Toward this end, it emphasizes an assessment of the problem in its particular context, seeking to decide which approaches are most relevant to the inquiry at hand.

By expanding the scope of reasoned argumentation, the informal logic of practical reason offers a framework for developing a multimethodological perspective. Most fundamental to practical reason is the recognition that the kinds of arguments relevant to different issues depend on the nature of those issues: what is reasonable in clinical medicine or jurisprudence is judged in terms different from what is 'logical' in geometrical theory or physics (Toulmin 1990). Basic to such judgment is a sensitivity to the contextual circumstances of an issue or problem. Practical reason, as such, distinguishes contextually between the world of theory, the mastery of techniques and the experiential wisdom needed to put techniques to work in concrete cases. In doing so, it supplies a conception of reason that more accurately corresponds to the forms of rationality exhibited in real-world policy analysis and implementation, concerns inherently centred around an effort to connect theory and techniques to concrete cases.

Practical deliberation thus seeks to bring a wider range of evidence and arguments to bear on the particular problem or position under investigation. As Hawkesworth (1988) explains, 'the reasons offered in support of alternatives marshal evidence, organize data, apply various criteria of explanation, address multiple levels of analysis with varying degrees of abstraction, and employ divergent strategies of argument'. But the reasons given to support 'the rejection of one theory do not constitute absolute proof of the validity of an alternative theory'. Through the processes of deliberation and debate, a consensus emerges among particular researchers concerning what will be taken as valid explanation. Although the choice is sustained by reasons that can be articulated and advanced as support for the inadequacy of alternative interpretations, it is the practical judgment of the community of researchers and not the data themselves that establishes the accepted explanation. Such practical judgments, rather than supposed reliance on proof unto itself, provides the mechanism for not only identifying the incompetent charlatan, but investigating the more subtle errors in our sophisticated approximations of reality. To be sure, practical reason cannot guarantee the eternal verity of particular conclusions, but the social rationality of the process is far from haphazard or illogical. Most important, it supplies us with a way of probing the much neglected contextual dependence of most forms of argumentation (Scriven 1987).

As a contextual mode of reason, practical reason takes place within a hermeneutic 'circle of reason' (Bernstein 1983). To probe specific propositions requires that others must be held constant. Such analysis, however, always occurs within a context of reference grounded in other sets of presuppositions. Moving outside of each framework to examine it from yet new frames permits the inquirer to step beyond the limits of his or her own languages and theories, past experiences and expectations. This increases the number of relevant perspectives, but need not lead to a hopeless relativism, as is often thought. Because the hermeneutic process is typically initiated by external stimuli in the object-oriented world, critical interpretations are 'world-guided' and can never be altogether detached from concrete experience (Williams 1985: 145).

That is, in the words of Bernstein (1983: 135), the process 'is "object" oriented in the sense that it directs us to the texts, institutions, practices, or forms of life that we are seeking to understand'. Such empirical stimuli cannot compel definitive interpretations, as the empiricist would have us believe, but they do work to limit the number of plausible interpretations. While the possibility of multiple interpretations remains, there are thus boundaries or limits to what can count. An interpretation that bears no plausible relationship to the object-world has to be rejected.

Given the limits imposed by fallibility and contingency, the informal probative logic of practical reason speaks directly to the kinds of questions confronted in most political and policy inquiry. Bringing together the full range of cognitive strategies employed in such inquiry, it judges both the application and results of such methods in terms of the contexts to which they are applied. Recognizing social context to be a theoretical construct, as well as the underdetermination of our available knowledge, practical deliberation focuses on the competing understandings of a particular problem and the range of methods appropriate to investigate them. Framing the analysis around the underlying presuppositions, postempiricist analysis seeks to anticipate and draw out the multiple interpretations that bear on the explanation of social and political propositions.

Policy-analytic implications: the empirical in normative context

The kinds of epistemological concerns presented above are quite different from those normally encountered in policy analysis and not at all well received in some quarters. In most cases the critical question raised rests with the status of the empirical: what happens to empirical research in a discursive approach? Although many postempiricist writers have not been clear enough on this question, one point is certain – a discursive model of policy inquiry must include empirical investigation. Indeed, rather than rejecting the empirical, the issue here concerns its relationship to the normative. How the empirical is situated in a larger set of normative concerns that give its findings meaning is the question that must be addressed.

What, then, does it mean to say that policy analysis should embrace this discursive or 'argumentative turn' (Fischer and Forester 1993)? From science studies we learn that scientific conclusions are in fact arguments designed to convince other scientists to see a particular phenomenon one way or another. Although findings are traditionally put forth in the language of empirical verification – advanced as evidence that a proposition is true or false – quantitative data are only a part of a broader set of factors that go into structuring the conclusion. As we have discussed earlier, behind these conclusions are a multitude of interpretative judgments, both social and technical. The conclusion as a whole can in fact be better understood as an argument rather than an inductive or deductive proof.

What does it mean for policy analysis to say that its social-scientific conclusions are arguments? One of the first policy scholars to call for such a reorientation is Majone. The structure of a policy argument, Majone (1989: 63) writes, is typically a complex blend of factual statements, interpretations, opinion and evaluation. The argument provides the links connecting data and information with the conclusions of an analysis. Having recognized the epistemological shift, however, Majone has not sufficiently clarified the normative dimensions that intervene between findings and conclusions. From the preceding discussion we can now formulate the task as a matter of establishing interconnections among the empirical data, normative assumptions (that structure our understanding of the social world), the interpretative judgments involved in the data collection process, the particular circumstances of a situational context (in which the findings are generated and/or to which the conclusions apply), and the specific conclusions. The acceptability of the conclusions ultimately depends on the full range of interconnections, not just the empirical findings. While neo-positivists argue that their approach is more rigorous and therefore superior to less empirical, less deductive methods, this model of policy argumentation actually makes the task more demanding and complex. Not only does it encompass the logic of empirical falsification, it includes the equally sophisticated normative questions within which it operates. The researcher still collects the data, but now has to situate or include it in the interpretative framework that gives it meaning. No longer is it possible to contend that such normative investigations can be ignored, as if they somehow relate to another field of inquiry.

Elsewhere I have suggested a multimethodological framework for integrating these concerns. In *Evaluating Public Policy*, I have offered a logic of four interrelated discourses that outline the concerns of a more comprehensively rational policy evaluation (Fischer 1995). Extending from the concrete questions concerning the efficiency of a programme up through its situational context and the societal system to the abstract normative questions concerning the impact of a policy on a particular way of life, the scheme illustrates how empirical concerns can be brought to bear on the full range of normative questions.

Towards a policy science of democracy: institutions and practices

Beyond the issues of methodology, the postempiricist model of practical deliberation has important implications for transforming institutional policymaking and the practices of governance more generally. Most important is its potentially democratizing influence on policy evaluation, an idea not as unique as it might sound. Although policy analysis has primarily emerged as a technocratic discipline, the concern for democracy has always been present. Indeed, as early as 1951 Lasswell put the discipline forward as the 'policy science of democracy'. Postempiricism is an effort to make good on that claim. In this closing section, we examine some of the larger normative and political issues that frame this effort.

First, a deliberative model of policy analysis extends the analytic goal beyond the technical efficiency of the governing institutions to include an assessment of the political interests and needs of the larger political community. From this perspective, the political community is inhabited by citizens who 'live in a web of interdependencies, loyalties, and associations' in which 'they envision and fight for the public interest as well as their individual interests' (Stone 1988: vii). Unlike most contemporary policy analysis, the postempiricism approach would not 'take individual preferences as "given"... but would instead have to account for where people get their images of the world and how they shape their preferences'. That is, in contrast to the mainstream approach which provides no meaningful way of talking about how people fight over visions of the public or community interest, a postempiricist approach emphasizes discourse as 'a creative and valuable feature of social existence' (Stone 1988: 4). Ideas thus move to the centre of policy evaluation. They are the fundamental media of all political conflicts; they make possible the shared meanings and assumptions that motivate people to action and weld individual striving into collective causes (Reich 1988). Policymaking, based on strategically crafted arguments, is thus reconceived as a constant struggle over the very ideas that guide the ways citizens and policy analysts think and behave, the boundaries of political categories, and the criteria of classification – what John Forester and I have elsewhere called the 'politics of criteria' (Fischer and Forester 1987). Basic to this approach must be the recognition that analytical concepts are themselves based on political claims and cannot be granted privileged status.

Because policy ideas are arguments that favour different ways of seeing and relating to social problems, their evaluation must include an assessment of their transformational impacts on the thought and deliberations of the political community. The enduring ideas of politics, offering criteria into which citizens read competing meanings, serve as measures against which community aspirations are interpreted and judged. The job of the deliberative analyst is to tease out the normative conflicts lurking behind the often equally plausible interpretations of the same abstract goal or value. In the process, various modes of defining policy problems have to be recognized as competing languages in which people offer and defend conflicting interpretations (Danziger 1995; Stone 1988). In particular, attention has to be paid to context. As Healey writes, 'knowledge for action, principles of action, and ways of knowing are actively constituted in the particularities of time and place'. 'Good' and 'right' actions are 'those we can come to agree on, in particular times and places, across our diverse differences in material conditions and wants, moral perspectives, and expressive cultures and inclinations'. The fundamental goal of such policy analysis can be reformulated as discovering ways of 'living together differently but respectfully' (Healey 1993: 238).

Especially important, in this view, is the need to rethink the relationships of the roles of the analysts, citizens and the decision-makers. As critical studies of social epistemology make clear, a more sophisticated understanding of the nature of an open and democratic exchange must confront the need to bring these roles together in a mutual exploration. Experts must establish a participatory or collaborative relationship with the citizen/client (Hawkesworth 1988; Healey 1997; Schön 1983). Methodologically, an approach capable of facilitating the kind of open discussion essential to a participatory context is needed. Such a method would provide a format and a set of procedures for organizing the interactions between policy experts and the lay citizens that they seek to assist. Albeit in quite different ways, writers such as deLeon (1992), Durning (1993), Laird (1993) and Fischer (1990) have called for such a 'participatory policy analysis'.

In this formulation, the expert serves as 'facilitator' of public learning and political empowerment, a concept that is not as strange as it might sound. In many ways, the practice can be interpreted as an extension of Dewey's argument in his book, *The Public and Its Problems* (1927), which sought to rejuvenate the possibility of democratic governance in a mass industrial society by calling on experts to facilitate public learning. The practice of facilitation and participatory policy inquiry more generally, as I argue in *Citizens, Experts, and the Environment: The Politics of Local Knowledge* (2001), can be seen as the practical implication of Dewey's political-theoretical argument. It would be a central practice of deliberative governance in a contemporary network society of the type envisioned by Hajer and Wagnaar in the Introduction.

Rather than providing technical answers designed to bring political discussions to an end, the task of the analyst-as-facilitator is to assist citizens in their efforts to examine their own interests and to make their own decisions (Caldwell 1975; Fischer 2001). The facilitator seeks to integrate the process of evaluation with the empirical requirements of technical analysis. Bringing together the analytical perspectives of social science and the competing normative arguments of the relevant participant in the policymaking process, the interaction can be likened to a conversation in which the horizons of both citizens and social scientists are extended through a mutual dialogue (Dryzek 1982).

The facilitation of citizen learning can be understood as enlarging the citizen/clients' abilities to pose the problems and questions that interest and concern them and to help connect them to the kinds of information and resources needed to help them (Brookfield 1986: 1–24). As a technique of empowerment and self-help, facilitation is defined as challenging learners with different ways of examining and interpreting their experience and presenting them with ideas and behaviours that assist them in critically exploring political issues in terms of their own ways of acting, their value systems and the assumptions by which they live. The assignment is to understand the conditions for citizen learning and to design and enable the setting within which citizens develop their own policy positions. Towards this end, professional experts must become specialists in how clients learn, clarify and decide. Emphasis is placed on creating the institutional conditions within which citizens draw on their own abilities and resources to solve their own problems. Essential to the practice, then, is the creation of institutional and intellectual conditions that help people to pose questions in their own ordinary (or everyday) languages and to decide the issues important to themselves.[6]

One approach to such a facilitative orientation has been called the 'counsel model'. Designed to outline a postempiricist concept of objectivity, Jennings (1987a) has put the model forward to reshape the relationship of policy analysts to both citizens and policymakers. The goal is to encourage a conversation with

---

[6] The central focus of such 'inquiring systems' is a process called 'problematization'. Problematization, as developed by Paulo Freire (1970), is the antithesis of technocratic problem-solving, seen 'to distort the totality of human experience'. Rather than reducing human experience to those dimensions amenable to treatment as mere difficulties to be solved, 'problematizing' helps people codify into symbols an integrated picture or story of reality that, in the course of its development, can generate a critical consciousness capable of empowering them to alter their relations to both the physical and social worlds. In the mainstream literature on professional expertise, the writings of Donald Schön (1983) take up the issue of problematization (or 'problem-posing' in his words), which he describes as a 'conversation with the situation'. Focusing in particular on naming situations and defining the problems that arise in them is part of a new postempiricist epistemological orientation sketched out in section three of this discussion.

many voices, adjudicated by the procedural standards of a discourse ethics. Taking this approach, the analyst first seeks 'to grasp the meaning or significance of contemporary problems as they are experienced, adapted to, and struggled against by the reasonable, purposive agents, who are members of the political community'. He or she then works 'to clarify the meaning of those problems' in a way 'that strategically located political agents (public officials or policymakers) will be able to devise a set of efficacious and just solutions to them'. Finally, the analyst attempts to guide 'the selection of one proffered policy from that set in light of a more general vision of the good of the community as a whole, as well as the more discrete interests of the policymakers themselves'. Emphasizing a *procedural* route to policy choice, the model strives to interpret the public interest in a way that can survive an open and undistorted process of deliberation and assessment. Importantly, in the process, *interpreting* the world and *changing* it are understood as complementary endeavours. The analyst-as-counsellor seeks to 'construct an interpretation of present political and social reality that serves not only the intellectual goal of explaining or comprehending that reality, but also the practical goal of enabling constructive action to move the community from a flawed present toward an improved future' (Jennings 1987b: 127).

Concluding remarks

This chapter has examined the postempiricist challenge to the conventional empiricist theory and practices in the social sciences and spelled out its implications for a non-technocratic reorientation of the theory and practice of policy analysis. Whereas empiricists have tried to minimize – if not eliminate – social and interpretative judgments, postempiricists have recognized their basic, constitutive role in any form of analysis. Rather than trying to control or hide their influence by turning to ever-more rigorous empirical research designs, the postempiricist positivist solution brings such judgments to the fore, acknowledging their centrality to the scientific process. For postempiricists there is no loss in terms of the scientific product; they seek only to supply a more accurate description of what is already taken as science. Postempiricism, in this sense, strives to offer a better *empirical* explanation of social scientific process.

Nowhere are the implications of this alternative understanding more important than in the contemporary policy curriculum. Still dominated by an outmoded conception of scientific epistemology, the social and policy sciences ill equip their students (especially doctoral students) for the world they are sent out to confront. Armed with empirical research designs and statistical methods, many often have little or no training in either understanding the normative and interpretative foundations of the tools they have learned to rely upon, or the social settings to which these techniques are to be applied. Some, to be sure, recognize these interpretative dimensions of the practice, but for reasons of examination and employment are compelled to concentrate on empirical methods. As students come to see the limits of these methods, as many do, the disciplinary neglect of these issues and concerns can breed more than a little cynicism. Some are simply turned off; others go through the academic ritual but turn away from – if not against – these methods after jumping over the requisite set of hurdles.

For a long time, the argument against changing the curricular focus has turned on the problem of alternatives. Given the absence of credible alternatives, so the argument has gone, it is better to hang on to the traditional – albeit problematic – methods than to step into a methodological void. But this no longer need be the case. Postempiricism, as we have shown here, outlines the beginnings of a new orientation. Not only does it offer a theory of the social sciences that is readily identifiable in our existing practices, it constitutes an incorporation of new methods and approaches rather than a simple rejection of old ones. By giving new life to our methods and practices, it opens the way to a richer and more productive approach to social and policy inquiry.

Beyond the methodology and curriculum, important implications for professional conduct and public understanding of the practice of science flow from postempiricism's discursive model of inquiry. Holding out the possibility of redeeming or realizing a policy science of democracy, it calls for participatory institutions and practices that open spaces for citizen deliberation on contextual assumptions, empirical outcomes and the social meaning of conclusions. The ultimate success of a postempiricist policy science will depend upon political and institutional reforms. The future of such an approach thus remains bound to progress in the struggle to further democratize political decision-making.

8

Accessing local knowledge
Dvora Yanow

Interpretative policy analysis rests on a long tradition of philosophical argumentation that stands on its own, without reference to positivist argument. Its hallmark is a focus on meaning that is situated in a particular context. The language of 'interpretative' policy analysis underscores the extent to which methodological choices, rather than being a disembodied repertoire of tools and techniques, are grounded in a particular set of epistemological and ontological presuppositions – in this case, those associated with interpretative schools of thought (such as hermeneutics, phenomenology, and some critical theory). This chapter elaborates on the importance to policy analysis of 'local' knowledge relative to a policy issue and sketches out some interpretative research methods for accessing and analysing it.

Policy analysis and communities of meaning

> The construction of diverse meanings for described political events shapes support for causes and legitimizes value allocations. The literature on the place of symbolism in politics explores the creation of meaning through political language and other actions . . . The student of symbolism is interested in how meanings are constructed and changed. Inquiry into the evocation of meanings entails seeing observers and the observed as part of the same

An earlier version of this chapter was presented at the Theory, Policy, and Society Symposium, Leiden University, 24–25, June 1999. I have benefited from subsequent discussions of parts of the argument at seminars at the University of Michigan's ICOS group and Maarten Hajer's group at the University of Amsterdam, and at several presentations among colleagues in the collective organizational learning community of scholars.

transaction rather than as subject and object, and it also recognizes that
values, theories, and facts are integrally intertwined with each other rather
than distinct concepts.

Murray Edelman[1]

The centrality of communities of meaning to policy analysis becomes evident
in what was initially called a 'cultural' approach to public policy processes,
including those organizational actions subsumed under implementation studies
(Yanow 1987, 1990). Such an approach entails an analytic focus on ways in
which policy and implementing agency language, legislative and implementory
acts, and the physical objects through which these are enacted (e.g. their pro-
grammatic vehicles and/or the buildings that house them) communicate meanings to various policy-relevant publics (Yanow 1993, 1996). In this focus,
policies are seen not just as tools for instrumental, goal-oriented, rational action.
Rather, this approach brings into view the ways in which public policies are
modes for the expression of human meaning – as, for example, when they constitute narratives of national identity (Schram and Neisser 1997; Yanow 1999).

'Culture' and 'interpretation': argumentation by metaphor

What was conceptually 'cultural' about such an approach was the situatedness
of what is meaningful to human actors, including the various artefacts embodying these meanings and facilitating their expression and communication. The
relationship is a symbolic one: the more concrete artefacts of language, objects
and/or acts represent the more abstract values, beliefs and/or feelings that comprise human meaning. This orientation towards the symbolic is what puts such
an analysis in the realm of culture, as anthropologists (and cultural or symbolic
anthropologists in particular, such as Clifford Geertz, e.g. 1973) understand
and use that term. This usage of 'culture' invokes more of a process orientation
towards meaning-making than its use in reference to race-ethnic or nationality
groups, where it tends to be a more objectified term, one that imputes a sense
of stability (that lived experience belies). The two denotations are nonetheless
related in that 'cultures'-as-noun are, at the same time, communities of meaning and communities of difference. That is, as the language of 'community'
suggests, they are bounded both by what they share (values, beliefs, feelings
and the artefactual manifestations of those meanings) and by what distinguishes
them from others (often, the self-same meanings and representations).

The focus on meanings and their representations is highly situation-specific:
although symbolic processes are generalizable, what specific artefacts will
represent what specific meanings is tied to the policy in question and its time

---

[1] In the afterword to the 1984 edition of *The Symbolic Uses of Politics* (Edelman 1964), pp. 195,
196.

and place. Such a context-specific, situated approach means that the range of meanings evoked and enacted in a policy situation cannot be pre-specified. That is the point of demarcation between this use of the concept of culture and that of the grid-group analysis developed by Mary Douglas (1982) and applied by her and others to various policy issues (e.g., Douglas and Wildavsky 1982; Ellis and Coyle 1994; Thompson, Ellis and Wildavsky 1990). Grid-group analysis is but one mode of understanding the use of 'culture' in application to policy issues. It retains positivist ontological presuppositions that there is a reality 'out there', external to the researcher, awaiting discovery, and that theory in some way can 'mirror' that reality.[2] It rests on positivism's insistence on universal principles; and by using pre-established, non-situation-specific 'conceptual boxes' into which policy 'nature' is 'forced' (Kuhn 1970: 5), it limits the scope of what can be discovered. To follow the presuppositions of interpretative philosophies and their associated applications, grid-group theory would have to relinquish its predetermined categorization of what is central across all policy issues, in favour of letting context-specific social and policy realities speak for themselves.

Interpretative understandings of policy realities, knowledge and research manifest influences from recent attention (among anthropologists, in particular) to the role of academic (and, by implication, practitioner) writing as a mode of 'worldmaking' (the phrase is Goodman's (1978); see, e.g., Brown 1976; Geertz 1988; Golden-Biddle and Locke 1993, 1997; Marcus and Fischer 1986; McCloskey 1985; van Maanen 1986; Yanow 1998); and to arguments in the philosophy of science (e.g., Kuhn 1970; Latour 1987) and other arenas of the so-called interpretative turn (e.g. Fish 1980; Rabinow and Sullivan 1979). Interpretative approaches have been developed quite widely within organizational studies (see, e.g., Gagliardi 1990; Kunda 1992; Pondy et al. 1983; Smircich 1983; Turner 1990). Within policy studies, Murray Edelman (1964, 1971, 1977) laid the groundwork in exploring the symbolic side of political language and acts. Interpretative approaches share a set of philosophical presuppositions with work that seeks to identify both the frames of reasoning and action that are operative in a given issue arena and the interpretative communities (that is communities of speech, thought, understanding) holding those frames (see, e.g., Chock 1995; Colebatch 1995; Gusfield 1963, 1981; Hofmann 1995; Linder 1995; Luker 1984; Maynard-Moody and Stull 1987; Pal 1995; Rein 1983a; Rein and Schön 1977; Schmidt 1993; Wynne 1992).

These philosophical presuppositions – articulated in some cases, implied in others – entail ontological, epistemological and methodological positions that explicitly draw on, emerge from or are implicitly in sympathy with the arguments of phenomenology, hermeneutics and (some) critical theory

---

[2] See Rorty (1979) on science and theory as the mirror of natural reality.

(see, e.g., Beam and Simpson 1984; Bernstein 1976; Dallmayr and McCarthy 1977; DeHaven-Smith 1988; Dryzek 1982; Fay 1975; Hawkesworth 1988; Healy 1986; Jennings 1983a, 1987; Kelly and Maynard-Moody 1993; Paris and Reynolds 1983; Torgerson 1985, 1986b). This is what makes situated, symbolic, meaning-centred analysis interpretative: its grounding in the life world of the actors in the policy situation (as a phenomenologist would have it), which is to say in situated 'knowers' and situated 'knowns'; its concern with legislative and agency texts and physical objects and acts and practices as 'text-analogues' for analytic-methodological purposes (in a hermeneutic approach; the phrase is Taylor's 1971; see also Ricoeur 1971); and its concern with the mutually (re)productive interactions between meanings and their artefactual representations, including institutions (a view of many critical theorists). It is this situated specificity of meaning that makes 'local' knowledge so central to the enterprise of policy analysis, and hence to its methods.[3] Analysts need to be trained in methods of accessing local knowledge – observing (with whatever degree of participating, as appropriate to the study), conversational (a.k.a. in-depth) interviewing, and close reading of documents – and in various methods of its analysis. This focus on accessing local knowledge moves the analytic enterprise away from the arena of technical expertise towards a more democratic undertaking (see Dryzek 1990b; Schneider and Ingram 1997 on the latter). Interestingly, as we shall see, attention to local knowledge reintroduces the concept of culture and underscores its conceptual utility.

It seemed necessary ten to twenty years ago for rhetorical purposes to draw on the language of 'culture' in designating this approach. The term worked in a metaphoric process, in which meaning is carried by and within words from their 'natural' sources into a new context. The borrowed source meanings, entire or partial, frame the perception of their applied focus. As Lakoff and Johnson (1980) observe, in this way we learn about something new, by drawing on existing knowledge of something known and familiar. It is not unusual for social theories to be informed by metaphorical borrowings, as Brown (1976) has noted. These, in turn, typically shape the reasoning process embedded in the theory, as they contain within them not only logics of description (models *of*) but also logics of prescription for ameliorative action (models *for*). This is particularly true of 'applied' social science, such as public policy analysis, planning and public administration (see Schön 1979 on this, and Miller's 1985 critique). Metaphoric reasoning is common in policy practices as well, serving both as models of prior conceptualizations of the issue and as models for subsequent action in respect of it. Indeed, as Stone (1988) argues, strategic reasoning by analogy – one form of metaphor, according to Miller (1985) – is

---

[3] *Local Knowledge* is also the title of a collection of essays by the anthropologist Clifford Geertz (1983).

the characteristic mode of political debate in the political community. These metaphoric logics of borrowing and application, these models of and models for, are typically not made explicit, either by theorists or by analyst-practitioners.[4] In reflecting on the theoretical argument about a 'cultural' policy analysis, I find the following underlying metaphoric reasoning.

Drawing on its source meanings in anthropology, 'culture' facilitated two modes of conceptualization. First, 'culture' enabled the ontological possibility of treating collectives – communities of meaning, for example – as 'real' for analytic purposes. Borrowing its reality status in anthropology eliminated the need to argue for collective policy activity as the aggregate of individuals – a more psychological approach – allowing for a conception of collective meaning-making to proceed. As Douglas (1986) so rightly noted, rather than seeing society as the individual writ large, we would do well to see the individual as society writ small. The metaphor of culture enables a treatment of public policies as expressions not only of individual meaning but of collective, societal meaning – emphasizing the situatedness of policy substance and process within their societal context – without having to argue that they are the sum of meanings made by each member of the polity.

Second, through the same metaphoric process, the 'culture' term carried meaning-focused, ethnographic methods from their source in cultural anthropology to the realm of policy practices. It facilitated an argument on behalf of methods appropriate for accessing the local knowledge of policy constituents – methods such as observation, participation, conversational interviewing and the close reading of 'local' documents (e.g., agency memos, neighbourhood newsletters) – as well as meaning-focused methods for analysing these data (such as semiotics, ethnomethodology, symbolic interaction, dramaturgy, metaphor analysis, category analysis and so on; see, e.g., Feldman 1994; Yanow 2000a).

In these ways, the culture metaphor implicitly argued for interpretative policy analysis as having the following characteristics: a focus on

- collectives
- and their situated acts (their policy-related practices, including interactions),
- engaging the artefacts (objects) that are the focus of these acts
- and the language used in engaging them,
- together with the site-specific meanings of these various artefacts to the actors engaging them,

---

[4] This was the area of disagreement between Schön and Miller. Schön argued that metaphoric reasoning could be made explicit and thereby eliminated – replaced by clearer thought. Miller argued, in effect, that metaphoric reasoning would always be with us. Following Lakoff and Johnson (1980), I agree with Miller: metaphors pervade thought and, as language is a form of thinking, all language; it is not possible to eliminate them.

- including the non-exclusively-cognitive (such as tacit, kinesthetic, and aesthetic knowledge);
- as well as the site- (or 'field-') based set of interpretative methods designed to access and analyse these data (Yanow 2000b).

These entailments of the culture metaphor imply the following in a policy analytic context:

1. That policy-relevant knowledge is held by policy-related actors together as a group – meaning that policy-relevant learning is relational and social, always rooted in a context of interaction, in addition to whatever individual cognition is entailed.
2. That policy-relevant learning is situated in ongoing policy-related practices.
3. That it is mediated by artefacts.
4. That it may include things known tacitly as well as explicitly, and that what is known is also at times communicated tacitly through its embodiment in (or representation by) artefacts.
5. That policy-relevant learning may also be engaged for purposes of sustaining existing policy-related practices and not only for changing them.
6. That what is learned is continually reproduced and negotiated, and hence always dynamic and provisional.

The methodological entailment of the metaphor is that site-specific meanings of artefacts (objects, language and acts) for organizational actors require interpretative research methods to access actors' situated 'local' knowledge (Yanow 2000b).[5] The situated embeddedness of these entailments in policy-relevant practices points the way towards the importance of both local knowledge and practical judgment in interpretative policy analysis, as noted in the next section.

The culture metaphor was, I think, useful in its time. Today, however, it is no longer necessary to rely on anthropology for justification of these ontological and methodological practices. Their roots within interpretative philosophies (hermeneutics, phenomenology and some critical theory in Europe; symbolic interaction and ethnomethodology in the USA) are much more widely known, and the argument itself is much broader. It is much more important today to bring into focus the vast, well-established philosophical traditions undergirding non-positivist approaches to policy analysis and to make explicit their methodological implications. For interpretative policy analysis is not a

---

[5] These are the characteristics of a collective, interpretative-cultural approach to organizational learning, which also draws on actor-network and activity theories; see also Blackler 1995; Blackler, Crump, and McDonald 2000; Cook and Yanow 1993; Engeström and Middleton 1996; Gherardi 2000; Gherardi, Nicolini and Odella 1998; Nicolini 1998; Nicolini, Gherardi and Yanow forthcoming.

'*post*'-positivist analysis in many important respects. While it has emerged as
an analytic form in policy studies only within the latter part of the twentieth
century, largely in a temporal response against the dominance of rational actor
and other positivist-informed analytic modes, it rests on a set of philosophical
antecedents that developed in the early twentieth century, many of which themselves drew on eighteenth-century Kantian ideas (especially his conception of
the role of *a priori* knowledge in sense-making). As I have argued elsewhere
(Yanow 1995b: 124), interpretative policy analytic theorizing has been almost
exclusively concerned with identifying the limits of positivist analysis. In this
context, alternatives have been presented in ways that linguistically locate them
as oppositions to positivist analysis. What today's persuasive efforts require
is developing 'interpretative policy analysis' in its own right – or analyses, as
there is a wide range of analytic modes beyond those used in accessing data.
Contemporary efforts should be directed toward naming and explicating the ontological and epistemological presuppositions that undergird various research
methods, including interpretative ones, and the rationale for claiming scientific
status for the latter. The rest of this chapter suggests some of that grounding for
interpretative analysis.[6]

Accessing local knowledge: conducting meaning audits and mapping architectures of meaning[7]

There is a realm of activity that policymakers need to have evaluated, systematically, rigorously, methodically, that centres not only on values but on other
forms of human meaning, including beliefs and feelings, as well. For example, a recent health policy survey sought to explore attitudes across American
race-ethnic groups toward sending infirm elderly parents to nursing homes. The
question was 'meaningless', however, to members of those groups that take it
as given that parents are cared for at home until death: they had no conceptual
framework within which to understand the question, which had been generated
from the context of a different meaning system of values, beliefs and feelings. In
another example, an American-initiated comparative study of US and Japanese
policies included the seemingly innocuous and factual question, 'What is your
age?' In light of American sensitivities about age, the question was placed at
the end of the questionnaire, with the thought (appropriate in an American
cultural context) that this would allow the researcher and the informant time
to establish some rapport that would 'cushion' the impact of the question's
'personal' nature. When used in Japan, however, this same placement cost

---

[6] For a fuller discussion of the philosophical grounding of interpretative policy analysis, see Yanow
1996: ch. 1 or 2000a: ch. 1 and the references there.
[7] The following sections are based on Yanow 2000a.

researchers key information relative to the elderly informants' status, age being more venerated in Japan than in the USA, broadly speaking, and this in turn led to miscues in the appropriate phrasing of preceding questions (which otherwise would have followed the age question and been framed more in keeping with local cultural meanings). Moreover, the comparative reliability of these data could be challenged: because of the link between age and status, Japanese answers are more likely to be chronologically accurate (the elderly having no reason to make themselves appear younger or older), whereas Americans are more likely not to respond or to bias their answers downwards, given the societal value placed on youth.[8]

In conducting a *meaning audit*, interpretative cultural analysis typically begins with the questions 'What does this proposed policy mean, and for whom does it have meaning?' The analyst anticipates that the policy would mean different things to different policy-relevant publics, and the first step is to begin to identify those different communities of meaning to discover what the policy means for each group. The analyst might begin by interviewing members of different constituencies, discovering, in this process, that the understandings of policy issues condensed in the terms 'nursing home' or 'age' are vast, complex, contradictory and emotionally charged, that even within a single population group, meaning is not uniform and the subject is hotly contested. The analytic report would map the *architecture of meaning* – situated, local meaning – and its modes of expression in the issue. In treating key policy words or programmes as symbols embodying potentially multiple meanings for different interpretative communities, the analyst can begin to identify the various ways the policy issue is being 'framed': identifying the details of what the term or object or act means, the specific language used to articulate those meanings, the different groups for which it holds those meanings, and what the conflicting interpretations are. Linder (1995) provides an example of such a mapping for five different communities of meaning in the context of electro-magnetic frequency emissions policy debates, and the architecture of meaning for each of those five.

In framing recommendations, the policy analyst focuses also on what meaning or meanings the decision-maker's act might have for the various policy-relevant communities of meaning.[9] The policy analyst might recommend that the decision-maker call a public forum on the matter or take some other form of action to discuss the issues publicly before she decides what action to take. A meaning audit goes beyond frame analysis, asking: what meanings, for whom,

---

[8] This example is based on a discussion of functional and conceptual equivalence in Peng, Peterson and Shui 1991: 101.

[9] In the first edition (1964) of *The Symbolic Uses of Politics*, Murray Edelman argued, drawing on the work of Sapir, for the distinction between condensation symbols and referential symbols. In the Afterword to the second edition (1984), he noted that he had given up this distinction. I concur with his revised view: empirical evidence does not support it.

with what consequences (for implementation and other aspects of the policy process)?

Policy analyses based on interpretative philosophical presuppositions put human meaning and social realities at their core. To understand the consequences of a policy for the broad range of people it will affect requires *local knowledge* – the very mundane, but still expert, understanding of and practical reasoning about local conditions derived from lived experience. Invoking 'local knowledge' draws a distinction between different forms of knowledge and their attendant sources: it embraces the subjective-experiential knowledge of phenomenology, the 'practical reasoning' of Aristotelian *phronesis*[10] and American pragmatics (see, e.g., Menand 1997; 2001), and Polanyi's (1966) tacit knowledge,[11] on the one hand, as distinct from university-based training in technical expertise, on the other.

Policy analysts have been trained since the 1970s largely in the technical tools of decision- and cost–benefit analysis. While these tools can be very useful in helping analysts think through their analyses more thoroughly and systematically, this training has created at least two (unintended) costs. First, emphasizing such technical and numerical proficiency has led to a dependence on the analytic expertise of the professional, concomitantly devaluing the typically non-quantitative expertise of policy clients/constituents which derives from their own intimate familiarity with the lived experience that the policy seeks somehow to alter (and which is typically expressed in narrative, rather than statistical, form) – that is, their local knowledge. Had researchers/analysts in the examples cited above first sought to understand from those in each situation about their values, beliefs and feelings (e.g., about parental ageing, about age) and then used that local knowledge in designing the surveys or the policy, the ensuing problems would likely have been avoided or at least anticipated and mitigated (to the extent possible). A prior condition for entertaining the possibility of seeking out situated understanding is an inclination to render it of value.

The lack of attention to (at best) or outright devaluing of (at worst) local knowledge has been a common occurrence in several policy issue areas. In development policy, drought remedies in a specific region had nomadic tribespeople dig more wells. Because of the meaning of livestock to a tribesman's reputation, adding wells encouraged them to increase their herd size. Policy analysts ignored or did not understand that local knowledge, and this exacerbated the drought-induced problem that the policy was intended to ameliorate.[12] In

---

[10] See Hawkesworth (1988: 54–57) and Ruderman (1997) for discussions of this concept and some of its contemporary exponents.

[11] Rudolph (2001: 2) includes moral knowledge along with 'imaginative, partial, contingent and spiritual truth'.

[12] Thurston Clarke, *The Last Caravan*, New York: Putnam, 1978; cited in Paris and Reynolds (1983: 199, n. 9).

technology policy, Schmidt (1993) writes of the disastrous collapse of a bridge after site-based engineers' 'intimate knowledge' about cement requirements under local conditions was dismissed by Washington, DC-based policymakers. In science policy, Wynne (1992) describes the local, implicit knowledge held by shepherds in northern England that was ignored by scientist-experts advising policymakers on fallout from Chernobyl, with detrimental economic results. In educational policy, had policymakers understood what 'bussing' meant to white parents, they might have pursued differently the policy that led to 'white flight', which undermined the policy's integrative purpose (Paris and Reynolds 1983: 180–181).[13]

'Location' within an agency's organizational structure, professional training and membership, sex and gender, and a myriad other possible dimensions lead to a set of values, beliefs and feelings that can bind people together in communities of meaning. Through a process of interaction, members of a community – whether it is a community of scientists or environmentalists or some other group – come to use the same or similar cognitive mechanisms, engage in the same or similar acts, and use the same or similar language to talk about thought and action. Group processes reinforce these, often promoting internal cohesion as an identity marker with respect to other communities: the familiar 'us–them' phenomenon. Cognitive, linguistic and cultural practices reinforce each other, to the point where shared sense is more common than not, and policy-relevant groups become 'interpretative communities' sharing thought, speech, practice and their meanings.[14] The shared point of view will depend on the policy in question, but some common points of beginning reference are those factors according to which a society or polity categorizes itself: race-ethnicity, class, age, religion, political ideology, professional or occupational experience, hobbies or pastimes, and so on. Such communities may be fluid, changing from issue to issue (although often with some overlap, e.g. according to positions along a spectrum of political or religious ideology). While the language of 'community' has its roots in a geographic locale – connoting similarities of position deriving from shared property-based interests, political views, race-ethnicity, class, religious or other commonalities – it is borrowed into a policy context with broader, non-place-specific reference points.

---

[13] Chock (1995), Colebatch (1995), Hofmann (1995), Linder (1995) and Pal (1995) provide other examples of the importance and use of local knowledge in a policy context.

[14] And individuals may, and do, belong to multiple interpretative communities. This approach reflects the two senses of 'paradigm' described by Kuhn (1970): it is both a worldview and the community of practitioners sharing and articulating that view. Members acquire it through education and training, experience and practice of their trade, profession or craft, as well as from familial, communal and societal or national backgrounds and personality. This also reflects a phenomenological approach (see, e.g., Berger and Luckmann 1966: part II; Schutz 1962). Incorporating thought and speech, on the one hand, and practice, on the other, perhaps accounts for this duality present not only in Kuhn's use of paradigm, but also in some accounts of the hermeneutic circle. See Lave and Wenger (1991) on communities of practice.

This suggests the potential existence of at least three communities of meaning in any policy situation: policymakers, implementing agency personnel, and affected citizens or clients. But from implementation and organizational studies, we know that agencies may contain any number of internal communities of meaning: directors, managers/administrators, groups of professionals, lower-level employees, street-level bureaucrats.[15] And from community studies we know that communities and neighbourhoods have internal divisions. We also know that the issues of policy debate do not die once a piece of legislation has been passed: they survive and resurface in subsequent debates, as well as in implementation actions (Baier, March and Saetren 1986; Yanow 1993). Moreover, there are potentially many other policy-relevant groups – community residents, cognate and competing agencies and professionals, interest groups, potential clients, unheard or silent voices; which ones are of analytic and decision-making concern will depend on the specific policy issue in question; and each one of them may interpret the policy differently from legislators' intent (if that can even be established as a single meaning). Policy analysts need to identify these communities and map the architecture of their 'structures' of interpretation and meaning – that is, the policy artefacts and what they stand for. This approach treats problem statements as contending interpretations of policy issues made by different communities of meaning, as Luker (1984) did in analysing abortion policy debates. Frame conflict occurs not only because different interpretative communities focus cognitively and rationally on different elements of a policy issue, but because they *value* different elements differently. The different frames reflect groups' values contending for public recognition and validation.[16]

Once the importance of local knowledge is accepted, appropriate methods for accessing it need to be developed. This is the second area that has been neglected in the focus on technical analyses. It has led to a methodological focus on tools for analysing data, without attending fully to methods for accessing data or to the epistemological and/or ontological presuppositions that such access entails. Interpretative methods of access include conversational interviewing, observing (with whatever degree of participation), and the close reading of policy- or agency-relevant documents. Interpretative policy analysis often begins with relevant document study, focusing initially on newspaper (and other media) coverage and extending to transcripts of committee hearings, various reports, legislation, and/or agency documents (depending on the policy issue and stage). These provide background information for conversational interviews with key actors (legislators, agency directors and staff, community members, interest

---

[15] See Raelin (1986) and Lipsky (1979).

[16] The use of 'frame' in such a cognitive sense seems to have originated with Bateson (1955). For applications to a policy context, see Rein and Schön (1977) and Schön and Rein (1994). See also Goffman (1974) for a more general social scientific application and Dery (1987), for example, on the facticity of policy 'facts'.

groups' representatives). These are typically identified through documentary sources and other interviews and selected through purposive choice designed to cast as wide a net as possible, vertically and horizontally, across an agency, a community or a policy issue.[17] In these interviews the analyst's provisional assumptions about the boundaries of interpretative communities, the important artefacts and their meanings can be corroborated or refuted. Document access and conversational interviews may be preceded by or supplemented with observation of (with varying degrees of participation in) legislative debates, interest group meetings, implementing agencies, and community groups.[18]

Observing what people do and how they do it, listening to how they talk about the issue, reading what they read and talking with them about their views will lead the analyst to a degree of familiarity with the issue and views on it from the perspective of those affected by it in whatever way. Out of this growing familiarity with local knowledge, the researcher-analyst will be able to identify the overlappings and commonalities that define borders between communities of different interpretative positions – the architectures of meaning according to which various parties to the debate frame the issue. All subsequent analysis depends on an immersion in the details of data accessed through these methods.

Analysing local knowledge

As policy analysts begin to access local knowledge, they also begin the process of analysing it. The analytic process entails two aspects: (1) a daily sensemaking, out of which (2) puzzles emerge (events or acts or interactions that contradict what the analyst expected, or which she cannot make sense of given what she knows at that moment, or which contradict one another).

In attempting to make sense of these puzzles or anomalies, the analyst may draw on specific tools or techniques for assistance. As aids to clearer thinking, they are methods of exploring data that the researcher already 'has' and which he usually has already begun to make sense of, to interpret. The tools enable a process of making these insights and understandings more explicit. In traditional field research methods texts these two processes are typically separated under

---

[17] This is often termed 'purposive sampling', but it is not sampling in the sense of random selection. It is akin to the 'snowball' process used in community studies.

[18] The literature on each of these methods of accessing data is vast. The following are some representative sources. On *interviewing*, see Holstein and Gubrium (1995: 38–51, 73–80), Spradley and McCurdy (1972: 41–56), Whyte (1984: 97–127). On *observing* see Spradley and McCurdy (1972: 4) and Whyte (1984: 83–96). On *document study* as well as observing and interviewing, see Murphy (1980). The classic methodological description of 'field work' – accessing local knowledge – is Whyte's appendix to the second edition (1955) of his 1943 work. For a discussion of theoretical concerns, see Geertz (1973). Gans (1976) provides an insightful reflection on the conduct of *participant-observation* and the continuum of roles between observer and participant.

the headings 'data collection' and 'data analysis,' although often they are neither
conducted separately in time nor separable in analysis (nor are they 'collected'
in the, say, biologist's sense of gathering field specimens to bring back to the
lab; in policy analysis the data usually remain in the field, and so it seems
more appropriate to speak, then, of accessing them). While the analyst is in the
process of interviewing, for instance, he is often analysing as well. Yet there
comes a time when the analyst feels that all key people have been interviewed
and interpretative communities identified (no new names are offered when the
analyst asks, 'With whom else should I speak?' and she feels that the policy
debate has been fully mapped). At this point, after data have been accessed,
there are many formal methods that may be engaged, often after the analyst is
no longer physically at the site that is the source of local knowledge.

For reasons of space, I cannot elaborate here on all of these. I will name
several, outlined by the primary artefact they engage, and point to other sources
that treat them in greater detail. This outline is intended to be suggestive of the
range of possibilities, rather than exhaustive.

Language-focused analytic methods are perhaps the most developed of the three
categories. They include:

1. *frame analysis*, in which the focus is on the structures of language use among
   different groups of policy-relevant actors, sometimes pointing to the implications for action of these various ways of thinking about the policy issue
   (see Linder 1995; Pal 1995; Rein 1983a; Rein and Schön 1977; Schön and
   Rein 1994)
2. *narrative and rhetorical analysis*, including an examination of 'talk' and of
   stories and their tellers (see Abma 1999; Chock 1995; the essays in Fischer
   and Forester 1993; Gusfield 1976; Maynard-Moody and Kelly 1993; Roe
   1994; Throgmorton 1991; analysis of 'talk' draws on work in ethnomethodology, see Feldman 1994);
3. *semiotics*, focusing on the structures of meaning of phrases and particularly how the choice of one implicates others in an oppositional mode (e.g.,
   Feldman 1994);
4. *metaphor analysis*, exploring the meanings carried by certain policy or implementing agency terms from their sources or contexts of origin into the
   issue domain, and the implications of these borne meanings for action (e.g.,
   Miller 1985; Schön 1979; Yanow 2000a: ch. 3);
5. *category analysis*, which examines the structures of inclusion and exclusion
   built into choices of category labels and their contents (Lakoff 1987; Yanow
   2000a: ch. 3, 2002).

Act-focused analytic methods draw on theoretical developments in symbolic
interaction as well as on Burke's (1969) dramatist framework, to focus on

ways in which legislative or implementing agency action itself, or its absence, communicates meaning (see Edelman 1964; Feldman 1994). Related to this are treatments of the ceremonial, ritual and mythic components of acts (see Floden and Weiner 1978; Yanow 2000a: ch. 5). Stein (2001), for example, calls attention to the ways in which school teachers would line students up when it was time for special sessions mandated by Title I of the Elementary and Secondary Education Act. The act of separating certain students out and setting them apart from their classmates conveyed meanings about poverty, minority-group membership, and family background – reinforced by teachers' language use and tone of voice in labelling these students – that policymakers did not foresee as part of policy implementation.

Lastly, analysis also focuses on physical *objects* that may figure in the communication of policy meanings. These may include aspects of the specific *programmes* established by legislation (e.g., the meaning of 'home ownership' in a housing policy) or the design of agency buildings or other forms of *space use* that house these programmes and play a central role in policy implementation (e.g., Lasswell 1979; Yanow 2000a: ch. 4).

Towards interpretative analyses: implications for professional practice

Interpretative methods are as scientific as quantitative-positivist ones, in the sense that 'science' requires procedural systematicity and a posture of doubt and disproof. The criticism of these methods as lacking reliability and validity evaluates them according to criteria grounded in positivist ontological and epistemological presuppositions. Interpretative methods hold to their own criteria of trustworthiness and dependability, an argument made extensively in Erlandson et al. (1993: 133, based on Guba and Lincoln 1985), which I will not recapitulate here.

There are, however, three other concerns about interpretative methods sounded by critics to undermine their scientific standing, which need to be addressed. First, 'interpretative' does not mean 'impressionistic'. Even though interpretative methods emphasize the centrality of human interpretation and, hence, subjective meaning – that is, meaning to the 'subject,' the actor and/or the researcher – they are, nonetheless, a method: systematic, step-wise, methodical. But because they rely on human meaning-making, which is of necessity responsive to the highly variable context of the research setting, the steps of these methods typically cannot be lined out in as discrete and regularized a fashion as those of cost–benefit or decision or regression or grid-group analysis and their counterparts. It is the rhetorical power of the orderly, seemingly finite steps of these latter methods that conveys the sense of their rigour, and, conversely, the absence of that rhetoric from interpretative methods that implies (to some) their lack of rigour. In practice, interpretative methods are as *formal* – 'conforming to accepted rules or customs' (*The Oxford Minidictionary*, 1981: 171) – as the others. And the latter entail as much human judgment and interpretation as the former.[19]

Second, there has been a tendency in some discussions of symbolic politics to treat that concept as distinct from 'real' politics, as if symbols and their meanings were not 'real' or as if material redistributions and instrumental actions were the only 'real' elements of political and policy acts. The distinction is erroneous and misleading. Policies and political actions are not either symbolic or substantive. They can be, and often are, both at once. Conceptually speaking, even purely instrumental intentions are communicated and apperceived through symbolic means. In practice, policies are intended to achieve something material or expressive, or both. To do so, they have recourse only to symbolic representations to accomplish their purposes, and these purposes can be understood only by interpretations of those representations. There can be no unmediated, directly apperceived policy or agency language, objects or acts.

Third, if methods based on a positivist ontology and epistemology also entail interpretative acts, why call the alternative described here 'interpretative', rather than 'qualitative', as they are still more commonly called? The positive (note: not positivist) answer is that the language of 'interpretation' signals and underscores the link between methods and their underlying philosophical presuppositions: the ways we go about accessing and analysing data derive from and reflect prior suppositions as to the reality status and knowability of the subject of our research. The negative answer – the reason not to call them 'qualitative' – is historical. That term emerged to distinguish a set of field-based, non-statistically grounded methods from 'quantitative' ones; but since 'qualitative' researchers also count, the distinction captured in those terms is increasingly meaningless. The quantitative–qualitative nomenclature is increasingly understood as connoting differences of philosophical presuppositions denoted by the positivist–interpretative distinction. Hence, interpretative policy analysis, standing on its own nomenclature, not looking backwards in time or philosophical space as a set of 'post'-positivist methods, but grounded in its own phenomenological-hermeneutic-critical writings of continental philosophy and American pragmatism.

---

[19] I reject the term 'rigour' as a criterion for interpretative analysis. It harks to one of the central differences between positivist-quantitative and interpretative methods: the latter do not, and cannot, proceed in the same step-wise fashion dictated by 'the scientific method'. When I am in the midst of a conversational (a.k.a. in-depth) interview, I need to respond to what I have just been told. Similarly, when I am observing (let alone participating) and the action moves to an unanticipated arena, I need to be free to move along with it. This flexibility is the precise opposite of the unbending, unyielding 'rigour'. That does not mean, however, that interpretative methods are not systematic and 'methodical'.

Interpretative methods often focus on 'puzzles' or 'tensions' of two related sorts. As noted above, the first is the difference between what the analyst expects to find and what she actually experiences in the policy or agency field. The expectations that one brings to a policy-analytic project derive from one's prior experience, education or training. When there is a 'mismatch', the ensuing puzzle or tension creates the opportunity to explain why the policy or agency is doing things 'differently'. The impulse, often, is to assume that the different way is 'wrong': 'they' don't know how to do things 'right'. An interpretative approach treats such differences as different ways of seeing, understanding and doing based on different prior experiences. This does not mean that all positions are necessarily 'right', but it does call on the analyst (if not contending parties) to accord different views and their underlying feelings serious respect (see Forester 1999; Roe 1994 on this point). Different views are not likely to be changed by appeal to facts alone (and coercive change is not an option). If the analyst can decouple 'different' from 'wrong', he can, in this view, proceed in another fashion. In analytic projects, the tension between expectations and present experience is potentially a source of insight and should be dwelled on, even cherished, although many analysts might be tempted to resolve the tension immediately. That tension is produced by the juxtaposition of the analyst's 'estrangement' from the analytic situation and his growing familiarity with that situation. By prolonging the balance between 'stranger-ness' and 'insider-ness' the analyst is able to move back and forth between seeing things as they are and seeing them as they are not.

The second sort of puzzlement that can spark interpretative analysis derives from the tension between word and act, captured in the saying 'Do as I say, not as I do' invoked so often by parents speaking to their children. Children (and sometimes workplace subordinates) are admonished in this way in face of the very anticipation that they will do precisely what they see their parents (or superiors) do, rather than following what they are told to do. When faced with a contradiction between word and deed, we tend to believe that the deed is closer to the 'truth' (or to the individual's intentions) than the word. Psychological research (e.g., Rosenhan, Frederick and Burrowes 1968) bears this out. In policy terms this translates into believing that what implementers do, rather than what the policy 'says' in its explicit language, constitutes the 'truth' of policy (and thereby the state's) intent. This is one of the points that Lipsky (1979) and his colleagues (Prottas 1979; Weatherly 1979) made in analysing street-level bureaucrats, their agencies and their clients.

One current task for theorists of interpretative policy analysis looking forward is to develop the relationship between these ideas and contemporary discourse theories. This needs to be worked out in three areas. First, the language of 'local knowledge' suggests a clear linkage with participatory democracy as that idea is being discussed in recent years (as distinct from its 1970s version, e.g. in participatory planning). This, in turn, suggests a link between the call for discourse and interpretative analysis, whose overlaps and differences need to be articulated. Third, it would be worth exploring whether the data-accessing methods of interpretative policy analysis are the ideal ones to draw on in practice to enable policy discourse (aside from their research role). I find parallels in technology and information studies, particularly in the areas of human–machine interface (HMI) and computer-supported cooperative work (CSCW). The emphasis there on 'participatory design', particularly among those taking more collective approaches to the study of the workplace (i.e. more anthropological and sociological than psychological), points to the importance for hardware designers of understanding the relevant work practices of those who would be using the machines in question. This calls on designers to attend to 'local' social practices, making sense of what is already in place and remaking it into something new. In organizational studies, and particularly in organizational learning, a related question is being asked: why are managers so little interested in the work of those they manage? Analysis focuses on the politics of expertise and of science and calls for changing the working definition of expertise to encompass local knowledge. Both of these point to the role of the expert – the designer, the manager – as translator, between local knowledge and technical-organizational knowledge (Yanow 2001). The interpretative policy analyst serves in much the same way. The challenge for the translator in all three instances is to 'disintermediate', so that those in possession of local knowledge can tell their own stories.

The ideas underlying the problem of ignoring or denigrating local knowledge are not new (nor is the phrase itself). They lie at the heart of theories of community organization as a professional practice (so called in the USA and developed and taught in graduate schools of social work, but also present, even earlier, in England as 'community' work and in France as *l'animation*). These practices date in the latter two instances to colonial occupations of Africa and Asia and to London's immigrant-populated slums; in the USA they date to the work of Jane Addams and her colleagues at Chicago's Hull House and elsewhere in the settlement movement – themselves influenced by Barnett's work in London's East End – and later to Saul Alinsky and the 'back of the yards movement', also in Chicago (Yanow 1976). The ideas recur in the citizen participation 'movement' of 1960s and 1970s US social policies (the Ford Foundation's 'grey areas' projects and subsequent OEO, HEW, and HUD programmes). In a sense, then, the present moment is their third incarnation. What is different this time is the evocation of the language of knowledge, because that shifts our focus from power- and institutionally based conflicts between agents of the state (e.g. community organizers) developing and implementing policies for its citizens, without asking them for their input – that is, from the state's noblesse oblige acting paternalistically toward its citizens in directed, and usually cooptive and/or cosmetic, efforts to 'empower' them – to a different framing of the issue: a knowledge-based frame.[20] The central implication for professional practice of living in a world of multiple communities of meaning, in which 'facts' are seen as constituted by policy contexts rather than as external, objective truths, is that policy analysts can no longer act as if they possessed certain knowledge. Instead, interpretive social 'realities' dictate that professionals, while charged with the passionate commitment to their ideas (and ideals), must maintain a sense of humility in the face of the possibility that they might be wrong. Policy analysts cannot be expected to produce 'usable knowledge' (Lindblom and Cohen 1979) on their own, sitting at their desks. Local knowledge must be accorded its place as central to the world of professional practice; and that practice must be conducted in the spirit of 'passionate humility' (Yanow 1997; Yanow and Willmott 2002).

When the problem is seen as differences in the bases of knowledge – technical-rational-university-based expertise versus lived-experience-based expertise – the terms of engagement change. Citizens are, in this view, no longer denied agency, linguistically-conceptually at least, as so many 'targets' of policy missiles (a metaphor common, still, in policy language).[21] This enlarges the range of action not only for policy analysis as a deliberative practice, in which non-traditionally expert citizens are nonetheless accorded respect for having expertise in their own lives and, hence, invited to participate in deliberations as partners; but it also recasts the role of policy analyst, from technical expert to expert in deliberative processes. Given the focus on communities of meaning and the importance accorded language, whether in storytelling or more simply as the mode of deliberative exchange (e.g. Forester 1999; Throgmorton 1993), the policy analyst may take on the role of translator, enabling interpretative communities to speak across the cultural divides of meaning and its expressive modes.

Policy analysis, in this view, cannot be restricted to policy language or ideas as understood and intended only by their authors. Others whose understandings of the policy are or will be central to its enactment are also of analytic concern. Interpretative policy analysis explores the contrasts between policy meanings as intended by policymakers – 'authored' texts – and the possibly variant and even incommensurable meanings – 'constructed' 'texts' – made of them by other policy-relevant groups.[22] Much of traditional policy analysis, especially *ex post* implementation or evaluation analysis, requires the establishment of policy intent as a benchmark against which to assess enactments or outcomes.

[20] I owe my clarity on this point to Ralph Hummel (2001).

[21] It derives in the USA from Robert McNamara's importation of PPBS from the Department of Defense to the Ford Foundation and the 1960s–1970s social policies that emanated from there.

[22] This line of reasoning is informed by work in literary analysis known as reader-response theory. See, e.g., Iser 1989; see Yanow 1995a for an application.

This is the sense of the policy as established by its creators – the authored text (or 'text'). But what interpretative analysis leads us to see is that it would be erroneous to assume that this is the only meaning appropriate or relevant for assessment. In this view, there is not a single locus of meaning: it does not reside solely in legislative language; *enacted interpretations* of written texts are just as important to analysis, and meaning may also be created in interactions among written texts, legislators' intent, and others' constructions of one or both of these. As implementation problems are often created by different understandings of policy language, it is as important for analysts to access these other interpretations – the local knowledge held by communities of meaning in constructed 'texts'.[23]

We come full circle, then: back to a role for the culture metaphor as a way of communicating aspects of these divisions of meaning. Seen this way, differences of meaning and interpretation cannot be seen as malevolent or as 'simple' stupidity (or cupidity): different people see things differently. Instead, such conceptual differences can be portrayed as differences of language-and-cultural-meaning groups, analogous to nationals of different countries, although these policy-relevant groups are residents of the same geographic locale. This suggests, then, the need for a philosophy of translation, not in a linguistic context narrowly conceived, but in an applied, everyday, practical one,[24] and for guidelines for the practice of 'applied translation' in a spirit of passionate humility.

---

[23] I am bypassing here the critical question of whether intent can even be established, as well as the point that policy language often contains elements of prior debates, such that more than one intent may be embedded there (see Baier, March and Saetren 1986 and Yanow 1993). This line of reasoning parallels that of 'original intent' arguments with respect to the US Constitution and the Founding Fathers, engaged publicly most recently around the nomination of Judge Robert Bork to the Supreme Court (see Teuber 1987).

[24] I have begun such an exploration in the context of organizational learning (Yanow 2001), drawing on the work of Mark Rutgers (1996, 1999) on the problem of translation in public administration.

Theoretical strategies of poststructuralist policy analysis: towards an analytics of government

Herbert Gottweis

When authors in the field of policy studies describe their approach as 'discourse analysis', many different things can be meant by this label, ranging from a Habermasian to a deconstructivist style of analysis. In this chapter I will draw some insights from poststructuralist theory for a discourse-analytical reading of the policy process. I will address a number of central, analytical questions that are raised by a poststructuralist perspective of the process of policymaking.[1] The approach I present is eclectic and draws on different theory traditions. I will show that poststructuralism offers a number of well-defined epistemological points of departure to develop a distinct set of conceptual tools which lead to a new understanding of the policy process. Furthermore, I will show how Foucault's analytics of government can inform policy analysis and sheds new light on the transformation of government practices in the emerging network society. Throughout my discussion I will draw on empirical examples from genetic engineering and medical policymaking to illustrate my argument.

The chapter goes from the general and theoretical to the specific and applied. The first part locates poststructuralist policy analysis within the larger context of current post-positivist social theory and methodology. I will then discuss how a discourse-analytical approach towards policymaking conceptualizes government and leads to a novel understanding of the policy process and the newly emerging topography of politics.

Points of departure I: policy analysis after Saussure

Poststructuralist policy analysis should be perceived as an expression of the larger, post-positivist movement in the social sciences. It has grown out of a

---

[1] See for a general outline of comparative poststructuralist policy analysis: Gottweis (1998).

critique of the positivist presuppositions that inform most empirical political science studies (George and Campbell 1990; Yanow 1996). While a number of different 'schools' of post-positivism share a focus on language, they differ significantly in their conceptualization of language, in the way they relate discursive to non-discursive phenomena, in their understanding of the actor-structure problem, and how they see their contribution to larger questions of social and political theory. In the first section of this chapter I will discuss a particular poststructuralist mode of political analysis which draws considerable influence from the work of Michel Foucault, Jacques Derrida and from the current sociology and philosophy of science. The unifying theme, which holds the work of these diverse scholars together, is that of creating a thinking space after structuralism and metaphysics. A theory of language and society in the tradition of post-Saussurian linguistics is of special importance for this project. Furthermore, the discussed approaches go beyond Saussure and, in general, mainly language-focused poststructuralist approaches by outlining new theoretical strategies to deal with human and non-human materials in social science analysis, and by developing a notion of signification which is not limited to language. As I will show, the development of a perspective of 'semiotic materialism' is of special importance for the analysis of the currently newly emerging regimes of government.

Classical structuralism, as paradigmatically developed in the work of Ferdinand de Saussure, constitutes one very important departure point of poststructuralism's critique of language and meaning. Saussure developed his notion of structure through the analysis of language.[2] For Saussure, structure refers to the ordering principle according to which the lexicon of a language is articulated. This is done in such a way that it can be recognized and mastered as the lexicon of one and the same national language. For Saussure structure is a system of pairs 'meaning–expression', i.e. signified/signifier – such that one and only one signified is assigned to every signifier. The individual signs are exact applications of an invariable law to which they are related; they cannot proliferate and become uncontrollable.

But it is exactly the concept of uncontrollability which poststructuralism brings into the debate. For Derrida, the idea of a closed structure reflects metaphysical thinking and a desire for control. Structuralism searches for general ordering principles and universal regularities which make the world capable of technological and scientific mastery, which give clear orientation in a world which otherwise would seem to be out of control. Derrida contests that structures can decompose, that we are entangled in structures and have no possibility of getting beyond our 'being-inside-structures'. He says, 'everything is

---

[2] For the following see: Derrida (1983), Frank (1989: 20–33), Welsch (1996: 245–255).

structure', but he does not mean 'everything' is taxonomy, but, rather, every meaning, every signification, every view of the world is in flux, nothing escapes the play of the differences and thus nothing can be tracked down and fixed in its meaning (Derrida 1976: 422–442).

This basic conceptualization of 'the world' has profound implications for policy analysis. Probably the central implication is that policy analysis cannot depart from a fixed, given and stable world (of politics, of economics, of society, of nature), but must assume that social, political or natural phenomena and, inseparably from them, their meanings, are constantly moving, changing and shifting in various directions.

Points of departure II: policy analysis and the 'real'

Poststructuralism's Saussurian point of departure underscores the importance of the study of language and such related phenomena as texts, narratives and discourses as critical for policy analysis. Whereas the (neo-positivist) representationalist/correspondence theory of truth believes that there 'is a truth out there' which can be represented through the neutral medium of language, the anti-representationalist view of poststructuralism rejects such a 'picture theory' of language in which the physical properties of the world are considered fixed while language is in the business of meeting the needs of their description (Rorty 1989: 5).

What does that mean for the analysis of the kind of phenomena that are typical for policy analysis? It means that we must conceptualize policy phenomena such as inflation, social welfare or degraded environments as articulations rather than facts, as the outcome of complicated processes of inscription, of re-presentation, rather than as 'given' structures, tendencies or situations. Neither the truth of 'hazards of genetically modified organisms', nor the policy-problem of a 'significant increase of Creutzfeldt-Jakob patients', nor a 'high technology-gap' (to give some empirical examples) is simply 'out there' and only needs to be discovered or studied.

However, poststructuralist analysis does not necessarily lead to the view of 'reality' as a simple 'product' of language. Rather, what constitutes a 'risk', 'high-technology' or an 'increase of patients with a particular disease' is the result of historically specific and ongoing constitutive practices of writing and inscription. Consequently, the 'truth' of an event, a situation, or an artefact will always be the contingent outcome of a struggle between competing language games or discourses which transform 'what is out there' into a socially and politically relevant signified (Daly 1994; Rorty 1989).[3]

---

[3] Important examples for the 'linguistic turn' in political science are: Fischer and Forester (1993), Jobert and Muller (1987), Patzelt (1987).

While poststructuralism believes in the power of representation, it does not reduce signification to language. What precisely is meant by this?

At this point we need to be more specific about some terminology we have already started to use, in particular with respect to the terminology of writing and inscription. Writing in the theory of poststructuralism is the process by which human agents inscribe order into their world, it is a way of fixing the flux and flow of the world in spatial and temporal terms. Government programmes, political speeches and party platforms are excellent examples of such attempts to create order. They strive to give sense and coherence to the otherwise confusing or contradictory realities of political life. A Minister of Research who gives a speech in which he explains why biotechnology is very important for society, and thus needs to be strongly supported by government programmes, tries to offer orientation in the complex and ambiguous world of genetic engineering. Likewise, the determination of entities such as the state or the economy and the delineation of their boundaries cannot count on any prediscursive settlements, but is based on processes of writing or articulation.[4]

But this is not the end of the story. For Derrida, writing has material potency. It is described as the action of inscribing notations, marks or signs on a surface which bring representation into being, be it a sheet of paper or a DNA sequence. Writing is not concerned with the meaning and content of messages, but with the structure and organization of representations. Accordingly, ministries, political parties or social movements can be regarded as symbolic productions which emerge from being 'written' and constituted by those who observe and participate in them (Cooper 1989; Linstead and Grafton-Small 1993).

But Ministers of Research or processes of industrial development are still mainly social phenomena. Many phenomena of policy analysis belong to what is usually called 'nature', such as brains, the structure and function of the double-helix of DNA, or a foetus. How does a poststructuralist mode of policy analysis deal with these phenomena? Important insights for this difficult task can be gained from the current sociology of science as represented by authors such as Bruno Latour and Michel Callon.

Essentially, following the work of Latour and Callon and others (discussed below), we can say that nature is not different from society once it becomes the object of human interest. The history of science and technology offers ample proof for this argument. In this context, Ian Hacking has pointed out, the birth of the Baconian Programme of the seventeenth century signalled the ascendance of a science whose prime aim was to manipulate and control nature for the utility of man, thereby collapsing the distinction between representation and intervention. Hence in the analysis of science we should focus on the interlocking

---

[4] For key contributions to poststructuralist political theory see Connolly (1991), Laclau and Mouffe (1985).

between representing and intervening (Hacking 1984). In a similar vein we can argue that nature or phenomena of human–nature interaction need to be conceptualized as the outcome of complex processes of production. Scientists who do research in biology write texts on life which at the same time shape life. For example we can understand the practices of scientists working in biology as a process of writing texts on life by using experimental systems. For biologists experimental systems are the smallest functional units of research, designed to give answers to questions which we are not yet clearly able to ask. Hans-Jörg Rheinberger has suggested that we interpret experimental systems as comprising two different yet inseparable structures or components: the first component is the scientific object, or the epistemic thing; the second component is the technological object.[5] The scientific object is a physical structure, a chemical reaction, or a biological function whose elucidation is at the centre of the investigative effort. It cannot be fixed and we can say it is something like a questioning machine. The technological object, in contrast, can be compared to an answering machine: it is determined and performs within and according to known regularities. The technological object contains scientific objects, embeds them, restricts them, and controls the proliferation of their meanings. Technological objects are – to stay with molecular biology – gels, ultracentrifuges or electron microscopes, which determine the mode of representation of the epistemic thing. At the same time this very operation of the control of meaning, the representation, constitutes the framework for intervening into life. In this sense, representation is intervention. Genetically modified plants, hybrid animals and recommendations based on prenatal screening are expressions of such interventions.

The 'semiotic-material character' of scientific practice becomes clear when we begin to understand that an experimental system creates a space of representation for things that otherwise cannot be grasped as scientific objects. Usually it is said that such a representation presents a model of what is going on 'out there in nature'. Thus 'in-vitro systems' are models for 'in-vivo systems.' But one can only know what goes on out there when one has a model for it. Consequently the reference point of any model can be nothing else but another model. It is impossible to go behind a signifying chain, for representations do not merely disclose some underlying reality, but actually constitute it. Hence, a scientific object realizes itself as a kind of writing, a tracing, a graphematic display, an ecriture, as Rheinberger argues. Through measuring devices and technical arrangements, the scientist creates the basis for a material textual structure. In other words, the realized representation is an epistemic thing which relies on a particular technical and instrumental background. At the same time this representation works within a historically contingent discursive formation,

---

[5] See for this and the following, Rheinberger (1992a, 1992b).

such as modern molecular biology. If the scientific object does not produce immediately visible traces, 'tracers' are introduced into it: radioactive or fluorescent markers, pigments, etc. A particular sequence of DNA is 'read' as a ladder of black bars in four adjacent columns on the autoradiograph of a sequencing gel. Temporally and spatially the object is an inscription. The experimenter uses such elements as a chromatogram or a DNA sequencing gel to arrange these graphemes and to compose a model. It is this graphematic reality in which the scientist is immersed. 'Nature' is an object of experimentation only insofar as it is already representation, insofar as it itself is an element, however marginal, of the game. Hence, what goes on is neither a 'reading' of the 'book of nature', a depicting of reality, nor a deliberate constructing of reality. Scientific representation is not expressing something intrinsic; instead, what occurs is graphematic activity: it is the shaping and arranging of material entities along partitions which are neither revealed (imposed by the existing world), nor prescribed through our actions. In short, science is a form of writing.

Likewise, technology is a way of structuring and organizing nature, or bodies. For example, the body of a foetus is not simply 'there', but is the result of the intervention of an ultrasound scanner, which produces signs called 'baby'. The representation of the body of the foetus, which at the same time constitutes a technological intervention, becomes 'the body'. In this process of semiotic materialization representational practices become inseparable from bodies, subjects, technologies. The Roslin Institute's cloned sheep Dolly is as much biotechnological as biological. In this sense Dolly is as cultural as she is natural, a heterogeneous construction of technologies and nature.

In conclusion, we can say the following: while representation often comes in the form of words, often it does not, and takes on the form of instruments, technical objects and other more or less hybrid material forms (Callon and Law 1995). The realities of the world, bodies, genes or sheep cannot be reduced to language, nor to technology, nor to nature. They are both semiotic and material, the result of complex processes of intermediation between the semiotic and the material and thus heterogeneous constructions. Likewise, regimes of government, as I will discuss them below, can be precisely understood as practices in which diverse phenomena of language, discourse, artefacts, technologies and contexts are inseparably interconnected.

Poststructuralist policy analysis: an approach without actors and structures?

After having dealt with the very general question of what constitutes the 'real' of policy analysis, we now can move on to a reconsideration of some basic concepts of policy analysis. In this section I want to address what constitutes a core problem of political analysis, and, in general, of social theory: the actor-structure relationship.[6] Any type of policy analysis is guided by a specific conceptualization of the role of actors and structures in the political process, for example by its view of policymaking as a struggle of competing groups, or a game played by rational actors, or as mainly determined by institutional structures.

Whereas conventional schools of political science privilege either actors or structures in their accounts, poststructuralist modes of political analysis tend to avoid such a dichotomization by offering a language or discourse-analytical perspective which acknowledges the importance of structural phenomena and contexts for the understanding of politics, without reducing actors to 'outcomes of structures'. From a poststructuralist perspective, subjects or actors cannot be viewed as the origin of social relations, because they depend on specific discursive conditions of possibility. For example, those who 'write' and create organizations or policy programmes should not be conceptualized as autonomous, rational actors. In what Derrida criticizes as the 'logocentric tradition' of thinking, self-conscious, rational minds produce thoughts. These thoughts provide meaning which is articulated by speech. Speech itself is inscribed by writing. The unmediated presence of consciousness is privileged over speech (logocentrism), and speech in turn is privileged over writing. This means that meaning is more authentic the closer it is to the origin, the immediate consciousness. Derrida overturns this logocentric conception of writing and argues that speech would not be possible without writing. He thus directs our intention to the specific and multilayered textual processes by which subjects come into being. He shows that writing determines consciousness, which is not immediate and unreflective, but the result of a relationship made with what has already been inscribed, the trace of previous individual or collective experience (Linstead and Grafton-Small 1993: 341–342).

In this perspective the self-conscious modern subject begins to be replaced by the idea of an intertwined and fragmented texture as the place for the emergence of subjectivity. For example, gender, though constructed, is not necessarily constituted by an 'I' or a 'we' who precedes that construction in any spatial or temporal sense. As Judith Butler writes, 'Subjected to gender, but subjectivated by gender, the "I" neither precedes nor follows the process of this gendering, but emerges only within and as the matrix of gender relations themselves' (Butler 1993: 7). Therefore, instead of talking about subjects it is preferable to talk about subject positions, which are contingent and strategic locations within a specific discursive domain. Actors do not have stable subject identities but constantly develop their subjectivity in a discursive exchange (Hajer 1994: 5; Laclau and Mouffe 1985: 115). From a logocentric view, the human agent represents a holistic and clearly bounded universe. But self-consciousness is never pure,

---

[6] See for a general outline of this argument in the social sciences, Smart (1982).

authentic and unmediated experience as, for example, rational choice theory
believes. Social and historical traces enter into the structuring of consciousness. In this way individual subjects or actors are constituted through symbolic
systems which fix and differentiate them in place while remaining outside of
their control. This is not a 'cultural dope' conception of human agency, but a
perspective which points out that human agency is produced reality (Linstead
and Grafton-Small 1993: 343; Smart 1982: 135). Also, this perspective does
not imply that there are no human actors in politics or that we have to pause
to talk about agency as we analyse political processes. There is no question,
for example, that a particular high-level administrator in the European Commission is in a powerful position and can act to mobilize support for his goal
to impose strict regulations protecting the environment from hazards related to
genetically modified organisms. And we can, and should certainly analytically,
follow his actions. But we have to understand that this administrator does not act
independently from European environmental policy discourse which in many
ways provides a critical influence on how this administrator views the world,
defines his goals and structures his actions.

   Likewise, we cannot simply assume the 'prediscursive existence' of entities
such as institutions, 'unified' subjects of policymaking and political identities.
There is, for example, no reason to deny the importance of the structure of the
German parliament for the shaping of the 1990 Genetic Engineering Act. But
how can we explain the strong involvement of the German parliament in the
shaping of the legislation in the first place? What created the dynamics for a
policymaking process leading to legislation? Here purely (neo-)institutionalist
arguments, for example, seem to be insufficient. Thus, poststructuralist policy
analysis pays great attention not only to the organization of politics, but also
to the politics of organization, not only to the actors of politics, but also to the
politics of actors, in other words, to the semantic struggles and discursive constructions which define who counts as an actor in a particular policy setting –
and who does not; which institutions are legitimized and authorized to take
part in the shaping or the implementation of policymaking – and which are
not. My argument here is not that actors don't have goals which they pursue
or that institutions don't matter in policymaking. Actors do things in politics
and institutions shape policymaking. But these processes need to be understood
within the discourses where actors are constituted and institutions framed as
relevant in a given policy field. These are extremely important analytic considerations which address dimensions of power widely ignored in conventional
policy analysis. Power is not only articulated in interactions between actors,
in institutional biases or ideologies. In addition, discourses, representations,
scientific statements, or 'public philosophies' are critical articulations of power
which construct subjectivity and position individual or institutional actors in
the socio-political field and thus deserve a prominent place in policy analysis.

Policymaking and the analytics of government

In this section I will show that a poststructuralist conceptualization of the actor-structure problem implies a rethinking of what constitutes the proper domain and the objects of policy analysis. This redefinition of the domain of policymaking is also related to a new understanding of government as a regime of practices. In this context, Michel Foucault's late work about government as the 'conduct of conduct' plays an especially important role (Burchell, Gordon and Miller 1991; Dean 1999; Foucault 1991a).

In conventional political science usage, government is associated with the activities of political authorities (such as the Cabinet or a ministry). Traditionally, policy analysis focuses on the activities of the state and its surrounding institutions. It seeks to understand how the machinery of the state and political actors interact to produce public actions (John 1999: 1). Recently the study of governance has pointed to the currently emergent patterns arising out of complex negotiations between a variety of groups and actors, public and semi-public institutions. The concept of governance indicates that, besides the state, there are other important (private) mechanisms of governance, such as community and market with their guiding principles of spontaneous solidarity and dispersed competition.[7]

The analytics of government in the tradition of Foucault is not interested in describing newly emerging fields of institutions or patterns. It is a perspective concerned with the analysis of the specific conditions under which particular entities emerge, exist and change (Dean 1999: 20; Foucault 1991b). The focus is on the heterogeneity of authorities which seek to govern conduct, the heterogeneity of the strategies, devices and technologies used for governing, the conflicts between them and the ways in which the present is characterized by such struggles (Rose 1999: 21). Thus, the analytics of government goes even beyond the relatively broadly focused governance concept. From a Foucauldian perspective, the focus of government is on practices: on those mechanisms and techniques which, in the name of truth and the public good, aspire to inform and adjust social and economic activities. Regimes of practices are objects of the analytics of government insofar as they concern the direction of conduct. Government, then, refers to the activities which are undertaken by a multiplicity of authorities and agencies that seek to shape our conduct by working through our desires, interests, aspirations and beliefs (Dean 1999: 11).

In this respect, government dominated by the state must be seen as a particular historical phenomenon in need of explanation rather than as a given fact. According to Foucault, the ascent of the state as the central government institution can be understood as the 'governmentalization of the state' (Foucault

---

[7] See, for example, Streeck and Schmitter (1985), Hollingworth and Schmitter (1994).

1991b), the development by which the state came to take on the function of the care of populations and individuals from the nineteenth century on. This process involved the invention and assembly of a multitude of technologies which connected the political centre with those decentralized points and fields where the administrative, financial, social and judicial agendas of the state were exercised. As I will argue in the last section of this chapter, it is the historical-contingent character of this 'governmentalization of the state' which is being called into question in the currently emerging network society.

At this point it should be also pointed out that government carries a concern with truth and rational problem-solving; in this way it is typically intrinsically linked to knowledge: to scientific theories, technological practices, experiments or economic forecasts.[8] This 'knowledge dependence' of government has important implications for policymaking. As the legitimacy of policymaking relies often on technical and scientific arguments, power becomes intertwined with knowledge: the exercise of power is predicated upon the deployment of knowledge. At the same time knowledge is always underdetermined – i.e. that, faced with choices, policymakers tend to adopt interpretations, theories, lines of research or arguments that enable them to monopolize areas of problem definition, dismiss interpretations of competitors or answer to the social demands of a particular class, the state, a political party, or a church. This underdetermination is overcome by non-scientific power interests which relate power internally and essentially to scientific knowledge, a phenomenon described by Foucault as the power–knowledge nexus (Kusch 1991: 150, 162–163). Not only actors and institutions matter, but discourses, ideas, technologies, scientific theories, representations and, in general, knowledge. Since these phenomena are seen as important forces which shape the process of policymaking, the analytics of government views the different fields where these communications originate as important sites of power. They are conceptualized as being in a relationship of exchange and interaction with other more traditional centres of power, such as parliaments, ministries or interest groups.

In this perspective, from the nineteenth century on the state is one important site of government next to others. There are sites of government which influence policymaking but have nothing to do with the state and its institutions. Thus, the focus on repressive modes of the exercise of power as visualized by the Hobbesian state is supplanted by the perspective of the 'multiple regime of government' relativizing the notional boundary between the state and society (Gordon 1991: 36). Markets, research institutes, biotechnology companies, financial institutions (in other words, knowledge-producing institutions of civil society whose practices define and structure social and economic realities,

---

[8] For a most illuminating discussion of a 'Foucauldian government analysis' see Rose and Miller (1992: 183).

but which are usually constituted as being 'non-political') are not necessarily 'objects' of state intervention but may coexist in a relationship of intimate symbiosis with state strategies and tactics (Hunt 1992: 27). In short, they govern, contribute to making things governable and are part of a larger structure.

The perspective of the analytics of government has major implications for our understanding of policymaking. We can say that policymaking is situated at the intersection between the different sites of a regime of government. Regimes of government are systems of practices in which people, individuals, nature and artefacts interact and are transformed into objects of intervention and become 'governable'. Hence, the analytics of government focuses on sets of practices in a relatively stable field of correlations of visibilities, mentalities, technologies and agencies. The objects of government (such as pregnancy, genes, the economy or global warming) co-emerge at a number of different locations that are not necessarily considered to be 'political' (such as in hospitals or research institutes), but nevertheless are sites where significant influence on the logic and the rationales of a policy field can be taken.

This leads us to an important redefinition of the nature of policymaking. I defined policymaking as situated at the intersection between forces and institutions deemed 'political' and those apparatuses that shape and manage individual conduct in relations to norms and objectives yet are constituted as 'non-political', such as science or education. Policies are often guided and informed by ideas, theories and knowledge that originate outside the political realm. This implies that policy analysis needs to extend its focus of interest from what is traditionally considered to constitute a political phenomenon to other areas, such as laboratories or the complexities of scientific expertise. I am not arguing, for example, that everything that occurs in a genetics lab deserves the attention of policy analysis. But certainly, if we try to understand genetic engineering regulation or the controversy over BSE, we have to pay considerable attention to the arguments and technologies originating in laboratories, their histories, discursive constructions and the underlying strategic goals. If BSE is caused by a virus, the policy-strategies to be pursued are very different from a scenario where BSE is seen as a prion disease. This 'micro-politics' of meaning which originates in a number of diverse sites from laboratories to parliaments is instrumental in creating, structuring and prioritizing the range of possibilities considered open to the government agencies involved in the policymaking process. It is predicated upon representations of nature, technology, economy and society in scientific and political discourse and the construction of policy narratives which established relationships between elements such as economic growth and molecular biology, recombinant DNA hazards and technologies, or collective identity and international economic competitiveness.

This theoretical perspective requires that policy analysis takes seriously the variety of practices underlying many policies ranging from health to biotechnology. Public policy questions such as what is responsible for the return of tuberculosis in many western countries or what causes Creutzfeldt-Jakob disease should not be black-boxed as issues of scientific opinion or controversy, but need to be addressed in policy analysis as issues in which scientific practices have become inseparable from expressions and structures of power. Today from economic to social and agricultural policy there is hardly a policy field whose operations and rationales are not in some way or other justified, explained and legitimized by reference to knowledge-based arguments. This is not to say that power is causally related to knowledge. Peter Haas, for example, in his approach to 'epistemic community' conceptualizes the power of experts as based on their access to information. In this reading, knowledge and interests are understood as distinct phenomena. As a result, science is conceptualized as potentially transcending politics and thus can help to make politics more rational (Haas 1992). Poststructuralist analysis is less optimistic about science as some sort of neutral judge in policy disputes. It underscores that today the legitimacy of political power relies increasingly on support from scientific or technical expertise. But policy analysis as an analytics of government is also aware of the fragility and openness of any regime of government. In the currently emerging network society a variety of actors, ideas and groups call into question established 'conducts of conduct' and how conduct is being shaped and directed. These groups, actors or ideas do not necessarily find political expression as lobby or interest groups within the established policy channels. In the field of health policy, for example, a multitude of actors and movements from traditional Chinese medicine to holistic medicine have developed a variety of new practices which question interpretations of health and disease and related treatments of health problems as offered by western medicine. Such problematizations can have a powerful impact on important and well-defined health policy institutions such as hospitals and insurance companies.

Policymaking as 'ordering activity'

After having rethought what constitutes the proper domain of policy analysis and the space of government, we are now in a position to further specify our notion of government as a regime of practices. In many ways, generations of policy scholars have struggled with the question of whether policymaking is mainly a reaction to structures, contexts and pressures or something more active and 'independent'. If the latter holds true, then policy analysis by definition must go beyond the identification of 'simple causalities' and put special emphasis on the study of those discursive phenomena which are a critical part in the semiotic-material construction of the world of government. Furthermore, an 'active' conceptualization of the process of policymaking further underscores the importance of paying special attention to narratives and counter-narratives in policymaking, and in general to those fields and sites where the meanings of government are negotiated and renegotiated.

In this context some of our earlier reflections are important. If language only reflects reality, its contribution to the creation of the political world can only be marginal. However, if language and representation are constitutive of politics, the picture changes. In this perspective, politics and political phenomena or society do not 'simply exist'. Their borders are always drawn (Gieryn 1995: 405) and thus we can view politics as an 'empty space' until demarcated and partitioned by means of struggles of boundary drawing.[9] These boundaries, for example, separate the 'political' from the 'non-political'. They define what is the legitimate space for policymaking and what not. Is experimental medical research such as xenotransplantation work 'political', and thus subject to public scrutiny, or is it 'non-political' and protected by the principle of the freedom of research? Answers to such questions involve complicated constructions of discursive spaces. It is through practices of articulation and inscription that nodal points are constructed which partially fix meaning and construct political spaces as different from other spaces, such as the space of medical science. These processes of boundary drawing which involve representations such as narratives, technologies (such as gels and ultrasound devices) or graphs do not create a single, stable order, but something more plural and incomplete. They can be seen as plural processes of social and political ordering (Law 1994). There is no such thing such as 'society', or 'politics', or 'the state' which constitutes a totality and as such is linked together, or 'sutured', to form a unity of some kind and capable of 'interactions', like 'state–society interactions'. There is no such thing as a single order, the dream and nightmare of modernity. There is no single underlying principle, such as the mode of production (Marx) or the process of rationalization (Weber), identified as responsible for connections and relations among groups and, in that way, constituting the whole field of differences. Rather, social, economic and political 'reality' are constructions made possible through articulatory or writing practices involving human (such as words) and non-human (such as a DNA-sequencing gel) materials.[10] Cloned sheep Dolly is referred to and re-presented by the Roslin Institute as a 'bioreactor'. Signifying Dolly is as much a product of language as of technology. If the signifier 'bioreactor' refers to a cloned sheep named Dolly, this designation of meaning collapses the distinction between technology and nature. At the same time the technology of cloning Dolly determines its re-presentation as 'bioreactor'. Such re-presentations can originate in different sites, like the Roslin Institute. But policymakers might also participate in the rewriting of

---

[9] See for pioneering work on the importance of boundary drawing in science politics Jasanoff (1990).

[10] For important contributions to this perspective from organization sociology see Cooper (1989), Hassard and Parker (1993), Reed and Hughes (1992).

the meaning of a particular new sheep. In policymaking, practices of articulation consist of the construction of nodal points, 'bridges of meaning', partially fixing meaning. In the process of policymaking, the unification of a political space through the instituting of nodal points constitutes a successful hegemonic attempt to define a political reality, subject identities and modes of action. Such constructions describe, for example, political rationalities and particular distributions of labour in the field of science policy. Thus they are processes of social and political ordering.

Practices of social and political ordering are inherently precarious processes. The boundaries of politics, society, nature and economy are always temporary phenomena and the relational system defining the identities of a given political space can undergo processes of weakening. This may result in the proliferation of floating elements of discourse and a (hegemonic) crisis of signification. The debate about the desirability of regulating the Internet raises questions concerning the boundaries between legitimate scrutiny and surveillance which undermines core liberties of civil society. Such boundary disputes often lead to redefinitions of what constitutes the field of the state, what the field of society.

Policymaking, then, comes across as a performative process which uses and mobilizes complex, heterogeneous systems of representations to fix the meaning of transient events (such as an economic recession). In doing so, it is possible to move them in space and time and make them susceptible to evaluation, calculation and intervention. An event such as a recession enters a government document in the form of statistical data and can be used, for example, to raise taxes or to distribute resources for investment. The economy in general is, of course, not something we can talk meaningfully about simply by looking at it. Many researchers and civil servants have to fill out long questionnaires and lists which need to be treated by computers. Only after this long process of tabulation, calculation and representation can the economy can be made visible (or re-presented) in the form of charts, lists, tables, numbers. Further simplification and computation yields more general data about the economy of a country, like its GDP or balance of payments, which then are placed within a story about the characteristics and needs of a market economy (Latour 1990: 38). The risks of genetic engineering are expressed in tables, categories and host-vector systems which become the basis for regulatory decision-making. This ordering activity of heterogeneous systems of representation is precisely what creates governability, which, for example, transforms the anarchic and multiple activities of an economy or of genetic engineering into a body of knowledge and markers which create the basis and orientation for political intervention. Instead of assuming governability and practices of policymaking, they must be posed as a problem. How do things and phenomena become objects of government and policymaking? These questions cannot be answered by pointing to actors, groups or other social forces, but require attention to various forms of re-presentation, such as narratives, indices, computations and procedures of assessment. Policymaking, then, must be studied as a material practice which does not simply react to its environment, but inscribes itself into its texture, and creates/rewrites order by drawing from a multitude of discursively available narratives, modes of representations, artefacts and technologies, a process which entails intermediation and translation between different social and non-social worlds and realms of perception.

Hence, what usually comes across as political order is the result of the operation of multiple ordering activities of which processes of policymaking are an important part. Every instance of policymaking can be described as an attempt at social and political ordering: to manage a field of discursivity, to establish a situation of stability and predictability within a field of differences, to maintain a specific system of boundaries such as between the state, science and industry, and to construct a centre that fixes and regulates the dispersion of a multitude of combinable elements. For example, the order of the policy field of medical policymaking seems to imply that scientists in medical schools do research, doctors give their patients state-of-the-art treatments, the sick get well, better and better cures become available, and politicians, civil servants and insurance companies distribute the money necessary for running the medical system. Everybody has a role and seems to be happy with it. But the fact is that this distribution of roles and functions is not stable and can be challenged at any time. The stability of the system is only temporary, the dominant feelings of what constitutes 'being sick' and what 'being healthy' are only transitory, even human bodies rather seem to be the result of complex interventions and re-presentations than stable entities. The clear boundaries between politics, medicine, patients and bodies are the result of continuous work and efforts mobilizing complex systems of re-presentation.

The elements which policymakers intend to stabilize originate in different sites of a regime of government and are frequently elements that policymakers find difficult or impossible to control. In the case of science policy, laboratories or scientific journals are typical sites for the production and interpretation of scientific and technological facts and artefacts which, far from being stable in their meaning, continue to be reframed and transformed in the process of policymaking. In medical policymaking hospitals, patient groups, doctors, ultrasound equipment and managed health care institutions are important sites where the nature of a policy problem is being defined. Ultimately, what is of importance in policymaking is the intermediation between heterogeneous systems of re-presentation, discursive constellation (or discursive economy), and the broader discursive context. The 'success' of policymaking depends as much on the construction of heterogeneous systems of re-presentation which organize political realities as on their translation into policy narratives, the inscription of these policy narratives into the given discursive constellation and the capability of these policy narratives to mediate between competing codes by which nature, economic, scientific or political reality (context) is assigned meaning. However, this attempt to mobilize actors, interpretations, meanings, technologies and artefacts and to stabilize a political space by means of a hegemonic narrative is usually only temporarily successful and open to challenge: government is a fundamentally unstable and conflict-ridden operation. Policy narratives are constant objects of interpretation and reinterpretation, as different readings are brought to bear upon the text of politics. The process of writing the political intertext, the determination of the structure and organization of representations of 'the political', is grounded in the multiplicity of meanings of any text, the dissemination and dispersions/instabilities of meanings as an inherent feature of intertextuality. As much as (semiotic) structures may influence action, they remain the effect of precarious stabilizations and thus inherently uncontrollable. The analytical tools of poststructuralist policy analysis focus especially on the attempts of policymaking to create order and structure under conditions of instability that would seem to undermine such efforts.

Policymaking and reflexive government

The reconceptualization of the policy process based on poststructuralist theorizing and an analytics of government also has important implications for a new understanding of the nature of policymaking and leads to a new perception of the currently emerging forms of government.

As I showed, the image of 'struggle' is an important one for poststructuralism's view of the policy process. Different modes of ordering reality seem to compete against each other and different narratives or stories lead to different perceptions of policy problems and, hence, different strategies to address these problems. I have argued that politics can be seen as an 'empty space' until demarcated and partitioned by struggles of boundary drawing. In this process, policy narratives and related political metanarratives serve as interpretations of the topography of a policy field. Certain narratives have a good chance of becoming hegemonic for a particular period of time and of defining the nature of a policy problem and the actors and institutions that should be involved in its handling. But there is also ample evidence that under postmodern conditions such hegemonic definitions of political reality tend to be short lived and become rather quickly objects of contest and destabilization.

The analytics of government helps us to sharpen our understanding of these processes. They articulate a displacement of what I called with Foucault the 'governmentalization of the state'. As mentioned, 'governmentalization of the state' refers to the process by which the state came to take on the function of the care of populations and individuals from the nineteenth century on, a process articulated in various policy fields from social to economic policies. In the interpretation of the analytics of government much of what is being discussed as the 'move from government to governance' or 'the rise of the network society' can be understood as a process in which the 'governmentalization of the state' is being called into question and reinscribed and recoded in a process where the mechanisms of government themselves become the subject of problematization and scrutiny. Hence, developments such as lack of social unity and the rise of a culture of dissent can be seen as problematizations of government practices which reflect a step in the creation of a 'reflexive government' (Dean 1999). The imperative of 'reflexive government' is to render government institutions efficient, accountable, democratic by a variety of technologies from the creation of deliberative spaces to various forms of auditing (Dean 1999: 193). This development is also related to the working of the post-metaphysical culture of our time which has given up the search for general ordering principles, laws of history, fixed notion of right-holders, and ultimate foundations of knowledge (Daly 1994). In this new culture the idea that there is one 'truth' which can be revealed by means of the 'grand narratives' of science or ideology is rejected in favour of the idea that society is an ongoing process of reinvention which should be able to draw on the plurality of the culturally available stories which deal with the social and political problems we face. Business organizations are not conceptualized as monolithic structures, but as texts written by a plurality of authors ranging from consumers to producers and regulators (Boje and Gepart 1996; Linstead 1993: 59–60). Democracy is not understood as an already given narrative which simply needs to be 'read' or revealed by certain 'specialists' so that people may discover their objective interests and what they were really intended for. Instead, democracy is a deliberative process, something which is 'written' by the democratic subject which is not a passive consumer of a given narrative, but the unstable locus for identities and responsible for the constitution of democracy as such (Daly 1994). Nor is science the unquestionable authority whose narratives can settle policy conflicts. In this reading, democracy is configured as a Janus-faced phenomenon which can create the space for the expression of alter-identities, or be a medium by which the dogmatization of identity and the elimination of dissensus are politically legitimized (Connolly 1991).

Reflexive government would imply acknowledgement of the importance of tolerance for the multiplicity of stories available in a policy field. To accept the elusiveness of the search to define the 'true' nature of a policy problem and to come up with a generally acceptable solution for it might be a crucial step in the direction of what ultimately could turn out to be a more efficient style of policymaking. Obviously, in Britain and Germany the strategy of biotechnology policymakers to represent genetically modified food as a blessing for society failed miserably in the market place, where consumers 'voted with their feet' against this form of technological innovation. More attention to voices critical of biotechnology would have saved government agencies and companies from substantial misinvestments and loss of credibility.

Instead of insisting on the possibility of finding 'one truth' or 'the way' and to impose it on to society, reflexive government acknowledges that modernity is a project which is fundamentally incompletable. This does not imply that policymaking is impossible or cannot find points of orientation. Postmodern policymaking takes up themes and logics of the modern, but without recourse to a telos or ultimate foundation (Daly 1994: 183). Critical elements of this style of policymaking are more tolerance for the multiple ways to tell the story of a policy problem, the acknowledgement that today it is increasingly difficult to distinguish between culture and nature, or the openness to negotiate frames of meaning and political realities. While some see in cloned Dolly a sheep, others regard it as a technology, still others as a tortured creature. They all mobilize technologies, language, images, people. Hence, democracy is not understood as an expression of a social totality, but a way of responding to politics and its many uncertainties and anxieties. It is a strategy to articulate and negotiate political issues and to keep them contestable, not to deny their controversial character or vilify certain critical groups and their positions (Warren 1996: 244–250).

There are a number of different, well-known techniques available to keep problems, practices, anxieties and issues contestable in a democracy (Warren 1996: 266). One way is to create deliberative spaces throughout the institutions of state, economy and civil society for the social negotiation of concerns and grievances. Different authors such as Ulrich Beck and Frank Fischer (Beck 1993: 189–203; Hajer 1995: 286–292; Fischer 1995: 207–226) have argued for the importance of institutionalizing new public spaces which facilitate communication between different semiotic universes which deal with alternative descriptions of the realities of policymaking. Certainly, such new institutional platforms for the public negotiation of policy problems would be useful improvements in the democratic process. Deliberative spaces could also be created by a reform of the existing institutions, in particular by empowering hitherto excluded groups and individuals to participate in the negotiation of policies. Often policy decision-making takes on features of what Ulrich Beck calls a subpolitics of science and technology not because there were in principle no institutional sites available for the social negotiation of, for example, genetic engineering policies. Rather, what was often missing were the public spaces within the confines of institutional politics which would allow for the articulation of alternative readings of policy problems. In other words, it was not so much a lack of institutions per se which impeded better communication between opposing conceptualizations of policy problems, but a lack of empowerment of important groups and actors to engage in such a dispute between different cognitive worlds. Hence, democratic policymakers would be well advised to create spaces within existing and in proposed new institutions to keep policy issues ranging from genetic engineering to pensions reform politically contestable and negotiable. Failure to do so would not only create political alienation, but also different forms of grievances and resistance such as excessive anxieties concerning the risks of new technologies or consumer boycotts against products. Such public spaces of reflection and communication, for example in the field of food regulation (BSE, genetic engineering, etc.), would be characterized by more permeable boundaries between science and 'non-science', between experts and non-experts. Science would not be conceptualized as some sort of metanarrative to solve policy disputes. This would probably make many processes of scientific and technological decision-making more complicated and time consuming. But it would also liberate policymaking from mobilizing science into endless and delegitimizing cycles of expertise and counter-expertise. Without the burden of the 'truth claim' and as one story next to others, the often elegant and elaborated narratives of science might develop a new value in the orientation of policymaking. In addition, the negotiation of these boundaries would be a public process with a specified place in the political-institutional framework.

It should be pointed out that recent institutionalizations of 'reflexive government' are not confined to deliberative forms of policymaking such as public inquiries but can be seen in a broad variety of articulations such as various mechanisms to render government agencies accountable and transparent or to initiate the devolution of financial budgets. Reflexive government implies a reinvention of the topography of politics from health care to the welfare state in a way which operationalizes the capacities of diverse associations, movements and groups in a novel way. Neo-liberal policies fit into this emerging regime of government just as deliberative practices do. In the United States the reconfiguration of health by the marketization of health care provision co-exists with the emergence of participatory forms of policymaking. Managed Health Care Organizations which in the last two decades transformed the system of health maintenance exist next to newly created deliberative bioethics committees which negotiate new experimental medical practices such as embryonic stem-cell research. In both cases existing government practices have been called into question and problematized by actors and voices of different motivations. As the 'conduct of the conduct' takes on new expressions and the 'governmentalization of the state' is being called into question, any policy analyst interested in shedding new light on the ways that governing occurs today needs to pay careful attention to the different meanings, aspects and implications of the emerging network society.

References

Abele, F. 1983, 'The Berger Inquiry and the Politics of Transformation in the Mackenzie Valley', Ph.D. thesis, Toronto: York University

Abma, T. A. 1999 ed., *Telling Tales: On Narrative and Evaluation*, Advances in Program Evaluation 6, Greenwich, CT: JAI Press

    2001, 'Narratieve Infrastructuur en Fixaties in Beleidsdialogen: de Schiphol discussie als casus (Narrative Infrastructure and Fixations in Policy Dialogues: The Case of Schiphol Airport)', *Beleid & Maatschappij* 28(2): 66–80

Abrams, P. 2000, 'Overcoming Challenges to Implementing Community-Based Collaborative Governance of Natural Resources: The Case of the Clayoquot Sound Central Region Board', unpublished paper, School of Resource and Environmental Management, Burnaby, BC: Simon Fraser University

Ackerman, B. 1992, *We, the People: Foundations*, Cambridge, MA: Harvard University Press

Allison, G. and P. Zelikow 1999, *Essence of Decision: Explaining the Cuban Missile Crisis*, New York: Longman

Amin, A. and N. Thrift 1994 eds., *Globalisation, Institutions and Regional Development in Europe*, Oxford: Oxford University Press

    1995, 'Globalisation, "Institutional Thickness" and the Local Economy', in Healey, P., S. Cameron, S. Davoudi, S. Graham and A. Madanipour (eds.), *Managing Cities*, Chichester: John Wiley, pp. 91–108

Amy, D. 1987a, 'Can Policy Analysis Be Ethical?', in Fischer and Forester, pp. 45–67

    1987b, *The Politics of Environmental Mediation*, New York: Columbia University Press

Archibald, K. A. 1980, 'The Pitfalls of Language, or Analysis through the Looking Glass', in Giandomenico, M. and E. S. Quade (eds.), *Pitfalls of Analysis*, New York: Wiley, pp. 179–199

Arendt, H. 1958, *The Human Condition*, Chicago: University of Chicago Press

Argyris, C. 1993, *Knowledge for Action: A Guide to Overcoming Barriers to Institutional Change*, San Francisco: Jossey Bass

Axelrod, R. 1984, *The Evolution of Cooperation*, New York: Basic Books

Axelrod, R. and M. Cohen 1999, *Harnessing Complexity: Organizational Implications of a Scientific Frontier*, New York: Free Press

Bachrach, P. and M. S. Baratz 1970, *Power and Poverty: Theory and Practice*, New York: Oxford University Press

Bacon, F. 1960[1620], *The New Organon*, New York: Macmillan

Bacow, L. S. 1993, 'Waste and Race: No Easy Answers', *Forum for Applied Research and Public Policy* Spring: 43–48

Bacow, L. S. and J. R. Milkey 1982, 'Overcoming Local Opposition to Hazardous Waste Facilities: The Massachusetts Approach', *Harvard Environmental Law Review* 6: 265–305

Baier, V. E., J. G. March and H. Saetren 1986, 'Implementation and Ambiguity', *Scandinavian Journal of Management Studies* 2: 197–212

Bailey, N. 1995, *Partnership Agencies in British Urban Policy*, London: UCL Press

Bailey, R. W. 2000, 'Quine, Davidson, Putnam and Policy Analysis: Constructing a Post-Positive Policy Analysis on the Remnants of Realism', paper presented at the Convention of the American Science Association, Atlanta

Bakhtin, M. 1968, *Rabelais and His World*, tr. Hélène Iswolsky, Cambridge, MA: MIT Press

1981, 'Discourse in the Novel', in Bakhtin, M., *The Dialogical Imagination*, tr. C. Emerson and M. Holquist, Austin: University of Texas Press, pp. 257–422

Banfield, E. C. 1961, *Political Influence: A New Theory of Urban Politics*, New York: Free Press

Bang, H. P. and Sörensen, E. 1999, 'The Everyday Maker: A New Challenge to Democratic Governance', *Administrative Theory & Praxis* 21(3): 325–361

Bardach, E. 1977, *The Implementation Game: What Happens After a Bill Becomes a Law*, Cambridge, MA: MIT Press

Bateson, G. 1955, *Steps to an Ecology of Mind*, New York: Ballantine

Baumol, W. J. 1991, 'Toward a Newer Economics: The Future Lies Ahead!', *Economic Journal* 101: 1–8

Beam, G. and D. Simpson 1984, *Political Action*, Chicago: Swallow Press

Beck, U. 1992, 'Modern Society as Risk Society', in Stehr, N. and R. V. Ericson (eds.), *The Culture and Power of Knowledge. Inquiries into Contemporary Societies*, Berlin: Walter de Gruyter, pp. 199–214

1993, *Die Erfindung des Politischen. Zu einer Theorie reflexiven Modernisierung*, Frankfurt am Main: Suhrkamp Verlag

1999, *World Risk Society*, Cambridge: Polity Press

Beck, U., A. Giddens and S. Lash 1994, *Reflexive Modernization*, Cambridge: Polity Press

Beck, U., M. A. Hajer and S. Kesselring 1999 eds., *Der unscharfe Ort der Politik. Empirische Fallstudien zur Theorie der reflexiven Modernisierung*, Opladen: Leske

Benhabib, S. 1986, *Critique, Norm, and Utopia: A Study of the Foundations of Critical Theory*, New York: Columbia University Press

1990, 'Communicative Ethics and Current Controversies in Political Philosophy', in Benhabib, S. and F. Dallmayr (eds.), *The Communicative Ethics Controversy*, Cambridge, MA: MIT Press, pp. 330–369

1992, *Situating the Self: Gender, Community, and Postmodernism in Contemporary Ethics*, New York: Routledge

1996a ed., *Democracy and Difference: Contesting the Boundaries of the Political*, Princeton: Princeton University Press

1996b, 'Toward a Deliberative Model of Democratic Legitimacy', in Benhabib, pp. 67–94

Berger, P. L. and T. Luckmann 1966, *The Social Construction of Reality*, New York: Anchor

Berger, T. 1977, *Northern Frontier, Northern Homeland: The Report of the Mackenzie Valley Pipeline Inquiry*, 2 vols., Ottawa: Supply and Services Canada

Berkel, C., A. Bosch and P. Clausman 1994, *Natuurbeleid in de peiling: Een tussentijdse balans van het Natuurbeleidsplan*, The Hague: LNV

Berlin, I. 1997, 'The Pursuit of the Ideal', in Hardy, H. and R. Hausheer, *Isaiah Berlin, The Proper Study of Mankind: An Anthology of Essays*, London: Chatto & Windus, pp. 1–16

Berman, M. 1988, *All that Is Solid Melts into Air*, New York: Penguin Books

Bernstein, R. J. 1976, *The Restructuring of Social and Political Theory*, New York: Harcourt Brace Jovanovich

1983, *Between Objectivism and Relativism: Science, Hermeneutics, and Praxis*, Philadelphia: University of Pennsylvania Press

Berten, H. 1995, *The Idea of Postmodernism: A History*, London: Routledge

Blackler, F. 1995, 'Knowledge, Knowledge Work, and Organizations', *Organization Studies* 16(6): 1021–1046

Blackler, F., N. Crump and S. McDonald 1999, 'Organizational Learning and Organizational Forgetting', in Easterby-Smith, M., L. Araujo and J. Burgoyne (eds.), *Organizational Learning and the Learning Organization*, London: Sage, pp. 194–216

2000, 'Organizing Processes in Complex Activity Networks', *Organization* 7(2): 277–300

Bobrow, D. B. and J. S. Dryzek 1987, *Policy Analysis by Design*. Pittsburgh: University of Pittsburgh Press

Bohm, D. 1996, *On Dialogue*, ed. Lee Nichol, London: Routledge

Boje, D. M. and R. R. Gepart Jr. 1996 eds., *Postmodern Management and Organization Theory*, London: Sage

Boltanski, L. and L. Thevenot 1999, 'The Sociology of Critical Capacity', *European Journal of Social Theory* 2(3): 359–377

Booher, D. E. and J. E. Innes 2001, 'Network Power in Collaborative Planning', *Journal of Planning Education and Research* 21(3): 221–236

Bostock, D. 2000, *Aristotle's Ethics*, Oxford: Oxford University Press

Bourdieu, P. 1977, *Outline of a Theory of Practice*, Cambridge: Cambridge University Press

1990, *In Other Words: Essays Towards a Reflexive Sociology*, Stanford, CA: Stanford University Press

Bourdieu, P. and L. J. D. Wacquant 1992, *An Invitation to Reflexive Sociology*, Chicago: University of Chicago Press

Bouwens, A. M. C. M. and M. L. J. Dierikx 1996, *Op de Drempel van de Lucht (On the Threshold of the Skies)*, The Hague: SDU Uitgevers

Braybrooke, D. and C. E. Lindblom 1970, *A Strategy of Decision*, New York: Free Press

Brookfield, S. D. 1986, *Understanding and Facilitating Adult Learning*, San Francisco: Jossey-Bass

Brown, Norman 1977, *Perception, Theory and Commitment: The New Philosophy of Science*, Chicago: Precedent Publishing

Brown, R. H. 1976, 'Social Theory as Metaphor', *Theory and Society* 3: 169–197

Brown, S. L. and K. M. Eisenhardt 1998, *Competing on the Edge: Strategy as Structured Chaos*, Boston, MA: Harvard Business School Press

Brubaker, R. 1993, 'Social Theory as Habitus', in Calbourn, C. et al. (eds.), *Bourdieu: Critical Perspectives*, Cambridge: Polity Press, pp. 211–233

Bryson, J. M. and B. C. Crosby 1992, *Leadership for the Common Good: Tackling Public Problems in a Shared Power World*, San Francisco: Jossey Bass

Bullard, R. 1990, *Dumping in Dixie: Race, Class, and Environmental Quality*, Boulder: Westview

    1993, 'Waste and Racism: A Stacked Deck?', *Forum for Applied Research and Public Policy* Spring: 29–35

    1994 ed., *Unequal Protection: Environmental Justice and Communities of Color*, San Francisco: Sierra Club Books

Burchell, G., C. Gordon and P. Miller 1991 eds., *The Foucault Effect: Studies in Governmentality*, London: Harvester

Burke, K. 1969[1945], *A Grammar of Motives*, Berkeley: University of California Press

Burke, T. 1994, *Dewey's New Logic. A Reply to Russell*, Chicago: University of Chicago Press

Burney, L. 1996, 'Sustainable Development and Civil Disobedience: The Politics of Environmental Discourse in Clayoquot Sound', MA Thesis, Trent University, Peterborough, ON

Bush, R. Baruch and Joseph P. Folger 1994, *The Promise of Mediation: Responding to Conflict Through Empowerment and Recognition*, San Francisco: Jossey Bass

Butler, J. 1993, *Bodies that Matter: On the Discursive Limits of 'Sex'*, New York: Routledge

Caldwell, L. K. 1975, 'Managing the Transition to Post-Modern Society', *Public Administration Review* 35(6): 567–572

Callon, M. and J. Law 1995, 'Agency and Hybrid Collective', *The South Atlantic Quarterly* 94: 481–507

Caloren, F. 1978, 'Getting Berger in Focus', *Our Generation* 12(3): 45–56

Camagni, R. 1999, 'La Ville comme milieu: de l'application de l'approche GREMI à l'évolution urbaine', *Revue d'Economie Regionale et Urbaine* 3: 591–606

Cars, G., P. Healey, C. A. Madanipour and C. de Magalhaes 2002, *Urban Governance, Institutional Capacity and Social Milieux*, Aldershot: Ashgate

Castells, M. 1996, *The Rise of the Network Society*, Oxford: Blackwell
  1997, *The Power of Identity*, Oxford: Blackwell
  1998, *End of Millennium*, Malden: Blackwell
Chock, P. 1995, 'Ambiguity in Policy Discourse: Congressional Talk about Immigration', *Policy Sciences* 18: 165–184
Clarke, L. 1989, *Acceptable Risk? Making Decisions in a Toxic Environment*, Berkeley: University of California Press
Clinton, W. J. 1994, *Federal Actions to Address Environmental Justice in Minority and Low-Income Populations*, Executive Order 12898
Cobb, S. 2001, 'Liminal Spaces in Negotiation Process: Crossing Relational and Interpretive Thresholds in a Family Business Negotiation', unpublished paper
Cohen, J. 1993, 'Moral Pluralism and Political Consensus', in Copp, D. et al. (eds.), *The Idea of Democracy*, Cambridge: Cambridge University Press, pp. 270–291
Colebatch, H. K. 1995, 'Organizational Meanings of Program Evaluation', *Policy Sciences* 18: 149–164
Coleman, J. 1988, 'Social Capital in the Creation of Human Capital', *American Journal of Sociology* 94, Supplement S: 95–120
Collins, Harry M. 1985, *Changing Order: Replication and Induction in Scientific Practice*, Beverly Hills: Sage
  1992, *Changing Order: Replication and Induction in Scientific Practice*, Chicago: University of Chicago Press
Committee for Spatial Development 1999, *The European Spatial Development Perspective*, Luxembourg: European Commission
Communities for a Better Environment 1998, *Holding Our Breath: The Struggle for Environmental Justice in Southeast Los Angeles*
Connecticut Legislative Program Review and Investigations Committee 1992, *Siting Controversial Land Uses*
Connick, S. forthcoming, 'The Use of Collaborative Processes in the Making of California Water Policy', Ph.D. thesis, Environmental Sciences, Policy and Management, University of California Berkeley
Connick, S. and J. Innes 2001, 'Outcomes of Collaborative Water Policy Making: Applying Complexity Theory to Evaluation', technical report, Berkeley, CA: Institute of Urban and Regional Development, forthcoming in *Journal of Environmental Planning and Management*
Connolly, W. E. 1983, *The Terms of Political Discourse*, Princeton: Princeton University Press
  1991, *Identity/Difference: Democratic Negotiations of Political Paradox*, Ithaca: Cornell University Press
Cook, S. D. N. 1982, 'Part of What a Judgment Is', Department of Urban Studies paper, Massachusetts Institute of Technology
  1994, 'Autonomy, Interdependence, and Moral Governance, Pluralism in a Rocking Boat', *American Behavioral Scientist* 38(1): 153–171
Cook, S. D. N. and J. S. Brown 1999, 'Bridging Epistemologies: The Generative Dance between Organizational Knowledge and Organizational Knowing', *Organization Science* 10(4): 381–400

Cook, S. and D. Yanow 1993, 'Culture and Organizational Learning', *Journal of Management Inquiry* 2(4); reprinted in Cohen, M. D. and L. Sproull (eds.), *Organizational Learning*, Newbury Park, CA: Sage, 1995, pp. 373–390

Cooper, R. 1989, 'Modernism, Post Modernism and Organizational Analysis 3: The Contribution of Jacques Derrida', *Organizational Studies* 10: 479–502

Corburn, J. 2001, *Bringing Local Knowledge into Environmental Decision-Making, Improving Urban Planning for Communities at Risk*, draft manuscript

Coulter, J. 1979, 'Transparency of Mind: The Availability of Subjective Phenomena', in Coulter, J., *The Social Construction of Mind: Studies in Ethnomethodology and Linguistic Philosophy*, Totowa, NJ: Rowman and Littlefield, pp. 35–62

Crozier, M., S. P. Huntington and J. Watanuki 1975, *The Crisis of Democracy: Report on the Governability of Democracies to the Trilateral Commission*, New York: New York University Press

Dallmayr, F. R. and T. A. McCarthy 1977 eds., *Understanding and Social Inquiry*, Notre Dame: University of Notre Dame Press

Daly, G. 1994, 'Post-metaphysical Culture and Politics: Richard Rorty and Laclau and Mouffe', *Economy and Society* 23: 173–200

Danziger, M. 1995, 'Policy Analysis Postmodernized: Some Political and Pedagogical Ramifications', *Policy Studies Journal* 23(3): 435–450

Davis, R. L. F. n.d., 'Creating Jim Crow: In-Depth Essay', http://www.jimcrowhistory.org/history/creating2.htm

Dean, M. 1999, *Governmentality: Power and Rule in Modern Society*, London: Sage

de Bono, E. 1977, *Lateral Thinking: A Textbook of Creativity*, Harmondsworth: Penguin Books

DeHaven-Smith, L. 1988, *Philosophical Critiques of Policy Analysis*, Gainesville: University of Florida Press

deLeon, P. 1988, *Advice and Consent: The Development of the Policy Sciences*, New York: Russell Sage Foundation

1992, 'The Democratization of the Policy Sciences', *Public Administration Review* 52: 125–129

1997, *Democracy and the Policy Sciences*, Albany: State University of New York Press

DeLeuze, G. and F. Guatani 1988, *A Thousand Plateaus*, London: Athlone Press

DeRoux, G. I. 1991, 'Together Against the Computer: PAR and the Struggle of Afro-Colombians for Public Services', in DeRoux, G., *Action and Knowledge: Breaking the Monopoly with Participatory Action-Research*, New York: Apex Press, pp. 37–53

Derrida, J. 1976, 'Die Struktur, das Zeichen und das Spiel im Diskurs der Wissenschaften vom Menschen', in Derrida, J., *Die Schrift und die Differenz*, Frankfurt am Main: Suhrkamp Verlag, pp. 422–442

1983, *Grammatologie*, Frankfurt am Main: Suhrkamp Verlag

Dery, D. 1987, 'Knowing: The Political Way', *Policy Studies Review* 7(1): 13–25

Dewey, J. 1920, *Reconstruction in Philosophy*, New York: Henry Holt

1922, Review of Walter Lippmann, 'Public Opinion', in *John Dewey: The Middle Works* 13, ed. Jo Ann Boydston, Carbondale and Edwardsville: Southern Illinois University Press, 1983, pp. 337–344

1927, 'The Public and Its Problems', in *John Dewey: The Later Works* 2, ed. Jo Ann Boydston, Carbondale and Edwardsville: Southern Illinois University Press, 1984, pp. 235–372

Di Chiro, G. 1998, 'Environmental Justice from the Grassroots: Reflections on History, Gender, and Expertise', in Farber, D. (ed.), *The Struggle for Ecological Democracy: Environmental Justice Movements in the United States*, New York: Guilford Press, pp. 104–136

Dodge, W. R. 1996, *Regional Excellence: Governing Together to Compete Globally and Flourish Locally*, Washington, DC: National League of Cities

Dodge, W. R. and K. Montgomery 1995, *Shaping a Region's Future: A Guide to Strategic Decision Making for Regions*, n.p.: National League of Cities

Dosman, E. J. 1975, *The National Interest: Politics of Northern Development 1968–75*, Toronto: McClelland and Stewart

Douglas, M. 1982[1973], *Natural Symbols*, New York: Pantheon
1986, *How Institutions Think*, New York: Syracuse University Press

Douglas, M. and A. Wildavsky 1982, *Risk and Culture*, Berkeley: University of California Press

Dreyfus, H. L. and P. Rabinow 1983, *Michel Foucault: Beyond Structuralism and Hermeneutics*, 2nd edn, Chicago: University of Chicago Press

Drucker, P. 1989, *The New Realities in Government and Politics/In Economics and Business/In Society and World View*, New York: Harper and Row

Dryzek, J. S. 1982, 'Policy Analysis as a Hermeneutic Activity', *Policy Sciences* 14: 309–329
1987a, 'Complexity and Rationality in Public Life', *Political Studies* 35: 424–442
1987b, 'Discursive Designs: Critical Theory and Political Institutions', *American Journal of Political Science* 31: 656–679
1987c, *Rational Ecology: Environment and Political Economy*, London: Basil Blackwell
1989, 'Policy Sciences of Democracy', *Polity* 22(1): 97–118
1990a, 'Designs for Environmental Discourse', in Paehlke, R. and D. Torgerson (eds.), *Managing Leviathan: Environmental Politics and the Administrative State*, Peterborough, ON: Broadview Press, pp. 97–111
1990b, *Discursive Democracy: Politics, Policy and Political Science*, Cambridge: Cambridge University Press
1993, 'Policy Analysis and Planning: From Science to Argument', in Fischer and Forester, pp. 213–232
1994, 'Ecology and Discursive Democracy: Beyond Liberal Capitalism and the Administrative State', in O'Connor, M. (ed.), *Is Capitalism Sustainable? Political Economy and the Politics of Ecology*, New York: Guilford Press, pp. 176–197
1996a, 'Political and Ecological Communication', in Mathews, F. (ed.), *Ecology and Democracy*, London: Frank Cass, pp. 13–30
1996b, *Democracy in Capitalist Times*, Oxford: Oxford University Press
1996c, 'Democracy and Environmental Policy Instruments', in Eckersley, R. (ed.), *Markets, the State and the Environment*, London: Macmillan, pp. 294–308

1996d, 'Strategies of Ecological Democratization', in Lafferty, W. M. and J. Meadowcroft (eds.), *Democracy and the Environment*, Cheltenham: Edward Elgar, pp. 108–123

1997, *The Politics of the Earth – Environmental Discourses*, Oxford: Oxford University Press

1999 'Transnational Democracy', *Journal of Political Philosophy* 7: 30–51

2000, *Deliberative Democracy and Beyond*, Oxford: Oxford University Press

Dunn, W. N. 1993, 'Policy Reforms as Arguments', in Fischer and Forester, pp. 254–290

Dunne, J. 1993, *Back to the Rough Ground: 'Phronesis' and 'Techne' in Modern Philosophy and in Aristotle*, Notre Dame: University of Notre Dame Press

Durning, D. 1993, 'Participatory Policy Analysis in a Social Service Agency: A Case Study', *Journal of Policy Analysis and Management* 12: 297–322

Dyrberg, T. B. 1997, *The Circular Structure of Power*, London: Verso

Eagleton, T. 1983, *Literary Theory*, Minneapolis: University of Minnesota Press

EDAW 1996, *Grainger Town Regeneration Strategy*, Glasgow: EDAW Consulting

Edelman, M. 1964, *The Symbolic Uses of Politics*, Chicago: University of Illinois Press

1971, *Politics as Symbolic Action*, Chicago: Markham

1977, *Political Language*, New York: Academic Press

1988, *Constructing the Political Spectacle*, Chicago: University of Chicago Press

Eeten, M. van 1999, *Dialogues of the Deaf: Defining New Agendas for Environmental Deadlocks*, Delft: Eburon

Elliot, M. 1999, ' "Making Sense of Places": The Use of "Sense of Place" in Public Participation', MTP thesis, Department of Town and Country Planning, University of Newcastle upon Tyne

Ellis, R. and D. Coyle 1994, *Politics, Policy and Culture: Applications of Group/Grid Theory*, Boulder: Westview

Elmore, R. F. 1996, 'Getting to Scale with Good Educational Practice', *Harvard Educational Review* 66(1): 1–26

Elster, J. 1999, *Strong Feelings: Emotion, Addiction, and Human Behavior*, Cambridge, MA: MIT Press

Engeström, Y. 1993, 'Developmental Studies of Work as a Testbench of Activity Theory: The Case of Primary Care Medical Practice', in Chaiklin, S. and J. Lave (eds.), *Understanding Practice: Perspectives on Activity and Context*, Cambridge: Cambridge University Press, pp. 64–103

Engeström, Y. and D. Middleton 1996 eds., *Cognition and Communication at Work*, Cambridge: Cambridge University Press

EPA Region One 2001, 'The EPA New England Environmental Justice Action Plan for Fiscal Years 2001 and 2002', 1 October, http://www.epa.gov/NE/steward/ejprog/ej_external.pdf

Eriksen, E. O. and J. E. Fossum 2000 eds., *Democracy in the European Union: Integration through Deliberation*, London: Routledge

Erlandson, D. A., E. L. Harris, B. L. Skipper and S. D. Allen 1993, *Doing Naturalistic Inquiry*, Newbury Park, CA: Sage

Esping-Anderson, G. 1990, *The Three Worlds of Welfare Capitalism*, Cambridge: Polity Press

Eyerman, R. and A. Jamison 1991, *Social Movements: A Cognitive Approach*, Edinburgh: Edinburgh University Press

1998, *Music and Social Movements – Mobilizing Traditions in the Twentieth Century*, Cambridge: Cambridge University Press

Falco, M. 1973, *Truth and Meaning in Political Science*, Columbus, OH: Merrill

Fay, B. 1975, *Social Theory and Political Practice*, London: George Allen and Unwin

1976, *Social Theory and Political Practice*, New York: Holmes and Meier

Feldman, M. S. 1994, *Some Interpretive Techniques for Analyzing Qualitative Data*, Beverly Hills: Sage

Finkelstein, L. S. 1995, 'What is Global Governance', *Global Governance* 1(1): 367–372

Fischer, F. 1980, *Politics, Values, and Public Policy: The Problem of Methodology*, Boulder: Westview

1990, *Technocracy and the Politics of Expertise*, Newbury Park, CA: Sage

1992, 'Participatory Expertise: Toward the Democratization of Policy Science', in Dunn, W. N. and R. M. Kelly (eds.), *Advances in Policy Studies since 1950*, New Brunswick, NJ: Transaction Publishers, pp. 351–376

1993, 'Policy Discourse and the Politics of Washington Think Tanks', in Fischer and Forester, pp. 21–42

1995, *Evaluating Public Policy*, Chicago: Nelson-Hall

1996, 'But Is it Scientific? Local Knowledge in Postpositivist Perspective', manuscript, New York

2001, *Citizens, Experts and the Environment: The Politics of Local Knowledge*, Durham, NC: Duke University Press

Fischer, F. and J. Forester 1987 eds., *Confronting Values in Policy Analysis: The Politics of Criteria*, Newbury Park, CA: Sage

1993 eds., *The Argumentative Turn in Policy Analysis and Planning*, Durham, NC: Duke University Press

Fischer, F. and M. Hajer 1999 eds., *Living with Nature – Environmental Politics as Cultural Discourse*, Oxford: Oxford University Press

Fischler, R. 2000, 'Communicative Planning Theory: A Foucauldian Assessment' *Journal of Planning Education and Research* 19(4): 358–368

Fish, S. 1980, *Is there a Text in this Class? The Authority of Interpretive Communities*, Cambridge, MA: Harvard University Press

Fisher, R. and W. Ury 1981, *Getting to Yes: Negotiating Agreement Without Giving In*, Boston: Houghton Mifflin

Floden, R. E. and S. S. Weiner 1978, 'Rationality to Ritual: The Multiple Roles of Evaluation in Governmental Processes', *Policy Sciences* 9: 9–18

Flyvbjerg, B. 1998, *Rationality and Power: Democracy in Practice*, Chicago: University of Chicago Press

Forester, J. 1985, 'The Policy Analysis–Critical Theory Affair: Wildavsky and Habermas as Bedfellows?', in Forester, J. (ed.), *Critical Theory and Public Life*, Cambridge, MA: MIT Press, pp. 258–280

1993a, *Critical Theory, Public Policy, and Planning Practices*, Albany: State University of New York Press

1993b, 'Learning from Practice Stories: the Priority of Practical Judgment', in Fischer and Forester, pp. 186–212

1999, *The Deliberative Practitioner: Encouraging Participatory Planning Processes*, Cambridge MA: MIT Press

Foucault, M. 1970, *The Order of Things – An Archeology of the Human Sciences*, New York: Vintage Books

1980, *Power/Knowledge: Selected Interviews and Other Writings 1972–77*, ed. C. Gordon, Brighton: Harvester

1986, 'Of Other Spaces', *Diacritics* Spring: 22–27

1991a, 'Governmentality', in Burchell et al., pp. 87–104

1991b, 'Questions of Method', in Burchell et al., pp. 73–86

Fox, C. J. and H. T. Miller 1996, *Postmodern Public Administration: Toward Discourse*, Thousand Oaks, CA: Sage

Fox-Keller, E. 1985, *Reflections on Gender and Science*, New Haven, CT: Yale University Press

Frank, M. 1989, *What Is Neostructuralism?* Minneapolis: University of Minnesota Press

Fraser, N. 1989, *Unruly Practices: Power, Discourse, and Gender in Contemporary Social Theory*, Minneapolis: University of Minnesota Press

1992, 'Rethinking the Public Sphere: A Contribution to the Critique of Actually Existing Democracy', in Calhoun, G. (ed.), *Habermas and the Public Sphere*, Cambridge, MA: MIT Press, pp. 109–142

Freire, P. 1970, *Pedagogy of the Oppressed*, New York: Seabury Press

Friends of Clayoquot Sound 1998, *Implementing the Scientific Panel: Three Years and Counting*, Tofino, BC (www.island.net/~focs)

Fukuyama, F. 1995, *Trust: The Social Virtues and the Creation of Prosperity*, London: Penguin Books

Fung, A., B. Karkkainen and C. Sabel 2001, 'After Backyard Environmentalism: Towards a New Model of Information Based Environmental Regulation', paper prepared for Conference on Information Based Environmental Regulation: The Beginning of a New Regulatory Regime, http://www.law.columbia.edu/sabel/papers/intro10_fin5.htm

Fung, A. and E. O. Wright 2001, 'Deepening Democracy: Innovations in Empowered Participatory Governance', *Politics & Society* 29(1): 5–41

Gagliardi, P. 1990, 'Artifacts as Pathways and Remains of Organizational Life', in Gagliardi, P., *Symbols and Artifacts*, New York: Aldine de Gruyter, pp. 3–38

Galison, P. 1997, *Image and Logic: A Material Culture of Microphysics*, Chicago: University of Chicago Press

Gamble, D. J. 1979, 'The Berger Inquiry: An Impact Assessment Process', *Science* 199: 946–952

Gamson, W. 1999, 'Meta-Talk', unpublished mimeo

Gans, H. 1976, 'On the Methods Used in this Study', in Golden, M. P. (ed.), *The Research Experience*, Itasca, IL: F. E. Peacock, pp. 49–59

Garvin, T. and J. Eyles 1997, 'The Sun Safety Metanarrative: Translating Science into Public Health Discourse', *Policy Sciences* 30: 47–70

Gee, J. 1990, *Social Linguistics and Literacies: Ideology in Discourses*, Basingstoke: Falmer

Geertz, C. 1973, *The Interpretation of Cultures*, New York: Basic Books

1983, *Local Knowledge*, New York: Basic Books

1988, *Works and Lives*, Stanford: Stanford University Press

Geiser, K. and G. Waneck 1994, 'PCBs and W. County', in Bullard, pp. 43–52

George, J. and D. Campbell 1990, 'Patterns of Dissent and the Celebration of Difference: Critical Social Theory and International Relations', *International Studies Quarterly* 34: 269–293

Gherardi, S. 2000, 'Practice-based Theorizing on Learning and Knowing in Organizations', *Organization* 7(2): 211–223

Gherardi, S., Davide Nicolini and Francesca Odella 1998, 'Toward a Social Understanding of how People Learn in Organizations', *Management Learning* 29(3): 273–298

Gibbons, M. T. 1987 ed., *Interpreting Politics*, Oxford: Blackwell

Gibbs, L. 1982, *Love Canal: My Story*, Albany: State University of New York Press

1994, 'Risk Assessments from a Community Perspective', *Environmental Impact Assessment Review*, special issue, 14(5/6): 327–335

Giddens, A. 1984, *The Constitution of Society: Outline of the Theory of Structuration*, Berkeley: University of California Press

1991, *Modernity and Self-identity*, Cambridge: Polity Press

1992, *Human Societies: An Introductory Reader in Sociology*, Cambridge: Polity Press

1995, *New Statesman and Society*, 7 April

Gieryn, T. F. 1995, 'Boundaries of Science', in Jasanoff, S. et al. (eds.), *Handbook on Science, Technology and Society*, Newbury Park, CA: Sage, pp. 393–443

Gleick, J. 1987, *Chaos Theory: Making a New Science*, New York: Viking

Gloin, L. 1989, 'Words: Functional Digital Options', *Saturday Magazine, The Toronto Star*, 25 February: M2

Goffman, E. 1974, *Frame Analysis*, Cambridge, MA: Harvard University Press

Golden-Biddle, K. and K. Locke 1993, 'Appealing Work: An Investigation in how Ethnographic Texts Convince', *Organization Science* 4(4): 595–616

1997, *Composing Qualitative Research*, Thousand Oaks, CA: Sage

Goodman, N. 1978, *Ways of Worldmaking*, Indianapolis: Hackett

Gordon, C. 1991, 'Government Rationality: An Introduction', in Burchell et al., pp. 1–51

Gottweis, H. 1995, 'Genetic Engineering, Democracy, and the Politics of Identity', *Social Text* Spring: 127–152

1998, *Governing Molecules: The Discursive Politics of Genetic Engineering in Europe and in the United States*, Cambridge, MA: MIT Press, pp. 11–38

Gowler, D. and K. Legge 1983, 'The Meaning of Management and the Management of Meaning', in Earl, M. (ed.), *Perspectives on Management: A Multidisciplinary Analysis*, Oxford: Oxford University Press, pp. 197–231

Gray, B. 1991, *Collaborating: Finding Common Ground for Multiparty Problems*, San Francisco: Jossey Bass

Grossman, K. 1994, 'People of Color Environmental Summit', in Bullard, pp. 272–297

Gualini, E. 2001, *Planning and the Intelligence of Institutions: Interactive Approaches to Territorial Policy-Making between Institutional Design and Institution-Building*, Aldershot: Ashgate

Guba, E. G. 1990, *The Paradigm Dialog*, Newbury Park, CA: Sage

Guba, E. G. and Y. S. Lincoln 1985, *Naturalistic Inquiry*, Beverly Hills: Sage
1989, *Fourth Generation Evaluation*, London: Sage

Guitierrez, G. 1994, 'Mothers of East Los Angeles Strike Back', in Bullard, pp. 220–233

Gumperz, J. J. 1982, *Discourse Strategies*, Cambridge: Cambridge University Press

Gunsteren, H. van 1998, *A Theory of Citizenship, Organizing Plurality in Contemporary Democracies*, Boulder: Westview

Gusfield, J. R. 1963, *Symbolic Crusade*, Chicago: University of Illinois Press
1976, 'The Literary Rhetoric of Science', *American Sociological Review* 41: 16–34
1981, *The Culture of Public Problems*, Chicago: University of Illinois Press

Gutman, A. 1994 ed., *Multiculturalism – Examining the Politics of Recognition*, Princeton: Princeton University Press

Haan, H. de 1998, 'Signs in the Landscape: The Construction of Identities in the Hoeksche Waard', in Anon, *New Landscape Frontiers*, Rotterdam: Air Southbound, pp. 54–79

Haas, P. 1990, *Saving the Mediterranean*, New York: Columbia University Press
1992, 'Introduction: Epistemic Communities and International Policy Coordination', *International Organization* 46: 1–36

Habermas, J. 1970a, 'On Systematically Distorted Communication', *Inquiry* 13: 205–218
1970b, 'Toward a Theory of Communicative Competence', *Inquiry* 13: 360–375
1979, 'What Is Universal Pragmatics?', in Habermas, J., *Communication and the Evolution of Society*, tr. T. McCarthy, Boston: Beacon Press, pp. 1–68
1981, *The Theory of Communicative Action: Reason and the Rationalization of Society*, tr. T. McCarthy, Boston: Beacon Press
1984/87, *The Theory of Communicative Action*, tr. T. McCarthy, 2 vols., Boston: Beacon Press
1990, 'Discourse Ethics: Notes on a Program of Philosophical Justification', in Habermas, J., *Moral Consciousness and Communicative Action*, tr. C. Lenhardt and S. Weber Nicholsen, Cambridge, MA: MIT Press, pp. 43–115
1992, 'Further Reflections on the Public Sphere', in Calhoun, G. (ed.), *Habermas and the Public Sphere*, Cambridge, MA: MIT Press, pp. 421–461
1996, *Between Facts and Norms: Contributions to a Discourse Theory of Law and Democracy*, tr. W. Rehg, Boston: MIT Press

Hacking, I. 1984, *Representing and Intervening: Introductory Topics in the Philosophy of Natural Science*, Cambridge: Cambridge University Press

Hajer, M. A. 1994, *Managing the Metaphors. Global Environmental Constructs and the Missing Public Domain*, paper prepared for the workshop 'Science Studies, International Relations and the Global Environment', Cornell University, 16–18 September

1995, *The Politics of Environmental Discourse: Ecological Modernization and the Policy Process*, Oxford: Oxford University Press

2000a, *Politiek als Vormgeving*, inaugural lecture, Amsterdam: Vosius Pers

2000b, 'Transnational Networks as Transnational Policy Discourse: Some Observations on the Politics of Spatial Development in Europe', in Salet, W. and A. Faludi (eds.), *The Revival of Strategic Spatial Planning*, Amsterdam: KNAW, pp. 135–142

2002, *Policy Analysis and the Institutional Void*, under review

Hajer, M. and F. Fischer 1999, *Beyond Global Discourse: The Rediscovery of Culture in Environmental Politics*, in Fischer and Hajer

Hajer, M. and S. Kesselring 1999, 'Democracy in the Risk Society – Learning from the Politics of Mobility in Munich', *Environmental Politics* 8(3): 1–23

Hajer, M. A. and A. Reijndorp 2001, *In Search of New Public Domain*, Rotterdam: NAi Publishers

Hall, P. and R. Taylor 1996, 'Political Science and the Three Institutionalisms', *Political Studies* 64: 936–957

Harding, A. 1995, 'Elite Theory and Growth Machines', in Judge, D., G. Stoker and H. Wolman (eds.), *Theories of Urban Politics*, London: Sage, pp. 35–53

Harvey, D. 1996, *Justice, Nature and the Geography of Difference*, Oxford: Blackwell

1999, 'The Environment of Justice', in Fischer and Hajer, pp. 153–185

Hassard, J. and M. Parker 1993, *Postmodernism and Organizations*, London: Sage

Hastings, A. 1996, 'Unravelling the Process of "Partnership" in Urban Regeneration Policy', *Urban Studies* 33: 253–268

1999, Special issue on Discourse and Urban Change, *Urban Studies* 36(1)

Hatch, C. 1994, 'The Clayoquot Protests: Taking Stock One Year Later', in Hatch, C. et al., *Clayoquot and Dissent*, Vancouver, BC: Ronsdale Press, pp. 199–208

Hawkes, T. 1977, *Structuralism and Semiotics*, Berkeley: University of California Press

Hawkesworth, M. E. 1988, *Theoretical Issues in Policy Analysis*, Albany: State University of New York Press

Healey, Patsy 1993, 'Planning through Debate: The Communicative Turn in Planning Theory', in Fischer and Forester, pp. 233–253

1997, *Collaborative Planning: Shaping Places in Fragmented Societies*, London: Macmillan

1998, 'Building Institutional Capacity Through Collaborative Approaches to Planning', *Environment and Planning B* 30: 1531–1546

2002, 'Place, Identity and Governance: Transforming Discourses and Practices', in Hillier, J. and E. Rooksby (eds.), *Habitus: A Sense of Place*, Aldershot: Avebury, pp. 173–202

Healey, Patsy, A. Khakee, A. Motte and B. Needham 1997 eds., *Making Strategic Spatial Plans: Innovation in Europe*, London: UCL Press

Healey, Patsy, C. de Magalhaes and A. Madanipour 1999, 'Institutional Capacity-Building, Urban Planning and Urban Regeneration Projects', special issue of *FUTURA*: Urban Futures: A Loss of Shadows in the Flowing of Spaces, Helsinki: Finnish Society for Futures Studies: 117–137

Healey, Patsy, C. de Magalhaes, A. Madanipour, and J. Pendlebury 2000, 'Place, Identity, and Local Politics: Analyzing Partnership Initiatives', reproduced as chapter 2 in the present volume

Healey, Patsy, A. Madanipour and C. de Magalhaes 2002, 'Shaping City Centre Futures: Conservation, Regeneration and Institutional Capacity', Centre for Research in European Urban Environments: University of Newcastle

Healy, Paul 1986, 'Interpretive Policy Inquiry', *Policy Sciences* 19: 381–396

Heidenheimer, A. J. 1986 'Politics, Policy and Policey as Concepts in English and Continental Languages: An Attempt to Explain Divergences', *Review of Politics* 48(1): 3–30

Heiman, M. 1990, 'From "Not in My Backyard!" to "Not in Naybod's Backyard!" Grassroots Challenge to Hazardous Waste Facility Siting', *Journal of the American Planning Association* 56(3): 359–362

Heineman, R., W. T. Bluhm, S. A. Peterson and E. N. Kearny 1990, *The World of Policy Analysis: Rationality, Values, and Politics*, Chatham, NJ: Chatham House

Held, D. 1995, *Democracy and the Global Order: From the Modern State to Cosmopolitan Governance*, Cambridge: Polity Press

Helling, A. 1998, 'Collaborative Visioning: Proceed with Caution! Results from Evaluating Atlanta's Vision 2020 Project', *Journal of the American Planning Association* 64(3): 335–349

Henriques, J., W. Holloway, C. Urwin and C. Venn 1984, *Changing the Subject: Psychology, Social Regulation and Subjectivity*, London: Methuen

Héritier, A. 1993, *Policy Analyse: Kritiek und Neuorientierung*, Opladen: Westdeutscher Verlag

Hirschman, A. 1982, *Shifting Involvements: Private Interest and Public Action*, Princeton: Princeton University Press

1991, *The Rhetoric of Reaction: Perversity, Futility, Jeopardy*, Cambridge, MA: The Belknap Press of Harvard University Press

Hofferbert, R. I. 1990, *The Reach and Grasp of Policy Analysis*, Tuscaloosa: University of Alabama Press

Hofmann, J. 1995, 'Implicit Theories in Policy Discourse: Interpretations of Reality in German Technology Policy', *Policy Sciences* 18: 127–148

Holland, J. 1998, *Emergence: From Chaos to Order*, Reading, MA: Addison-Wesley

Hollingworth, J. R., P. C. Schmitter and W. Streeck 1994 eds., *Governing Capitalist Economies: Performance and Control of Economic Sectors*, Oxford: Oxford University Press

Holstein, J. A. and J. F. Gubrium 1995, *The Active Interview*, Thousand Oaks, CA: Sage

Honig, B. 1993, *Political Theory and the Displacement of Politics*, Ithaca: Cornell University Press

Honneth, A. 1992, *Kampf um Anerkennung. Zur moralischen Grammatik sozialer Konflikte*, Frankfurt am Main: Suhrkamp Verlag

Houser, N. and C. Kloesel 1992 eds., *The Essential Peirce*, vol. 1, Bloomington: Indiana University Press

Hummel, R. 2001, 'Kant's Contributions to Organizational Knowledge: Do Workers Know Something Managers Don't?', paper presented to the Annual Conference of the Public Administration Theory Network, Leiden, 21–23 June

Hunt, A. 1992, 'Foucault's Expulsion of Law: Toward a Retrieval', *Law and Social Inquiry* 17: 1–38

Imrie, R. and M. Raco 1999, 'How New is the New Local Governance?', *Transactions of the Institute of British Geographers* 24(1): 45–63

Innes, J. 1992, 'Group Processes and the Social Construction of Growth Management: Florida, Vermont and New Jersey', *Journal of the American Planning Association* 58(4): 440–453

1995 'Planning Theory's Emerging Paradigm: Communicative Action and Interactive Practice', *Journal of Planning Education and Research* 14(4): 183–189

1996a, 'Indicators for Collective Learning: Rethinking Planning for Complex Systems', paper prepared for presentation at the 50th Anniversary Conference, Department of Town and Country Planning, University of Newcastle, October

1996b, 'Planning through Consensus Building: A New View of the Comprehensive Planning Ideal', *Journal of the American Planning Association* 62(4): 460–472

1998, 'Information in Communicative Planning', *Journal of the American Planning Association* 64(1): 52–63

Innes, J. and D. E. Booher 1999a, 'Consensus Building and Complex Adaptive Systems: A Framework for Evaluating Collaborative Planning', *Journal of the American Planning Association* 65(4): 412–423

1999b, 'Consensus Building as Role Playing and Bricolage: Toward a Theory of Collaborative Planning', *Journal of the American Planning Association* 65(1): 9–26

1999c, 'Indicators for Sustainable Communities: A Strategy Building Complexity Theory and Distributed Intelligence', Working Paper 99–04, Institute of Urban and Regional Development, Berkeley: University of California, September, published 2000 in *Planning Theory and Practice* 1(2): 173–186

1999d, 'Metropolitan Development as a Complex System: A New Approach to Sustainability', *Economic Development Quarterly* 13(2): 141–156

2000a, 'Planning Institutions in the Network Society: Theory for Collaborative Planning', in Salet, W. and A. Faludi (eds.), *Revival of Strategic Spatial Planning*, Amsterdam: Elsevier/Oxford University Press, pp. 175–189

2000b, 'Public Participation in Planning: New Strategies for the 21st Century', Working paper 2000–07, Institute of Urban and Regional Development, University of California Berkeley August

Innes, J. and S. Connick 1999, 'San Francisco Estuary Project', in Susskind, McKearnon and Thomas-Larmer, pp. 801–827

Innes, J. and J. Gruber 2001a, *Bay Area Transportation Decision Making in the Wake of ISTEA: Planning Styles in Conflict at the Metropolitan Transportation Commission*, University of California Transportation Center, http://www.uctc.net/papers/papersalpha.html#I

2001b, 'Planning Styles in Conflict at the San Francisco Bay Area's Metropolitan Transportation Commission', working paper no. 2001–09, Institute of Urban and Regional Development, University of California Berkeley, http://www-iurd.ced.berkeley.edu/pub/abstract_wp200109.htm

Innes, J., J. Gruber, M. Neuman and R. Thompson 1994, *Coordinating Growth and Environmental Management through Consensus Building*, California Policy Seminar, CPS Report: A Policy Research Program Report, University of California: Berkeley

Isaacs, W. 1999, *Dialogue and the Art of Thinking Together*, New York: Doubleday

Iser, W. 1989, *Prospecting: From Reader Response to Literary Anthropology*, Baltimore: Johns Hopkins University Press

Jameson, F. 1972, *The Prison House of Language: A Critical Account of Structuralism and Russian Formalism*, Princeton: Princeton University Press

Jamison, A. 2002, *The Making of Green Knowledge*, Cambridge: Cambridge University Press

Jänicke, M. 1996, 'Democracy as a Condition for Environmental Policy Success: The Importance of Non-Institutional Factors', in Lafferty and Meadowcroft, pp. 71–85

Jasanoff, S. 1990, *The Fifth Branch: Science Advisers as Policymakers*, Cambridge, MA: Harvard University Press

Jennings, B. 1983, 'Interpretive Social Science and Policy Analysis', in Callahan, D. and B. Jennings (eds.), *Ethics, the Social Sciences, and Policy Analysis*, New York: Plenum, pp. 3–36

   1987a, 'Interpretation and the Practice of Policy Analysis', in Fischer and Forester, pp. 128–152

   1987b, 'Policy Analysis: Science, Advocacy, or Counsel?', in Nagel, S. (ed.), *Research in Public Policy Analysis and Management*, vol. 4, Greenwich, CT: JAI Press, pp. 50–85

Jobert, B. and P. Muller 1987, *L'Etat en action. Politiques publiques et corporatisms*, Paris: Presses Universitaires de France

John, P. 1999, *Analysing Public Policy*, London: Pinter

Johnson, B. L. 1994, 'Is Health Risk Assessment Unethical?', *Environmental Impact Assessment Review* 14(5/6): 377–384

Johnson, D. W. and F. P. Johnson 1997, *Joining Together: Group Theory and Group Skills*, 6th edn, Boston: Allyn and Bacon

Johnson, S. 2001, *Emergence: The Connected Lives of Ants, Brains, Cities and Software*, New York: Scribner

Jonsen, A. R. and S. Toulmin 1988, *The Abuse of Casuistry: A History of Moral Reasoning*, Berkeley: University of California Press

Jordan, A. 1999, 'The Implementation of EU Environmental Policy: A Policy Problem without a Political Solution?' *Environmental and Planning C: Government and Policy* 17: 69–90

Kahne, M. J. and C. Schwartz 1978, 'Negotiating Trouble: The Social Construction and Management of Trouble in a College Psychiatric Context', *Social Problems* 25(5): 461–475

Kahneman, D. and A. Tversky 1981, 'The Framing of Decisions and the Psychology of Choice', *Science* 211: 453–458

Kaplan, T. J. 1993, 'Reading Policy Narratives: Beginnings, Middles, and Ends', in Fischer and Forester, pp. 167–185

Kathlene, L. and J. A. Martin 1991, 'Enchancing Citizen Participation: Panel Designs, Perspectives and Policy Formation', *Journal of Policy Analysis and Management* 10: 46–63

Kauffman, S. 1995, *At Home in the Universe: The Search for the Laws of Complexity*, London: Viking

Kekes, J. 1993, *The Morality of Pluralism*, Princeton: Princeton University Press

Kellert, S. H. 1993, *In the Wake of Chaos: Unpredictable Order in Dynamic Systems*, Chicago: University of Chicago Press

Kelly, K. 1994, *Out of Control: The Rise of the Neobiological Civilization*, Reading, MA: Addison-Wesley

Kelly, M. and S. Maynard-Moody 1993, 'Policy Analysis in the Post-positivist Era', *Public Administration Review* 53(2): 135–142

Kelman, H. C. 1996, 'Negotiation as Interactive Problem Solving', *International Negotiation* 1: 99–123

Keulartz, J. 1999, 'Engineering the Environment: The Politics of Nature Development', in Fischer and Hajer, pp. 83–102

Keulartz, J., S. Swart and H. van der Windt 2000, *Natuurbeelden en natuurbeleid*, The Hague: NWO

Kickert, W. J. M., E. Klijn and J. Koppenjan 1997, *Managing Complex Networks: Strategies for the Public Sector*, London: Sage

King, C. S. and C. Stivers 1998 eds., *Government Is Us: Public Administration in an Anti-government Era*, Thousand Oaks, CA: Sage

King, G., R. O. Koehane and S. Verba 1994, *Designing Social Inquiry: Scientific Inference in Qualitative Research*, Princeton: Princeton University Press

Knill, C. and A. Lenschow 2000 eds., *Implementing EU Environmental Policy: New Directions and Old Problems*, Manchester: Manchester University Press

Knorr-Cetina, K. and M. Mulkay 1983 eds., *Science Observed: Perspectives on the Social Study of Science*, London: Sage

Kolakowski, L. 1968, *The Alienation of Reason: A History of Positivist Thought*, Garden City, NY: Doubleday

1969, 'The Priest and the Jester', in Kolakowski, L., *Toward a Marxist Humanism*, tr. J. Kielonko Peel, New York: Grove Press, pp. 9–37

Krauss, C. 1993, 'Blue Collar Women and Toxic-Waste Protests: The Process of Politicization', in Hofrichter, R. (ed.), *Toxic Struggles: The Theory and Practice of Environmental Justice*, Philadelphia: New Society Publishers, pp. 107–117

1994, 'Women of Color on the Front Line', in Bullard, pp. 256–271

Kuhn, T. 1970, *The Structure of Scientific Revolutions*, Chicago: University of Chicago Press

1977, 'Second Thoughts on Paradigms', in Kuhn, T. A., *The Essential Tension: Selected Studies in Scientific Tradition and Change*, Chicago: University of Chicago Press, pp. 293–319

Kunda, G. 1992, *Engineering Culture*, Philadelphia: Temple University Press

Kundera, M. 1992, 'Les Chemins dans le brouillard', *L'Infini* Winter: 42–64

Kusch, M. 1991, *Foucault's Strata and Fields: An Investigation into Archeological and Genealogical Science Studies*, Dordrecht: Kluwer

Kusterer, K. C. 1978, *Know-How on the Job: The Important Working Knowledge of 'Unskilled' Workers*, Boulder: Westview

Laclau, E. and C. Mouffe 1985, *Hegemony and Socialist Strategy: Toward a Radical Democratic Politics*, London: Verso

Lafferty, W. and J. Meadowcroft 1996 eds., *Democracy and the Environment: Problems and Prospects*, London: Edward Elgar

Laird, F. 1993, 'Participatory Policy Analysis, Democracy, and Technological Decision Making', *Science, Technology, and Human Values* 18: 341–361

Lakoff, G. 1987, *Women, Fire, and Dangerous Things*, Chicago: University of Chicago Press

Lakoff, G. and M. Johnson 1980, *Metaphors We Live By*, Chicago: University of Chicago Press

Larmore, C. E. 1987, *Patterns of Moral Complexity*, Cambridge: Cambridge University Press

Lash, S., B. Szerszinski and B. Wynne 1996 eds., *Risk, Environment and Modernity: Towards a New Ecology*, London: Sage

Lasswell, H. D. 1926, 'Review of Walter Lippmann, *The Phantom Public*', *American Journal of Sociology* 31: 533–535

1941, *Democracy through Public Opinion*, Menasha, WI: George Banta

1951, 'The Policy Orientation', in Lasswell, H. D. and D. Lerner, *The Policy Sciences*, Stanford: Stanford University Press, pp. 1–15

1971, *A Pre-View of Policy Sciences*, New York: American Elsevier

1979, *The Signature of Power*, New Brunswick, NJ: Transaction Publishers

Latour, B. 1987, *Science in Action*, Cambridge, MA: Harvard University Press

1990, 'Drawing Things Together', in Lynch, M. and S. Woolgar (eds.), *Representation in Scientific Practice*, Cambridge, MA: MIT Press, pp. 18–68

Latour, B. and S. Woolgar 1979, *Laboratory Life*, Newbury Park, CA: Sage

Laudan, L. 1977, *Progress and Its Problems*, Berkeley: University of California Press

Lauria, M. 1997 ed., *Reconstructing Urban Regime Theory: Regulating Urban Politics in a Global Economy*, London: Sage

Lave, J. 1988, *Cognition in Practice: Mind, Mathematics and Culture in Everyday Life*, Cambridge: Cambridge University Press

1993, 'The Practice of Learning', in Chaiklin, S. and J. Lave, *Understanding Practice: Perspectives on Activity and Context*, Cambridge: Cambridge University Press, pp. 3–34

Lave, J. and E. Wenger 1991, *Situated Learning: Legitimate Peripheral Participation*, Cambridge: Cambridge University Press

Law, J. 1994, *Organizing Modernity*, Oxford: Blackwell

Laws, D. 1998, 'Bargaining in the Shadow of the Future', Ph.D. Dissertation, Department of Urban Studies and Planning, Massachusetts Institute of Technology

Laws, D. and L. Susskind 1991, 'Changing Perspectives on the Facility Siting Process', *Maine Policy Review* 1(1): 29–44

Lax, D. A. and J. K. Sebenius 1986, *The Manager as Negotiator*, New York: Free Press

Lemert, C. 1995, *Sociology after the Crisis*, Boulder: Westview

Lenzer, G. 1975 ed., *Auguste Comte and Positivism: The Essential Writings*, Chicago: University of Chicago Press

Lewis, J. 1994, 'Foreword', in Bullard, pp. vii–x

Lincoln, Y. S. and E. G. Guba 1985, *Naturalistic Inquiry*, Newbury Park, CA: Sage

Lindblom, C. E. 1958, 'Policy Analysis', *American Economic Review* 48: 298–312

1990, *Inquiry and Change*, New Haven, CT: Yale University Press

Lindblom, C. and D. Cohen 1979, *Usable Knowledge: Social Science and Social Problem Solving*, New Haven, CT: Yale University Press

Linder, S. H. 1995, 'Contending Discourses in the Electromagnetic Fields Controversy', *Policy Sciences* 18: 209–230

Linstead, S. 1993, 'Deconstruction in the Study of Organizations', in Hassard, J. and M. Parker (eds.), *Postmodernism and Organization*, London: Sage, pp. 49–70

Linstead, S. and R. Grafton-Small 1993, 'On Reading Organizational Culture', *Organization Studies* 13: 331–355

Lipsky, M. 1979, *Street-level Bureaucracy*, New York: Russell Sage Foundation

LNV (Ministry of Agriculture, Nature Conservation and Fishery) 1990, *Natuurbeleidsplan*, The Hague: LNV

LNV/IPO (Ministry of Agriculture, Nature Conservation and Fishery, IPO) 1999, *Evaluatie van het natuur-, bos- en landschapsbeleid*, The Hague: LNV/IPO

LNV/VROM (Ministry of Agriculture, Nature Conservation and Fishery/Ministry of Public Housing, Spatial Planning and the Environment) 1992, *Structuurschema Groene Ruimte*, The Hague: SDU

Lovins, A. B. 1977, 'Cost–Risk–Benefit Assessments in Energy Policy', *George Washington Law Review* 45: 911–943

Lowi, T. J. 1964, 'American Business, Public Policy, Case-Studies, and Political Theory', *World Politics* 16(4): 677–715

1972, 'Four Systems of Policy, Politics and Choice', *Public Administration Review* 32(4): 298–310

Luke, T. 1999, 'Eco-Managerialism: Environmental Studies as a Power/Knowledge Formation', in Fischer and Hajer, pp. 103–120

Luker, K. 1984, *Abortion and the Politics of Motherhood*, Berkeley: University of California Press

Lynch, M. 1985, *Art and Artifact in Laboratory Science: A Study of Shop Work and Shop Talk in a Research Laboratory*, London: Routledge and Kegan Paul

Maanen, J. van 1986, *Tales of the Field*, Chicago: University of Chicago Press

Machiavelli, N. 1963, *The Prince*. tr. C. Detmold, ed. G. Crocker, New York: Washington Square Press

MacIntyre, A. 1981, *After Virtue: A Study in Moral Theory*, Notre Dame: University of Notre Dame Press

MacNaghten, P. and J. Urry 1998, *Contested Natures*, London: Sage

MacRae, Jr., D. 1993, 'Guidelines for Policy Discourse: Consensual versus Adversarial', in Fischer and Forester, pp. 291–318

Magnusson, W. and K. Shaw 2002 eds., *Disrupting the Political: Reading the Global through Clayoquot Sound*, Minneapolis: University of Michigan Press

Majone, G. 1989, *Evidence, Argument and Persuasion in the Policy Process*, New Haven, CT: Yale University Press

Mak, G. 1994, *Hoe God verdween uit Jorwerd*, Amsterdam: Atlas

Malbert, B. 1998, *Urban Planning Participation: Linking Practice and Theory*, Gothenburg: School of Architecture, Chalmers University

Malmberg, A. and P. Maskell 1997, 'Towards an Explanation of Regional Specialisation and Industry Agglomeration', *European Planning Studies* 5(1): 24–41

Manin, B. 1997, *The Principles of Representative Government*, Cambridge: Cambridge University Press

Mansbridge, J. 1996, 'Using Power/Fighting Power: The Polity', in Benhabib, pp. 46–66

March, J. G. 1989a, 'Footnotes to Organizational Change', in March, J. G., *Decisions and Organizations*, Oxford: Basil Blackwell, pp. 167–186

    1989b. 'The Technology of Foolishness,' in March, J. G., *Decisions and Organizations*, Oxford: Basil Blackwell, pp. 253–265

March, J. G. and J. P. Olsen 1995, *Democratic Governance*, New York: Free Press

    1998, 'The Institutional Dynamics of International and Political Orders', *International Organization* 52(4): 943–969

March, J. and H. A. Simon 1958, *Organizations*, New York: John Wiley

Marcus, G. E. and M. Fischer 1986, *Anthropology as Cultural Critique*, Chicago: University of Chicago Press

Marks, G., F. W. Scharpf, P. C. Schmitter and W. Streeck 1996, *Governance in the European Union*, London: Sage

Marsh, G. P. 1864, *Man and Nature*, New York: Scribner

Massachusetts Hazardous Waste Facility Site Safety Council 1987, *Policy on Determination of Need for New Hazardous Waste Facility Capacity in Massachusetts*

Massachusetts Siting Policy Task Force 1990, *Final Report on Hazardous Waste Facility Siting Process Improvements*

Maynard-Moody, S. and M. Kelly 1993, 'Stories Public Managers Tell about Elected Officials: Making Sense of the Politics–Administration Dichotomy ', in Bozeman, B. (ed.), *Public Management: The State of the Art*, San Francisco: Jossey Bass, pp. 71–90

Maynard-Moody, S. and D. Stull 1987, 'The Symbolic Side of Policy Analysis', in Fischer and Forester, chapter 11

Mayntz, R. 1999, 'Nieuwe Uitdagingen voor de Governance Theory (New Challenges for Governance Theory)', *Beleid & Maatschappij* 26(1): 2–13

McCarthy, T. 1978, *The Critical Theory of Jürgen Habermas*, Cambridge, MA: MIT Press

McCloskey, D. N. 1985, *The Rhetoric of Economics*, Madison: University of Wisconsin Press

McClurg, S. 2001, 'Conjunctive Use: Banking for a Dry Day', *Western Water* (Sacramento, CA), July/August: 4–13

Melucci, A. 1996, *Challenging Codes: Collective Action in the Information Age*, Cambridge: Cambridge University Press

Melzner, A. J. 1976, *Policy Analysts in the Bureaucracy*, Berkeley: University of California Press

Menand, L. 1997, *A Pragmatism Reader*, New York: Vintage

    2001, *The Metaphysical Club*, New York: Farrar, Straus and Giroux

Meppem, T. and S. Bourke, 1999, 'Different Ways of Knowing: A Communicative Turn Toward Sustainability', *Ecological Economics* 30: 389–404

Merriam, C. E. 1931, *New Aspects of Politics*, 2nd edn (1st edn 1925), Chicago: University of Chicago Press

Mill, J. S. 1835, 'Tocqueville on Democracy in America (vol. 1)', in Himmelfarb, G. (ed.), *Essays on Politics and Culture*, Gloucester, MA: Peter Smith, 1973, pp. 172–213

    1865, *Considerations on Representative Government*, 3rd edn, Indianapolis: Bobbs-Merrill, 1958

Miller, D. C. 1991, *Handbook of Research Design and Social Measurement*, Newbury Park, CA: Sage

Miller, D. F. 1985, 'Social Policy: An Exercise in Metaphor', *Knowledge* 7(2): 191–215

Morgan, K. 1997, 'The Learning Region: Institutions, Innovation and Regional Renewal', *Regional Studies* 31(5): 491–503

Morris, E. 1998, *Urban Redevelopment and the Emerging Community Sector*, Ph.D. thesis, University of California: Berkeley

Mouffe, C. 1996, 'Democracy, Power, and the "Political"', in Benhabib, pp. 245–256

Moulaert, F. 2000, *Globalisation and Integrated Area Development in European Cities*, Oxford: Oxford University Press

Muller, P. and Y. Surel 1998, *L'Analyse des politiques publiques*, Paris: Montchestien

Murphy, J. T. 1980, *Getting the Facts*, Santa Monica: Goodyear

Natter, W., T. Schatzuku and J. P. Jones III 1995 eds., *Objectivity and its Other*, New York: Guilford Press

NEJAC 2000, 'Environmental Justice and Community-Based Health Model Discussion', Meeting Report in 5 sections, http://es.epa.gov/oeca/main/ej/healthreport.pdf

Nelson, B. 1996, 'Public Policy and Administration. An Overview', in Goodin, R. E. and H.-D. Klingemann (eds.), *A New Handbook of Political Science*, Oxford: Oxford University Press, pp. 551–592

Newcastle City Council 2000, *Going for Growth: A Citywide Vision for Newcastle 2020*, Newcastle upon Tyne: Newcastle City Council

Nicolini, D. 1998, 'Situated Learning, Local Knowledge, and Action: Social Approaches to the Study of Knowing in Organisations', symposium proposal to the Managerial and Organizational Cognition Interest Group, Academy of Management Annual Conference, San Diego, 8–11 August

Nicolini, D., S. Gherardi and D. Yanow forthcoming, *Knowing in Organizations: A Practice-based Approach*, Armonk, NY: M. E. Sharpe

Novotony, P. 1994, 'Popular Epidemiology and the Struggle for Community Health in the Environmental Justice Movement', in Bullard, pp. 137–158

Nussbaum, M. C. 1990, *Love's Knowledge: Essays on Philosophy and Literature*, Oxford: Oxford University Press

Nuu-Chah-Nulth Tribal Council 1990, *Nuu-Chah-Nulth Land Question: Land Sea and Resources*, Port Alberni, BC, September

O'Donnell, A. 1987, Letter to Joseph W. Walsh Jr. in *Comments for the Massachusetts Audubon Society on the Draft Policy on Determination of Need for New Hazardous Waste Facility Capacity in Massachusetts*

Offe, C. 1972, 'Political Authority and Class Structures', *International Journal of Sociology*, 2: 73–108

1977, 'The Theory of the Capitalist State and the Problem of Policy Formation', in Lindberg, L. N. and A. Alford Lexington (eds.), *Stress and Contradiction in Modern Capitalism*, Lexington: D. C. Heath, pp. 125–144

O'Hare, Michael, Lawrence Bacow and Deborah Sanderson 1983, *Facility Siting and Public Opposition*, New York: Van Nostrand Reinhold

Olson, M. 1965, *The Logic of Collective Action: Public Goods and the Theory of Groups*, Cambridge, MA, Harvard University Press

Orr, J. E. 1996, *Talking About Machines: An Ethnography of a Modern Job*, Ithaca: Cornell University Press

Osborne, D. and T. Gaebler 1992, *Reinventing Government: How the Entrepreneurial Spirit is Transforming the Public Sector*, Reading, MA: Addison-Wesley

Ostrom, E. 1990, *Governing the Commons: The Evolution of Institutions for Collective Action*, Cambridge: Cambridge University Press

Otway, H. 1992, 'Public Wisdom, Expert Fallibility: Toward a Contextual Theory of Risk', in Krimsky, S. and D. Golding (eds.), *Social Theories of Risk*, Westport, CT: Praeger, pp. 215–228

Ozawa, C. 1991, *Recasting Science: Consensual Procedures in Public Policy Making*, Boulder: Westview

Ozonoff, D. 1994, 'Conceptions and Misconceptions about Human Health Impact Analysis', *Environmental Impact Assessment Review* Special Issue, 14(5/6): 499–515

Pal, L. 1995, 'Competing Paradigms in Policy Discourse: The Case of International Human Rights', *Policy Sciences* 18: 185–207

Paller, B. T. 1989, 'Extending Evolutionary Epistemology to "Justifying" Scientific Beliefs', in Halweg, K. and C. A. Hooker (eds.), *Issues in Evolutionary Epistemology*, Albany: State University of New York Press, pp. 231–257

Paris, D. C. and J. F. R. Reynolds 1983, *The Logic of Policy Inquiry*, New York: Longman

Pateman, C. 1971, *Participation and Democratic Theory*, Cambridge: Cambridge University Press

Patzelt, W. J. 1987, *Grundlagen der Ethnomethodologie. Theorie, Empirie und politikwissenschaftlicher Nutzen einer Soziologie des Alltags*, Munich: Wilhelm Fink Verlag

Penchaszadeh, A. 1998, 'Tell Me a Story: How a Community-based Organization Learns from its History through Reflective Storytelling', MA thesis, Department of Urban Studies and Planning, Massachusetts Institute of Technology

Peng, T. K., M. F. Peterson and Y. Shui 1991, 'Quantitative Methods in Cross-national Management Research', *Journal of Organizational Behavior* 12: 87–107

Perrow, C. 1999, *Normal Accidents: Living with High Risk Technologies*, Princeton: Princeton University Press

Peters, G. B. 1998, *Comparative Politics: Theory and Methods*, New York: New York University Press

Peterse, A. 1995, 'The Mobilization of Counter-Expertise: Using Fischer's Model of Policy Inquiry', *Policy Sciences* 28: 369–373

Pierre, J. 2000 ed., *Debating Governance*, Oxford: Oxford University Press

Piller, C. 1991, *The Fail-Safe Society: Community Defiance and the End of American Technological Optimism*, New York: Basic Books

Planologische Kernbeslissing Schiphol en Omgeving (PKB) 1993–1995, 4 vols.

Polanyi, M. 1958, *Personal Knowledge: Towards a Post-critical Philosophy*, Chicago: University of Chicago Press

1966, *The Tacit Dimension*, New York: Anchor, Doubleday

Pondy, L. A., P. J. Frost, G. Morgan and T. C. Dandridge 1983 eds., *Organizational Symbolism*, Greenwich, CT: JAI Press

Popper, F. 1991, 'LULUs and Their Blockage: The Nature of the Problem, the Outline of the Solution', in Dimento, J. and L. Graymeyer (eds.), *Confronting Regional Challenges: Approaches to LULUs, Growth, and other Vexing Governance Problems*, Cambridge, MA: Lincoln Institute for hand Policy, pp. 13–30

Popper, K. 1959, *The Logic of Scientific Discovery*, London: Heinemann

Postone, M., E. LiPuma and C. Calhoun 1993, 'Introduction: Bourdieu and Social Theory', in Calhoun, C., E. LiPuma and M. Postone, *Bourdieu: Critical Perspectives*, Cambridge: Polity Press, pp. 1–13

Pressman, J. L. and A. Wildavsky 1979, *Implementation: How Great Expectations in Washington Are Dashed in Oakland*, Oakland Project, Berkeley: University of California Press

Prigogine, I. and I. Stenger 1984, *Order out of Chaos*, New York: Bantam

Proctor, R. N. 1991, *Value-Free Science? Purity or Power in Modern Knowledge*, Cambridge, MA: Harvard University Press

Prottas, J. M. 1979, *People-processing*, Lexington: D. C. Heath

Putnam, H. 1995 *Pragmatism: An Open Question*, Cambridge, MA: Blackwell

Putnam, R. 1985, 'Creating Facts and Values', *Philosophy* 60(2): 187–204

1993, *Making Democracy Work: Civil Traditions in Modern Italy*, Princeton: Princeton University Press

Putt, A. D. and J. F. Springer 1989, *Policy Research: Concepts, Methods, and Applications*, New York: Prentice-Hall

Quine, W. V. O. 1961, 'Two Dogmas of Empiricism', in Quine, W. V. O., *From a Logical Point of View*, Cambridge, MA: Harvard University Press, pp. 20–46

1969, 'Ontological Relativity', in Quine, W. V. O., *Ontological Relativity and Other Essays*, New York: Columbia University Press, pp. 26–68

Rabinow, P. and W. M. Sullivan 1979 eds., *Interpretive Social Science: A Reader*, Berkeley: University of California Press

Raelin, J. A. 1986, *The Clash of Cultures*, Boston: Harvard Business School Press

Raiffa, H. 1982, *The Art and Science of Negotiation*, Cambridge, MA: The Belknap Press of Harvard University Press

1985, 'Creative Compensation: Maybe "In My Backyard"', *Negotiation Journal*, July: 197–203

Ravetz, J. and S. O. Funtowicz 1993, 'Science for the Post-Normal Age', *Futures* 25(7): 735–755

Rawls, J. 1971, *A Theory of Justice*, Cambridge, MA: Harvard University Press

Reed, M. and M. Hughes 1992, *Rethinking Organization: New Directions in Organization Theory and Analysis*, London: Sage

Reich, R. 1988, 'Policy Making in a Democracy', in Reich, R., *The Power of Public Ideas*, Cambridge, MA: Ballinger, pp. 123–156

Rein, M. 1976, *Social Science and Public Policy*, New York: Penguin

1983a, 'Action Frames and Problem Setting', in Rein, M., *From Policy to Practice*, London: Macmillan, pp. 221–234

1983b, 'Value-Critical Policy Analysis', in Callahan, D. and B. Jennings (eds.), *Ethics, the Social Sciences, and Policy Analysis*, New York: Plenum Press, pp. 83–112

Rein, M. and W. Gamson 1999, notes from a joint course on 'Discourse in Social Policy', MIT, Spring

Rein, M. and D. Schön 1977, 'Problem Setting in Policy Research', in Weiss, C. (ed.), *Using Social Research in Policy Making*, Lexington, MA: Lexington Books, pp. 235–251

1996, 'Frame-Critical Policy Analysis and Frame Reflective Policy Practice', *Knowledge and Policy* 9(1): 88–90

Rein, M. and S. White 1977, 'Policy Research: Belief and Doubt', *Policy Analysis* 3: 239–271

Rheinberger, H.-J. 1992a, 'Experiment, Difference, and Writing, Part I', *Studies in History and Pholospohy of Science* 23: 305–331

1992b, 'Tracing Protein Synthesis, Part II: The Laboratory Life of Transfer RNA', *Studies in History and Philosophy of Science* 23: 389–422

Rhodes, R. A. W. 1996, 'The New Governance: Governing without Government', *Political Studies* 44: 652–667

1997, *Understanding Governance: Policy Networks, Governance, Reflexivity and Accountability*, Milton Keynes: Open University Press

2000, 'Governance and Public Administration', in Pierre, pp. 54–90

Ricoeur, P. 1971, 'The Model of the Text: Meaningful Action Considered as Text', *Social Research* 38: 529–562

Roe, E. 1994, *Narrative Policy Analysis: Theory and Practice*, Durham, NC: Duke University Press

Rorty, R. 1979, *Philosophy and the Mirror of Nature*, Princeton: Princeton University Press

1983, 'Nineteenth-century Idealism and Twentieth-century Textualism', in Rorty, R., *Consequences of Pragmatism*, Minneapolis: University of Minnesota Press, pp. 139–159

1989, *Contingency, Irony, and Solidarity*, Cambridge: Cambridge University Press

Rose, N. 1999, *Powers of Freedom: Reframing Political Thought*, Cambridge: Cambridge University Press

Rose, N. and P. Miller 1992, 'Political Power Beyond the State: Problematics of Government', *British Journal of Sociology* 43: 172–205

Rosenhan, D., F. Frederick and A. Burrowes 1968, 'Preaching and Practicing', *Child Development* 39: 291–301

Rosenau, J. N. 1995 ed., *Governance Without Government: Order and Change in World Politics*, Cambridge: Cambridge University Press

Rouse, J. 1987, *Knowledge and Power: A Political Philosophy of Science*, Ithaca: Cornell University Press

Ruderman, R. S. 1997, 'Aristotle and the Recovery of Political Judgment', *American Political Science Review* 91(2): 409–420

Rudolph, L. I. 2001, 'Let a Hundred Flowers Bloom, Let a Hundred Schools of Thought
Contend: Arguments for Pluralism and against Monopoly in Political Science',
paper presented to the American Political Science Association Annual Meeting,
San Francisco, 31 August

Rutgers, M. R. 1996, 'The Meanings of "Administration": Translating across Boundaries', *Journal of Management Inquiry* 5(1): 14–20

1999, 'Comparison and Translation', unpublished ms.

Sabatier, P. and H. Jenkins-Smith 1993 eds., *Policy Change and Learning: An Advocacy
Coalition Approach*, Boulder: Westview

Sabel, C. 1993, 'Constitutional Orderings in Historical Context', in Scharpf, F.
(ed.), *Games in Hierarchies and Networks*, Frankfurt am Main: Campus Verlag,
pp. 65–123

1994, 'Learning by Monitoring: The Institutions of Economic Development', in
Smelser, N. J. and R. Swedberg (eds.), *The Handbook of Economic Sociology*,
Princeton: Princeton University Press, pp. 137–165

Sabel, C., A. Fung and B. Karkkainen 1999, 'Beyond Backyard Environmentalism:
How Communities Are Quietly Refashioning Environmental Regulation', *Boston
Review*, October/November: 4–10

Salter, L. and D. Salco 1981, *Public Inquiries in Canada*, Science Council of Canada,
Background Study 47, Ottawa

Sandweiss, S. 1998, 'The Social Construction of Environmental Justice', in Camacho,
D. E. (ed.), *Environmental Injustices, Political Struggles*, Durham, NC: Duke
University Press, pp. 31–57

Saxenian, A. 1994, *Regional Advantage: Culture and Competition in Silicon Valley and
Route 128*, Cambridge, MA: Harvard University Press

Schiffrin, D. 1994, *Approaches to Discourse*, Oxford, Blackwell

Schiphol, TOP 1999, *Nieuwsbrief Platform 13, Bibliotheek Tijdelijk
Overleg Platform Schiphol*, http://www.tnli.org/clients/onl/onl.nsf/
1efacd93ee7063cec125659b005el7c2/b8fe66a524, accessed 11 September 2001

Schlosberg, D. 1999, *Environmental Justice and the New Pluralism: The Challenge of
Difference for Environmentalism*, Oxford: Oxford University Press

Schmidt, M. R. 1993, 'Grout: Alternative Kinds of Knowledge and Why They Are
Ignored', *Public Administration Review* 53(6): 525–530

Schneider, A. L. and H. Ingram 1997, *Policy Design for Democracy*, Lawrence:
University Press of Kansas

Schön, D. A. 1979, 'Generative Metaphor', in Ortony, A. (ed.), *Metaphor and Thought*,
New York: Cambridge University Press, pp. 254–283

1983, *The Reflective Practitioner*, New York: Basic Books

Schön, D. A. and M. Rein 1994, *Frame Reflection: Toward the Resolution of Intractable
Policy Controversies*, New York: Basic Books

Schram, S. F. 1993, 'Postmodern Policy Analysis: Discourse and Identity in Welfare
Policy', *Policy Sciences* 26: 249–270

Schram, S. F. and P. T. Neisser 1997 eds., *Tales of the State*, New York: Rowman and
Littlefield

Schutz, A. 1962, *Collected Papers*, vol. 1, ed. M. Natanson, The Hague: Martinus Nijhoff

Schwandt, T. A. 2000a, 'Further Diagnostic Thoughts on what Ails Evaluation Practice', *American Journal of Evaluation* 21(2): 225–229

2000b, 'Meta-Analysis and the Everyday Life: The Good, the Bad, and the Ugly', *American Journal of Evaluation* 21(2): 213–219

Scientific Panel for Sustainable Forest Practices in Clayoquot Sound 1995a, *First Nations' Perspectives Relating to Forest Practices Standards in Clayoquot Sound*, Report 3, Victoria, BC: Cortex Consultants Inc.

1995b, *First Nations' Perspectives Relating to Forest Practices Standards in Clayoquot Sound*, Appendices V and VI, Victoria, BC: Cortex Consultants Inc.

1995c, *Sustainable Ecosystem Management in Clayoquot Sound*, Report 5, Victoria, BC: Cortex Consultants Inc.

1995d, *A Vision and Its Context: Global Context for Forest Practices in Clayoquot Sound*, Report 4, Victoria, BC: Cortex Consultants Inc.

Scott, J. C. 1998, *Seeing Like a State: How Certain Schemes to Improve the Human Condition Have Failed*, New Haven, CT: Yale University Press

Scriven, M. 1987, 'Probative Logic', in Eemeren, F. H. van et al. (eds.), *Argumentation: Across the Lines of Discipline*, Amsterdam: Foris, pp. 7–32

Seidel, G. 1985, 'Political Discourse Analysis', in Dijk, T. A. van (ed.), *Handbook of Discourse Analysis*, vol. 4, London: Academic Press, pp. 43–60

Senge, P. M. 1990, *The Fifth Discipline: The Art and Practice of the Learning Organization*, New York: Doubleday

Simon, H. A. 1976 [1947], *Administrative Behavior*, 3rd edn, New York: Free Press

Smart, B. 1982, 'Foucault, Sociology, and the Problem of Human Agency', *Theory and Society* 11: 121–141

Smircich, L. 1983, 'Concepts of Culture and Organizational Analysis', *Administrative Science Quarterly* 28: 339–358

Smith, R. Y. 1997, '*Hishuk ish ts'awalk* – All Things Are One: Traditional Ecological Knowledge and Forest Practices in Ahousaht First Nation's Traditional Territory, Clayoquot Sound, BC', MA thesis, Trent University, Peterborough, ON

Society of Professionals in Dispute Resolution 1997, *Best Practices for Government Agencies: Guidelines for Using Collaborative Agreement-Seeking Processes*, Washington, DC: Society of Dispute Resolution Professionals

Spradley, J. P. and D. W. McCurdy 1972, *The Cultural Experience*, Palo Alto: Science Research Associates, Inc.

Stein, S. 2001 'These Are Your Title I Children', *Policy Sciences* 34: 135–156

Stewart, M., S. Goss, R. Clarke, G. Gillanders, J. Rowe and H. Shaftoe 1999, *Cross-cutting Issues Affecting Local Government*, London: Department of the Environment, Transport and the Regions

Stockman, N. 1983, *Anti-Positivist Theorists of the Sciences: Critical Rationalism and Scientific Realism*, Dordrecht: D. Reidel

Stokey, E. and R. Zeckhauser 1978, *A Primer for Policy Analysis*, New York: W. W. Norton

Stone, D. 1988, *Policy Paradox and Political Reason*, Boston: Little, Brown

1997, *Policy Paradox: The Art of Political Decision Making*, New York: W. W. Norton

Storper, M. 1997, *The Regional World*, New York: Guilford Press

Strauss, A. L. 1993, *Continual Permutations of Action*, Hawthorne, NY: Aldine de Gruyter

Streeck, W. and P. C. Schmitter 1985 eds., *Private Interest Government: Beyond Market and State*, London: Sage

Sunstein, C. R. 1997, *Free Markets and Social Justice*, New York: Oxford University Press

Susskind, L. and P. Field 1996, *Dealing with an Angry Public: The Mutual Gains Approach to Resolving Disputes*, New York: Free Press

Susskind, L., S. McKearnon and J. Thomas-Larmer 1999 eds., *Consensus Building Handbook*, Thousand Oaks, CA: Sage

Swaffield, S. 1998, 'Contextual Meanings in Policy Discourse: A Case Study of Language Use Concerning Resource Policy in the New Zealand High Country', *Policy Sciences* 31: 199–224

Swidler, A. 1995, 'Cultural Power and Social Movements', in Johnston, H. and B. Klandermans (eds.), *Social Movements and Culture*, Minneapolis: University of Minnesota Press, pp. 25–40

Sylvia, R. D., K. Meier and E. Gunn 1991, *Program Planning and Evaluation for the Public Manager*, Prospect Heights, IL: Waveland

Tamanaha, B. Z. 1997, *Realistic Socio-Legal Theory*, Oxford: Clarendon Press

Tarlock, A. D. 1984, 'State versus Local Control of Hazardous Waste Facility Siting: Who Decides in Whose Backyard?', reprinted from *Zoning and Planning Law Report*, in Lake R. (ed.), *Resolving Locational Conflict*, New Brunswick, NJ: Center for Urban Policy Research, pp. 137–158

Tarrow, S. 1994, *Power in Movement*, Cambridge: Cambridge University Press

Taylor, C. 1971, 'Interpretation and the Sciences of Man', *Review of Metaphysics* 25: 3–51

  1977, 'Interpretation and the Sciences of Man', in Dallmayr and McCarthy, pp. 101–131

  1994, 'The Politics of Recognition', in Gutman, pp. 25–73

  1995a, 'Explanation and Practical Reason', in Taylor, C., *Philosophical Arguments*, Cambridge, MA: Harvard University Press, pp. 1–19

  1995b, 'Overcoming Epistemology', in Taylor, C., *Philosophical Arguments*, Cambridge, MA: Harvard University Press, pp. 34–60

Taylor, M. 1995, *Unleashing the Potential: Bringing Residents to the Centre of Regeneration*, York: Joseph Rowntree Foundation

  2000, *Top-down Meets Bottom-up: Neighbourhood Management*, York: York Publishing Services

Tennberg, M. 1998, *The Arctic Council: A Study in Governmentality*, Rovaniemi: University of Lapland Press

Teuber, A. 1987, 'Original Intent', unpublished ms.

Thissen, F. and J. Droogleever Fortuijn 1998, 'Sociale cohesie en dorpsverenigingen op het Drentse platteland', AME working paper, University of Amsterdam

Thompson, M., R. Ellis and A. Wildavsky 1990, *Cultural Theory*, Boulder: Westview

Throgmorton, J. A. 1991, 'Rhetorics of Policy Analysis', *Policy Sciences* 24: 153–179

1993, 'Survey Research as Rhetorical Trope: Electric Power Planning Arguments in Chicago', in Fisher and Forester, pp. 117–144

Torgerson, D. 1980, *Industrialization and Assessment: Social Impact Assessment as a Social Phenomenon*, Toronto: York University Press

1985, 'Contextual Orientation in Policy Analysis: The Contribution of Harold D. Lasswell', *Policy Sciences* 18: 241–261

1986a, 'Between Knowledge and Politics: Three Faces of Policy Analysis', *Policy Sciences* 19: 33–59

1986b, 'Interpretive Policy Inquiry', *Policy Sciences* 19: 307–405

1990, 'Limits of the Administrative Mind: The Problem of Defining Environmental Problems', in Paehlke, R. and D. Torgerson (eds.), *Managing Leviathan: Environmental Politics and the Administrative State*, Peterborough, ON: Broadview Press, pp. 115–161

1992, 'Priest and Jester in the Policy Sciences: Developing the Focus of Inquiry', *Policy Sciences* 25: 225–235

1993, 'The Paradox of Organizational Rationality: Uncertainty Absorption and the Technology of Foolishness', paper presented at the School of Business, Queen's University, Kingston, ON

1995, 'Policy Analysis and Public Life: The Restoration of *Phronesis*?', in Farr, J., J. S. Dryzek and S. T. Leonard (eds.), *Political Science in History: Research Programs and Political Traditions*, Cambridge: Cambridge University Press, pp. 225–252

1996, 'Power and Insight in Policy Discourse: Postpositivism and Problem Definition', in Dobuzinskis, L., M. Howlett and D. Laycock (eds.), *Policy Studies in Canada: The State of the Art*, Toronto: University of Toronto Press, pp. 266–298

1997, 'Policy Professionalism and the Voices of Dissent: The Case of Environmentalism', *Polity* 29: 358–359

1999a, 'Images of Place in Green Politics: The Cultural Mirror of Indigenous Traditions', in Fischer and Hajer, pp. 186–203

1999b, *The Promise of Green Politics: Environmentalism and the Public Sphere*, Durham, NC: Duke University Press

Toulmin, S. 1982, 'The Construal of Reality: Criticism in Modern and Postmodern Science', in Mitchell, W. J. T. (ed.), *The Politics of Interpretation*, Chicago: University of Chicago Press, pp. 99–117

1990, *Cosmopolis: The Hidden Agenda of Modernity*, Chicago: University of Chicago Press

Tribe, L. H. 1972, 'Policy Science: Analysis or Ideology?', *Philosophy and Public Affairs* 2: 66–110

Turner, B. A. 1990 ed., *Organizational Symbolism*, New York: Aldine de Gruyter

Turner, S. 1994, *The Social Theory of Practices: Tradition, Tacit Knowledge and Presuppositions*, Cambridge: Polity Press

Tversky, A. and D. Kahneman 1981, 'The Framing of Decisions and the Psychology of Choice', *Science* 211: 453–458

US EPA 1992, *Environmental Equity: Reducing Risk for all Communities*, vols. I and II, EPA Document 230-R-92-008 n.d., 'The EPA's Environmental Justice Strategy', http://www.epa.gov/grtlakes/ seahome/grants/src/strategy.htm

Varney, Robert W. 2001, 'EPA New England Regional Policy on Environmental Justice', 1 October, http://www.epa.gov/NE/steward/ejprog/ejpolicy.html

Vickers, S. G. 1995[1965], *The Art of Judgement*, London: Sage

Vigar, G., P. Healey, A. Hull and S. Davoudi 2000, *Planning, Governance and Spatial Strategy in Britain*, London: Macmillan

Wacquant, L. 1999, 'Urban Marginality in the Coming Millennium', *Urban Studies* 36(10): 1639–1648

Wagenaar, H. 1995, 'Het onbedoelde gebruik van beleid (The Unintended Use of Public Policy)', in Aarts, L., P. de Jong, R. van der Veen and H. Wagenaar, *Het Bedrijf van de Verzorgingsstaat. Naar Nieuwe Verhoudingen tussen Staat, Markt en Burger*, Amsterdam/Meppel: Boom, pp. 234–259

1997, 'Verhalen in de beleidspraktijk (Narrative and Policy Practice)' *Beleid & Maatschappij* 24(1): 2–7

1999, 'Value Pluralism in Administrative Practice', *Administrative Theory & Praxis* 21(4): 441–454

Wagenaar, H. and R. Hartendorp 2000, 'Oedipus in the Welfare Office. Practice, Discourse and Identity in Public Administration', in Wagenaar, H. (ed.), *Government Institutions: Effects, Changes, and Normative Foundations*, Dordrecht: Kluwer Academic, pp. 147–178

Wagner, P. 1994, 'Dispute, Uncertainty and Institution in Recent French Debates', *Journal of Political Philosophy* 2(3): 270–289

1995, 'Sociology and Contingency: Historicizing Epistemology', *Social Science Information* 34(2): 179–204

2001, *Theorizing Modernity: Inescapability and Attainability in Social Theory*, London: Sage

Wallace, H. and A. R. Young 1997 eds., *Participation and Policy-making in the European Union*, Oxford: Clarendon Press

Wallerstein, I. 1996, *Open the Social Sciences*, Report of the Gulbenkian Commission on the Restructuring of the Social Sciences, Stanford: Stanford University Press

Warren, M. 1992, 'Democratic Theory and Self-Transformation', *American Political Science Review* 86(1): 8–23

1996, 'What Should We Expect from More Democracy? Radically Democratic Responses to Politics', *Political Theory* 24: 241–270

1999, *Democracy and Trust*, Cambridge: Cambridge University Press

Weatherley, R. 1979, *Reforming Special Education*, Cambridge, MA: MIT Press

Weiss, C. 1990, 'Policy Research: Data, Ideas or Arguments?', in Wagner, P. et al. (eds.), *Social Sciences and Modern States*, Cambridge: Cambridge University Press

Welsch, W. 1996, *Vernunft. Die zeitgenoessische Vernunftkritik und das Konzept der transversalen Vernunft*, Frankfurt am Main: Suhrkamp Verlag

1998, *Communities of Practice: Learning, Meaning and Identity*, Cambridge: Cambridge University Press

Westerman, F. 1999, *De Graanrepubliek*, Amsterdam: Atlas

Wheeler, M. 1993, 'Regional Consensus on Affordable Housing: Yes in My Backyard?', *Journal of Planning Education and Research* 12(2): 139–149

1994, 'Negotiating NIMBYs: Learning from the Failure of the Massachusetts Siting Law', *Yale Journal of Regulation* 11: 241–291

White, H. 1987, *The Content of the Form: Narrative Discourse and Historical Representation*, Baltimore: Johns Hopkins University Press

White, R. 1984, *Fearful Warriors: A Psychological Profile of US–Soviet Relations*, New York: Free Press

Whyte, W. F. 1943/1955, *Street Corner Society*, Chicago: University of Chicago Press
1984, *Learning from the Field*, Newbury Park, CA: Sage

Wildavsky, A. 1979, *Speaking Truth to Power: The Art and Craft of Policy Analysis*, Boston: Little, Brown

Wilkinson, D. and E. Appelbee 1999, *Implementing Holistic Government*, Bristol: Policy Press

Wilkinson, S. 1992, 'Towards a New City? A Case Study of Image-Improvement Initiatives in Newcastle upon Tyne', in Healey, P., S. Davoudi, M. O'Toole, S. Tavsanoglu and D. Usher (eds.), *Re-building the City: Property-led Urban Regeneration*, London: E. & F. N. Spon, pp. 174–211

Williams, B. 1985, *Ethics and the Limits of Philosophy*, Cambridge, MA: Harvard University Press

Williams, B. A. and A. R. Matheny 1995, *Democracy, Dialogue, and Environmental Disputes: The Contested Languages of Social Regulation*, New Haven, CT: Yale University Press

Wilson, J. 1998, *Talk and Log: Wilderness Politics in British Columbia*, Vancouver: University of British Columbia Press

Wilson, P. 1997, 'Building Social Capital: A Learning Agenda for the Twenty-first Century', *Urban Studies* 34(5/6): 745–760

Wolman, H. C. and Page, E. C. 2000, *Learning from the Experience of Others: Policy Transfer among Local Regeneration Partnerships*, York: York Publishing

Woolgar, S. 1988, *Science: The Very Idea*, London: Tavistock

Woozley, A. D. 1949, *Theory of Knowledge*, London: Hutchinson

World Bank 1997, *World Development Report 1997*, New York: Oxford University Press

WRR 1999, *Spatial Development Policy*, The Hague: SDU

Wynne, B. 1992, 'Sheep Farming after Chernobyl', in Lewenstein, B. (ed.), *When Science Meets the Public*, Washington, DC: American Association for the Advancement of Science
1996, 'May the Sheep Safely Graze', in Lash et al., pp. 44–88

Yankelovich, D. 1999, *The Magic of Dialogue: Transforming Conflict into Cooperation*, New York: Simon and Schuster

Yanow, D. 1976, 'Community Organization: A History of Ideas', unpublished paper
1987, 'Toward a Policy Culture Approach to Implementation Analysis', *Policy Studies Review* 7: 103–115
1990, 'Tackling the Implementation Problem: Epistemological Issues in Policy Implementation Research', in Palumbo, D. J. and D. J. Calista (eds.), *Implementation and the Policy Process*, Westport, CT: Greenwood Press, pp. 213–227
1993, 'The Communication of Policy Meanings: Implementation as Interpretation and Text', *Policy Sciences* 26: 41–61

1995a, 'Built Space as Story: The Policy Stories that Buildings Tell', *Policy Studies Journal* 23(3): 407–422

1995b, 'Practices of Policy Interpretation', editor's introductory essay to the special issue, 'Policy Interpretations', *Policy Sciences* 28(2): 111–126

1996, *How Does a Policy Mean? Interpreting Policy and Organizational Actions*, Washington, DC: Georgetown University Press

1997, 'Passionate Humility in Interpretive Policy and Administrative Analysis', special issue on 'Interpretive and cultural theories in administration', ed. S. J. Jong, *Administrative Theory and Praxis* 19(2): 171–177

1998, 'Space Stories; Or, Studying Museum Buildings as Organizational Spaces, while Reflecting on Interpretive Methods and their Narration', *Journal of Management Inquiry* 7(3): 215–239

1999, 'Public Policies as Identity Stories: American Race-Ethnic Discourse', in Abma, pp. 25–52

2000a, *Conducting Interpretive Policy Analysis*, Newbury Park, CA: Sage

2000b, 'Seeing Organizational Learning: A "Cultural" View', special issue 'Knowing in Practice', ed. S. Gherardi, *Organization* 7(2): 247–268

2001, 'Translating Local Knowledge at Organizational Peripheries', paper presented to the Interdisciplinary Committee on Organizational Studies (ICOS) Seminar, University of Michigan, Ann Arbor, 30 March

2002, *Making American 'Race' and 'Ethnicity': Category Failures in Policy and Administrative Practices*, Armonk, NY: M. E. Sharpe

Yanow, D. and H. Willmott 2002, 'Passionate Humility: Toward a Philosophy of Ethical Will', in Jong, S. J. (ed.), *The Future Challenges of Administrative Theory: Looking Ahead to the Next Century*, Westport, CT: Praeger, pp. 131–140

Young, I. M. 1987, 'Impartiality and the Civic Public', in Benhabib, S. and D. Cornell (eds.), *Feminism as Critique*, Minneapolis: University of Minnesota Press, pp. 57–76

1990, *Justice and the Politics of Difference*, Princeton: Princeton University Press

Young, O. R. and G. Osherenko 1993, *Polar Politics. Creating International Environmental Regimes*, Ithaca: Cornell University Press

Subject index

accountability 9
act-focused analysis 240
action 173
  in politics and policy analysis 140
  and practice 149–150, 153, 155
  preferences 142
activity system 150, 166
actors, non-governmental 2, 101
administrative rationality 125
ambiguity, in policy practices and discourse 29
argument, figures of 29
argumentative turn, in policy analysis 7, 14, 17, 211, 222
authority 1, 5, 9
  state 5
autonomy 57

behavioural disposition 17
belief 174, 175
  reframing of 173
  system 8–9, 173
  within a frame 174
bias, mobilization of 67, 116, 117, 124
bureaucratic structures 8

capital building
  institutional 26, 62–65, 83
  intellectual 55, 63, 71
  social 63, 71
category analysis 240
change, macro-sociological 4
citizenship, capacities for 3
cleavages 89

coherence theory 217
collaborative policy dialogues 2, 25, 26, 34–36, 39, 42–44, 50, 55, 56, 58
  creativity 46
  exclusion 40
  facilitator 37, 40
  identity 47
  inclusiveness 39
  interdependence 39–42
  learning 44
  reciprocity 42
  relationships 42–43
  social capital 43
  system adaptations 47
  trust 44
  see also interactive policymaking; learning; legitimacy
communicative infrastructure 75
communicative rationality 35, 116, 119, 124, 128, 132, 135
communities 21, 237
  of action 11
  of difference 229
  epistemic 108, 258
  of fate 97, 98
  interpretative 230, 235, 237–238, 245
  language of 237
  of meaning 229, 235, 238, 245–246
  political 89, 223
  and practice 150
  of practice 109, 148, 151
  scientific 215
conflict resolution, new modes of 11
constitutionalism, liberal 27, 159

Author index